DATE DUE

Unless Recalled Earlier

ILL 10-8-93

JAN 27 1998

DEMCO 38-297

A RESPONSIVE SOCIETY

AMITAI ETZIONI

A
Responsive
Society

COLLECTED ESSAYS ON GUIDING DELIBERATE SOCIAL CHANGE

Jossey-Bass Publishers

San Francisco   •   Oxford   •   1991

A RESPONSIVE SOCIETY
Collected Essays on Guiding Deliberate Social Change
by Amitai Etzioni

Copyright © 1991 by: Jossey-Bass Inc., Publishers
                        350 Sansome Street
                        San Francisco, California 94104
                                    &
                        Jossey-Bass Limited
                        Headington Hill Hall
                        Oxford OX3 0BW

Library of Congress Cataloging-in-Publication Data

Etzioni, Amitai
    A responsive society : collected essays on guiding deliberate
social change / Amitai Etzioni.
        p.   cm. — (The Jossey-Bass management series)
(The Jossey-Bass social and behavioral science series)
    Includes bibliographical references and index.
    ISBN 1-55542-378-7
    1. Social change. 2. Social movements. 3. Community. I. Title.
II. Series.   II. Series: The Jossey-Bass social and behavioral
science series.
HM101.E79 1991
303.4—dc20   91-25603
                                                    CIP

Manufactured in the United States of America

The paper in this book meets the guidelines for
permanence and durability of the Committee on
Production Guidelines for Book Longevity of the
Council on Library Resources.

JACKET DESIGN BY WILLI BAUM
FIRST EDITION

Code 9177

2414 1832
6/10/92 KB

A joint publication in
The Jossey-Bass
Management Series
and
The Jossey-Bass
Social and Behavioral Science Series

CONTENTS

Contents

PREFACE

I must admit that I have a hidden purpose in putting these essays together. The popular press has more than once referred to the fact that I have been shifting from topic to topic over the years. *Time* magazine went so far as to call me "the Everything Expert." Under that heading, their statement reads:

> Sometimes Amitai Etzioni seems to be a one-man profession. A professor of sociology at Columbia University and director of New York City's Center for Policy Research, Etzioni, 46, has written two books on foreign affairs, debated Wernher von Braun on the space race, helped Betty Friedan start a "think tank" for women, testified as an expert on an abortion bill, and received a National Book Award nomination for a book on genetics. Two weeks ago he was hailed by a New York *Daily News* headline writer as a "sexpert" for a talk on sexual ethics, and the same day he was named a staff director of a politically sensitive investigation of New York State's spreading nursing home scandal [*Time*, Feb. 17, 1975, p. 68].

But no academician would accept that designation as flattering. This volume may substantiate the claim that I deal with a wide range of topics—the collection, in four parts that span seven chapters and nineteen essays, includes discussions of genetics, economics, power politics, ethics, and other subjects. However, underlying all these treatments are a limited number of concepts, linked by an overarching theory. All the essays are concerned with the opportunities and limits of guided (or deliberate) social change. The essay that best summarizes my overall approach is "A Theory of Societal Guidance."

With two exceptions—the first essay and the last, which are new—the essays in this collection were first published elsewhere. I have not included two kinds of essays: those dealing with compliance theory and those dealing with socioeconomics. My essays on compliance theory have often been reprinted and summarized, and my most recent work on socioeconomics is readily available.

The question of how a society can influence its future, rather than being subject to the whims of historical and environmental forces beyond its control, has been of great interest since the advent of modernity. With secularization and the rise of science, including social science, societies have developed the idea and ambition of being masters in their own houses, rather than being fatalistic and relying on the supernatural or submitting to foreign powers or domestic elites. Whether we are speaking of the dissenters who left Europe to join in the building of a free society in North America, the Zionists who wished to create a Jewish state, or the socialist-communist experiment in the U.S.S.R., the underlying goal was the same: to introduce major social changes in line with a master concept, although not necessarily with a detailed plan. In a more modest way, all public policies, from those that introduce tax changes to those that encourage saving and investments to programs that combat AIDS, are attempts at deliberate societal change.

The subject has received much renewed debate since the dramatic changes in Eastern Europe. At the center of the debate have been the twin questions of how previously communistic societies can change market economies and how they can alter their policy toward democracy. Whether these societies fail or not, the various courses followed (for example, by Poland, which sought to accelerate change, or by Hungary, which proceeded more gradually) will be studied for many years to come. Guidance theory provides a major framework for analyses of such attempts to change.

Equally important is the movement to form communities out of nations, as in the unification of the two Germanys and in the attempts to turn Western Europe into one community. In other areas, from Canada to the U.S.S.R., efforts to maintain societies in view of forced ethnic movements are the other side of the same coin. Guidance theory provides one frame of reference for trying to come to grips with these important societal changes.

Most of the other essays in this volume concern elements of guidance or constraints. For example, on the surface, the essay "Normative-Affective Factors: Toward a New Decision-Making Model" deals with the psychology of emotions. In effect, however, it examines under what conditions we are governed, for better or worse, by factors other than pure reason. Likewise, the essays in social philosophy, in Chapter Four, seem to deal with individual rights and social responsibilities, but they are also concerned with the conditions under which people can still enforce their historical will, both alone and in groups, while they are subject to social forces that they neither understand nor control.

At the same time, I must make two admissions. First, I have seen no reason to limit my interests to what is technically called "sociology." Like many of my colleagues, I have found that several of the topics we explore carry us into social psychology (if not psychology proper), political science, some parts of economics, and social philosophy. Moreover, there are often more commonalities now among the economists, public-choice political scientists, and exchange sociologists who call themselves neoclassicists than there are among all the other members of any one of these disciplines—say, among sociologists. The borders among these disciplines were created many decades ago and, in my judgment, have lost much of their justification. Work that breaks through the disciplinary boundaries more often seems productive. One may, of course, be severely critical of this or that author who works across disciplines, but the approach itself, it seems to me, has merit. As I showed in my book *The Moral Dimension: Toward a New Economics,* this approach is more predictive, theoretically justifiable, and ethically sound.

Colleagues and students in a wide variety of fields find guidance concepts of interest. These people include not only

those whose speciality is social change or the study of contemporary America and other societies undergoing intensive
change but also those who fashion public policy, people in
government and society programs in business schools, students and teachers of social work (especially those concerned
with communities and their change), and a fair assortment of
others, who have never explained to me their reasons for cit-
ing this line of work and contributing to its development;
nor is there a particular reason for them to do so. This is
clearly a line of approach that many have come to share, and
if the concepts advanced here are of service, then I am richly
rewarded.

As for the second admission, I readily recognize that
my work has changed over time and become ever more explicitly concerned with moral considerations. My work was
never value-free, nor is that of any other social scientists I
know. (Indeed, my first book, *A Diary of a Commando Soldier,*
published only in Hebrew when I was twenty, extols the value
of peace and highlights the agony of war.) My work in compliance theory discusses the evils of coercion and the merits
of normative involvement. The central issue of guidance
theory is the conditions under which society is authentically
responsive to all its members. Only in the last five years or so,
however, have I dared to weigh in explicitly on the side of a
particular body of ethical theory—a moderate version of
deontology. This view holds that we experience certain moral
statements as binding moral duties, compelling from within,
and examines the foundations and implications of such statements. I see this development as a sign of growth and matu-
ration—hardly as a change of heart.

Washington, D.C.   Amitai Etzioni
September 1991

THE AUTHOR

Amitai Etzioni is the first University Professor of the George Washington University. He received his B.A. (1954) and M.A. (1956) degrees from the Hebrew University, Jerusalem, and his Ph.D. degree (1958) from the University of California, Berkeley. He is editor of the journal *The Responsive Community: Rights and Responsibilities.*

From 1987 to 1989, Etzioni served as Thomas Henry Carroll Ford Foundation Professor at the Harvard Business School. Previously, he was senior advisor to the Carter administration from 1979 to 1980. For twenty years (1958–1978), he was professor of sociology at Columbia University and for part of that time was chair of his department. He founded and was the first president of the Society for the Advancement of Socio-Economics.

He is the author of fourteen books, including *The Moral Dimension, Capital Corruption, An Immodest Agenda, Social Problems, Genetic Fix, The Active Society, Political Unification, Modern Organizations,* and *A Comparative Analysis of Complex Organizations.*

In 1968 Etzioni founded the Center for Policy Research, a not-for-profit corporation dedicated to public policy, and has been its director since its inception. In 1976, the American Revolution Bicentennial Administration awarded him a certificate of appreciation for his outstanding contributions to the bicentennial commemoration. He has also been awarded honorary degrees by Rider College, Trenton, New Jersey, and the University of Utah, Salt Lake City.

Part One

THE NEED
FOR
SOCIAL CHANGE

1

Facing the Slings and Arrows: Personal Reflections on a Life of Social Activism

Goal? To Change the World

In the second half of 1990, I was working feverishly to bring about the publication of a new journal, *The Responsive Community: Rights and Responsibilities.* Friends warned me that it would be tough to raise the funds, obtain a steady flow of good articles, and rise above the noise level to get the message out. When I pushed on anyway, a professional fund raiser tried to help. To find out what we would be trying to accomplish with the new publication, she persistently probed: "What slice of the market are you aiming at? How much circulation do you hope to build up the first year? How much profit? What are you trying to achieve?" "None of the above," was my admittedly immodest response. "I want to change the world." She was more than a little taken aback; others may well consider the response naive if not preposterous.

But what am I to say? I made more money than anyone has a right to; additional income per se (as distinct from raising funds for a cause) moves me rather little. Power has never

Note: The author is indebted to Judith Lurie for several editorial suggestions regarding this essay.

3

been my thing. I cannot control my own office; give me a say in a larger endeavor and I know that I will just foul things up. What gets me going and keeps me coming is that occasionally I see the handwriting on the wall, trends in the world—the quicksand that the war in Vietnam was turning into; the fact that corporations are about to close in on a commission set up by Congress and the president to impose new penalties on corporate crime—that trouble me greatly and move me to try to intervene, like someone realizing that a child is about to fall from a tree.

I can practically hear some of my colleagues chiding me for a "paternalistic" position. "People have a right to decide what they wish to decide; they are *not* small children." "What you are trying to do is to substitute your values for theirs!" And "Even if their course is erroneous, they have a right to follow it, fail, and learn from their mistakes." These points might apply to someone commanding much power, a ruler able to force a course on a people or even the sole adviser of a ruler. However, in our pluralistic world, with "inputs" flying left and right, from all comers, it seems proper to add one's voice to the cacophony. That a particular voice carries a bit further than some others on some occasions is merely a sign that people are convinced by the merits of the position. I am hardly in a position to make them heed my council.

True, I often feel quite strongly that this or that group (for example, the Democratic Party in the 1980s, supply-siders in the Reagan era and beyond), is following a poor strategy, the dire consequences of which can be readily foretold. During those "attacks" of hubris, possibly a prerequisite for being a committed activist, it never ceases to amaze me that not everybody immediately sees how unwise or unfair it is to introduce this or that societal change (such as the advice to Poland in 1989 to "jump" from Communism to capitalism). Most times, though, I realize that future events are hard to forecast with any certitude. And I see that my effectiveness (such as it is) has been set back, on more than one occasion, by my being more confident about what I see is about to happen than any social scientist has a right to. But what would you do if you were sure that if society further dismembers the nuclear family . . . insists on focusing on cognitive teaching of the young instead of educating them as full persons . . . accelerating the arms race . . . allowing special interests to eat up the commons . . . ? Would you jump in with both feet?

Some Academic Life

What have these observations, right or wrong, to do with the life of an academic? Why put them at the beginning of a collection of academic essays? Indeed, I was brought up to believe that academic life was contemplative, detached, out of the rough-and-tumble of the real world—in a word, academic. When I was appointed assistant professor at Columbia University upon graduating from Berkeley and wrote a movie review of *Hiroshima Mon Amour* with a slightly disguised peace message, let alone after participating in a student demonstration against nuclear weapons, I was taken aside by some of my elders (and imposing figures those used to be!) and warned that there was no glory or future in these kinds of activist pursuits. A sociologist especially, I was scolded, must watch his or her steps, because the academic standing of sociology is often questioned by both the public at large and the harder sciences. Keeping our noses clean was essential if we were not to be treated, god forbid, like "social workers"! C. Wright Mills, who was also in the department in those days, was practically excommunicated. Another activist, Alvin Gouldner, was held up like a red devil, not to be emulated. Well, thirty years later, I am telling you that one can be an active academic, one that is engaged in the world around us in a variety of ways, from being a presidential adviser to being a witness before congressional committees, a voice on op-ed pages and network TV, and a speaker at massive rallies—without losing one's academic credentials. Scores of scholars do it, from Daniel Bell to Herb Kelman, from Roger Fisher to Cynthia Epstein. And if it did set back the careers of some, it seems a price well worth paying.

In effect, academia provides some special opportunities to be active, such as tenure that ensures that one has freedom of expression and one's basic livelihood, as well as intellectual constructs and conceptions that, we shall see, guide action and make it less likely that it will be mindless. Moreover, academic work can benefit rather than suffer when one draws on one's experiences and actions to improve these constructions, conceptions and approaches. Theory nourishes practice, but practice enriches theory. The following pages explore the role of an active academic as seen by one who has drawn on social sciences and evolved them in the process.

Starting the Ball Rolling: Vietnam

Sociology helps one to realize that there is little to the great leadership theory. Under all but rare exceptional circumstances, such as the coming apart of a society as seen in Germany after World War I and Russia in 1917, an individual, however charismatic, cannot move a society much unless the followers are willing to move themselves. Guiding change is hence much more a matter of catching and riding or detecting societal trends than creating them de novo. Relating to social trends, in turn, requires the coming together of many people and the proper historical circumstances. And this, in turn, requires someone to start building the ideas that frame the new endeavor, a Betty Friedan, a Rachel Carson, a Ralph Nader. And these are often preceded by lesser lights. Someone has to start and see whether he or she can get the ball rolling, to mix the metaphor. I was one of those very early lesser lights when I published an article against the war in Vietnam in 1964 in the *Washington Post*. In the years that followed, I became somewhat of a stock speaker at rallies against the war. None of these got me into more serious pickles than one at Stanford. The students were looking for a government building in front of which to rally in their protest. There was none in sight, so they picked the U.S. Post Office in down-town Palo Alto, as pleasant a suburb as they come. There was, of course, no podium from which to deliver speeches, so talks were given from the top of a painter's ladder held up by some juniors. I may have been sure of what I was saying but certainly not of my footing. These were followed with public debates with the war's proponents (from Madam Nu to Herman Kahn), participation in what were called teach-ins, carrying banners in demonstrations, and an odd event where several of us stood beside the highway in front of the Fountainbleu Hotel in Miami Beach, on a strip between rac-ing Cadillacs and limos on one side and yachts on the other, to say "Honk if you are against the war." Fourteen years later and following the commitment and efforts of many hundreds of thousands of activists, many on the campuses, we did get the United States out of Vietnam. Societal changes almost never come about easily, nor should they; otherwise, one in-tellectual, opinion leader, or demagogue would turn a soci-ety around. The efforts go into finding support; that is, build-ing a democratically sound base for the needed change.

A Question of Motivation

Inactive academicians live for a publication, a research find-ing, a footnote, a sign of recognition by colleagues (did you ever see how an academic opens a new book? Index first, to see whether he or she is cited), but they are fueled much less by the world at large. (Nobel prizes are an exception; most of the many awards given annually by the various social science disciplines have no currency outside academia.) In effect, too much off-campus attention makes one suspect on campus, whatever one's scholarly credentials. Active academicians, while far from immune to these intracampus incentives, are deeply engaged in causes that transcend the campus and its internal battles.

In my later work (on socioeconomics), I found that neoclassical economists argue that whatever one does, it is always to satisfy oneself. They recognize only a one-dimensional world, one in which individuals seek to enhance their pleasures and avoid pain. In contrast, I presented data and arguments to demonstrate that people are propelled by additional forces, foremost by moral causes, by considerations of what they sense as being right and wrong, which are fundamentally different from pleasure and pain. Indeed, doing what is right often is not pleasurable at all. While I buttressed my position with data and reasoning, I had a fundamental sense of the difference between the call of moral causes and the sensation of pleasures. Advancing societal causes is typically a rather arduous and taxing task. If one could draw an economist-like balance sheet of costs and benefits, the pain of efforts versus the pleasure of rewards, this would be revealed as a prime area to avoid.

Looking at my own endeavors, I feel right about what I did against the war in Vietnam. It is not some kind of egomania, a crazy sense of grandeur that I "caused" the United States to do what was right. It is the participation on the side of the angels, being one of many, and one of the first, doing my part, even leading the way. At first, those few of us who spoke up were jeered, considered unpatriotic, called "pink," "lefty," and worse, shunned by many, and quite a bit isolated. Two incidents, rather trivial on their own, illustrate the marshmallow nets that some of us were ensnared in (fortunately, though, I never received the harsher treatment of losing my job, being jailed, and so on). The FBI, my file shows, sabotaged my presentation at America House in Frankfurt, Germany, by, for example, making sure that no notices were put up, and Reagan people put me an a blacklist that prevented me from being chosen by the U.S. government to be a speaker overseas; the resulting "deprivations" were minor to trivial (I had only a small audience in Frankfurt and gave fewer speeches and paid my own way). The jeering never got to me, because I had an inner guide that told me that the cause I was pursuing was right. The main difficulty was keeping at it, year after year, through the tedium of explaining one more time that the United States had no reason to intervene in Southeast Asia, that we were causing more casualties by mixing in than would be inflicted if we stayed out, that we were supporting a corrupt regime, and so on.

Economists who are out to explain that whatever one does must be done for selfish reasons sometimes argue that if such endeavors are not explained by outright gains and pay-offs, they are rewarded by psychic income, that they are pro-pelled by a quest for recognition, prestige, or such. But in the first years, the prestige was largely negative, and when we finally were winning, and more and more leading Ameri-cans—who had not previously been heard from or who had straddled the fence or were hacks—joined the antiwar move-ment, they received the accolades. I occasionally was some-what perturbed about that, but it did not rob from me the feeling that I had done the right thing and would do it again, when the call came. If you set out to change the world, you had better expect little other reward than the inner feeling that comes with doing what is right.

Indeed, in a sense the anti-Vietnam endeavor was un-usually "rewarding." Here, the long efforts, in the end, led to a constructive conclusion; we were able to get the United States to do what is right. It is more difficult to be at peace with oneself when calamity cannot be averted. I had surely more experiences of this kind—hard work yielding failure—than of the other, successful kind. My endeavors against the flood of private money into public offices, which in my judg-ment corrupts the American local and national government (see "Special Interest Groups Versus Constituency Represen-tation" in Chapter Five and my book *Capital Corruption*), have been, to date (I have not stopped yet), more than unsuccess-ful. The role of PACs has substantially increased since a few of us weighed in. I have been unsuccessful in convincing Common Cause and Congress Watch that the matter needs to be tackled less legislatively and more by building up a so-cial movement (the way Mothers Against Drunk Driving did). My writing on the subject did not elicit nearly the same kind of response that my other works did. (Americans seem to have a hard time accepting that the problem is one of defects in tne system rather than of individual rascals whom they can throw out, and to the extent that they do not blame the system, they do not believe that it can be fixed: "All politicians are corrupt.")

Very early in my upbringing, someone—it is so long ago that I do not remember who—drummed into me the notion that life is but a train ride. If you expect stations at which banners will unfurled and bands will play to mark your arrival, you will be repeatedly disappointed. Even if there are such stops, still, the ride continues. Life should be led so that the ride is meaningful, which can be achieved not by Sisyphian pleasures but by dedication to service to transcendental causes, compelling values that serve the commons, not the transient self.

A Failure That Propels

A scorching failure was my attempt in the White House, during the Carter administration, to prevent a recession from being forced in order, one more time, to slow down inflation. The details and the social science reasoning involved are discussed in "Mass Psychology in the White House." I did not, though, report in that essay the extent of my disappointment with myself, my sense of incompetence. Here I was, involved, albeit at the margins, in a decision that cost twenty million people their jobs, robbed many more millions of their livelihood, drove thousands into mental institutions and suicide, and yet—as right as my position was, as events that followed showed—I could not marshal evidence, arguments, and support sufficient to prevent the ensuing economic and political calamity.

After a period of being crestfallen about it, I tried to invest my feelings more constructively. Upon leaving the White House, I started my work on socioeconomics, to try to ensure that if ever a social scientist found him- or herself in a situation like that again, he or she would have more ready-made evidence, arguments, and support. Thus, this is a case where an action failure "in the world" led to renewed *academic* efforts, although there were nonacademic motives for those efforts. The two are thus rather intertwined.

The need to do research well ahead of decision time, when the need for it cannot be anticipated, the kind of research that academicians can do but others might be hard-pressed to, contains a lesson of greater import than it might seem. Frequently when high-level decisions are made, they are in response to a crisis, there is no time for studies, lengthy evaluations of facts, and sorting out of experts. These all need to be done ahead of time. While it is impossible to anticipate specific issues that are going to arise, the general structure can be foretold. Hence, it is possible to prepare studies of deliberate societal change and what is to be done and try to help persuade colleagues, opinion leaders, and the public at large that certain directions are more promising than others.

We are not quite there yet, but we are more ready than before. From a small workshop at the Harvard Business School, the Society for Advancement of Socio-Economics grew into a major international society, headquartered at George Washington University in Washington, D.C., with representatives in scores of countries, an active council, committees, annual meetings, journals, and books. It is now on its way to developing concepts, findings, and the other wherewithal needed for more realistic, ethically sound advice to policy makers than that provided by neoclassical economists.

Submersion and Success

One of the subtle differences between pure academics and those acting within the world is that on campus, using someone else's material is a cardinal sin. To always properly footnote one's sources is drilled in, is elementary. Off campus, most articles and speeches delivered by public, business, and labor leaders are not written by them, and their writers are rarely acknowledged. Indeed, because the essence of the work is building consensus and mobilizing coalitions, to gain even a chance of success writers must be willing to submerge their contributions in speeches delivered by others, questions prepared for a senator to raise during a congressional hearing, or "eyes only" policy suggestions offered to a presidential

candidate. In effect, it might be said that the more widely
endorsed the societal change one favors, the less likely one is
to be credited with contributing to the change.

I learned this lesson early. In a series of articles, books,
and briefings in Washington during the early sixties, a well-
known psychologist, Charles Osgood, and I argued for a form
of psychological disarmament that we believed could reduce
the tensions of the cold war to a level at which multilateral
arms reductions could be possible. (We differed here both
from pacifists, who believed that unilateral disarmament by
the United States was the only way to proceed, and from the
prevailing consensus that the balance of terror, whereby each
side threatens the other with severe destruction, is the only
way to prevent nuclear war.) At first, we received the usual
treatment—criticism from all sides and little attention from
major policy makers. Eventually, however, for reasons that are
not yet completely clear to me, President Kennedy decided
to embrace the course that we suggested. To the extent that
he was able to follow it, it worked very much as expected.
There was little mention of the work that Osgood and I had
done on the subject. Indeed, given the way in which decisions are made—on the basis of many inputs, changes in public opinion, and other factors—even we cannot tell with any
certitude what role we played in the change, although there
seems to have been no one else who advocated the change
before it occurred. Certainly, one would rather have one's
role clearly determined and recognized, but after a brief period of disappointment, one moves on to the next project,
wiser. Those who seek to become active academics should not
expect their names to be engraved on societal improvements—especially significant ones that involve, as they usually do, casts of thousands.

The Curse of Dichotomies and Single-Factor Theories

In academia, recognizing gradations and subtleties is a mark
of a thinking person, surely of a scholar. On careful examination, one finds few things to be black and white. Off campus,

however, the world tends to think in terms of dichotomies. Moreover, in one major way, the task of those who seek to support one course of societal change and to deflect others in the real world has become more difficult over the decades. Television, which was a new technology when the earliest of the essays in this book were first published, gained ever more influence over the years, especially over the younger generation and, as they grew older, over ever larger portions of the society. It fed into a general tendency to simplify and to dichotomize (you are a hawk or dove, liberal or conservative, and so on). As a realist, I recognize that approaches that are inherently complex tend to lose out to single-factor analyses. Thus, a suggestion that the United States needs to fix seven elements of infrastruture, each with its own list of specifications, can hardly compete with the notion that all we need is less government intervention. The concept that deliberate societal change requires the coming together of wise policies with upward support, consensus formation, and coalition building and the complex ways in which these upward flows may be combined with some "downward" directional signals has a hard time competing with the notion that a clever Madison Avenue ad campaign can get people to "Just Say No" to drugs, curb the spread of AIDS, and so on. Unfortunately, the theory of societal guidance lacks a way to build the tolerance for complexities that is needed for most responsible societal change.

The lack of tolerance for complex and graduated positions made it difficult for the gradual way to peace to gain a full hearing when the public debate was divided between doves and hawks, between those who favored unilateral disarmament (who believed that if the West would just lay down its arms, others—especially the much feared U.S.S.R.—would follow) and those who believed in the need to keep the level of nuclear forces high and continuously update them to maintain the balance of terror and mutual deterrence. In matters of economic policy, the debate was divided between the free market and planning (or, later, industrial policy); the position I advance of semitargeting, favoring activities such as saving but not specific industries, did not find an easy place.

Never was this reality more evident than when I tried to help develop the social-philosophical positions of a communitarian movement. The essence of the position was that the individual's rights need to be balanced with concern for the community, a position that seemed to me elementary, almost self-evident (see the essay in Chapter Four on "Liberals and Communitarians"). However, those of us who raised that issue were very soon challenged from the libertarian side as "majoritarians" and authoritarians who wished to impose the community on individuals and by social conservatives as hidden individualists, unwilling to bite the bullet of social order. Even those who were willing to grant the abstract need for some balance between the particular and the commons strongly favored one-sided public policies when it came to questions such as whether carriers of the HIV virus should be expected to inform their sexual contacts or railroad engineers should be tested for drugs, vigorously defending one side or the other, as the ACLU and the Moral Majority did. This is despite the fact that the positions that can be best justified ethically and socially lie in intermediary positions between these two simplistic poles. It became necessary to defend the intermediary positions with the recognition that it is much more difficult to advocate such positions than to present an issue as a simple one-sided conception.

Sociology: A Happy Choice

Often when I read a newspaper, listen to talk shows on my car radio, or turn on the television, I feel distressed that sociology is not given—and is not giving—more of a hand. I am confident that if the world would listen more to sociology and if sociology would speak more to the world, it would be a much better—and safer—place. It hurts me to see billions of dollars squandered, millions of people made miserable, whole continents endangered because elementary sociological principles are ignored.

One may well ask at this point: What sociology? Is there one sociology on which one can draw? And are not sociologists' internal conflicts—indeed, our tendency to mutual scorn—a major reason sociology does not have much of the impact that it deserves? I join here Randall Collins's (1986) excellent essay "Is 1980s Sociology in the Doldrums?" Collins shows quite conclusively that while it is true that there currently is more sociological pluralism, at least within the United States, than there was, say, in the early 1960s, there has been considerable progress in many of the specialties or particular branches of sociology. Among those he lists are mathematical, historical, and economic sociologies; the study of emotion, sex and gender; and the study of micro-macro relations. Others could surely be added. In short, pluralism has enriched sociology, rather than impoverished it.

The internal conflicts and the sense of superiority with which all too many sociological camps eye one another may be an inevitable part of intellectual and disciplinary exchanges, but they are also vastly overdone. Sociology and its ability to serve would benefit from a considerable toning down of the fervor with which positions are espoused and greater respect for other avenues of progress; for example, the important work done by a variety of nonacademic practicing sociologists and by those who use qualitative methods.

What are some of the merits of sociology that I see that lead me to urge greater visibility for and use of sociological findings, concepts, methods, and insights? By and large, sociology has maintained a good balance between reality testing and theory development, between induction and deduction. Other social sciences have contributed more to one side than to the other. Mainstream Western economics, for example, has become highly mathematical and deductive. Nobel Prize-winning economist Wassily Leonteif examined the articles that appeared in the *American Economic Review* during much of the 1970s. He found that half of all the articles "represented mathematical models without any empirical data. Twenty-two percent of the articles contained empirical information, but it was essentially not information based on direct observations. They contained parameters which were derived by very complicated processes of indirect statistical inference. In short, most of the data were cooked up. Of the four or five articles based on direct observations made by the authors, one dealt with pigeons and the other with mice" (Leonteif, 1985, pp. 29–30).

The work of many psychologists, in contrast, is highly inductive. They conduct thousands of experimental studies, each covering a very limited range. Indeed, many psychologists have given up on concepts such as personality and group (or even attitude, emotions, and persuasion) as too global, too deductive (Zajonc, 1980, p. 152). Political science is increasingly swept by neoclassical models, while anthropology—to the extent that it has not been sociologized—is still largely a field of case studies and, by anthropologists' own accounts, one of storytelling (Schweder, 1986, p. 1). True, there are quite a few sociologists whose work is either highly mathematical or quite empirical, but this is beside the point. As a field or series of subfields that share knowledge, sociology's contribution is to combine a systematic collection of quantitative or qualitative data *and* theory building. It is the most balanced social science, not a small matter, because excessive deduction makes theories irrelevant, and excessive induction undermines generalization.

In an age of growing egocentrism, interest-group politics, and radical individualism, sociology is the disciplinary custodian of the commons, of institutions, value systems, and even the polity, the "we's" into which all those "I's" must fit. Radical sociologists may fairly argue that society has a conservative bias and that the existing society (its institutions and values) may be an imposed one. But even if one maintains that a fundamentally different community needs to be constructed, one still holds to a concept of the commons, a concept lost in the analyses that merely aggregate individual behavior, as in economics, or are preoccupied with individual behavior, as in psychology.

One could readily extend the list of the strong conceptual and methodological features of sociology, but it is time to turn to the core questions: Why is society not more attentive? What would it take for sociology to be drawn on more frequently by society, whether it be Washington, self-help movements, labor unions, or some other group?

Until the matter is systematically studied, one hazards some guesses. Part of the problem is obviously image. Other disciplines have publications that carry their messages to the world (for example, *Psychology Today*); we are still in the process of evolving one. Other disciplines have been more active in ensuring that their members participate in various private and public councils of policy making; we do not have the same resources that the American Psychological Association commands, and we must overcome the rift between academic and practicing sociologists to be able to do more in these areas.

One way or another we must find ways to tell our story better and to ensure that sociologists have more opportunities to show what they can do. Former Executive Director of the American Sociological Association William D'Antonio's idea to make sociology the lead in a campaign to deal with the public health aspects of AIDS is an excellent illustration of what might be done. Case studies of sociological "success stories" might be another avenue. There must be others. I do not have at my fingertips a list of steps that could ensure for sociology the opportunity to better serve society and to itself further develop in the process, which both society and sociology require. And, given the limits of sociology's investment in self-analysis, some steps that may be tried will initially fail and new suggestions arise. But without continued and increased effort to enhance sociology's service to society, both society and sociology will be the losers.

A Minority of One

On rare occasions, it has been necessary for me to hold on to a position that no one else, at least in my intellectual and social circles, shared. This isolation is regrettable; my communication skills must have been defective and my effectiveness quite limited if I could not convince even like-minded people of the merits of my positions on the questions at issue.

In some instances (for example, in advocating my position on gun control), I tried to trim sails at the edges to see whether the approach would sail better this way without compromising the basic course. This proved to be impossible, however, when I dealt with moral relativism. Here, mine is a position that most everyone I know, other than those who are religiously committed, subscribes to implicitly if not explicitly. Indeed, for a long time, holding this position has been considered part of being sophisticated or enlightened, if not culturally superior. It is considered one of the great liberalizing experiences resulting from the study of anthropology and sociology that we learn to realize that our values tend to color our views of others, that others have their own sets of values, to which they are just as committed as we are to ours, that there is no appropriate reason to believe that our values are superior to theirs, and so on.

Strong utilitarian tendencies further support this approach by suggesting that what is right depends on calculation of costs and benefits. This was highlighted by a discussion that took place at the Harvard Business School. During a class discussion of a case concerning Braniff Airlines, which was facing bankruptcy, a student wondered whether the CEO should not have lied to a potential customer about the airline's prospects. The instructor was not sure how to respond and discussed the question with other faculty members, who were also puzzled. As a result, a cross-faculty seminar was created to come up with an answer (I served as one of the four organizers). Most members of the seminar endorsed the notion of a calculus of harm. That is, they argued that if the CEO felt that more people were going to be harmed by telling the truth than by lying, the CEO should have lied, and vice versa. This explicit form of moral relativism by cost-benefit analysis is very close in concept to the more often implicit popular one.

I advanced during the seminar the deontological position that we have an obligation not to lie. Of course, we do not always live up to our moral commitments, but that does not make them relativistic. And there are special circumstances, whose moral principles can be articulated, that modify our basic commitment. For instance, we recognize that a lie told strictly to help the person lied to—for example, when we encourage a patient about to go into surgery by being more cheerful about the outcome than we have a scientific reason to be—is morally much more acceptable than a lie told to advance our interests at the other's expense. I found only a few active supporters of this view in the seminar—or outside it. (In the United States, deontology is much less widely subscribed to than is utilitarianism.)

In the essay in Chapter Four on "Basic Human Needs, Alienation, and Inauthenticity," I argue that we are all god's children in the sense that we are created in the same basic manner and acquire the same basic human needs. All people are subject to the process of socialization; this process, in turn, builds into us specific universal human needs, such as the need for the approval of others. Once internalized and individually honed, these needs become the basis of our inner moral voice. Evidence for this view is seen in the fact that when a societal structure is constructed that works against basic human needs (or human nature), people come to resent it and, when possible, fight it or change it rather than learning to appreciate whatever pattern the particular society comes up with. That is, we cannot be successfully socialized into structures that are incompatible with our nature. (All of that was written long before human nature won dramatically against Communist regimes after decades of socialization.)

In the decades that followed the first publication of that essay, I repeated its points to numerous students and colleagues and argued them in the popular press and in faculty meetings, in which the question "whose values are we going to teach?" is often used as a kind of trump argument to stop the teaching of ethics. I never heard a counterargument that I found compelling (as I did in other areas). Indeed, unlike the many areas in which I tend to stir up either support or spirited opposition, here the most common response is silence. I hence feel justified in my position that seeing people as having different basic human needs is a major step toward racism. It is easy to see that if we assume, for instance, that African Americans have needs different from the needs of white Americans, it follows that they may be differently treated. While consensus building and intellectual give-and-take may be called for in some areas, when it comes to fundamental moral issues, one must stick to one's position. I hence present the case for basic human needs here one more time, as Luther put it, because I cannot do otherwise.

References

Collins, R. "Is 1980s Sociology in the Doldrums?" *American Journal of Sociology,* May 1986, pp. 1336–1355.

Etzioni, A. "Mass Psychology in the White House." *Society,* Nov./Dec. 1980.

Leonteif, W. "Interview: Why Economics Needs Input-Output Analysis." *Challenge,* Mar–Apr. 1985, pp. 29–30.

Schweder, R. A. "Storytelling Among the Anthropologists." *New York Times Book Review,* Sept. 21, 1986, p. 1.

Zajonc, R. B. "Feeling and Thinking: Preferences Need No Inferences." *American Psychologist,* 1980, *35* (2), 152.

2

Conditions for Guiding Change: Author's Note

Guidance theory deals with the conditions under which societies are able to guide themselves, understand their condition, and control their fate. It asks questions similar to those that Communist leaders in the early 1990s have asked as they try to steer their countries toward democracy and freer economies; its queries mirror those of Western European nations as they attempted to form a united states of Europe and of Margaret Thatcher during a decade of efforts to turn Britain into a laissez-faire society. These are only a few of countless efforts to deliberately change society, many of which are less drastic and visible—endeavors to change race relations, to evolve new gender roles, and to flatten the class structure.

Guidance theory differs from other studies of societal change in that it focuses on deliberate changes as distinct from those that merely occur. It focuses on changes that reflect public policies, social movements or interest groups, rather than, say, subtle but cumulative changes in the work ethic, family values, or other areas that no one planned on, wished for, or was even aware were occurring. These types of changes are as different from one another as a free flowing mountain river is from a cement lined canal equipped with locks and pumps.

At the same time, this is hardly a theory of social engineering or control; it is not a theory of cybernetics. In part, it is dedicated to exploring the conditions under which the "downward" signals and flow of power are responsive to and reflect "upward" flows (the consensus and power of those governed). It is a deeply democratic theory of societal change, not merely a formal one. The theory is based not only on occasional votes but also on the authentic engagement of society's members in the formation and implementation of social policies and structural changes.

It might be said that this theory grew out of my experiences at Berkeley on the eve of the 1960s. More likely, its roots lie in my upbringing in Israel, serving on a kibbutz, and my experience as a member of a Zionist movement dreaming about and then forming the state of Israel. While some of my colleagues in those days were Communists who later became socialists, then liberals, and eventually ended up neoconservatives, I joined the youth section of MAPI (the Labor Party) at age fifteen and have been quite at home with its social-democratic ideals ever since. While the two core elements of guidance theory do not represent any particular ideological or political position, the combination of an active social agenda with a thoroughly democratic approach does reflect a social science "processing" of my earlier roots.

The presentation of the guidance theory here is necessarily brief (a full text is found in *The Active Society*). It stands at the front of this collection to suggest that it provides a framework for much that follows.

A Theory of
Societal Guidance

A 1987 conference on institutional design organized by
Vernon W. Ruttan, Leonid Hurwicz, John P. Campbell, and
Styam Sunder provided the participants with a discussion out-
line that included the following text:

> How free is the society to choose the path of institutional
> change that it will follow? Is society as free as planners fre-
> quently assume when they design new institutions? Or is in-
> stitutional design dominated by historical or evolutionary
> forces such as changing resource and cultural endowments?

The answer, as we see it, lies between the voluntarist
pole (of an actor "free" to design at will, which assumes a
very malleable social system or a very powerful overlay) and
the determinist pole (which assumes little or no ability to
guide). The productive question is: Under what conditions is
the ability to guide enhanced?

After implicitly ignoring or explicitly challenging the
need to study institutions (North, 1987, p. 2), select followers
of the neoclassical paradigm are turning to study it, in their
way. They treat institutions as designed and fashioned at will
by freestanding, rational individuals, seeking to maximize
their utilities. For example, hierarchical institutions (corporations) are said to be introduced, when they are needed,
because "decentralized" markets are found to be inefficient
when the volume of transactions that need coordination is
high and the knowledge needed to coordinate is great
(Williamson, 1975; Heiner, 1983). Other societal-historical
factors are treated in the same manner: value systems

Note: Adapted from "Toward a Theory of Societal Guidance," *American Journal of Sociology,* 1967, *73*(2), 173–187.

(Ullmann-Margalit, 1977) norms (Field, 1984), rules (Baumol and Quandt, 1964; Frank, 1987), societal structures, and even the unfolding of history itself (North, 1981).

The philosophical roots of this approach are Lockean. The image that permeates these writings is of a state of nature that preceded society and its institutions, a state in which individuals join to form commons out of rational deliberations and in line with their interests. Locke and others, who drew on this image, realized quite well that history did not evolve in that way, but used the image for heuristic purposes. It might hence be quite unnecessary to argue that historically the commons preceded the individuals and to a large extent fashioned them. The pivotal question, though, remains: What is the validity of the paradigm, which the heuristic devices serve to chart?

The neoclassical design school of institutions, broadly understood, may well be partially valid. Its deepest problems arise not from the factors it encompasses, but from those it does not embrace. The resulting partial view, we shall see, is seriously flawed. The highly voluntarist, individualist and rationalist perspective ignores deterministic, collective, and nonrational factors, which *together* with those the design school does encompass, may account for much of the dynamics of institutions, society, and history.

In effect, whether one takes the viewpoints of a single actor (an individual) or a collective one (as embodied in the White House, a legislature, or other such organs), the actor faces major non-designable factors, including historical forces, environmental factors, and *other actors* not necessarily cooperative. Corporate executives may lay out hierarchical blueprints, but power flows within corporations, in part, along "informal," often horizontal, undesigned, and uncontrollable, lines. Legal experts may fashion contracts, laws or international treaties, but societal forces bend them in ways difficult to anticipate and impossible to prevent. Victorious social movements, such as the Communists in 1917 in the U.S.S.R., may seek to design a society without religion, family, hierarchy, coercion, or stratification, but advance a society with strong and growing elements of all the factors they sought to undo.

There is no reason to embrace the opposite extreme, the neoromantic perspective, a view of society and history as governed by forces we are neither able to comprehend nor to control (Shweder, 1986), or to assume that collective interventions are bound to fail (Wildavsky and Pressman, 1986). It seems most productive to presuppose a perpetual, in part creative, conflict between the forces of design and those of inertia and opposition, to see social systems as in part guided by a cybernational overlay, and as in part an underlay composed of collective bodies, of societal bonds, values, institutions, and powers that resist guidance. Once the key elements of both parts are specified, we are ready to ask the pivotal question those who seek to design must face: Under what conditions are the guiding factors *relatively* more powerful? What renders a society *relatively* more malleable?

A brief terminological digression is necessary here. The use of the term "design" provides an image we suggest one ought to avoid. It produces an image of a world that is a *tabula rasa*, like the paper on which an architect draws his or her design, a subject without "designs" or attributes of its own, or power to resist being drawn upon. The term *control* has similar although less extreme, voluntaristic, omnipotent implications. We prefer to use the term *guidance*, to stress that whatever the designers indicate is but one source of the resulting dynamics; it reflects a combination of "downward" control efforts and "upward" flow of societal consensus, which both sustains and limits control. Institutions, values, society, and history can be guided but not controlled, let alone "designed."

The Key Elements

The concept that societies (and sub-societies such as communities, races, and ethnic groups) have cybernatorial capacities is highlighted by the fact that—via their organizational embodiments—they set goals, form policies, and seek to guide social processes, including changes in their own structures, even in their guiding mechanisms. Governments, headquarters and local offices of professional and voluntary associations, lobbies, and corporate hierarchies are cases in point. The processes of such organizational expressions of societal collectivities are akin to individual decision-making in that knowledge is used, inferences are drawn, and so on.

The organizational embodiments which provide the cybernatorial overlay typically contain cybernatorial heads, which generate policies, which in turn are transmitted to their "bodies" for implementation. The "bodies" typically consist of so-called bureaucracies or organizational structures, which—at the direction of the "heads"—seek to introduce the decisions made into the underlay. (In effect, the "bodies" often affect the "heads"; that is, the implementing bodies affect the decisions that guide them, but this is a subject for another occasion.) Only highly voluntaristic theory assumes that it is enough to fashion a plan, or to emit a signal, and it will not require specialized implementation efforts, investments, and structures. It may seem unrealistic in the extreme to make such assumptions, but much of economic theory used to assume, and significant segments still do, that information travels at the speed of light, is instantly absorbed, and without cost (Thurow, 1983). Political scientist Karl Deutsch (1963) called his book *The Nerves of Government* to contrast it with the use of muscle or power. He pointed out that if you know how to choose the right key to a door, it will readily open; there is no need for power. More generally, he expected that knowledge and communication, in the postmodern society, will replace power. In contrast, it is assumed here that there are no transactions among equals (that is, all transactions are affected by power differentials) (Etzioni, 1988, part III), and at least a marginal power advantage is a necessary prerequisite of implementation.

The main structures of implementation are hierarchies (whether those of public agencies, private corporations or voluntary associations), regulation, and other forms of intervention in the market and society (for example, subsidies).

While these structures draw on persuasion and information, power often plays a key role. For example, a government agency that seeks to curb drunken driving uses not only dissemination of public service announcements and driver education to call attention to the dangers of driving while intoxicated but also fines and incarceration. The need to apply power to enhance the introduction of a policy, to be able to guide under most circumstances, is an indication of the existence of resisting factors that must be overcome if they cannot be won over, so that implementation may take place.

The collective bodies, into which the guiding signals and forces are injected, are typical of organized groupings and their linkages, not atomized individuals. These groupings include local communities, ethnic groups, neighborhoods, and other such social bodies the members of which are bound to one another by social bonds and value commitments. They often have guidance mechanisms of their own (labor unions are an example) which often act as constraints rather than serve as resources for guidance from the viewpoint of the actor under study, because these "other" actors tend to follow their own course.

The Cybernatorial/Collective Ratios

A list of propositions follows, all of which have the same structure: Factors are listed that are expected to increase guidability and the reasons for this expectation are provided.

Effectiveness of the Cybernational Head

Knowledge: Working Hypotheses. Societal units differ in their capacity to collect, process, and use information. This holds not only for corporations that compete over a market, but also other social units, for example, political parties (Kennedy is believed to have used social sciences more effectively than Nixon in the 1960 campaign), federal agencies (the Air Force is thought to be superior in this respect to the Navy and the Army), and civic organizations.

We suggest that the input of knowledge into a societal unit follows the same basic patterns other inputs do; that is, it might be blocked (and hence partially or completely lost for action purposes) at each stage of the process. Societal units have varying facilities for collecting information (raw material input). This capacity seems to be associated with economic affluence but not in a one-to-one relationship. If we were to order countries or other societal units by their per capita income and then score their information collection capacity, say in terms of expenditure on research, we would expect the most affluent units to have much higher capacity than the next affluent ones, and all the other units would have few such capacities. In short, patterns of interunit distribution of knowledge assets seem significantly more inegalitarian than are those of distribution of other economic assets. All other things being equal, the lending units in knowledge assets should have a guidance advantage.

The ratio of collecting information to processing information is an indicator of the sophistication of the cybernatorial overlayer and the knowledge-strategy to which the particular unit subscribes. The United States and Great Britain, it seems, tend to invest relatively highly in data collection; France, at least until recently, has stressed relatively more processing.[1] A societal unit that emphasizes disproportionately the collection of information will, we expect, have a fragmented view of itself and its environment; it will have many bits but no picture, like a survey study before tabulation. Such processing will tend to be associated with drifting (or passivity) as information that is not sufficiently processed is in effect not available for active societal guidance.

On the other hand, a unit that overemphasizes processing is expected to have an unempirical view of itself and its environment, because it will tend to draw more conclusions from the available information than are warranted; it is similar to acting on the basis of a poorly validated theory. Thus, overprocessing is expected to be associated with hyperactivity, as the actors assume they know more than they do. Master plans used to guide economic development are typically hyperactive in their assumptions. Finally, societal units whose collection and processing are relatively balanced (not in absolute amounts but in terms of intrinsic needs of their guidance mechanisms) are expected to have comparatively more effective controlling overlayers, all other things being equal, and to be active without being hyperactive.

Information that has been processed might still be wasted as far as the societal unit is concerned if it is not systematically introduced into the unit's decision-making and implementation overlayer where the main conflictive consumption of information takes place (Homans, 1950, pp. 364–414). Two major variables seem useful for characterizing the different arrangements societal units have for interaction between the knowledge-producing and the decision-making units; one concerns the relative degree of autonomy of production, the other, the effectiveness of communications of the product. It is widely believed that structural differentiation between the producers and consumers of information is necessary; fusion of the two kinds of units—for instance, in the management of a corporation—is viewed as dysfunctional both for production of knowledge and for decision making. For societal units whose knowledge and decision-making units are differentiated, various modes and forms of articulation and communication exist whose relative effectiveness remains to be explored. Here we can touch on only one aspect of this intricate subject.

The controlling overlayer itself has layers upon layers; processing is superimposed on the collecting of information, both in the logical sense that the one presupposes the other, and in the structural sense that those engaged in processing tend to have higher ranks and more power to mold the societal input of knowledge than those who collect information (Hilsman, 1956).

Differences in the internal structure of the control overlayer affect the total action capacity of societal units. The division between those who work within a given knowledge framework and those who seek to transform it, and the structural relations between them, seem to be of much cybernatorial importance. Consumption and, to a degree, processing of knowledge are inevitably in part political processes.

That is, which part of the available knowledge is used and what conclusions are reached on the basis of the knowledge are in part determined by political factors. These include consideration of the knowledge producers in terms of the internal politics of the organizations in which knowledge is processed, their affiliations with political groupings in the society at large, and the differential absorption by various political actors of the knowledge produced, according to its political rather than its intrinsic value. The core of the politicization of knowledge lies often not in deliberate or subconscious slanting of facts but in the interpretive and judgmental elements most items of knowledge include. It is not, as some students of administration would have it, that knowledge-units produce information and the political decision-making elites add the judgment. The producers of knowledge play an active role in formulating the judgments. (All these issues were highlighted during the CBS-Westmoreland trial which dealt with the information about the war in Vietnam that the military provided to the White House, Congress, and the public.)

Within this context, one issue is of special significance for the study of societal guidance: the effect of the relative investments in two sections of the cybernatorial overlayer, namely transforming versus stable knowledge production. Transforming knowledge rechecks and potentially challenges the basic assumptions of a system. Stable knowledge elaborates and respecifies, even revises, secondary assumptions within the framework of a basic set which is taken for granted. Most decision-making elites most of the time seem to prefer stable over transforming knowledge production, to seek closure on basic knowledge assumptions precisely because they cannot be selected and reviewed on wholly empirical grounds. Hence, once consensus has been reached on the basic assumptions of a world-view, a self-view, a view of others, strategic doctrine, and the like, it is expensive politically, economically, and psychologically for the elites to transform these assumptions (Janis, 1972). Therefore they tend to become tabooed assumptions, and knowledge production tends to become limited to specifics within the limits of the assumptions. At the same time, the ability to transform basic perspectives is sharply reduced and with it the capacity for societal self-transformation. The societal units survive as long as the range of tolerance of their knowledge and societal pattern allows for sufficient adaptation to environmental changes, but such adaptation tends to become increasingly inadequate and costly.

More active units have supralayers that can be activated to review and transform tabooed assumptions. A comparison of corporations that have shifted to a new line of products, restructured their internal organization, and found new markets when their old markets were gradually lost, with those whose sales and profits declined or "died" because of lack of innovations, suggests that transforming corporations maintained units which were not only exempt from the tabooed assumptions but were also, among other things, expected sporadically to review these assumptions. That is, part of their institutionalized role was to engage in search behavior precisely where the decision-making elites would otherwise settle for "satisficing" solutions.

The societal parallel of this cybernatorial arrangement is not difficult to see. The intellectual community acts as a series of societal knowledge units, as critical examiners of tabooed assumptions. Under what economic, political, and sociological conditions it can fulfill this function and what, if any, functional alternatives exist, are questions social scientists have strong feelings about—but there is surprisingly little systematic research (Coser, 1965).

At first blush, it would seem obvious that the more knowledge an actor commands, the more the actor is able to guide a social system. Thus, an Agency for International Development (A.I.D.) project conceived by experts is expected to be much more effective than one conceived by amateurs. And, it is expected for experts to be more able to design a program against a problem about which they know a great deal (for example, traffic congestion) than one about which they know little (for example, mental illness) because there is a more extensive body of knowledge about the causes and cures of the first social problem than the second. However, on closer examination, the question of the knowledge of the societal guide turns out to be a rather complex matter, and not merely a question of the amount of knowledge the cybernatorial overlay commands.

One complexity emerges out of the tension between specialization and comprehensiveness. Expert knowledge tends to be specialized; however, social systems are multi-faceted and as a rule it is not possible to significantly modify one element without either modifying the others or dealing with linkages to the others. Otherwise, the untreated elements become the source of "irrational," "unanticipated" reactions. For example, if one introduces an austerity program into a less developed country (LDC) to curb inflation without attention to the political consequences, the result of an attempt to improve the economy may be a military dictatorship. On another front, the result of more effective border patrols to intercept shipments of controlled substances may be urban crime waves; the price of drugs rises as supplies are reduced.

Effective guidance, it seems, requires both knowledge that is *expert* (valid, well-formulated, advanced, and typically specialized) and *encompassing* (covering the main relevant variables—something training in policy "sciences" and experience is more likely to provide than highly specialized training). I offer a discussion of the difficulties entailed in combining specialized knowledge to make encompassing knowledge and ways to proceed elsewhere (Etzioni, 1985).

Furthermore, the question concerning which knowledge is "valid" is far from a simple one. Knowledge is often produced in analytic frameworks that define the criteria of validation but this does not mean that such knowledge is useful for guidance purposes. For instance, "findings" by neoclassical economists often reflect a combination of assumptions and weighted regression analyses, which are "validated" by dovetailing the conclusions of one analysis with those of a similarly composed other, but do not necessarily serve as a reliable base for intervening in the economy. Thus, attempts to enhance saving by providing tax incentives with All-Savers certificates, and more recently IRAs, generated little if any net gain in saving.

In short, while knowledge may well be the most "rational" component of the cybernational overlay, it contains major difficulties, which if not insurmountable, render guidance a far from straightforward or "rational" endeavor, one that *requires at least some trial and error* to adjust the course as factors not understood come into play rather than relying on the course indicated by the original analysis. That is, if one could understand fully a situation and the consequences of one's interventions in that situation, one could plan, in detail, what must be done to engineer a desired change. Or, if one knew nothing, one could seek random interventions. However, the fact that knowledge is often *partial* (not to be confused with "imperfect" knowledge) suggests that the preliminary formulations of a policy are to be followed by *focused* trial and error (within a range defined by knowledge, not a random search); this, in turn, will lead to frequent revisions of one's policy. That is, policies ought to be treated as little more than working hypotheses in which one has limited confidence. This may seem "obvious" but is a point frequently ignored by many policy advocates, planners, and active citizens. Indeed, liberals in the 1960s focused on passing legislation rather than how and if it was implemented, one of the greatest failings of the New Frontier and the Great Society.

"Appropriate" Decision-Making Strategy. The ability of actors to guide is affected by their choice of decision-making strategies. There are no universally appropriate decision-making strategies; they must be suited to the given level of knowledge and to the task. Thus, while in the abstract decision-making strategies that scan widely and deeply (examining a wide range of options, each in detail) may seem superior to those that scan less, this often is not the case, for instance, when knowledge is costly. Indeed, recently Frank (1987) called attention to the advantages of "searching" less, even

adopting what otherwise may seem to be quite unsatisfying solutions, when search costs are high.

Another factor is the complexity of the task. Very simple tasks allow for highly rationalistic decision making (one may be able to find the perfect solution) although even for a game of checkers this is a rather daunting task. Complex tasks, which all societal tasks are, require much less exacting decision-making strategies; for example, mixed scanning rather than full scanning decision makers, who apply a mixed scanning strategy, first examine major sectors in a generalized way, choose which sectors to examine in detail, and explore more fully only options that fall into the chosen sections. While such strategies will yield non-optimal choices, they are much less taxing than full scanning (Etzioni, 1986).

Also, the decision-making strategy used must fit the actor's other capabilities. Thus, the U.S.S.R. chose in 1917 a highly detailed form of centralized planning, before the use of computers and without a sophisticated data base, extremely overloading its national guidance system.

One typical decision which those in charge of guided change often have to make, at what are relatively critical turning points, is between acceleration and deceleration of the processes of change they guide. When a societal change is initiated—whether it be collectivization of farms, federation, or desegregation—resistance tends to accumulate because existing patterns are upheld by vested interests which are often threatened by the changes. As a change is being advanced, there is often at least one critical turning point at which resistance rises to a point where it challenges those in control: the president thinks he might not be reelected; a government believes it might be overthrown, or a part of the country might secede. The decision those in power then face is between acceleration, in hope of overpowering the opposition and reaching a stage at which the support of those that will benefit from the new pattern will rise, or slowing down to give more time for the opposition to be worked out, circumvented, educated, or otherwise dealt with. Wrong decisions made at such junctions are particularly detrimental to effective guidance.

Cybernational Power

The basic neoclassical paradigm has no place for the concept of power. This point is usually expressed by saying that no firm has an ability to affect the market. As Stigler puts it: "The essence of perfect competition, therefore, is the utter dispersion of power" (1968, p. 181). He adds that in this way power is "annihilated . . . just as a gallon of water is effectively annihilated if it is spread over a thousand acres".[2] Nor do other voluntarist, rationalist paradigms have a concept of power. In effect, even a cursory examination of incidents of guidance shows that aside from the wisdom of the decisions made, students of guidance and its architects must know by how much power decisions are backed, to overcome resistance. Power is defined as the ability of *a* to make *b* follow *a*'s instructions. In this context, cybernational power refers to the relative strength of the overlay over the underlay, such as management versus workers or labor unions or the government versus those governed.

A central predisposition of societal guidance is that the relationship between assets and power is a loose one—that is, the amount of assets a societal unit commands is a poor predictor of how much societal power the unit has. The amount of power generated depends significantly on the allocation of a unit's assets among alternative usages. A unit poor in assets can, in principle, command more power than a much more affluent one, if the poor unit assigns more of its assets to power "production." (With half the GNP the Soviet Union long maintained a defense budget similar to that of the United States.)

What fraction of the assets a unit possesses is converted into power is itself influenced by the societal context and not freely set by the societal actor (for example, the fact that Black Americans were politically less active than Jewish Americans up to the 1960s was in part due to differences in educational opportunities). However, we suggest, the degree of intraunit assignment of assets to power is a relatively more malleable attribute than the amount of assets the unit possesses (at any given point in time). It is here that an important element of

voluntarism enters the societal structure. A comparison of colonial societies in the years immediately preceding the takeoff
of national independence movements with those immediately
after they won their independence suggests that the takeoff
involved more change in the relative use of assets for power
than in the assets base. Similarly, the American civil rights
movement, which between 1953 and 1965 transformed important segments of the American Black community from a passive to an active grouping, entailed much more of a change in
mobilization of power than in amount of assets, (Wilson,
1965, esp. pp. 5–7).

Each societal unit has at any given point in time a level
of activation which we define as the ratio of its assets that are
available for collective action to its total assets. The percent
of the GNP spent by the government, the percent of the labor force employed by it, and the percent of knowledge producers that work for it are crude indicators of national activation level. Mobilization refers to an upward change in the
level of activation, to an increase in the fraction of the total
assets possessed by a unit that are made available for collective action by that unit. (Demobilization refers to a reduction
in that level.)

The level of activation of most societal units most of
the time is very low; if all their assets are taken into account,
usually less than ten percent are available for unit action.
Hence relatively small percentage changes in the level of mobilization may largely increase the action capacity of a unit.
For example, an increase of ten percent in the assets of a
unit that are mobilized might more than double its action
capacity. Major societal transformations, such as revolutions
and the gaining of national independence, usually involve
relatively high mobilization. The secret of the power of social
movements lies in part in the relatively high mobilization
which their asceticism and the intense commitment of their
members allow for.

To some extent, the amount of power applied, the level
of knowledge used, and the appropriateness of the decision-
making strategy that is applied can be traded off. For instance, a poorly conceived decision can be implemented if

backed by much power, and a wise decision requires less power backing. However, there are clear limits on such trade-offs, and as a rule all three guidance elements must be mobilized as much as possible, because typically the overlay is very short on all, in view of the severe limits of the ability to know, to decide rationally, and to mobilize power, and in view of the typically strong inertia or resistance of the underlay.

The Cybernatorial Underlay

The underlay, the part of the system subject to the overlay at which its signals and interventions are largely aimed, is the body society, or the corporate employees (bound into groups, informal organizations, culture, and associations), depending upon which system we study. We already noted that the underlay is quite powerful, quite often more so than the overlay. One main reason for this power differential is that the underlay often contains actors that have some cybernational capacities of their own, largely aimed at the overlay (for example, workers vs. management). And, frequently the course these actors seek to follow is not supportive of that of the overlay.

So far, guidance of change has been explored from a downward view, from the controlling overlayer to the controlled underlayer; even the discussion of subject resistance has been from the viewpoint of a controlling center. The main difference, though, between the societal and electronic cybernetic is that in the societal we take into account systematically that the controlled units have some of the controlling capacities themselves: they input knowledge, make decisions, pursue goals, and exercise power. Hence the capacity of any one unit to act is determined only in part by its ability to control the others; it is similarly affected by the degree of consensus, that is, the degree to which the goals it has chosen to pursue and the means it employs are compatible or in conflict with those preferred by other units.

Consensus, the congruence of preferences of the units concerned, is viewed by typical deterministic theories as largely given (or changing under the impact of ongoing processes); voluntaristic theories tend to view it as open to manipulation by charismatic leadership and/or mass media. From the viewpoint of the societal guidance theory evolved here, consensus is the result of a process in which both given preferences expressed "upward" (for example, via elections) and downward efforts (government campaigns such as "just say no" to drugs) affect the outcome, resulting in a changing consensus. Many studies have applied such a perspective; in societal guidance it finds a theoretical home. How much consensus is actually achieved changes with a variety of socio-political factors that cannot be explored here.

As a direct result, the extent to which the total system is guidable depends highly on two factors: First, the extent to which the goals of the overlay and of the underlay are to begin with, or can be made to be, compatible. One way compatibility can be advanced, is for the overlay to mobilize the support of the underlay. Such an endeavor presupposes a highly persuasive overlay, able to gain the voluntary support of the underlay. This kind of mobilization is found when a nation is engaged in what the citizens perceive as a just way, or in revolutionary movements, when a social movement takes over a government like the Nazis in Germany in the late 1930s or the Communist movement in 1917 U.S.S.R., or movements of national liberation, after World War II. However, such high ability of the overlay to mobilize the underlay is quite rare. Under most circumstances, the ability of even totalitarian, let alone authoritarian and demoralistic, governments to mobilize their citizens is quite limited. Governments seek to combat alcoholism and corruption (as seen recently in the U.S.S.R.), but they remain rampant; the United States seeks to enhance democracy in other countries, but it remains highly unstable (for example, in Argentina, Haiti and the Philippines); the IMF, the World Bank, and local governments seek to curb inflation but it keeps breaking through (in Israel and in many other countries). Recently, Gorbachev was forced to slow down his grand reforms in the face of widespread resistance. The U.S.S.R.—despite being a totalitarian power—could not impose its designs on Afghanistan any more than the United States could on Vietnam.

A higher degree of compatibility is achieved the other way around, when the overlay is responsive to goal inputs from the underlay in well functioning representative governments. This, in turn, presupposes high consensus among the various component parts of the underlay, or in authoritarian countries, a high level of *intra* underlay power concentration, which renders ineffectual those unheeded.

Indeed a major, if not *the* major, difference between the concept of guidability and those of design and of control is that guidability assumes that a significant role is played by the body society in its governance, in setting public policies and in form and reform of the structures that influence these policies. It is not "downward" process but a combination of "upward" process with "downward" flows, with the role of upward signaling and application of power often exceeding those of the "downward" ones. However, because of internal divisions within both layers (but especially the underlay) and between them, guidance is a complex undertaking, quickly overloaded and often rather slow, costly, cumbersome, and far from effectual.

There is a trade-off curve between control and consensus; that is, for any given level of activation, the greater consensus, the less need for control. Which mix is used is, of course, not without consequences; it affects the level of alienation and of resistance, and hence the future capacity to guide. It is important to realize that when both consensus and control are relatively high, more change can be guided than when both are lower, without an increase in alienation. (The additional consensus absorbs the additional alienation which the additional control would generate.)

To illustrate a societal guidance approach to the study of consensus formation, we briefly compare built-in to segregated consensus formation structures. In a built-in structure consensus formation is by and large the output of ongoing interactions among the societal units. For example, consensus formation in smaller and less complex preliterate tribes seems to rely largely on ongoing interaction among the member families. In the Soviet society, consensus is to a degree produced in the process of interaction among factory manager, union leaders, and party officials, though the prime function of these interactions is not consensus formation but is economic and administrative in nature (in the downward guidance sense of the term). (see Berlinger, 1957, and Brzezinski and Huntington, 1965, pp. 124–190.) In a segregated structure, political units (such as parties and legislatures) exist as distinct from societal ones, and societal differences are translated into political ones before consensus concerning collective action is worked out. Segregated structures seem more effective for consensus formation than built-in ones, though they can produce only enough to back up comparatively low levels of activation. They are like a sophisticated machine that cannot be used for heavy duty.

In the search for a structure that would allow for more guided change and higher consensus, a search that is far from completed, voluntary planning has been developed in France in the postwar years and by the European Economic Community. In such planning, there is less segregation of political and societal units than in the segregated structure (typical of traditional democracies) but more than in built-in structures (typical of totalitarian regimes). Above all, the knowledge input units are related not only to the decision-making units but also to the consensus-forming process, thus informing the controlled and not just the controlling units, and remodeling the judgments that information units produce—on the basis of interaction with both groupings.

Conclusion

The more we understand the factors that determine the ability to guide, the more we realize that the capacity is typically limited. Far from being highly subject to design, far from being highly malleable, societies (and sub-societies) typically are highly resistant to guided change. The extent to which societies are malleable depends to a significant extent not merely or even firstly on the attributes of the controlling parts, but significantly on those of the guided units, and their relations to the controlling overlay. Hence, the importance of a conception that encompasses both kinds of attributes.

Notes

1. This is one meaning that is implied when the Anglo-Saxon tradition is characterized as pragmatic and the French as rationalistic. For some evidence related to differences in economic planning, see Andrew Shonfield. *Modern Capitalism: The Changing Balance of Public and Private Power.* New York: Oxford University Press, 1965, pp. 151–175.
2. Neoclassical theories have been advanced that draw on the concept of power, including studies of industrial organization, and those of monopolistic behavior. The extent to which these theories are successful and remain with the basic paradigm is a subject not explored here.

References

Baumol, William J. and Richard E. Quandt. 1964. "Rules of Thumb and Optimally Imperfect Decision". *American Economic Review.* Vol. 54 (March), pp. 23–46.

Berlinger, Joseph. 1957. *Factory and Manager in the USSR.* Cambridge: Harvard University Press.

Brzezinski, Zbigniew and Samuel P. Huntington. 1965. *Political Power: USA/USSR..* New York: Viking.

Coser, Lewis. 1965. *Men of Ideas.* New York: Free Press.

Deutsch, Karl W. 1963. *The Nerves of Government.* New York: Free Press.

Etzioni, Amitai. 1985. "Making Policy for Complex Systems: A Medical Model for Economics." *Journal of Policy Analysis and Management.* Vol. 4, No. 3, pp. 383–395.

Etzioni, Amitai. 1986. "Mixed Scanning Revisited." *Public Administration Review.* Vol. 46, No. 1 (Jan./Feb.), pp. 8–14.

Etzioni, Amitai. 1988. *The Moral Dimension. Toward a New Economics.* New York: Free Press.

Field, Alexander James. 1984. "Microeconomics, Norms and Rationality." *Economic Development and Cultural Change.* Vol. 32, No. 4 (July), pp. 683–711.

Frank, Robert H. 1987. "Shrewdly Irrational." *Sociological Forum.* Vol. 2, No. 1 (Winter), pp. 21–41.

Heiner, Ronald A. 1983. "The Origin of Predictable Behavior." *American Economic Review.* Vol. 73, No. 4 (Sept.), pp. 560–595.

Hilsman, Roger. 1956. *Strategic Intelligence and National Decisions.* New York: Free Press.

Homans, George E. 1950. *The Human Group.* Orlando, Fla.: Harcourt Brace Jovanovich.

Janis, Irving. 1972. *Victims of Group Think.* Boston: Houghton Mifflin.

North, Douglas C. 1981. *Structure and Change in Economic History.* New York: Norton.

North, Douglas. 1987. "Institutions and Economic Growth." Paper presented at Conference on Knowledge and Institutional Change, University of Minnesota.

Shweder, Richard A. 1986. "Divergent Rationalities," in R.W. Fiake and R.A. Shweder (eds.). *Metatheory in the Social Sciences: Pluralisms and Subjectivities.* Chicago: University of Chicago Press.

Stigler, George J. 1968. "Competition." *International Encyclopedia of Social Science.* Vol. 3. New York: Macmillan, pp. 181–182.

Thurow, Lester C. 1983. *Dangerous Currents.* New York: Random House.

Ullmann-Margalit, Edna. 1977. *The Emergence of Norms.* Oxford: Clarendon Press.

Williamson, Oliver E. 1975. *Markets and Hierarchies: Analysis and Antitrust Implications.* New York: Free Press.

Wildavsky, Aaron B. and Jeffery L. Pressman, 1986. *Implementation.* Berkeley: University of California Press.

Wilson, James Q., 1965. *Negro Politics: The Search for Leadership.* New York: Free Press.

Part Two

THE ELEMENTS
OF
SOCIAL CHANGE

3

Decision Making and Social Change: Author's Note

Any societal actor, whether it is a government, a major corporation, a labor union, or a coalition of environmental groups, will have one or more decision-making units in which knowledge about the setting in which action is to take place is collected and processed. This knowledge, in turn, is usually fed into distinct units in which plans are devised, substantive strategies are laid out, and decisions are made. These units, though they are often unaware of it, face preliminary decisions about which decision-making approach to apply. The approach must be suited to their intellectual capabilities. If these are meager, detailed decision making (planning) is extremely unlikely to succeed, because it assumes a very high capacity to gain and process information and to draw proper conclusions from it. This is a very daunting task even for rather simple endeavors, such as playing a game of cards. In contrast, if the unit does command a fair level of intellectual capacities, relying on random choices is not necessary.

Indeed, most decision-making units find themselves somewhere in between the two extremes, and require a decision-making strategy that is not as demanding as detailed planning or as uninformed and wasteful as random or muddled choices. Mixed scanning, the combination of wide but not deep examination of facts and options with more detailed study of select sub-sectors, chosen in the first or second round of scanning, provides such a strategy.

A discussion of mixed scanning, an integral part of guidance theory, was included in my book *The Active Society* and was the subject of an article published in 1967. The approach triggered a fair amount of discussion and research. The essay on this topic that is presented here, "Mixed Scanning Revisited," provides the original material plus an overview of the findings of twenty-five years of research on mixed scanning.

Detailed master planning is usually associated with socialist theories because it is assumed that only governments engage in it. However, corporations, many of which manage assets that are considerably greater than those managed by many governments, also practice it. Rationalism is usually associated with corporate decision making, although it is also considered in the context of public administration, that is, government. Though it is often overlooked, there is a deep link between detailed planning and rationalism. Both assume a highly knowledgeable actor (indeed, in some cases, an actor who is able to gain perfect information) who operates on such knowledge without being sidetracked by considerations of values, effects of power, or affect. As evidence has mounted over the years showing that actors do not command such intellectual capabilities, many subscribers to rationalism have simply pronounced or assumed that the actors must be rational and creatively invented other factors which the actors "must have" considered in order to account for decisions that clearly ignored facts and were not based on deliberations. For example, it has been assumed (but not demonstrated) that actors forgo deliberations and follow "rules of thumb" under many conditions because such conduct is more economical, which assumes that actors can make at least these calculations rationally. In contrast, incrementalists have argued that rational actors have never existed, have not been and cannot be approximated, and that the human race is fumbling through history "putting one drunken foot in front of the other."

The essay, "Rationality Is Anti-Entropic," after briefly considering matters of definition, argues that it is productive to treat the rationality of actors as a variable, not as a given. Actors are not rational or irrational, but are rational in varying degrees. The essay then explores the psychological and sociological conditions under which actors are relatively more or less rational. This, by the way, is a subject about which we know much less than is, well, rational. It seems that it would be advisable to dedicate more resources to this and related questions.

So far, I have adhered to a long tradition of making rationality the standard and asking to what extent we are able to live up to its demands. However, there are strong and cumulative bodies of data showing that typically we are unable even to approximate rational thinking or decision making, supporting the notion that it may be wiser to start from a different base line. This is attempted in the essay "Normative-Affective Factors: Toward a New Decision-Making Model." Here the theory starts from the assumption that most choices are made on the basis of emotional involvements and normative commitments (say, to friends or causes) and that rational deliberations play a rather small role in many decisions, in part because they too are affected by our emotions and values. Such decision-making processes apply not merely to the selection of goals but also to the selection of means. From this vantage point, the essay on normative-affective factors is a preliminary attempt to evolve a new decision-making model, one based on values, habit, and emotions rather than on high-power information processing.

Mixed Scanning Revisited

An article on mixed scanning as a "third" approach to decision making published in the *Public Administration Review* (Etzioni, 1967), which was awarded the William Mosher Award, generated a steady stream of discussion, criticisms, and applications but very little empirical research. The approach was developed in contrast to rationalist models of decision making and to incrementalism. Rationalist approaches were held to be Utopian because actors cannot command the resources and capabilities required by rationalist decision making. Incrementalism was shown to overlook opportunities for significant innovations and to ignore the empirical fact that incremental decisions are often, in effect, made within the context of fundamental decisions. For example, once the U.S. embraced the Truman Doctrine after World War II, and decided to contain the U.S.S.R. (rather than either allow it to expand or have the U.S. attempt to free countries within the Soviet Bloc), numerous incremental decisions were made in Greece, Turkey, and Iran. However, these were implemented and guided by the fundamental context-setting decision and cannot be properly understood without taking into account the basic decision.

Mixed Scanning: Definition and Illustrations

Mixed scanning is a hierarchical mode of decision making (Goldberg, 1975, p. 934) that combines higher-order, fundamental decision making with lower-order, incremental deci-

Note: This essay was originally published in the *Public Administration Review*, 1986, *46* (1), 8–14. The author is grateful to Janet Shope for research assistance. Copyright © 1986 by the American Society for Public Administration (ASPA) 1120 G Street NW. S500, Washington, DC 20005. All rights reserved. Reprinted with permission.

sions that work out and/or prepare for the higher order ones. The term scanning is used to refer to search, collection, processing, and evaluation of information as well as to the drawing of conclusions, all elements in the service of decision making. Mixed scanning also contains rules for allocation of resources among the levels of decision making and for evaluation, leading to changes in the proportion of higher- versus lower-levels of scanning based on changes in the situation.

For example, chess players, unable to review all the options (Haynes, 1974, pp. 7–8) and seeking to do better than merely thinking one or two steps ahead, running from trouble or toward a seeming opportunity, divide their time and psychic energy between first deciding among fundamental approaches ("ready to attack" vs. "need to further develop the forces"; "attack on the queen or king side") and then examining in detail options only within the chosen approach. (In effect, this form of scanning may take place on more than two levels, e.g., choosing a major strategy, a substrategy, and then examining in detail some options within that substrategy.) Rules for allocation are illustrated in chess when the game must be completed within a given time period. Players will then engage in less higher-level scanning, i.e., allot it less time, as the game progresses, although it may be granted "extra" time if the strategy followed runs into difficulties.

This approach is less demanding than the full search of all options that rationalism requires, and more "strategic" and innovative than incrementalism. It was suggested in the 1967 publication that it is both empirically supported, in that the most effective decision makers are expected to use mixed scanning, and the most suitable, i.e., normatively correct, approach.

Mixed scanning, it was suggested in the original publication, is akin to scanning by satellites with two lenses: wide and zoom. Instead of taking a close look at all formations, a prohibitive task, or only at the spots of previous trouble, the wide lenses provide clues as to places to zoom in, looking for details. In the years that passed, a new technology was developed which applies the "double-lens" approach to mixed scanning, Decision Information Discipline System (DIDS). The system provides computer graphic displays of geodata, usually in the form of a map. The system has a zoom capacity that allows its users to zero in instantaneously on subunits (or subsets of variables), for example, states within the U.S.A. and counties within these states. Wallace (1983) studied the 10 uses of the system as instances of mixed scanning. In one case a wide scan established that some areas were losing population although they were in parts of the county that by general trends should have been experiencing population growth. The zoom revealed these to be places in which military bases were being closed. In four, possibly five, of the ten cases the approach led to what Wallace calls "unexpected" findings (1983, p. 318). The broad scanning was more economical than detailed (zoom-in) scanning of all counties. At the same time, the zoom-in scanning of counties, singled out by the broad scanning, prevented the loss of information that would have ensued if only broad scanning would have taken place.

Operationalization

A significant part of the works that followed spelled out the mixed-scanning model in programmatic terms, terms that can be used as a guide for decision makers, as a starting point for a computer program, and as a basis for research designs. Etzioni (1968, pp. 286–288) started this elaboration:

> a. *On strategic occasions* (for definition see d below) (i) list all relevant alternatives that come to mind, that the staff raises, and that advisers advocate (including alternatives not usually considered feasible).
> (ii) Examine briefly the alternatives under (i) (for definition of "briefly" see d below), and reject those that reveal a "crippling objection." These include: (a) utilitarian objections to alternatives which require means that are not available, (b) normative objections to alternatives which violate the basic values of the decision-makers, and (c) political objections to alternatives which violate the basic values or interests of other actors whose support seems essential for making the decision and/or implementing it.

(iii) For all alternatives not rejected under (ii), repeat (ii) in greater though not in full detail (for definition of scale see d).

(iv) For those alternatives remaining after (iii), repeat (ii) in still fuller detail (see d). Continue until only one alternative is left, or randomize the choice among those remaining (and ask the staff in the future to collect enough information to differentiate among all the alternatives to be reviewed).

b. *Before implementation* (i) when possible, fragment the implementation into several sequential steps (an administrative rule).

(ii) When possible, divide the commitment to implement into several serial steps (a political rule).

(iii) When possible, divide the commitment of assets into several serial steps and maintain a strategic reserve (a utilitarian rule).

(iv) Arrange implementation in such a way that, if possible, costly and less reversible decisions will appear later in the process than those which are more reversible and less costly.

(v) Provide a time schedule for the additional collection and processing of information so that information will become available at the key turning points of the subsequent decisions, but assume "unanticipated" delays in the availability of these inputs. Return to more encompassing scanning when such information becomes available and before such turning points.

c. *Review while implementing.* (i) Scan on a semi-encompassing level after the first sub-set of increments is implemented. If they "work," continue to scan on a semi-encompassing level after longer intervals and in full, over-all review, still less frequently.

(ii) Scan more encompassingly whenever a series of increments, although each one seems a step in the first direction, results in deeper difficulties.

(iii) Be sure to scan at set intervals in full, over-all review even if everything seems all right, because: (a) a major danger that was not visible during earlier scanning but becomes observable now that it is closer might loom a few steps (or increments) ahead; (b) a better strategy might now be possible although it was ruled out in earlier rounds (see if one or more of the crippling objections was removed, but also look for new alternatives not previously examined); and (c) the goal may have been realized and, therefore, need no further incrementation. If this occurs, ask for new goal(s), and consider terminating the project.

d. *Formulate a rule for the allocation of assets and time among the various levels of scanning.* The rule is to assign "slices" of the available pie to (i) "normal" routines (when incrementing "works"); (ii) semi-encompassing reviews; (iii) over-all reviews; (iv) initial reviews when a whole new problem or strategy is considered; (v) a time "trigger," at set intervals, to initiate more encompassing reviews without waiting for a crisis to develop; and (vi) an occasional review of the allocation rule in the over-all review, and the establishment of the patterns of allocation in the initial strategic review.

Janis and Mann (1977, p. 37) introduced a major improvement of the program. They point out that while in the initial scanning, all those options that have no "crippling objections" are held over for closer scanning, which amounts to a "quasi-satisficing" approach, "each time the surviving alternatives are reexamined, the testing rule might be changed in the optimizing direction by raising the minimum standard (from crippling objections to more minor objections)."

They also expanded the range of decision making to which mixed scanning may be applied: "Although intended for policy makers, the same program, with minor modifications, could be applied to an individual's work-task decisions and to personal decisions involving career, marriage, health or financial security" (1977, p. 38). For such applications, they indicated, step a(i) must be modified: the staff and advisers would be replaced by family or friends.

Starkie (1984, p. 75) concurs with Etzioni that a mere accumulation of numerous incremental changes is not expected to yield the equivalent of a contextual or fundamental decision, because the incrementalist model provides no guidelines for the accumulation; it is likely to be random or scattered. In contrast, in mixed scanning, the fundamental decisions provide such guidance. Starkie correctly points out that Etzioni's suggestion that an "incremental 'creep' followed by a sudden change when existing policies are no longer sustainable by modification alone" is but one possible pattern of a combination of incremental and fundamental decisions; incrementation may *follow* a fundamental decision, just as readily as the other way around. Chadwick (1971) relates the various methods of decision making to different purposes and techniques of decision making. He sees rationalism as related to attempts to explore the long range and sees its techniques as either normative forecasting or exploration and simulation; that is, lacking in empirical content. He sees the purpose of mixed scanning as the "provision of alternative sets of action policies," using evaluation, the design methods, and something he calls "planning balance sheet" (p. 340). No details are provided concerning these techniques and Chadwick's endorsement of mixed scanning "as a highly acceptable meta-procedure" is based on his judgment that it is flexible but not on an empirical study. Wright (1977) follows a similar tack.

How a fundamental decision can be told from an incremental decision properly concerned several who examined the mixed-scanning model. Lee (1979, p. 486) agrees with the basic approach, to wit, "it is more rational in practice to be selective and systematic about a number of feasible options than to 'rationally' examine all the choices." He adds, however, that the theory "does not tell us at what point the selection ceases to be rational." Cates (1979, p. 527) writes: "my problem is trying to identify a big or little decision. Appearances are deceiving." (See also Falcone, 1981.)

On the other hand, Alexander (1972, p. 327) does not experience this difficulty: he finds that an example Braybrooke and Lindblom use to show how a policy is determined by incremental decisions, the 1940 "state of emergency" declared by F. D. Roosevelt prior to U.S. entry into World War II, was in effect an incremental step implementing his prior fundamental decision, to involve the United States in the war, one way or another.

One way to differentiate between incremental and fundamental decisions is *relative* size. For example, Fenno (1966) used the fact that Congress tends to make only 10 percent or less changes in the budgets of numerous federal agencies, each year, to argue that it is only incrementing. Ten percent or less may amount to billions of dollars but in the context may be considered small or incremental. Etzioni, in turn, used the same rule of thumb, i.e., 10 percent or less is marginal, to show that many of the actual decisions made were nonincremental: 211 out of the 444 decisions Fenno studied (12 years, 37 agencies) were actually changes of 20 percent or larger, within one year; 24 decisions entailed a budget change of 50 percent or more; seven 100 percent or more (Etzioni, 1968, p. 289). Other changes were small, but only following a major change. For example, the U.S. defense budget increased at the beginning of the Korean War from 5.0 percent of the Gross National Product in 1950 to 10.3 in 1951.

Another way to distinguish between incremental and fundamental decisions is to check for a nestling relationship. If an incremental decision requires or draws on a contextual decision, this is the fundamental one. For example, R&D review committees that authorize funds for federal projects act incrementally if they review each project, of which there are many, on its own merits. They engage in mixed scanning if they first form some guidelines as to what lines of research they wish to promote and heed these when they render specific decisions. Indeed, some projects that do not qualify by the criteria chosen may not need to be reviewed in detail at all.

Positive and Normative

All three approaches to decision making are not only positive, in the sense that they claim to describe the ways decision makers actually act, but also normative approaches in that they prescribe how effective decisions ought to be made. Alexander (1972) would add here, "under the given circumstances," because he does not believe that there is one appropriate decision-making strategy for all circumstances. Janis and Mann (1977, p. 38) suggest that different types of decision makers will find different strategies suitable to their divergent personalities and levels of education and training. In contrast, I hold that these situational and actor differences will be reflected in the relative investment among the various scanning levels. For instance, those with less education will tend to invest less in higher scanning. However, no actor, under any realistic circumstances, can abide by the rationalist approach. And, all actors under all but highly unlikely circumstances would lose by merely incrementing, although if the situation is very stable and the actors happen to use the best strategy to begin with, the damage would be smaller than under other circumstances.

Parkinson (1980) applies the mixed-scanning approach in an attempt to develop a new policy-making model for the educational system in Ohio, superior to the existing one. The approach used in the educational system before Parkinson's endeavor was relatively incremental; contextual consider-ations were neglected (1980, p. 161). Following the mixed-scanning approach, Parkinson developed a model that de-fines policy first on a broad level and then evaluates policy on an incremental level. To incorporate the mixed-scanning approach, Parkinson suggested that there is a need to estab-lish a meta policy group with the capability to maintain broad perspectives needed for longer range planning. "The collec-tion and maintenance of broad policy information and its ready availability to all would enlarge the policy view to incor-porate more than the current preoccupation with imme-diacy—that is solving the problems of the moment—without destroying the need for individuals and groups to research and provide information on specific policy issues which are of particular interest to themselves" (1980, p. 169). Parkinson's study is normative in that it is prescriptive; he did not study the results of shifting to the mixed-scanning model he favored in his study.

Hackett (1980) offers a model for the use of power by administrators. Much of his work does not concern mixed scanning but the way "assets" (resource, personality) are con-verted into intraorganizational power. However, one of the major components of his power model is the use of mixed scanning. He integrates it into his model by tying sweeps of scanning to the development of plans to deploy or "activate" the administrator's power assets. Thus, for example, if scanning reveals a loss of cooperation, power assets have to be deployed to regain cooperation (or to force one's way), or, presumably, to modify one's approach (1980, p. 102; see also p. 14).

Seen in a wider perspective, differences in normative models tie to differences in general world views. Rationalists tend to be philosophically attuned to *laissez-faire*, classical liberal, and libertarian perspectives. They are also highly optimistic in that they see the individual decision maker as highly self-reliant and able. In that sense they are also highly optimistic, utilitarian, and Utopian (Bradley, 1973, pp. 297–298). Incrementalists favor conserving the status quo, because they are blind to opportunities for radical departures (Dror, 1969) or to major reforms. They are also highly pessimistic about human capacity to know and to act sensibly.

Mixed scanning is most compatible with a progressive, innovative viewpoint. It assumes a capacity of the actors to adapt to changing circumstances, even major changes, including the structure of the actors themselves. Revolutionary changes, which entail a breakdown of the old regime and the rise from the ashes of a new one, may occur in a poorly scanning actor but, under most conditions, can be avoided by proper scanning if the findings of the scanning undertaken are heeded and proper adaptations are made. At the same time the hyperoptimism of fine-tuned planning and rationalist models is avoided. (Indeed, Dyson, 1975, reports that the model "stimulated S.P.D. intellectuals." The S.P.D. referred to is the German Social Democratic Party.) As Bradley (1973, p. 298) puts it: "Mixed-scanning seeks to avoid the most serious problems of both the overly rationalistic model and the excessively pragmatic model. . . . Normatively, it provides for the standing and predictability, which at least in the long run, is necessary to a decent society as well as acceptance of needed major innovations. . . ."

Others have questioned whether mixed scanning avoids the twin traps. Hanna (1980) depicted incrementalism as compatible with market economies and those who champion them; rational planning as reflecting "value authorizationism," and mixed scanning as "ignoring normative issues." He does not provide the reasons for reaching this conclusion. Smith and May (1980, p. 153) pose a more serious challenge:

But in fact it is not clear that the unrealistic and conservative shortcomings would actually be avoided. They might merely be confined or moved to different sectors of the decision making process. There is no guarantee that within these confines they might not even be accentuated. We would need to examine mixed scanning in practice before we could judge. Other issues are side-stepped. For example Etzioni retains the presumption that decision makers can summarize and rank their values, at least ordinarily. As we have mentioned, it has been argued with conviction that values are ordered only in contexts of specific choice.

Indeed, whether or not values can be "summarized" is an empirical question which unfortunately has not been studied, at least in this context.

Structural Factors

The original article (Etzioni, 1967) and the following elaboration (Etzioni, 1968) stressed the role of structural factors. Decisions are not made in a vacuum; they are deeply affected by the position and relative power of the decision makers and their relation to one another.

Rationalism assumes an all-powerful actor, as reflected in the notion that actors ought to set their goals and set about implementing them, without asking about their place in various power hierarchies or the strategies needed to deal with them. For instance, a subordinate may need to act differently than a high ranking executive. Incrementalism is most compatible with the acceptance of existing power relations. As Bradley (1973, p. 298) put it: "The unorganized, and others who lack control over adequate decision-making resources, have no role to play in the game of partisan mutual adjustment." (Mutual adjustment is usually associated with incrementalism.) Mixed scanning sensitizes the decision maker to taking into account *other* actors; one of the major factors scanning encompasses is the posture of other actors and the relations among them.

The structural element received little attention in the more than 50 publications that deal with mixed scanning, possibly due to a widespread tendency to treat decision making as a disembodied strategy. (A full list of references is available from the author.) Wimberley and Morrow (1981), one of the few who examined this factor, concluded that incrementalism leans toward consensus whereas rationalism tends toward optimization and hence to disregard of consensus. Mixed scanning is viewed as seeking to provide a "compromise" of the two approaches. The authors see mixed scanning as "involved" and "time consuming" (p. 504) but deem these features as unavoidable if the need to scan sufficiently, not to overlook a major opportunity, without being burdened down with insurmountable details, is to be attended to. They hence conclude that mixed scanning is "most suitable for the full range of decisions" (p. 506).

A structural point was made by Snortland and Stanga (1973) when they applied mixed scanning to the relations among courts. The higher courts (like higher ranking executives) attempt to reserve for themselves the fundamental decisions and expect the lower courts to increment. When the lower courts deal with incremental cases in contexts the higher courts have not passed on, this becomes "a matter of concern" for the higher ones.

A similar relationship has been observed between federal agencies and other agencies and private agents. Cardinal (1973) explored a specific act from a mixed-scanning viewpoint; namely the National Environmental Policy Act of 1969, focusing on its implementation. Special attention is paid to Section 4332(c) that provides for an institutionalization of the scanning levels. The "generalist policy leadership is seen as coming from the EPA . . . to be the primary line agency to create and complement policies. . ." (p. 469). Detailed implementation and related incremental decisions are often left to other agencies: states, localities, or corporations.

Berry (1974, pp. 358–359) examines what he calls "community relations" under different decision-making strategies, specifically in the context of the relations between Comprehensive Health Planning Agencies and their councils. The rationalists' plan, he finds, is "technically sophisticated" and hence requires a "rather stable" environment. This, in turn, requires council members who are technically competent *and* "following approval of this document [the master plan] community reaction and debate would be discouraged. . . ." Incrementalism requires a high level of consensus building; hence great attention must be paid to a council that is based upon fair representation. Mixed scanning requires deep public awareness of *the fundamental* decisions and of the main alternative schemes (but, by implication, less involvement in incremental decisions).

Some Evidence

Snortland and Stanga (1973, pp. 1021–1031) applied mixed scanning to the study of the law. First they found the model applied to the Constitution.

> The second phase of the incorporation of the Bill of Rights provides an illustration of mixed-scanning. While the first phase proceeded absent-mindedly, the second involved fundamental decisions by the Court within a mixed-scanning framework of both fundamental and bit decision. *Mapp* v. *Ohio,* and certainly *Gideon* v. *Wainwright,* appear to represent major and conscious fundamental decisions to incorporate provisions of the Bill of Rights into the fourteenth amendment. Within a few years after these decisions, the Court virtually completed the process of incorporation by incremental decision-making. The Court did not adopt Justice Black's position, which called for immediate and complete incorporation. Rather, the Court made a fundamental choice on the incorporation question, but ensured that the process could be halted if it proved to be deleterious to the administration of criminal justice. The Court retained the freedom to reevaluate this major policy decision and to retrench, if necessary. This is precisely the process that is prescribed by the mixed-scanning model.

Snortland and Stanga show the relevance of mixed scanning to two major Supreme Court decisions: *Miranda* and *Brown.* In the case of *Miranda,* the context setting decision involved both formulating guidelines and selecting the incrementing case. In the case of *Brown,* the fundamental decision both followed and set the context to incremental ones.

The Court clearly was aware that its first decision on inter-
rogations and confessions after *Escobedo* would be an important one. The case takes on an even greater significance, in
terms of mixed-scanning, when it is realized that *Miranda*
and the companion cases "were as representative of police
interrogation situations as *Escobedo* had been unique."
Miranda involved not only a conscious decision of a fundamental question but also a selection of cases that would encourage a broad application of the new policy to interrogation and confession cases.

. . . The *Brown* decision provides a useful example of the
application of the mixed-scanning model. *Brown* was preceded by a series of cases that strongly eroded the "separate
but equal" doctrine. Because of the incremental nature of
these cases, the outcome in *Brown* should have been a sur-
prise to no informed observer. Yet it is clear that *Brown* was
a major policy decision of fundamental importance. It was
not an incremental decision, although it is likely, as Shapiro
suggests, that the Court had already resolved to outlaw segregation. Many aspects of racial discrimination were left un-
answered by *Brown*. The questions were to be worked out
incrementally, as is shown by the second *Brown* decision.

Many additional detailed points made by the two authors cannot be recaptured here.

Wiseman (1979) examined the design and development of planning processes used within the Scottish health
service. Various decision-making approaches are examined
and "for reasons set out below, a mixed-scanning approach
was felt to be most relevant" (p. 104). The subject of the
study is the Scottish Home Health Department (SHHD) that
encompasses 15 district health boards and a headquarters
that contains an administrative and a planning unit. Before
reorganization, the focus of the study, the SHHD was "very
much geared to the administration and management of existing health services and the development of policies was
mainly undertaken in response to external stimuli" (p. 105).
Issues arose on an ad hoc basis, with no systematic evaluations of the situation, and decision making was largely one of
incrementalism, although sporadic and futile attempts to introduce rationalisms occurred. For example, an attempt was
made to use management science techniques for manpower

planning purposes. Disappointment with the results of this approach led to a search for a more effective approach.

> A rational comprehensive approach was rejected at an early stage because of the limited planning resources available, the complexities of a changing environment, the multiple interests and the multiple accountability of individuals within the health service. On the other hand, there was also a desire to introduce more rationality and more balance into policy-making than had been possible in the past. This inevitably meant searching for a middle course which would improve on past practice. A mixed-scanning approach was proposed which embodied three key components (Wiseman, 1979, p. 107).

The first element was the introduction of a scanning process, whose purpose was to review from time to time "what had been happening, to identify and where possible anticipate major issues for possible detailed attention and in general to provide an overview on which the future directions for the development of health services could be considered" (*ibid.*). To ensure that the process would not be rationalistic it was agreed that "the review process would consider the field of health services in broad terms but not in depth and would not attempt to produce detailed policies or plans for any one specific aspect" (*ibid.*, p. 107).

The second element was a selection procedure, to sort out which of the fundamental issues identified by the review process would be subject to detailed study and planning, taking into account the limited resources. The third element entailed detailed planning of the relatively small subset of issues selected for incrementalization. Wiseman (1979, p. 104) reports that the plan was implemented but provides no observations on its effectiveness. (Two other publications, Wiseman, 1978 and 1980, deal with the same effort but provide no more detail on the outcome of the introduction of mixed scanning.)

Berry (1974, pp. 351–353) suggests briefly how mixed scanning can be applied to a variety of situations, including the decision of an owner of several newspapers in small communities of whether or not to include a given additional town in his chain, and the use of sudden changes in death or morbidity data to initiate various levels of scanning by public health authorities (scope of search depends on the relation of departure of the data from the established norms). Berry proceeds to suggest the amount of resources and time various approaches to decision making require: The rationalist approach requires "maximum time and funds before action"; incremental least; mixed scanning relatively few funds but more than incrementalists and "moderate time"; the radical approach is as taxing and time consuming as the rationalist ones (p. 356).

Deshler (1974) trained 56 educational administrators in mixed scanning and observed their behavior both before and after the training and attained information from them by the use of questionnaires and interviews. He found that practically all those studied scanned broadly "naturally," before they were exposed to mixed scanning (p. 89). However, before they were introduced to mixed scanning about half limited their scanning to local issues, ignoring state and federal ones; and most tended to scan downward, not upward, and internally and not externally. Mixed scanning enhanced the scope of their scans upward and outward. It also decreased their tendency to attach the label of "excellent" to whatever was established practice and enhanced their tendency to consider alternatives. "The process enables you to think about the issue in greater depth. It removes your tunnel vision. It stimulates cross-disciplinary thinking, and opens up new areas for consideration," interviewers told Deshler (Deshler, 1974, p. 101).

DeVall, Bolas, and Kang (1976) compared the three approaches to the decision making in their study of the utilization of applied social research in 240 projects. They developed a measure of "overall policy impact" based on interviews with policy makers. (The measure has five elements the correlations among which were examined. For details see *ibid.*, appendix B.) Testing next showed that the rationalist approach, defined as explicitly, fully spelled-out "policy norms," has a poor policy impact. The impact was 12.56 when the norms were clearest; 13.40 when they were unclear, and 19.07 when they were not explicitly indicated.

Incrementation, operationalized as adjusting closely the policy research to the "ongoing, day-to-day processes of decision making," showed considerable policy impact (highest, 17.60). Mixed scanning was operationalized as full scanning, rather than merely diagnosing the problem or merely identifying policy goals also encompassing implementation options. It was associated with the most intense use of the applied social research. The policy impact reading was 23.67.

Conclusion

Mixed scanning seems to have an intuitive appeal to a fair number of scholars and action-oriented students of decision making. The ways it might be operationalized for the purpose of research or implementation have been clarified over the years, and the essential difference between fundamental and incremental decisions seems not to pose great difficulties. The links between the three different approaches of decision making and various intra- and interorganizational power structures, as well as between power approaches versus consensus building, have been explored. However, it remains to be empirically substantiated if, indeed, rational models are more suitable for totalitarianism or high-power approaches (e.g., master planning); incrementalism to highly pluralistic, special-interest dominated polities; and mixed scanning to systems that combine a balanced commitment to the collectivity with pluralism (Etzioni, 1984). The alternative hypothesis would be that rationalism does not work even for highly centralized systems (as the recent changes in the U.S.S.R. and China suggest) and that incrementalism reinforces the weakness of pluralism without a collective framework. All may require mixed scanning, albeit using different mixtures of higher and lower levels of scanning.

Above all, mixed scanning is still very short of case studies and quantitative studies of situations in which decision-making strategies were changed from either rationalist or incrementalist ones to mixed scanning. More needs to be known of the results in terms of effectiveness and of the factors that hindered or fostered the use of mixed scanning.

References

Alexander, Ernest R., "Choice in a Changing World," *Policy Sciences*, vol. 3 (September 1972), pp. 325–337.

Berry, David E., "The Transfer of Planning Theories to Health Planning Practice," *Policy Sciences*, vol. 5 (September 1974), pp. 343–361.

Bradley, Michael, "Decision-Making for Environmental Resources Management," *Journal of Environmental Management*, vol. 1 (1973), pp. 289–302.

Cardinal, Thomas E., "Comment—The National Environmental Policy Act of 1969 and Its Implementation: A Socio-Political-Legal Look at the 'New' Environmental Planning," *Journal of Urban Law*, vol. 50 (1973), pp. 465–485.

Cates, Camille, "Beyond Muddling: Creativity," *Public Administration Review*, vol. 39 (November/December 1979), pp. 527–532.

Chadwick, George F., *A Systems View of Planning* (New York: Pergamon Press, 1971).

Deshler, John David, "Utilizing Mixed-Scanning as a Strategy for Administrative Decision-Making," Ph.D. dissertation (University of California, Los Angeles, 1974).

DeVall, Mark Van, Cheryl Bolas, and Tai S. Kang, "Applied Social Research in Industrial Organizations: An Evaluation of Functions, Theory, and Methods," *Journal of Applied Behavioral Science*, vol. 12 (April/May/June 1976), pp. 158–177.

Dror, Y., "Muddling Through—Science or Inertia?" In Amitai Etzioni, ed., *Readings on Modern Organization* (Englewood Cliffs, N.J.: Prentice-Hall, 1969).

Dyson, K. H. F., "Improving Policy-Making in Bonn: Why the Central Planners Failed," *The Journal of Environmental Management*, vol. 1 (May 1975), pp. 289–302.

Etzioni, Amitai, "Mixed Scanning: A 'Third' Approach to Decision Making," *Public Administration Review,* vol. 27 (December 1967), pp. 385–392.

Etzioni, Amitai, *The Active Society: A Theory of Societal and Political Processes* (New York: Free Press, 1968).

Etzioni, Amitai, *Capital Corruption* (Orlando, Fla.: Harcourt Brace Jovanovich, 1984).

Falcone, David, "Health Policy Analysis: Some Reflections on the State of the Art," *Policy Studies Journal,* vol. 9 (Special Issue, No. 1, 1981), pp. 188–197.

Fenno, Richard F., *The Power of the Purse* (Boston: Little, Brown, 1966).

Goldberg, M. A., "On the Inefficiency of Being Efficient," *Environment and Planning,* vol. 7 (December 1975), pp. 921–939.

Hackett, John Allen, "A Theoretical Model for the Predictive Analysis of Power," Ph.D. dissertation (George Peabody College for Teachers, Vanderbilt University, 1980).

Hanna, Allan Alexander, "Settlement and Energy Policy in Perspective: A Theoretical Framework for the Evaluation of Public Policy," Ph.D. dissertation (University of Western Ontario, 1980).

Haynes, Paul A., "Towards a Concept of Monitoring," *Town Planning Review,* vol. 45 (January 1974), pp. 6–29.

Janis, Irving, and Leon Mann, *Decision Making* (New York: Free Press, 1977).

Lee, Kenneth, "Health Care Planning, Policies, and Incentives," *Futures* (December 1979), pp. 482–490.

Parkinson, Geoffrey William, "Policy-Making at the State Level for K–12 Education," Ph.D. dissertation (Ohio State University, 1980).

Smith, Gilbert and David May, "The Artificial Debate Between Rationalist and Incrementalist Models of Decision Making," *Policy and Politics,* vol. 8 (April 1980), pp. 147–161.

Snortland, Neil E. and John E. Stanga, "Neutral Principles and Decision-Making Theory: An Alternative to Incrementalism," *The George Washington Law Review,* vol. 41 (July 1973), pp. 1006–1032.

Starkie, David, "Policy Changes, Configurations, and Catas-
trophies," *Policy and Politics,* vol. 12 (January 1984), pp. 71–
84.

Wallace, Doris Nadine, "An Exploratory Study of the Utility
of the Decision Information Display System for Decision
Making and Policy Analysis," Ph.D. dissertation (American
University, 1983).

Wimberley, Terry and Allyn Morrow, "Mulling Over 'Muddling Through' Again," *International Journal of Public Administration,* vol. 3 (1981), pp. 483–508.

Wiseman, Colin, "Selection of Major Planning Issues," *Policy
Sciences,* vol. 9 (February 1978), pp. 71–86.

Wiseman, Colin, "Strategic Planning in the Scottish Health
Service—A Mixed Scanning Approach," *Long Range Planning,* vol. 12 (February 1979), pp. 103–113.

Wiseman, Colin, "Policy-Making for the Scottish Health Services at National Level," *Scottish National Yearbook 1980*
(1980), pp. 135–160.

Wright, Kevin, "An Exchange Strategy for the Interface of
Community-Based Corrections into the Service System,"
Human Relations, vol. 30 (October 1977), pp. 879–897.

Rationality Is Anti-Entropic

The Thesis

No matter how many challenges are thrown at the rationalist assumptions entailed in the notion of "economic man" (and macro-economic theory which assumes rational decision making), it is understandable that many economists continue to base their analyses on these postulates. Every scientific paradigm faces challenges and it is reasonable not to abandon a paradigm until a more productive one is found; otherwise the result is theoretical anarchy. If one abandons the rationality postulates, what should one adopt in their place? That people's economic behavior is non-rational? Irrational? Biologically determined?

This article examines the merits of one alternative concept, the notion that *rationality is anti-entropic*. That is, the "normal" (or base-line) state of human behavior is assumed to be non-rational; for behavior to be rational even in part, forces must be activated to pull it in the rational direction. Moreover, following such an activization, behavior "strives" to return to the entropic state. (For a previous, well-known, attempt to relate economic theory to entropy, see Georgescu-Roegen, 1971.) Hence, to remain rational requires continued investment of resources and effort. The analogue is limited to one major point: it takes special forces to pull the situation or behavior away from its natural, entropic, non-rational state.

Note: This essay was originally published in *Journal of Economic Psychology*, 1986, 7, 17–36. Reprinted with permission from Elsevier Science Publishers, Physical Science and Engineering Division. I am indebted to Arthur Snow and Lucy Ferguson for their comments and to Kathy Wilson and James Baldwin for research assistance.

The "normal" state is one in which behavior is not purposive, noncalculative, governed by emotions and values, potentially inconsistent and conflict-ridden, indifferent to evidence, and under the influence of "group-think" (i.e., individuals defer in their thinking to group-defined facts, interpretations, and conclusions even if they diverge significantly from objective reality).

To put it differently: non-rational behavior is natural; rational conduct is artificial, it must be manufactured. I turn below to point to various well-known bodies of data which are compatible with the thesis advanced here. It will become evident that because rationality is artificial, i.e., manufactured, it has a *cost*. The fact that resources must be sacrificed to gain rationality provides empirical evidence that rational behavior is a product.

It should be noted that the position undertaken here is far from a radical departure. Williams and Findlay, the former a professor of administrative science and the latter of finance, concluded their 1981 review of the relevant social science literature with the statement that "it is becoming increasingly obvious from the research conclusions of other [non-economic] disciplines (psychology, philosophy, political science, and sociology in particular) that the simplistic notion of 'economic man' posited so often in economic literature, is more fancy than fact" (Williams and Findlay, 1981: 17). Lovejoy found that "man's 'reason' has, at most, a secondary and very small influence upon his conduct and irrational or nonrational feelings and desires are the real efficient causes of all, or nearly all, of men's actions" (Lovejoy, 1961: 64). Many others have taken similar positions (for extensive bibliography see Williams and Findlay, 1981). In comparison the position taken here is rather moderate. It is not assumed that rationality is rare, only that it is costly.

It might be argued that it does not matter how common rational behavior is, one can use the concept of a rational actor (or "economic man") as an ideal type, the way the concept of a frictionless slope serves the physicist. In contrast, the author suggests that it is more productive to use a concept that is apparently characteristic of most behavior, rather than an extreme uncharacteristic concept, and that the factors which cause deviation from the norm (e.g., friction) must be included in a productive model. The norm used here is non-rationality; the forces which move behavior from the norm are investments in producing rational behavior (cf. Day, 1967).

Rationality Defined

As there is no single agreed upon definition of rationality, it seems necessary to indicate which definition is followed here and the reasons for selecting it. One way to approach the subject is to view the varying definitions as ranked from less to more strict. One definition requires the actor to be consistent (that his or her choice behavior is transitive). This demand is not easy to meet; indeed there is some evidence people do not meet it (Maital, 1982: 168, *passim*). Still, consistency is at best a necessary but not a sufficient condition for most behavior which is commonly referred to as rational, because consistency does not necessarily involve reason, or even being conscious (Becker, 1976: 7; March, 1978: 593). Indeed, low species, whose behavior is determined by genetic codes and conditioning, might be much more consistent than human beings.

A more demanding definition of rationality assumes an ability to collect, assess and interpret information, and draw proper conclusions from it. It is sometimes referred to as calculative rationality (March, 1978: 589) or intentional rationality (ibid.) or procedural rationality (Simon 1976: 131). A careful reading of numerous usages of the term rationality, whose steps cannot be retraced here, suggests that this is the meaning most often implied when the term is used (Simon 1976: 130; Kunkel, 1970: 62–64; Lee, 1972: 6ff.). We hence follow it here.

(The distinction between automatically consistent non-calculative rationality and the conscious, calculative one does not parallel the often cited opposition between "best" and "proper" choice, or optimal and "satisficing." Indeed, theoretically both optimal and satisficing behavior might be achieved either automatically or via deliberations. Empirically we go a step beyond Simon: we expect most decision making to be less than satisfying. Coping might be an appropriate term.)

Reference is to decision making, not to behavior, to what some psychologists call "reasoned action" (Ajzen and Fishbein, 1980). The reason is that well thought out decisions may run into unexpected events (e.g., oil price "shocks") which in retrospect may make a decision seem non-rational even if at the time it was made all the available information was used and the proper conclusions were drawn. And poor decisions may luck out of trouble.

The deeper source of the difference between rational decision making and behavior is where they take place. Decision making takes place within a person's mind, corporate meetings, computer programs—in the realm of intellectual processes and symbolic transactions. Behavior takes place within the world of nature and society, of objects and people. There are significant inherent differences between these realms: the symbolic one can be much more easily manipulated and rationalized than the other (albeit not necessarily easily). One can readily think about a horse with wings; to breed one is a rather different matter. (For additional discussion, see Etzioni, 1968: ch. 2.)

Rationality: A Variable, Not a Characterization

From the viewpoint represented here it makes little sense to ask whether or not people "are" rational. Rationality is viewed as a continuous variable; that is, people are more or less rational depending on their abilities, the strength of the activating forces (discussed below) and environmental circumstances, which may help or hinder these forces. To the extent that evidence shows that as activization forces rise, so does rationality, and that it subsides as these forces slacken, the basic approach advanced here is supported.

Several leading economists have moved in the opposite direction, protecting the claims of universality of the rationality assumption. Faced with the growing chorus of criticism that it is unreasonable to assume that people are rational, they responded by relaxing the criteria of what rationality entails. First, actors who use "only" all the information accessible to them (rather than all that might be used) have been defined as rational (March, 1978). Then those who stop their search short of finding the optimum solution were added. These economists also attempted to show that all kinds of behavior which at first seem to be non-rational, in effect, are rational, including pathological behavior, because psychoanalytical literature "explains the patient's illness in terms of the functions it performs for him" (Simon, 1978: 3).

In such economic writing the question is not put in terms of *how* rational people are, but people are said "to be" rational and arguments are advanced against those who maintain otherwise. "Everybody in this prosaic universe (the world according to economists) is rational" (Lekachman, 1976: 108). "Economic theory is usually predicated on the premise that, given their schedules of preferences for goods and services and leisure, individuals behave consistently and 'rationally'" (Tobin, 1971: 18). "Economics . . . the discipline is founded on the rational man premise. Even most non-'mainstream' economists who are uneasy with both the methods and conclusion of neoclassicism unhesitatingly adopt assumptions about human behavior that are increasingly questioned elsewhere . . ." (Williams and Findlay, 1981: 18–19).

Such statements which characterize a whole species as having certain shared attributes are found in other disciplines, but are regarded as preliminary, poor first approximations, because science builds not on such characterizations which apply to all the incidents of a category under study, but on recognizing variations, on variables (Nisbett and Ross, 1980: 8; Musgrave, 1981). Thus it is of little interest to note that people's blood is warm unless one compares them to some species whose blood is cold. When one studies people, interest focuses on *differences* in temperature, not on the shared range. Drawing on this general view of how scientific knowledge advances it seems productive to treat rationality not as a trait all people share but to ask to what extent is the behavior of various groups (subaggregates) of people rational, and under what conditions is their behavior more or less rational.

Rationality Equals Effort

To seek the most effective and efficient means to advance one's goals, to act rationally, entails effort. The term *effort* is used here in a broad sense to include commitment of resources, energy, time, and dedication. (It is much broader than the term *costs*, at least as usually understood. It encompasses such elements as developing self-discipline, and moderation of self or collectivity.) In contrast, entropy, the state of nature, is effortless. It involves no setting of goals or their pursuit; ongoing processes are not interfered with, like rivers running downhill. Similarly, to act impulsively in line with one's prejudices, "urges", habits—in disregard of information, without analysis or deliberation—requires no effort. In contrast rationality entails three kinds of effort:

(1) the search for effective means (including preparations for searching), to be referred to as *cognitive work;*
(2) the development of *personality and societal foundations* that are required in order to be able to undertake extensive research and search that is relatively autonomous from irrelevant constraints and interruptions; and
(3) the balancing of maintenance and adaptation of the appropriate resources and procedures (such as computers and R&D staff). The differences among these three kinds of efforts are briefly indicated for individuals, organizations and societies before evidence about the correlation between effort-levels and rationality-levels is cited.

Cognitive Work

One kind of effort expected to be associated with rationality is the *commitment of resources for cognitive work* needed to assemble, analyze and apply relevant information. Cognitive work encompasses both efforts expended directly on search behavior (for example, how many dealers an individual visits before he or she buys an auto) and efforts entailed in preparations (for instance, does a new investor in the stock market first study economics and participate in an investment workshop before he or she decides to search for which particular stock to invest in).

Cognitive work for a person may entail gaining access to information (for instance, purchase of a guide book), to information processing technologies, or to experts. For a corporation it may involve increasing the investment in R&D or increasing the staff-to-line ratios. For a society it may entail increasing the reliance on a professional civil service and reducing the role of political considerations in the selection of means.

Personality and Societal Development

Personality and societal development provide the non-cognitive foundations for rational behavior. Rational behavior does not take place in a vacuum; it requires appropriate personality and societal underpinnings. Although all individuals have the same potential to learn to act rationally, people are not born with the necessary motivation and personality traits to actually behave rationally. Indeed, societies differ significantly in their tolerance for rational decision making; in some, decisions are largely governed by myth, tradition, kinship and tribal obligations.

There is no agreement in the psychological and educational literature about the nature of the capabilities that allow some people to behave more rationally than others or how these capabilities are evolved. Without attempting to review the enormous literature on the subject, the following merely illustrates the nature of what, lacking a better term, is referred to as *non*-cognitive bases of rationality. Accordingly, we expect that people's cognitive capabilities are developed not merely by teaching specific skills (such as computer literacy) or general skills (such as the ability to calculate) but build on non-cognitive personality development. This is achieved through education beginning within the family before school. Specifically the ability to do cognitive work is hypothesized to be associated with the ability to defer gratification. To be able to think logically, to take in evidence, to interpret it properly, a person must be able to follow a set of procedures, as compared to "snap judgement," "intuition," or following what is traditional.

In modern societies, those parents who conform to the society's main values (as distinct from deviant subcultures) invest considerable efforts in developing in their children the capacity to defer gratification. Kindergarten, schools, and even colleges, further contribute to this development. This takes place when, for instance, the ability to work on one's own, to plan one's work, to work on schedule is rewarded. In a re-analysis of Coleman's data about American high schools, we found that high performance was correlated with homework. Homework is valuable because it allows a person to develop self-discipline, especially when the assignments are considered properly assigned and fairly evaluated (Coleman et al., 1982; Etzioni, 1982, 1984).

The main point for the thesis at hand is that certain kinds of personality development, prerequisites for rational conduct, require considerable and continuous investment, time, energy, and dedication, i.e., effort. The counterhypothesis is advanced by some radical critics of institutional education. Illich (1971) maintains that it would be best to close schools and allow children to follow their parents through their day of work. Holt writes: "children are by nature smart, energetic, curious, eager to learn and good at learning" (1972: 2). He would leave educators quite passive. "We teachers can see ourselves as travel agents. When we go to a travel agent, he does not tell us where to go. He finds out first what we are looking for. . . . Given some idea of what we are looking for, he makes some suggestions. . . . He does not have to take the trip with us" (Holt, 1970: 70–71).

To turn now to societies, they, too, are undergoing development (economic, educational, cultural) which allows them, acting as collectivities, to invest more in deliberations, in pursuit of rationality. The conditions under which a society develops have been analyzed in an enormous literature that has shown little tendency to reach a consensus. Most approaches, though, clearly show that development entails massive efforts. One school of thought emphasizes the need for capital formation. Typically this requires deferring consumption in order to enhance the capacity of the system, which strains the people of those countries. In contrast, to the extent the development is based on foreign aid or can be financed from the gains of enlarged trade, comparatively few sacrifices are required. There is, however, no evidence that development was ever fully or even largely achieved in this way.

Another school of thought, that of "human capital," stresses the role of education, training and R&D, i.e., that of investment in human capital, in achieving modernization. Because of the longer lead time between investment and yields the effort entailed according to this thesis is even larger than the one assumed by the capital formation school.

Maintenance and Adaptation

Rationality is not a habit which, like swimming, once acquired tends to be maintained without *continued* effort. On the contrary, it is our hypothesis that rationality is a self-degrading attribute. If no maintenance efforts are undertaken, the capacity to act rationally is expected to diminish over time. Moreover, the changing environment requires the adaptation of existing patterns of cognitive work, capabilities, even personality and societal foundations, if a given level of rationality is to be maintained. Physicians must attend workshops, follow journals. etc., to update their knowledge and skills. Corporations dedicate resources both to maintain their computers and to purchase "state of the art" software. Societies appropriate budgets to educate and train the new generation, both to transmit the stock of existing knowledge and to acquire new knowledge.

All said and done, while there are clearly counterhypotheses to the thesis advanced here, and while the voluminous research on personality and societal development does not speak to one conclusion, most lines of work clearly point to the correlation between extending efforts and acquiring, maintaining, and adapting rationality.

Theoretical Home

Several significant developments in economic thinking and research find a theoretical home in the thesis about the antientropic nature of rationality. In discussing these developments the purpose of the article is not to do justice to the many important works on each subject but only to point to theoretical links.

Information Costs

In early economic works, and in some recent work (especially that by the school of "rational expectations"), it was common to assume that information has no cost (Leman and Nelson, 1981: 99). This notion is implicit in the basic concept of a market. It assumes that all the buyers and sellers have uninhibited access to the information about all offers to buy and sell.

Economists have come to recognize that information is not free and gradually moved to integrate information costs into their analyses. Economists have incorporated information costs into the rationality model by suggesting that the "correct" point for terminating the search is realized when the marginal cost of additional learning equals the expected marginal improvement (Stigler, 1961: 213–215). Leaving aside the question of whether most actors most times can make such a calculation, let us note that, as Simon pointed out, these approaches treat "cavalierly" the costs of the search (1978: 10; Radner, 1975: 253). More than traveling from one auto dealer to another is involved. There are emotional "costs" (such as the need to agree with one's spouse about the demerits of each option rejected), and normative ones (e.g., check each item considered against the norms of one's group or groups), among others. That is, deliberations activate a wide range of complex considerations, far beyond mere price comparisons (cf. Stigler, 1962). And, as Simon (1978) and Lindblom (1965) pointed out, actors' limited computational and analytic capabilities are typically overloaded, long before the rationally correct point is reached.

Assuming these observations are correct, they suggest that information costs are considerably higher than is often assumed; they encompass much more than the actual costs of the search. It follows, from the preceding argument, that search behavior will often be much more limited than has been assumed to be "rational." Needless to say, the very existence of information costs is compatible with the anti-entropic thesis.

A conceptual clarification is necessary here. Information costs and transaction costs are not to be used as synonyms. Transaction costs include, aside from information costs, implementation costs. (This is implied by Nicholson (1978: 32), Kamerschen and Valentine (1981: 246), and Alessi (1983).) A search which cost x might lead to the conclusion that an investor ought to switch from, say, bond A to B, but if to implement the decision (say, for a small account) involves proportionally high brokerage costs, this may make the transaction not worthwhile. Indeed, implementation costs, especially in labor markets, are expected to often exceed information costs. Detroit workers may buy Houston newspapers to learn about jobs for 50 cents; this is a long way from paying for the move. It seems hence sensible to see transaction costs as the more encompassing category which involves information and implementation costs. The preceding discussion deals with information costs only. In contrast, price dispersion, widely used as an indicator of information costs (Stigler, 1961, 1962; Marvel, 1976) reflects both kinds of costs. (Cf. "price dispersion is a manifestation—and, indeed, it is the measure—of ignorance in the market" (Stigler, 1961: 214).)

If one focuses on information cost only, the fact that information costs vary a great deal from one area of economic behavior to another has significant consequences for what is rational behavior. All other things being equal, the higher the search costs, the less rational it is to engage in it.

Indeed, when the costs are high, randomizing one's choices may well yield results superior to informed choices. The greater information costs in dealing with labor vs. capital goods explains why the latter are often preferred by management and investors even in situations when otherwise investment in labor would seem preferable (e.g., given a relatively high cost of capital, as reflected in high interest rates). For the same basic reasons, the long lead time and uncertain payoffs, i.e., high information costs, are a reason the basic research part of R&D is neglected to a point at which it is commonly listed as one of the few areas in which the market is likely to fail and public investment is justified, even according to *laissez-faire* purists.

Power results from asymmetries; for instance, when few buyers face numerous sellers. It is also generated when actors possess different information or different abilities to acquire it. That is, the ability to overcome entropy is not equally distributed among all actors. For example, most sellers of used autos command more of it than most buyers (Akerlof, 1970). Market models that assume free information serve relatively poorly in these situations, and models that take into account differential access to information have only recently been advanced (Riley, 1979; Crocker and Snow, 1988).

Finally, the relative level of information costs and the role of power must be taken into account jointly. When both are high, markets do not work well at all. Most patients cannot judge most of the medical advice they are given, nor the merit of second opinions. The knowledge required for these assessments is both relatively expensive *and* highly asymmetric between physician and patient. In contrast, comparative shopping on *standardized* products is relatively low in cost, and relatively little asymmetry exists. Market models apply better here.

The Learning Curve

The learning curve is another phenomenon engineers, operation researchers and economists have discovered, and which finds a theoretical explanation in the anti-entropic nature of rationality; moreover, the three-part typology of efforts introduced above helps explain the particular shape various learning curves take. Basically, what is at work here is the fact that cognitive work and preparations, relevant personality and societal development, maintenance and adaptation are not free goods.

Early economic theory, which assumed information to be freely available and instantly absorbed and utilized, expected that learning will be instantaneous and effortless. This was often not explicitly stated but reflected in ignoring the time and costs learning entails (MacRae, 1978: 1245). Specifically, the disregard of the learning curve can be seen in the notion that the unit production costs (of the same product) will remain constant over time (assuming of course no change in input costs, such as labor and capital and in technology). As late as 1964 Hirschmann bemoaned that "although learning curves have been recognized in industries other than aircraft, they have not been as widely accepted. Instead, predictions are usually based on assumptions of level performance and constant costs" (1964: 125).

Industrial learning curves have been observed as early as 1925 (Hirschmann, 1964: 125; Wright, 1936), in the production of airplanes. As the management and workers gained experience with the production of the new technologies, unit cost declined significantly. The same was observed for other products (Andress, 1954). Not all the gain is due to learning; in part it is due to increases in production batches over time (Goddard, 1982) but there is clearly a significant learning factor.

What accounts for it is, in part, the cost of rationality. A new or modified technology or technique is rarely introduced into a plant fully developed. Experience (a major source of knowledge) forces numerous modifications. Resources must be dedicated to train the workers and to motivate them to learn. Structural changes, in work relations, between staff and line, and between levels of management, are often necessary but do not come about without effort. For example, while R&D staff often have an interest in trying new techniques, production managers frequently resist such innovations, and must be "bought off" (Dalton, 1950).

The fact that learning has costs supports the thesis that rational behavior is not free; the fact that learning is often slow and partial suggests that the cost of rationality is often high. It also suggests that most people will not be fully "learned" most times, especially in a changing environment.

Thurow (1983) points out that economists assume an equilibrium, which, if disturbed, will seek to reestablish itself. Hence, one cannot learn from periods of disruption about the "normal" situation. However, he wonders, if in a world of rapid changes learning is ever present and equilibrium never approximated, if one ought not to change one's assumptions about the working of the economy. In such a world, which we agree is prevalent, behavior will be substantially less rational than the equilibrium theory assumes.

Habit and Impulse Buying

In contrast to the assumption that actors rationally decide what to purchase, how much to save, and otherwise act rationally in economic matters, evidence has been accumulating that often this is not the case. People buy out of habit or on impulse. "The main alternative to such (rational) behavior (assumed by economists) was found to be habitual behavior" (Katona, 1975: 218). "Habitual behavior occurs much more frequently and whatever the origin of our habits, they do not exhibit the major features of rational behavior. People act as they have acted before under similar circumstances, without deliberating and choosing. Routine procedures and the application of rules of thumb by consumers as well as businessmen exclude the weighing of alternatives" (Katona, 1975: 218–219).

Studies of the purchase of major household appliances, i.e., expensive and enduring items infrequently bought and of relative importance, show they are acquired with relatively little deliberation (Katona and Mueller, 1954). For other items, for example new sport shirts, deliberation was found to be even more limited (Katona and Mueller, 1954). Factors governing the purchase were found to be a sense of an urgent need, preventing careful deliberation (say, one's refrigerator broke down beyond repair), and/or satisfaction with a similar article previously bought.

A classic study of the subject by Houthakker and Taylor (1970) analyzed consumer expenditures for 82 categories. Fifty were found statistically to be subject to habit formation. These 50 accounted for 58.4 percent of the total expenditure. In contrast, commodities subject to inventory adjustment accounted for 28.2 percent of total expenditure. As Houthakker and Taylor point out, prices (at many income levels) are relatively unimportant and so leave habits as the main explanation of why people (within a given income level) spend what they do. Houthakker and Taylor concluded that "habit formation quite *clearly predominates* in the United States consumption" (1970: 164, emphasis added). (For a challenge, which uses different time units, see Sexauer, 1977.)

While habit buying seems more common than impulse buying, the latter is far from uncommon. Such purchases are reported to represent over 33 percent of all purchases in variety stores and in drugstores according to several studies, and more in liquor stores (Hansen, 1972: 338). Still another study found unplanned purchases ranged from 38.7 percent to nearly two-thirds of all purchases in the supermarkets (Engel and Blackwell, 1982: 552). It should be noted that here, too, serious conceptual and methodological problems arise as to what is defined as impulse buying, which are not explored here. Explanations for impulse buying include persuasion ("in-store stimuli"), *inability* to make actual purchases in line with "measured purchase intentions," and *unwillingness* to invest time or effort.

When one moves from regular consumer items to other purchases, rational behavior is even less common. "Even people who are accustomed to buying cars on credit are often not able to say what the minimum requirement for down payment or the costs of credit are. Lack of information on life insurance is extensive, for instance, about the differences among different kinds of policies and their costs" (Katona, 1975: 222–223).

Addictions, to cigarettes or alcohol for instance, are an extreme example of habit formation. This has been reported in the form of a "kinked" demand curve. If a good is not affected by habit formation, one would expect the demand curve to be smooth and the elasticity of demand to be symmetric. For goods affected by addiction the demand response to price is expected to be asymmetric; in particular, one would expect the response to a price increase to be smaller than to a price decrease. Demand is inelastic to price increases and relatively elastic to price decreases (Scitovsky, 1978; Young, 1983).

Habits affect not merely purchasing. Changes in fiscal policy, say cuts in income tax, frequently are found not to have the expected effects on motivation to work "because the public may persist with previous economic behavior as though it were ignorant of these fiscal changes" (Lewis, 1982: 4). When Americans were offered a free "energy audit" (to establish how they could reduce their energy waste and hence expenditures) only a very small fraction of the public accepted the offer (Stern, 1984: 62).

The saving rate in the U.S.A. between 1951 and 1981 remained "surprisingly constant within a range of 16 to 18 percent of GNP" (Bosworth, 1984: 62). This despite the fact that in the period under study numerous changes were introduced in tax policies which presumably made it "rational" to change one's saving behavior, including significant changes in the general level of taxation and specifically taxes levied on capital gains. While the evidence for the post–1981 years is not yet in, it seems that supply-side tax cuts also did not change this basic conclusion.

All this is not to suggest that changes in prices, interest rates, or tax incentives have no effects. However, we hypothesize that (a) "no effect" (or a trivial one) is more common than having an effect, which supports the thesis advanced above that the norm (or ideal type) should be non-rational behavior, and (b) the size of the change (in prices, incentives, etc.) will affect the frequency and magnitude of the response, and, in turn, provides a measure of the relative costs of "producing" a specific level of rationality in a given area of behavior as compared to others, for a particular group of individuals (say, middle class) compared to some others.

All this suggests that the base-line assumption ought be "no effect." When effects do take place, there are special circumstances which account for them. For instance, when price changes are comparatively large, or otherwise administer a "shock," they are more likely to initiate search behavior than series of small or routine changes (Heberlein and Warriner, 1983).

Thurow (1983) gives examples of slow learning by the economy, not merely by individuals. When President Johnson decided to finance the war in Vietnam without raising taxes or cutting domestic spending, as his economists advised him, since the economy was already at full employment, inflation was expected. However, it took three years, much longer than his economic advisors expected, before inflation rose from 2.2% in 1965 (when Johnson acted) to 4.5% in 1968 (1983: 53–54). Thurow discusses a similar slow reaction to deflationary measures (1983: 54–55, 66).

The basic reason routine changes in prices, wages, tax incentives, and so on typically are unlikely to have an effect is that habit and impulse buying, and continued saving at the same level as in the recent past, require no cognitive work, preparation, development or adaptation, i.e., have no rationality costs, although they clearly exact economic ones. And, by the same token, the relative infrequency of highly rational behavior in buying and saving attests to the considerable efforts, high costs, that rational behavior entails.

Indifference Zone and Stress

Rationality entails efforts, not merely because information must be collected and used in decision making, but also because rationality as well as the alternatives to the course already followed to which it points are often emotionally and normatively negatively loaded. In addition, the search process itself provokes anxiety, that is, exacts emotional costs. To put it the opposite way, rational choice commands least effort (all other things being equal) when there are no emotional or normative objections to any of the means which objectively might be considered, or attachments and commitments to those actions previously chosen or considered. That is, rationality is highest when the means not only have the same emotive and normative status but it is one of *indifference;*[1] i.e., all alternatives reviewed have no or only a low loading. For instance, a person looking for the least costly auto within a given mile per gallon range and a given weight (for safety) will act most rationally—given a set amount of resources for search within a time frame—when he or she has no anti-German or anti-Japanese feeling and he or she does not "care" about color or "style."

This is not because buying a red sports car is irrational per se according to the definition used here, even if it is used exclusively in dense city traffic. If a man set out to buy a red sports car (say, to match his wife's evening gown and tiara) and chooses among the various kinds of such cars according to information relevant to his secondary criteria (e.g., speed), he would act rationally. If, on the other hand, he set out to buy a car for another purpose, say, fuel economy, and attributes *irrelevant* to his goal swayed him by evoking emotive, or normative commitments, then the act would be non-rational. Such factors may merely truncate the search, in which case the behavior will be similar to that when information is low, or completely prevent a search—"it must be a Porsche"—in which case the "choice" would be completely non-rational.

It follows that theoretically at least there is an indifference zone, in which two or more items are identical in the eyes of the actors in all but the differences relevant for rational choice (i.e., other differences, which always exist, are either not perceived or perceived to be of no emotive or normative significance). Most means, though, seem to have an emotive and/or normative "loading." As Katona (1975: 197) puts it, "There is hardly any knowledge lacking affective connotations." We further suggest that the higher the loading, the greater the efforts required to choose rationally because one must hold at bay one's feelings, value judgements, anxieties and group pressures.

Another way of approaching the same basic point is to suggest that rational behavior is what is referred to as "cool" behavior. Much of the personality and societal developments discussed above serve to evolve the ability to act "cool." Once established, such an ability is continually challenged, in the person—by fatigue, consciousness modifying drugs including alcohol, and stress; in society—by forces intolerant of rational deliberations (including most religious, social, and political movements). Efforts must therefore be exerted, costs incurred, if the ability is to be maintained.

The work of Janis and Mann (1977) on the psychology of choice is pivotal here. Janis and Mann integrated large bodies of findings gained from psychology and related disciplines in their work on the ways decisions are reached. It is important to note that Janis and Mann deliberately decided not to deal with "an endless round of minor, routinized decisions a person faces when he looks over a menu in a restaurant, selects a movie" (1977: 4), and, we would add, when a person selects among homogeneous products. They focus on more substantial decisions and find that they all are "worrisome" (ibid: 3) because a person typically finds that making a choice is "painful" (ibid: 6) because there are some expected costs and risks no matter which course of action he or she chooses (ibid). This leads to search avoidance or search limiting behavior, such as procrastination and rationalization (ibid). In short, to act "cool" or rationally is an effort, like advancing against currents of personality and societal forces; to act non-rationally is to float with the flow.

The "Quality" of Information

The preceding discussion of the conceptual association (or correlation) between the *amount* of efforts invested and the relative level of rationality attained by individuals, organizations, and societies, provides only a crude first approximation. The next step is to move beyond the simple assumption that by increasing the efforts, rationality will rise. Obviously, the law of declining marginal productivity applies, as it does for all other factors. Adding ever more computers, engineering, R&D, and so on, will yield ever less marginal improvements in rationality.

Less obviously, the "quality" of the inputs affects the outcome. Economists often discuss information in terms of the amounts available (as the author did in the preceding discussion). However, studies show that other attributes have a significant impact.

Price changes are often depicted by economists as market signals, as conveying information to which a rational actor will respond. A National Academy of Sciences study of consumer responses to information about the availability of finances to improve one's residential use of energy (e.g., through insulation) found non-financial features much more important than the size of the financial incentive. Given the *same* finance information coupled with different non-financial attributes (such as simpler vs. more complex implementation procedures; degrees of protection against shabby work) caused great differences in response ranging from less than 1 percent of households' approval to more than 40 percent, in one state; 8 percent to nearly 90 percent in another state (Stern 1984: 55).

It seems, though, misleading to refer to these attributes as "qualities" of information, because this implies some difficult to measure aspects, like the quality of food or education, as distinct from amounts of calories or years of education. The main point is that knowledge (and knowledge-resources) are multi-dimensional: i.e., often more than one attribute must be measured to assess the input. Thus, one needs to know not merely how much information a person has been given, but also how reliable it is. True, *some* of these "additional" attributes are qualitative or relatively difficult to measure, but many others are not. The need is for assessing multiple dimensions, covering both the relevant attributes to the problem at hand and the match between the actor's various knowledge components (more information without additional or more effective processing facilities will create overloads, i.e., diminish the marginal effect).

The study of the "qualities" of information is a highly complex and greatly underdeveloped field. It is not the purpose of this article to delve into it but merely to indicate its relevance to the issue at hand: the relationship between rationality and efforts.

Note

1. Barnard (1947: 167–169) uses the same term to denote an area in which an individual is willing to accept orders. Actions outside of the zone violate the person's sense of what ought to be obeyed.

References

Ajzen, I. and M. Fishbein, 1980. *Understanding attitudes and predicting social behavior.* Englewood Cliffs, NJ: Prentice-Hall.

Akerlof, G., 1970. "The market for lemons: qualitative uncertainty and the market mechanism." *Quarterly Journal of Economics* 84, 488–500.

Alessi, L., 1983. "Property rights, transaction costs, and x-efficiency: an essay in economic theory." *American Economic Review* 73, 64–81.

Andress, F.J., 1954. "The learning curve as a production tool." *Harvard Business Review* 32, 87–97.

Barnard, C., 1947. *The functions of the executive.* Cambridge, MA: Harvard University Press.

Becker, G., 1976. *The economic approach to human behavior.* Chicago, IL: University of Chicago Press.

Bosworth, B.P., 1984. *Tax incentive and economic growth.* Washington, DC: Brookings.

Coleman, J.S., T. Hoffer and S. Kilgore, 1982. *High school achievement—public, catholic and private schools compared.* New York: Basic Books.

Crocker, K.J. and A. Snow, 1985. "The efficiency of competitive equilibria in insurance markets with asymmetric information." *Journal of Public Economics* 26 (2), 207–219.

Cyert, R.M. and J.G. March, 1963. *A behavioral theory of the firm.* Englewood Cliffs, NJ: Prentice-Hall.

Dalton, M., 1950. "Conflicts between staff and line managerial officers." *American Sociological Review* 15, 342–351.

Day, R.H., 1967. "Profits, learning and the convergence of satisficing to marginalism." *Quarterly Journal of Economics* 81, 302–311.

Engel, J.F. and R.D. Blackwell, 1982. *Consumer behavior,* 4th ed. New York: Dryden Press.

Etzioni, A., 1968. *The active society: a theory of societal and political processes.* New York: Free Press.

Etzioni, A., 1982. *An immodest agenda.* New York: McGraw Hill.

Etzioni, A., 1984. *Self discipline, schools, and the business community.* Washington, DC: National Chamber Foundation.

Georgescu-Roegen, N., 1971. *The entropy law and the economic process.* Cambridge, MA: Harvard University Press.

Goddard, C.T., 1982. "Debunking the learning curve." *IEEE Transactions on Components, Hybrids, and Manufacturing Technology* 5/6, 328–335.

Hansen, F., 1972. *Consumer choice behavior, a cognitive theory.* New York: Free Press.

Heberlein, T. and K. Warriner, 1983. "The influence of price and attitude on shifting residential electricity consumption from on-to-off-peak periods." *Journal of Economic Psychology* 4, 107–130.

Hirschmann, W.B., 1964. "Profit from the learning curve." *Harvard Business Review* 42, 125–139.

Holt, J., 1970. *What do I do Monday?* New York: Dutton.

Holt, J., 1972. *Freedom and beyond.* New York: Dutton.

Houthakker, H.S. and I.D. Taylor, 1970. *Consumer demand in the United States, 1929–1970,* 2nd ed. Cambridge, MA: Harvard University Press.

Illich, I., 1971. *De-schooling society.* New York: Harper & Row.

Janis, I. and L. Mann, 1977. *Decision making: a psychological analysis of conflict, choice and commitment.* New York: Free Press.

Kamerschen, D. and L. Valentine, 1981. *Intermediate microeconomic theory,* 2nd ed. Hinsdale, IL: Dryden Press.

Katona, G., 1975. *Psychological economics.* New York: Elsevier.

Katona, G. and E. Mueller, 1954. "A study of purchase decisions." In: L. Clark (ed.), *Consumer behavior.* New York: New York University Press.

Kunkel, J., 1970. *Society and economic growth.* New York: Oxford University Press.

Lee, S.M., 1972. *Goal programming for decision analysis.* Philadelphia, PA: Auerbach.

Lekachman, R., 1976. *Economists at bay: why the experts will never solve your problems.* New York: McGraw Hill.

Leman, C. and R.H. Nelson, 1981. "Ten commandments for policy economists." *Journal of Policy Analysis and Management* 1, 97–117.

Lewis, A. 1982. *The psychology of taxation.* New York: St. Martin's Press.

Lindblom, D., 1965. *The intelligence of democracy.* New York: Free Press.

Lovejoy, A.O., 1961. *Reflections on human nature.* Baltimore, MD: Johns Hopkins University Press.

MacRae, D., Jr., 1978. "The sociological economics of Gary S. Becker" (review). *American Journal of Sociology* 83, 1244–1258.

Maital, S., 1982. *Minds, markets, and money.* New York: Basic Books.

March, J.G., 1978. "Bounded rationality, ambiguity and the engineering of choice." *Bell Journal of Economics* 9, 587–608.

Marvel, H., 1976. "The economics of information and retail gasoline price behavior: an empirical analysis." *Journal of Political Economy* 84, 1033–1060.

Musgrave, A., 1981. "'Unreal assumptions' in economic theory: the F-twist untwisted." *Kyklos* 34, 377–387.

Nisbett, R. and L. Ross, 1980. *Human inference.* Englewood Cliffs, NJ: Prentice Hall.

Nicholson, W., 1978. *Microeconomic theory,* 2nd ed. Hinsdale, IL: Dryden Press.

Radner, R., 1975. "Satisficing." *Journal of Mathematical Economics* 2, 253–262.

Riley, J.G., 1979. "Noncooperative equilibrium and market signalling." *American Economic Review* 69, 303–307.

Scitovsky, T., 1978. "Asymmetrics in economics." *Scottish Journal of Political Economy* 25, 237–277.

Sexauer, B., 1977. "The role of habits and stocks in consumer expenditure." *Quarterly Journal of Economics* 91, 127–142.

Simon, H., 1976. "From substantive to procedural rationality'. In: S.J. Latsis (ed.), *Method and appraisal in economics.* Cambridge: Cambridge University Press, pp. 129–148.

Simon, H., 1978. "Rationality as process and as product of thought." *American Economic Review* 68, 1–16.

Stern, P.C., 1984. *Improving energy demand analysis.* Washington, DC: National Academy Press.

Stigler, G.J., 1961. "The economics of information." *Journal of Political Economy* 69, 213–215.

Stigler, G.J., 1962. "Information in the labor market." *Journal of Political Economy, Labor Supplement* 70, 94–104.

Thurow, L.C., 1983. *Dangerous currents.* New York: Random House.

Tobin, J., 1971. *Money, wage rates and employment. Essays in economics, Vol. 1: Macroeconomics.* Chicago, IL: Markham.

Williams, E.E. and C.M. Findlay III, 1981. "A reconsideration of the rationality postulate." *American Journal of Economics and Sociology* 40, 17–36.

Wright, T.P., 1936. "Factors affecting the cost of airplanes." *Journal of Aeronautical Science* 3, 122–128.

Young, T., 1983. "The demand for cigarettes: alternative specifications of Fujii's model." *Applied Economics* 15, 203–211.

Normative-Affective Factors: Toward a New Decision-Making Model

Normative-Affective Persons

Intellectual circles in Europe were preoccupied for more than a century shadow boxing with the ghost of Karl Marx, trying again and again to show that history is not dominated by economic or materialistic factors, that ideas matter. Similarly, social scientists and attending intellectuals, on both sides of the Atlantic Ocean, have been preoccupied—and still are—with extolling, questioning, and attempting to shore up the notion of Rational Man (or *homoeconomicus*). Indeed, even those who challenge this notion often define their position in terms of various deviations from the rational model. This is evident in the frequent reference to their concepts as dealing with a residue realm, the "nonrational," rather than some category that may itself be positively defined. Moreover, nonrationality is often confused with irrationality and tends to carry a negative connotation. "The trouble is that once one starts to talk about rationality, it preempts the way we organize our views of human thought and behavior. We tend to think always in terms of default from a standard" (Abelson, 1976: 61).

Here an attempt is made to follow those who break out of the rationalist framework, by positing a different view of human nature, a concept of individuals governed by normative commitments and affective involvements, by norma-

Note: This essay was originally published in *Journal of Economic Psychology*, 1988, *9*, 125–150. Reprinted with permission from Elsevier Science Publishers, Physical Science and Engineering Division.

tive-affective (N/A) factors. The central thesis advanced here is that the majority of choices people make, including economic ones, are completely or largely based on normative-affective considerations not merely with regard to selection of goals but also of means, and that the limited zones in which other, logical-empirical (L/E), considerations are paramount are themselves defined by N/A factors that legitimate and otherwise motivate such decision making. Logical-empirical decisions are based on inferences and facts, a very widely used definition of rational decision making. (For additional discussion, see Etzioni 1986a.) Normative-affective factors are subject to logical-empirical research by observers, but those actors who make them draw on value-commitments and emotional involvements, not information or reason. Many decisions are based on a combination of N/A and L/E, but the categories per se are clearly distinct.

One of the virtues of the neoclassical paradigm is that it provides a clear, concise, and simple conception of the human nature it presupposes. Many of the social scientists who showed that this concept is extremely unrealistic and sought to posit an alternate view run into difficulties because the concept they advanced has been complex and fuzzy, because they enriched the basic concept with numerous qualifications and empirical observations. Here an attempt is made to provide a parsimonious conception, although admittedly it is not as simple as the notion of a rational utility-maximizing individual, a notion whose excessive simplicity one may well not seek to match (Hirschman, 1984: 11). The concept of normative-affective actors, whose choices are dominated by values and emotions, is an ideal type, a baseline concept. Once it is introduced, there is room to discuss the conditions under which behavior deviates from this basic concept. Neoclassical economists often referred to theorems about rational utility maximizers as akin to theorems about a frictionless slope (albeit, as a rule, they do not discuss the corrections the friction factor requires). The concept of normative-affective actors is our frictionless slope; friction is introduced later. Or, to push the point, since actors are viewed here as typically highly inefficient from the view-point of instrumental rationality (defined below), although not as ineffectual persons, the baseline used here might be viewed as 100 percent friction; the corrections to be introduced later concern those factors that alleviate friction. N/A factors thus provide the context within which L/E considerations find their place.

In keeping with the preliminary approach, only the barest outline of the conception is provided; findings are cited merely as illustrations without any attempt to provide one more review of the literature.

Only immoderate rationalists deny the role of normative-affective factors in the selection of goals or utilities. The main bone of contention is the role of normative-affective factors in the selection of means. One cannot argue about tastes, preferences, or values, runs a typical neoclassical argument (Stigler and Becker, 1977: 76). The desire to buy deodorants is not more "rational" (or irrational) than the desire to buy bread (let alone white bread). The question is, we are told, whether or not, given two comparable ("homogeneous") deodorants (or two indistinguishable breads), but one less costly than the other, the consumer will purchase the less costly one. That is, rationality enters when we come to the choice of means. The position advanced here is that *normative-affective factors shape to a significant extent decision making, to the extent it takes place, the information gathered, the ways it is processed, the inferences that are drawn, the options that are being considered, and those that are finally chosen.* That is, to a significant extent, cognition, inference, and judgment are not logical-empirical endeavors but governed by normative-affective (noncognitive) factors, reflecting individual, psychodynamic and, we shall see, collective processes. For instance, N/A factors determine to a considerable extent on which sources of information people draw (for example, whether or not they read newspapers or watch TV, and what they watch—news, sports, or soap operas), how they interpret what they see, and what they believe they ought to infer from what they believe they have learned about the situation at hand.

Toward an N/A Decision-Making Model

A Radical Departure

The neoclassical decision-making model draws on one variation or another of the information-processing means-end scheme. Individuals are assumed to have ends (clear and orderly) and to set out to collect, process and interpret information about alternative means to serve those goals, drawing proper inferences as to the most efficient means—the decision. We radically depart from this model here and see the majority of choices as involving no or only little information processing but largely or exclusively draw on affective involvements and normative commitments. Thus, the question whether to work in the U.S.A. or in Mexico or even Canada, for most Americans is not only or mainly a question of relative wages or tax rates but of national identity. Choices either entail no deliberation at all (the "right" choice is "self-evident"), or entail a rather different process, e.g., of evoking a value or weighing among them. Thus, the question whether a worker owes more loyalty to his or her work place or the labor union, is not only or mainly one of relative costs and benefits but of trying to judge which loyalty is more commanding. A minority of choices is based on L/E considerations but many of these, we shall see, are infused to one extent or another with N/A considerations. One may wish to keep the term *choice* to all selections among options, however limited the scope of information process, deliberation, and L/E considerations, while reserving the term *decision making* to deliberative choices. (For other attempts to develop "moral" decision-making models, see Schwartz, 1970a, 1970b; Simmons, Klein, Simmons, 1977: 237 ff.; Latane and Darley, 1970. The main difference between the present effort and these important prior ones is that they are closer than ours to the neoclassical decision-making model.)

An N/A choice making model is next outlined. While it has several segments, throughout N/A factors *and their dynamics* must be understood first if the ways choices are reached are to be explained. L/E factors (of the kind studied by neoclassicists) play a role, but within the framework defined by N/A factors.

The N/A L/E Choice Continuum

Normative-affective factors influence the selection of means by *excluding* the role of logical-empirical considerations in many areas (i.e., choice is made exclusively on normative-affective grounds); in other areas by infusing the deliberations in such a way that logical-empirical considerations play a relatively minor or secondary role to normative-affective factors; and in still others define the areas in which choices may be made largely or wholly on logical-empirical grounds, areas referred to here as normative-affective *indifference* zones. Together the three concepts, exclusion, infusion, and indifference, characterize three segments of a continuum of bases of choice. Note, though, that according to the thesis advanced here (a) the zone high in L/E considerations is itself eked out and defined by N/A factors, and (b) the segments are far from equal in size. For most individuals, in most societies, in most historical periods, the indifference zones are much smaller than the other two and the exclusion zone is the largest in behavior in general, economic behavior included. As Katona (1975: 197) put it: "there is hardly any knowledge lacking affection connotations." The three zones are next discussed in more detail.

Exclusion

One major way exclusion of L/E considerations takes place is by N/A-based fusion of a particular means to a particular end. When exclusion takes place all other means that L/E considerations might point to are treated as morally and/or emotionally "unthinkable" or irrelevant. To suggest that L/E considerations in this zone are seen as "unacceptable" is to understate the case, because it implies that they have been considered and rejected; as we see it, excluded options are not considered by the actors. They are blocked from conscious deliberation; their *consideration*—not merely their adoption—is tabooed. Thus, most shopkeepers do not consider bombing their competitors even when times are difficult and they believe they could get away with the criminal act.

Such a means to an end fusion is often found when a means commands a symbolic significance, i.e., embodies, concreticizes and illustrates a value. For example, a suggestion that an American flag with one star is more efficient than the official flag will not be taken as serious because only *one* particular format has taken a symbolic significance. Neoclassicists may counter that if the price of each star on the flag will rise significantly the notion of fewer stars will be open to consideration. While this may be true, it is also true that given the range of prices observable in the actors' experience (as distinct from those in some hypothetical model), difference in costs is *irrelevant*. This is what Durkheim (1954), Walzer (1983) and Goodin (1980) referred to as the "sacred" realm, as distinct from that of expedient morality: One of its characteristics is that L/E considerations are not considered more appropriate than money changers in the temple.

When N/A fully excludes L/E considerations actors choose a course of action without exploring alternatives, because it is the right way to go, because it feels right. They inform interviewers they did not deliberate and observers see no signs they did. The house on fire, children upstairs, their mother dashes in, without considering alternatives. Internalized moral values and emotions invested in the children fully form the choice. Studies of people asked to donate one of their kidneys to a sibling report that they responded positively and instantaneously. "Case 1: Donor (mother): Me? I never thought about it . . . I automatically thought I'd be the one. There was no decision to make or sides to weight" (Simmons, Klein, Simmons, 1977: 243). "Case 2: You mean did he think about it and then decide? No—it was just spontaneous. The minute he knew . . . it was just natural. The first thing he thought was that he would donate" (Simmons,

Klein, Simmons, 1977: 243). Let it be said that such "verbal responses" are unreliable, the studies show most people act on them by actually donating the kidney (Fellner and Marshall, 1970: 1249). The discussion so far focused on absence of deliberations before the choice; however, it is also absent during the choice. And after-choice justifications (reduction of cognitive dissonance), seem to be in part affective as well.

Exclusively N/A choices discussed so far concern situations in which the actor perceives only *one* course of action, although from the viewpoint of the observer there are at least two. It might be said that a mother "chooses" between running and not running into the fire; indeed, all acts may be compared to the option of not acting; however, the actor perceives only one option; nonaction is defined as "out of the question" by N/A factors. Beyond making the choice completely, N/A factors often make the choice even when actors perceive two or more options. A typical American teenager will not require any deliberation to choose between a serving of snails and Perrier and an order of hamburgers and Coke.

In still other situations N/A factors do not make the choice but exclude most options (rather than all) often by excluding from deliberation *major sub-sets* of facts, interpretations, and approaches that are L/E accessible (as deemed by scientific observers). Here, N/A factors instead of fusing a means to a goal, form what has been called a *tunnel vision* (Easterbrook 1959).

When the author suggested to a successful young Wall Street V.P. to look for a place to live in Brooklyn Heights (one subway stop away from his workplace) rather than in the much more expensive, distant, mid-Manhattan, the V.P. recoiled in horror: "To live in Brooklyn?!!" he exclaimed, rejecting out of hand the suggestion to "at least have a look." It might be said that the V.P.'s choice was "rational" because the prestige loss and the restrictions on his social life resulting from living in Brooklyn exceed the saving in real estate. However, as he refused to examine the Brooklyn option and had no knowledge of the size of saving in real estate, how many singles roam the Heights, the comparative number of discos, and so on, we maintain that stigma prevented the option from being considered. Given the low cost of a trip to Brooklyn, we score such choices as dominated by N/A factors, and as not rational.

College, career and job choices are often made only within N/A prescribed sub-contexts. To begin with, whole categories of positions are not considered at all by most young people who plan their job education and career from becoming street vendors to funeral parlor directors, or working in "feminine" occupations (by traditional males).

Partial exclusion of options is contextuating in the sense that it sets a normative/affective framework within which L/E considerations may take place. N/A loading and intrusions, discussed next, affect the specific choice made within the N/A context, further narrowing the range of L/E considerations. As a first approximation, the discussion here deals with the role of N/A factors in affecting choices as if they were a single factor. Additional elaborations require exploring the relations among N/A factors which leads to issues previously explored as substantive rationality (Weber, 1921–22/1968), moral reasoning (Kohlberg 1981 and 1983), and some aspects of what is called cognitive dissonance (Festinger, 1957 and 1964) but includes N/A factors. They are not explored here.

N/A Infusing

When actors are open to "search behavior," seek valid information and try to interpret it and draw inferences properly, they are often and extensively subject to N/A infusing. These take two main forms, loading and intrusions.

Normative-affective factors load (or "color") various facts, their interpretation, and inferences drawn with non-logical and nonempirical "weights." Unlike exclusion, which precludes certain facts, interpretations and inferences, and hence options, from consideration, loading only provides *dif-*

ferential normative-affective weights that rank options in ways that differ from their L/E standing.

For example, selling short a stock has the same basic L/E standing as buying one "long" (although there are differences in risk, and some other L/E considerations concerning payment of dividends and interest charged on marginal accounts, and tax considerations). However, for long periods many Americans, especially small investors, believed that selling short was unpatriotic, "selling America short," not believing in its future. We expect, although we know of no such study, that the more a person was committed to this view, the less likely he or she was to sell short. This example illustrates, in an area of economic behavior, a situation where the actors *perceive* two options, buying stock A or selling short stock B, as a way to improve their investments. However, they perceive one as morally less acceptable than the other and hence proceed in choosing B only if the return is much higher although there is no objective (or much less objective) reason for such behavior. People who buy on installment credit or use credit cards do not see themselves as engaged in borrowing money. They perceive it as "deferred payments" (Katona, 1975: 272). When people pay down their mortgages, they are unaware that they increased their assets, that they saved (Maital, 1982). Nominal wages are often more heeded than real wages ("money illusion").

Intrusions occur when N/A factors prevent the orderly completion of a specific L/E consideration. L/E considerations require completing a *sequence* that involves collecting facts, interpreting their meanings, and drawing inferences leading one to favor one option over others. A decision may entail several such sequences of considerations, one or more for each option, aside from the task of weighing the options themselves. N/A factors, aside from limiting the options that are considered or loading those that are, often cut short L/E considerations by skipping steps or inadequately completing them. Abelson (1976: 62) distinguishes between two kinds of intrusions: one in which the picture of reality used for decision making is distorted; the other where the reasoning used to deal with a current picture is distorted. As we see it, both are distorted by N/A factors and often both intrusions are present simultaneously.

Completing the sequence(s) exacts considerable psychic costs, requires a relatively high level of attention, concentration, and mobilization of self. The ability of self to mobilize is often more limited than the task requires. The reasons are in part intra-cognitive; e.g., people have a hard time keeping "enough" facts in their short term memories or combining two probabilities. However, N/A factors also play an important role. People's "stamina" (or "will power') may be insufficient for the task. They hence cut short the L/E processes impulsively (not the same as acting impulsively to begin with).[1] The interrupted sequences are found in many forms. In some, each step in the process of decision making is cut short; in others, individuals (and firms) collect numerous facts but under-analyze them, "jump" to conclusions. While L/E thinking is conducted "vertically," in sequences, N/A "considerations" using "lateral thinking" often "jump" to the solutions. Some writers tie the difference to that between the left and right hemisphere of the brain (Williams and Chapman, 1981). Other forms of intrusion have been established. For example, high stress has been shown to increase random behavior, increase error rate, generate regression to lower (more "primitive" or simpler) responses, induce rigidity, reduce attention and tolerance for ambiguity, diminish the ability to separate dangerous events from trivial ones and cut one's ability to think abstractly (Holsti, 1971; Torrance, 1954; Korchin, 1964). Compelling data about N/A loaded choices are available from studies of the ways graduates of universities, including MBAs, choose among job offers they receive. One study reports that the graduates spend a long time comparing the first and second satisfactory offers they receive, in the process subjecting one of the two to a perceptual distortion, as a way to make it easier for the students to pick the other (Soelberg, 1967). Two other studies that report that choices are made without much thought are Moment (1967) and Nisbet and Grant (1965). It should be noted, though, that some other studies found a higher degree of reliance on L/E considerations (e.g., Glueck, 1974).

Decisions are often discussed and studied as if they occur at one point in time. Actually most decisions are composed of series of steps, sub-decisions, or require repeated steps. A decision to stop smoking, for example, is rarely a once for all decision but a continuous one. The decision to invest in a stock for many is not a one-time occurrence, buy it and put it away, but one frequently reviewed and, in effect, remade. For such decisions there are often "relapses to nonpreferred alternatives" (Sjoberg, 1980: 123) as N/A factors undermine decisions previously made on L/E grounds, such as to diet, to stop drinking to excess, or to hold a stock despite short-term price fluctuations. (For additional discussion, see Elster, 1985a: 6 ff.)

On the other hand, when there are no strong counter pulls, people tend to stick to their decisions, once a commitment has been made, either publicly or even to self (Steiner, in Fishbein, 1980: 22). They react to desire not to be seen "frivolously inconsistent" (Steiner, 1980: 22). If new information that is adverse to their decision is introduced, people tend to deny they could have foreseen it (Steiner, 1980: 24). "The more a person is emotionally involved in his beliefs, the harder it is to change him by argument or propaganda—that is, through an appeal to intelligence—to the point of virtual impossibility" (Berelson and Steiner, 1964: 575). In short, N/A factors may intrude in many ways, but are rarely absent.

Various attempts have been made to incorporate N/A factors into the neoclassical paradigm by assuming that the actors are aware of these factors and respond to them in a calculating fashion, basically as if they were one more environmental constraint (Fishbein and Ajzen, 1975; Kelley and Thibaut, 1978). It is hence necessary to reiterate that it is assumed here that while actors under some conditions treat N/A factors in the said way, often these factors are internalized, i.e., they are absorbed by the person and shape the inner self. In the process they may well be modified by self, but when the process is complete the values, behavior, attitudes and emotions are what the person believes, feels, prefers and seeks—not something the person treats as external.

Legitimated Indifference Zones

Normative-affective factors *define specific, often quite limited* zones as appropriate or as demanding for a decision to be made largely (rarely exclusively) on L/E grounds. These zones are referred to (from here on) as *legitimated indifference zones*[2] to emphasize that they themselves are set and protected from intrusions by N/A factors—by N/A factors. A familiar example from everyday life is the situation in which parents berate teenagers for impulsive buying, or in the traditional family, in which husbands' (who often considered themselves to be more "rational" and budget minded than their wives) values (such as frugality and "smart" shopping) and affect (e.g., anger) are used to combat impulse and habit buying. Similarly, among homemakers, there is peer pressure to consult *Consumer Reports,* to shop in discount places, to find good "buys," and so on. The significance of these observations is that indifference zones do not simply exist, they are not the normal, obvious way people make consumer decisions, as neoclassical economics assumes, but rather, they are defined and set by N/A factors.

The limited scope of indifference zones even in purchase of consumer goods (less N/A loaded than other economic decisions such as investment or job choice) is highlighted by the following finding. An overview of numerous studies of consumer behavior distinguishes between "high-involvement" products (for most contemporary American consumers) and "low-involvement" ones (Engel and Blackwell, 1982: 21–22). High-involvement goods are those consumers consider not merely as products to consume but also as items that "send a message to the world" about the person and that are tied to the person's sense of self-esteem. Choosing among them involves decisions that are more "complex" and prolonged and N/A affected than deciding among items of low involvement, which entails no risk to self-esteem.

What is particularly important is that surprisingly numerous items fall into the high-involvement category. These include not only "big" purchases such as autos, houses, and most clothing but also coffee [the quality of which is viewed as indicating one's "ability" as a homemaker (Engel and Blackwell, 1982: 21)], medications (buying over-the-counter drugs rather than brand names is perceived as "taking a risk with one's family"), and many other items. Low-involvement items include ballpoint pens, light bulbs, aluminum foil, and other such relatively trivial items. Other studies have come up with different lists, but the role of N/A factors and the limited range of indifferent zones are clearly documented (Furnham and Lewis, 1986: 207ff; Morgan, 1978: 61).

Similarly, it is common to note that in public policy matters one ought to draw on expert "inputs," but that because of N/A factors decisions are often made by the policy-makers, who draw on "other" considerations, especially political ones. Only decisions of highly technical nature are left to experts, typically only within the context of choices made, in part, on N/A grounds.

A pointed way to make the same point is that L/E considerations are allowed to dominate those choices in which none of the options is N/A loaded, i.e., when all options have the same or a comparable N/A standing. Here, individuals are "cool" (Janis and Mann, 1977) and L/E considerations are allowed to govern. Only people are rarely very cool.

Are N/A Considerations "Disruptive"?

A Matter of Personality Theory

How one views the role of affect in decision making is framed by the personality theory to which one subscribes, if any. I say, "if any" because in recent decades the great difficulties in agreeing on one personality theory and in operationalizing such a theory have led many psychologists to abandon the use of personality theory and focus instead on the study of specific cognitive processes. Without attempting here to review the immense literature on personality theories, the main relevant points to the issue at hand are briefly indicated.

First, some personality theories, usually associated with Freud, see raw emotions or the *id* as wild forces that disrupt reason. While these forces can be "civilized," even used to energize the *super-ego* and *ego,* improper or incomplete socialization leaves emotions lurking in the dark recesses of the personality. They either break through, causing impulsive, regressive, infantile—i.e., irrational—behavior, or activate various unwholesome defensive mechanisms. In short, raw emotions are viewed as antithetical to reason. No wonder Freud's work is viewed as a grand challenge to the Age of Reason.

Similarly, implicit in the argument that L/E considerations are rational, at the core of the neoclassical paradigm, is the prescription that they are the correct ones to make. Indeed, it is widely acknowledged that neoclassical decision-making theories are much more prescriptive (or "normative") than descriptive. The role of affect, to the extent that it is not simply ignored, is depicted as negative, a factor that "twists" and "distorts" thinking. "When emotions are directly involved in action, they tend to overwhelm or subvert rational mental processes, not to supplement them" (Elster, 1985b: 379). Sjoberg (1980: 123) refers to "twisted reasoning" by "emotional stress." Toda (1980: 133) sees emotions as having a "disturbing" role, as "noisome, irrational agents in the decision-making process."

Literally hundreds of studies could be cited that follow these traditions, although often quite unaware of their theoretical or philosophical roots. A typical study establishes the role of affect in the estimation of probabilities. Wright and Bower (1981) tested the influence of mood on individuals' estimation of "blessed" and "catastrophic" events. Subjects were asked to evaluate the likelihood of various event on a scale of 1 to 100. They evaluated half the list in an induced happy state, the other half in a sad state. The control group evaluated the whole list in a neutral state. The neutral group evaluated the events as follows: Blessed .44; Catastrophic .43. The happy group rated Blessed at .52 and Catastrophic at .37, while the sad group rated Blessed at .38 and Catastrophic at .52. Thus, when sad, negative events are viewed as more likely and good outcomes as less likely than when the subjects are in a neutral mood. When happy, the subjects view good outcomes as more likely. Mood biases cognition. (For further evidence on the subjective editing of probabilities see Steiner, 1980: 23; and Edwards, 1954: 400.)

While the studies cited so far deal with elements of information processing and decision making (such as memory and estimation of probabilities), Janis and Mann deal with the role of affect in the whole process. Janis and Mann (1977: 10–11) concluded that it is very difficult to judge the efficiency of a decision maker by outcomes because the outcomes are numerous, many difficult to measure quantitatively. They hence developed a process model of seven steps efficient decision makers go through, drawing mainly on the work of Etzioni (1967, 1968), Katz and Kahn (1966), Simon (1976), and others. The steps included "thorough canvassing of a wide range of alternative courses of action"; "surveying full range of objectives"; careful aligning of consequences; "search for new information"; and "open assimilation of new information" (ibid., p. 11). Jointly these steps are referred to as vigilant decision making. Omission of any step will render a decision defective, and the more omissions, the more defective the decision.

Janis and Mann next reviewed numerous psychological studies to show that most decision making is not vigilant, because all significant decision making evokes anxiety, i.e., an emotional strain. People often fall into one of four defective patterns: inertia (sticking to a course, despite a challenge without proper decision making by the said criteria); unexamined shift to a new course of action; defensive avoidance; and hypervigilance. The study provides detailed analyses of each pattern and its antecedents. Anxiety is cardinal to all.

Freudian and other psychodynamic theories, that view raw affect as antithetical to reason, are usually contrasted with the work of Piaget (1965) which focuses on cognitive processes. Even when he deals with moral development, at the core is the development of judgments, not of commitments. Above all, a major trend in psychology, in recent decades, has been to view emotions as an unnecessary concept, to "treat emotions as the product of nonemotional processes, usually a synthesis of cognitive and automatic motor reactions" (Leventhal, 1982: 126). More on this below. However, the main alternative to Freudian and other such theories from the viewpoint of the issue at hand, is the position that affect provides a constructive basis for behavior and decision making, found in the work of humanistic psychologists, for example Abraham Maslow. People here are seen as motivated by the desire to satisfy basic human needs such as affection, self-esteem, and self-actualization. Affect here is depicted as wholesome and "normal" rather than destructive. Indeed, some see excessive preoccupation with reason as problematic. Spontaneity is valued over extensive deliberations.

The main view followed here is that raw emotions often do limit and interrupt reason, and socialization of emotions may never be complete. At the same time it is recognized that socialized emotions often, though not always, play significant positive roles. They can help ensure that other considerations than those of instrumental rationality be taken into account, including the primacy of ends over means, the selection of ethical means over others, help mobilize self, and in some instances enhance efficiency. On the other hand, affect may undermine rationality, especially when it sets tight decision-making contexts rather than relatively loose ones, and interrupts sequences the actor seeks to complete on L/E grounds. In short, whether affect is constructive or disruptive depends on the specific circumstances and the role it plays.

To illustrate: some studies suggest that the greater the emotional intensity, the narrower one's focus. For example, in an extreme state of fear, an individual will notice only the feared object. This narrowing is beneficial or detrimental depending on the nature of the task involved. The narrowing may exclude irrelevant facts and help an individual concentrate his or her intellectual powers. On the other hand, it may exclude highly relevant factors, preventing the proper analysis of available options.

Pieters and Van Raaij (1987) distinguish the following four major functions of affect:

(1) Interpretation and Organization of information about one's own functioning, and about the environment. Pain and fatigue indicate one's somatic constraints; fear and anxiety indicate psychic limits. Affect also provides a simple structure of the physical and social world, organizing objects, persons, and ideas on the basis of attractiveness.

(2) Mobilization and Allocation of resources is influenced by the affective state of the organism. In strong emotional states of the organism, somatic energy resources are mobilized (peak performance) or inhibited (freezing). A loud noise or a fast moving object creates an emergency reaction. Adrenaline output is enhanced, and allocated to the urgent task of coping with the danger. "Acting out" frustrations may be a consequence of blocking of a desired goal. This causes frustration and it may be therapeutic to act out one's frustrations in showing affect to others and to oneself.

(3) Sensation Seeking and Avoiding may occur in order to reach an optimal level of arousal. When stimulation levels are too low, they cause low levels of arousal (boredom). When stimulation levels are too high, they create high levels of arousal (stress). People try to avoid these extreme levels of arousal by actively seeking or avoiding stimulation (sensation).

(4) Affect is a way to communicate with others. Facial expressions, body postures, and exclamations all communicate one's feeling and preferences. Affect is a much more expeditious mode of communication than the cognitive system. The authors proceed to review scores of studies showing these varying effects of affects.

In short, the notion that affect necessarily, commonly or even typically subverts rational decision making is rejected. Affect often plays a positive role, although when it excessively restricts the decision-making context, heavily loads one option compared to others, or interrupts L/E deliberations it undermines rationality.

The Role of Values

Normative values (such as equality, justice, freedom), to distinguish from other values (for example, aesthetic ones), contain an affective element. Without it, values have no motivating force. On the other hand, values differ from sheer affective involvements in that they contain a justification and define a wider claim (e.g., others to whom the same right applies), while sheer affective states contain no such statements. (Love for mankind is a value; love for a particular person is an emotion.) Normative values may be internalized and thus become part of the actor's perception and judgment or they may remain external, and be part of the constraints the actor faces. Judgments based on normative values may be used to curb emotions or to legitimate them.

The relationships between normative values and rationality is in many ways akin to that of affect. Normative values may exclude some or most options, load others, and so on. For example, a study (Lefford, 1946: 141) has shown that normative loading limits logical reasoning. Students were given 40 syllogisms. Half of these dealt with socially controversial material, the other half with neutral material. Subjects were asked to state the validity of the syllogism as well as whether they agreed or disagreed with its conclusion. Most subjects were better able to judge neutral syllogisms than charged ones. And their reasoning was biased in the direction of their convictions. Moreover, the group of students who were given the neutral syllogisms first, followed by the charged ones, did better on both the neutral and emotionally charged syllogisms. Similarly, values lead to *selective exposure* to information. For example, during Watergate, McGovern supporters actively sought information about the event, while Nixon supporters avoided it (Chaiken and Stangor, 1987: 10).

Abelson (1976: 61) discusses the many functions served by holding beliefs "other than in the service of rationality.

Beliefs may be comforting, may protect against anxiety, may organize vague feelings, may provide a sense of identity, may be the prerequisite for participating in a cause, may provide something to say to avoid seeming uninformed, etc."

Last but not least, normative values—as factors that influence the choice of means—help ensure the primacy of ends. The preoccupation with means, with enhancing their strength, scope, quantity and quality, is the essence of industrialization, market economies and economics, technology and applied science, of modern man. However, this preoccupation, through a process known as goal displacement, tends to lead to primacy of means over ends. Studies of organizations are replete with reports of organizations designed to serve a specific goal. When the design proved to be inappropriate, rather than adjust it the goal is replaced, to suit the existing design (Sills, 1957). Multimillionaires work themselves to a frazzle to increase their income. Executives work "for their families," destroying their family life in the process. Societies undermine their fabric in order to accelerate economic growth. Normative values serve as an antidote to goal displacement because they rule out certain categories of means (which undermine ends) or excessive preoccupation with means or efficiency, to the neglect of other values. In short, the correct question hence is not do normative values play a positive role in decision making, but under what conditions are they contributing versus undermining instrumental rationality?

It is tempting to suggest that both values and emotions, that N/A factors, enhance decision making when they set contexts, and hinder them when they infuse, especially interrupt, L/E considerations. While such a statement may serve as a very crude first approximation, it must be noted that (a) the "tightness" of context is another factor: the less options it legitimates, the more it limits rationality, but (b) not all limits on rationality are dysfunctional. Also, (c) some interruptions of orderly decision making (e.g., in an emergency, when emotions instruct us to escape rather than deliberate) are highly functional. In short, the specification of the relation between the role of N/A factors and rational decision making is a task far from complete, but it is clearly established that both affect and normative values often play important positive functions and are not merely hindrances to reason.

On Definitions, Measurements, and Alternative Interpretations

Cognitive Interpretations of N/A Factors

Cognitive psychologists correctly challenged the notion that every deviation from instrumental rationality is due to an N/A factor. Indeed, they have provided robust evidence that L/E considerations are often limited or disturbed by intra-cognitive factors. It is argued here, though, that sometimes the approach is carried too far, to suggest that all or most limitations on L/E are cognitive, that N/A factors play no significant role. While we have no new evidence to present, the data available suggest that the role of N/A factors should not be ruled out.

Most of the cognitive studies choose tasks for their subjects that have two features of particular relevance for the issue at hand: They have one unequivocal solution (at least within the framework of Bayesian logic) and there are no normative-affective loadings attached to any of the options. For example, when subjects are asked whether X or 0 are more frequent in a random sequence (on which they tend to project a pattern), the correct answer—both are equally frequent—is not hindered by an affective attachment to, or normative judgment of, either X or 0. Hence, it is very plausible that the source of the bias that subjects exhibit is intra-cognitive.

In contrast, many facts, inferences, and judgments people make in real-life situations concern matters that have no clear-cut answers and which include items that evoke affects and normative judgments. Typically, facts individuals employ are more akin to those Americans have concerning whether the Soviet Union is trustworthy, or what inflation and interest rates will be ten years hence, that is, judgments that are anxiety-provoking (a mistake may cost one's home, or country). In some situations only intra-cognitive biases may be at work; in others both intra-cognitive and N/A based ones. I suggest that most real-life decisions are of the second kind.

Indeed, in those cognitive studies that deal with real-life situations, the N/A factors seem to us to stand out and provide a parsimonious explanation. For example, psychologists find that people are, in general, overconfident in estimating probabilities that affect their lives. They believe they are better-than-average drivers, more likely than the average person to live past 80, and less likely than the average person to be harmed by products (Slovic and Lichtenstein, 1982). This is explained as a matter of "availability," a cognitive phenomenon in which people respond more to "vivid" information than to "dull" statistics. Since people have little experience with major accidents, or their own death, they are said not to be "vivid" and hence are underestimated. It seems, though, plausible that *part* of the variance is to be explained by N/A factors such as people trying to protect or enhance their self-esteem ("I am a good driver") and by cultural pressures to display confidence. (Thus, one would expect such responses to be more common in boisterous cultures than in those in which self-effacing is the accepted norm. Compare British to American, for example.)

Similarly, most people's risk behavior defies economic assumptions. For instance, people prefer a sure gain over a larger but less certain gain even when according to the probabilities the value of the second option is considerably higher (Kahneman and Tversky, 1982: 160), they, in fact, prefer the smaller return. Conversely, when it comes to risk taking, people violate the economic assumptions that they will take a risk only if compensated for the risk. They prefer to gamble on a loss rather than accept a certain loss even if the potential loss is larger (of course taking into account the difference in probabilities). All these findings may find a parsimonious explanation in the relative loss to self-esteem of some outcomes over others. For example, a person may

prefer a sure, smaller gain over a probable, larger one because small but sure gain avoids the possibility of having to
criticize oneself if one was so "stupid" to "blow" the gain, a
prospect one must face only if one goes for the larger gain.
This line of analysis, motivation, in addition to cognitive
interpretation, may be validated if people with higher self-
esteem are found to be more inclined to take risks, and so
on. For a still different explanation, see Van Raaij (1985).

The difference in emphasis is highlighted in the discussion of prejudice. Nisbett and Ross (1980: 237–242) attack
the tendency to attribute racial or ethnic prejudice to motivational, emotional, or spiritual "defects," to a "triumph of the
heart over the intellect" (p. 237). The author sees the cause
of prejudice in various *cognitive* biases, for example, individuals who fit stereotypes are given disproportionate weight in
overall impressions of others, and infrequent incidents are
used to "validate" stereotypes (p. 240). Thus, those who see a
few lazy blacks, or loud Italians, and assume all are, are simply overgeneralizing. They may well, but why do they not
overgeneralize positive attributes? And why do they so often
focus their hostility on the vulnerable groups? Emotional
mechanisms seem also to be at work. For example, people
seem to split their ambivalence about others in such a way
that negative feelings are projected on the out-group and
positive ones on the in-group.

Affect: Definition and Operationalization

The terms affect and normative values have been used
throughout the preceding discussion, despite the fact that in
the mainstreams of recent psychological literature these
terms are deliberately avoided, although in the 1980s the concept of affect (or emotions) had a measure of a comeback.
(Not so, yet, for normative values.) Without going here into
details of the complex matters involved, it is necessary to indicate briefly the reasons the author draws heavily on such
unfashionable concepts.

Part of the answer lies in intellectual history. In the period between 1960 and 1980, mainstreams of psychology were preoccupied with establishing that intra-mind processes are valuable, in overcoming the behavioristic notions that behavior is externally driven, formed by inputs from the environment, with the person being viewed as a "black box" that need not be explored internally (Norman, 1980; 1–11). The internal processes that were highlighted were characterized as strictly cognitive, as if it were difficult enough to introduce such an ephemeral concept as cognition; there was little disposition to go even further and also re-introduce affect (Zajonc, 1980: 152). Indeed, emotions were either "shown" to be an unnecessary concept or viewed as reflecting cognitive interpretations of unspecific psychological arousal. The work of Schachter (1966, 1971) and his associates (Schachter and Singer, 1962) has been often cited to argue that emotions are nothing but physiological arousal and a cognitive coding of the situation that generates the arousal. What the person "feels" depends thus not on the inner sensation but on the situation that caused it and on the ways the person appraises the situation. The *same* arousal may be experienced as joy or anger depending on the cognition brought to bear. We note that many criticisms have been made of the original studies and that attempts to replicate them have not succeeded (Marshall and Zimbardo, 1979; Maslach, 1979), and that hundreds of studies have shown the role of affect (for a review work see Isen, 1984).

Another major reason emotions have been played down is that they have been difficult to define. It should, however, be noted that there are similar difficulties in defining the term *cognition* (Holyoak and Gordon, 1984: 37). Hence, definitional difficulties should not be used to favor one concept over the other.

Finally, researchers have encountered considerable difficulties in finding empirical measurements of emotions. However, we believe that a promising approach to measure affect is to combine several measurements, thus correcting for the weakness of each single one. For example, self-reports of emotional states tend to be problematic because they are subject to rationalization. (People buy more of a product when the background music is to their liking but when asked, report they bought the product because of its qualities.)

Physiological aspects of emotions, measured by electronic devices are unreliable because arousal may reflect other factors, e.g., changes in physical exertion. Behavioral measures such as smiling (when happy) and frowning (when concerned) are similarly unreliable when used in isolation.

However, when all three kinds of indicators point in the same direction, one may assume that the affect is indeed operative. And when the measurements are incompatible, this may be used to form a typology of different kinds of affect, such as declared emotions (only self-reported), physiological arousal without awareness, and so on. Those, in turn, may correlate with various psychological observations. For example, emotions limited to one of the possible three levels are expected to be less stable than those which encompass all three levels. For example, a person exhibiting only declared emotion but not arousal or emotional behavior may be expected to conform to social norms that have not been internalized (for example, saluting a flag when one is actually quite anti-patriotic). For additional discussion, definition and measurements of emotions, see Izard, Kagan and Zajonc (1984).

The concept of normative values may have fewer problems than that of affect, but is hardly free of methodological concerns. The concept is often challenged on the ground that values as states-of-mind are not observable, and provide poor predictions of behavior. However, in recent years approaches have been developed that measure values closer to behavior than the tradition was previously (for example, Schwartz, 1977; Ajzen and Fishbein, 1980; England, 1967; England and Lee, 1974; and Watson and Barone, 1976). Indeed, studies that include such variables often predict better than those that do not include attitudes (Hoch, 1985).

All this is not to say that the serious problems in defining and operationalizing affects and values have been solved. However, they also are evident in the other, widely used concepts and some promising leads seem to be at hand.

Can N/A Factors Be Incorporated into the Neoclassical Paradigm?

Neoclassicists argue that even if all these observations about N/A factors are valid, it is still unnecessary to evolve another paradigm because these factors can be incorporated into the prevailing paradigm. N/A factors can be included in preferences (especially as they affect goals) and in constraints (especially as they affect the choice of means). Value commitments and emotional involvements are said to be simply two of the many factors "reflected" in one's preferences. In a previous publication I argued that such incorporation of moral values is excessively parsimonious, unproductive, and ethically unacceptable (Etzioni, 1986a). Here additional arguments are brought to bear to support the thesis that N/A factors should be treated as a significant, distinct category, both for preferences and for constraints.

If N/A only curbed one's choice to a limited extent, these factors could be "modeled" as nothing more than one more factor that affects constraints (say Hindus are prohibited from purchasing cows but are free to trade in thousands of other items). However, the position taken here is that a good part of the choices made by individuals is made on N/A and not L/E grounds; i.e., an N/A factor is not simply one more factor, one member of a large batch, but it explains a significant proportion of the actual choices made, and hence needs to be studied distinctively if choices are to be explained.

Most important, neoclassicists treat preferences as stable and/or as given (Stigler and Becker, 1977). However, as N/A factors account for an important part of the variance among preferences and for changes in them, a productive

social science must be able to identify the factors that form
and that change these factors. Hence, cultural change, social
movements, rise and fall of leaderships, societal strains and
their resolution or reduction—all factors that explain N/A
changes—must enter into one's paradigm.

Also, as neoclassicists are stressing the merit of their
approach because it is highly parsimonious, it should be
noted that recognizing the role of N/A factors is especially
parsimonious because these factors affect both preferences
and constraints.

An example serves to illustrate all these points. From
1981 to 1986 in the U.S.A. there was a decline in the consumption of alcohol. A neoclassicist may seek to explain this
trend by a change in constraints, such as rising prices, new
taxes, rising drinking age, etc. However, the price of liquor
actually declined as compared to other products, and consumption declined even in states that did not raise the drinking age. The major reason was a change in preferences, the
result of a neotemperance movement (especially MADD and
SADD) coming on top of a rising fitness and health movement. *These same factors* also affected the price—they led to
some increase in taxes—and the age limit. Neoclassicists, uncomfortable with macro-explanations, not based on individual acts or choices, or their aggregation, may ask—what
caused these societal trends? While this question can be answered, two methodological points need to be made: (a) one
can always ask about any cause, or any paradigm, what caused
it, and thus slip into a never ceasing, unsolvable, dilemma
and (b) macro-concepts are acceptable explanations in the
paradigm at hand, because they treat macro-factors as primary (basic) causes. In short, N/A factors are significantly,
often macro, parsimonious explanatory factors both for societal trends and for micro individual choices and behavior.

Notes

1. The subject touched upon here deserves major attention:
    the difference in the neoclassical and deontological view

of concepts such as self-control, deferred gratification, will power or character. This must be left for another day.
2. Barnard (1947: 167–169) uses the term to denote an area in which an individual is willing to accept orders. Actions outside of the zone violate the person's sense of what ought to be obeyed. (See, also, Sherif, Sherif, and Nebergall, 1965.)

References

Abelson, R.P., 1976. "Social psychology's rational man." In: S.I. Benn and G.W. Mortimore (eds.), *Rationality in the social sciences*. London: Routledge and Kegan Paul.

Ajzen, Icek and Martin Fishbein, 1980. *Understanding attitudes and predicting behavior*. Englewood Cliffs, NJ: Prentice-Hall.

Barnard, Chester, 1947. *The functions of the executive*. Cambridge, MA: Harvard University Press.

Beckman, L., 1970. "Effects of students' performance on teachers and observers' attributions of causality." *Journal of Educational Psychology* 61, 75–82.

Berelson, Bernard and Gary A. Steiner, 1964. *Human behavior: An inventory of scientific findings*. Orlando, Fla.: Harcourt Brace Jovanovich.

Chaiken, Shelly and Charles Stangor, 1987. "Attitudes and attitudinal change." *Annual Review of Psychology* 38, 575–630.

Davis, W.L. and D.E. Davis, 1972. "Internal-external control and attribution of responsibility for success and failure." *Journal of Personality* 40, 123–136.

Durkheim, Emile, 1947. *The division of labor in society*. Glencoe, IL: The Free Press.

Durkheim, Emile, 1954. *The elementary forms of religious life*. New York: Macmillan.

Easterbrook, J.A., 1959. "The effect of emotion on cue utilization and the organization of behavior." *Psychology Review* 66, 183–210.

Edwards, Ward, 1954. "The theory of decision making." *Psychological Bulletin* 51, 380–417.

Elster, Jon, ed., 1985a. *The multiple self.* Cambridge: Cambridge University Press.

Elster, Jon, 1985b. "Sadder but wiser? Rationality and the emotions." *Social Science Information.* London: Sage, vol. 24, 375–406.

Engel, James F. and Roger D. Blackwell, 1982. *Consumer behavior,* 4th ed. Chicago, IL: The Dryden Press.

England, G.W., 1967. "Personal value systems of American managers." *American Management Journal* 10, 53–68.

England, G.W. and R. Lee, 1974. "The relationship between managerial values and managerial success in the United States, Japan, India, and Australia." *Journal of Applied Psychology* 59, 411–419.

Etzioni, Amitai, 1967. "Mixed scanning: A 'third' approach to decision-making." *Public Administration Review* 27, 385–392.

Etzioni, Amitai, 1968. *The active society.* New York: Free Press.

Etzioni, Amitai, 1986a. "The case for a multiple-utility conception." *Economics and Philosophy* 2, 159–183.

Etzioni, Amitai, 1986b. "Rationality is anti-entropic." *Journal of Economic Psychology* 7, 17–36.

Etzioni, Amitai, 1987. *The moral dimension: Toward a new economics.* New York: Free Press.

Feather, N.T., 1969. "Attribution of responsibility and valence of success and failure in relation to initial confidence and task performance." *Journal of Personality and Social Psychology* 13, 129–144.

Fellner, Carl H. and John R. Marshall, 1970. "Kidney donors—The myth of informed consent." *American Journal of Psychiatry* 126, 1245–1251.

Festinger, Leon, 1957. *A theory of cognitive dissonance.* Stanford, CA: Stanford University Press.

Festinger, Leon, 1964. *Conflict, decision, and dissonance.* Stanford, CA: Stanford University Press.

Fishbein, Martin and Icek Ajzen, 1975. *Belief, attitude, intention and behavior: an introduction to theory and research.* Reading, MA: Addison-Wesley.

Fitch, G., 1970. "Effects of self-esteem, perceived performance, and chance on causal attributions." *Journal of Personality and Social Psychology* 16, 311–315.

Freize, I. and B. Weiner, 1971. "Cue utilization and attributional judgments for success and failure." *Journal of Personality* 39, 591–606.

Furnham, Adrian and Alan Lewis, 1986. *The economic mind: the social psychology of economic behavior.* Brighton: Wheatsheaf.

Glueck, William F., 1974. "Decision making: organization choice." *Personnel Psychology* 27, 77–99.

Goodin, Robert E., 1980. "Making moral incentives pay." *Policy Sciences* 12, 131–145.

Heider, F., 1958. *The psychology of interpersonal relations.* New York: Wiley.

Hirschman, Albert O.,1984. "Against parsimony: Three easy ways of complicating some categories of economic discourse." *Bulletin: The American Academy of Arts and Sciences* 37, 8, 11–28.

Hoch, Irving, 1985. "Retooling the mainstream." *Resources* 80 (Spring), 1–4.

Holsti, Ole R., 1971. "Crisis, stress, and decision-making." *International Social Science Journal,* 23, 53–67.

Holyoak, Keith J. and Peter C. Gordon, 1984. "Information processing and social cognition." In: Robert S. Wyer, Jr. and Thomas K. Srull (eds.), *Handbook of social cognition,* vol. 1. Hillsdale, NJ: Erlbaum.

Isen, Alice M., 1984. "Toward understanding the role of affect in cognition." In: Robert S. Wyer, Jr. and Thomas K. Srull (eds.), *Handbook of social cognition,* vol. 1. Hillsdale, NJ: Erlbaum.

Izard, C.E., J. Kagan, and R.B. Zajonc, eds., 1984. *Emotion, cognition, and behavior.* Cambridge: Cambridge University Press.

Izard, C.E., 1977. *Human emotions.* New York: Plenum.

Janis, Irving and Leon Mann, 1977. *Decision making: a psychological analysis of conflict, choice and commitment.* New York: Free Press.

Johnson, T.J., R. Feigenbaum, and M. Weiby, 1964. "Some determinants and consequences of the teacher's perception of causation." *Journal of Experimental Psychology* 55, 237–246.

Jones, E.E. and K.E. Davis, 1965. "From acts to dispositions: The attribution process in person perception." In: L. Berkowitz (ed.), *Advances in experimental social psychology*, vol. 2. New York: Academic Press.

Kahneman, Daniel and Amos Tversky, 1982. "The psychology of preferences." *Scientific American* 246, 160–173.

Katona, George, 1975. *Psychological economics*. New York: Elsevier.

Katz, D. and R.L. Kahn, 1966. *The social psychology of organizations*. New York: Wiley.

Kelly, Harold H., 1967. "Attribution theory in social psychology." In: D. Levine (ed.), *Nebraska symposium on motivation: 1967*. Lincoln, NE: University of Nebraska Press, 192–241.

Kelly, Harold H. and John W. Thibaut, 1978. *Interpersonal relations: a theory of interdependence*. New York: Wiley.

Kohlberg, Lawrence, 1981. *Essays on moral development*. San Francisco: Harper-Collins.

Kohlberg, Lawrence, 1983. *Moral stages: a current formulation and response to critics*. New York: Karger.

Korchin, Sheldon J., 1964. "Anxiety and cognition." In: Constance Sheever (ed.), *Cognition: theory, research, promise*. New York: Harper-Collins.

Kozielecki, Jozef, 1975. *Psychological decision theory*. Dordrecht: Reidel.

Latane, B. and J.M. Darley, 1970. *The unresponsive bystander: Why doesn't he help?* New York: Appleton-Century-Crofts.

Lefford, Arthur, 1946. "The influence of emotional subject matter on logical reasoning." *Journal of General Psychology* 34, 127–151.

Leventhal, Howard, 1982. "The integration of emotion and cognition: a view from the perceptual-motor theory of emotion." In: Margaret Clark and Susan Fiske (eds.), *Affect and cognition*. Hillsdale, NJ: Erlbaum, 121–156.

Lewis, Michael, Margaret Wolan Sullivan, and Linda Michalson, 1984. "The cognitive-emotional fugue." In: Caroll E. Izard, Jerome Kagan, and Robert B. Zajonc (eds.), *Emotions, cognition, and behavior*. Cambridge, MA: Cambridge University Press, 264–288.

Maital, Shlomo, 1982. *Minds, markets, and money.* New York: Basic Books.

Marshall, G.D. and P.G. Zimbardo, 1979. "Affective consequences of inadequately explained physiological arousal." *Journal of Personality and Social Psychology* 37, 970–985.

Maslach, C., 1979. "Negative emotional biasing of unexplained arousal." *Journal of Personal Social Psychology* 37, 953–969.

Moment, David, 1967. "Career development: a future oriented historical approach for research and action." *Personnel Administration* 30, 4, 6–11.

Morgan, James N., 1978. "Multiple motives, group decisions, uncertainty, ignorance, and confusion: A realistic economics of the consumer requires some psychology." *American Economic Review* 68, 58–63.

Nisbet, J.D. and W. Grant, 1965. "Vocational intentions and decisions of Aberdeen arts graduates." *Occupational Psychology* 39, 215–219.

Nisbett, Richard and Lee Ross, 1980. *Human inference: strategies and shortcomings of social judgement.* Englewood Cliffs, NJ: Prentice-Hall.

Norman, D.A., 1980. "Twelve issues for cognitive science." In: D.A. Norman (ed.), *Perspectives on cognitive science: talks from the La Jolla conference.* Hillsdale, NJ: Erlbaum.

Piaget, Jean, 1965. *The moral judgment of the child.* New York: Free Press.

Pieters, Rik G.M. and W. Fred van Raaij, 1987. "The role of affect in economic behavior." In: W. Fred van Raaij, Gery M. van Veldhoven, and Karl-Erik Warneryd (eds.), *Handbook of economic psychology.* Amsterdam: North-Holland.

Schachter, Stanley, 1966. "The interaction of cognitive and psychological determinants of emotional state." In: Charles D. Spielberger (ed.); *Anxiety and behavior.* New York: Academic Press, 193–224.

Schachter, Stanley, 1971. *Emotion, obesity, and crime.* New York: Academic Press.

Schachter, Stanley and J.E. Singer, 1962. "Cognitive, social and psychological determinants of emotional state." *Psychology Review* 69, 379–399.

Schwartz, Shalom H., 1970a. "Moral decision making and behavior." In: J. Macaulay and L. Berkowitz (eds.), *Altruism and helping behavior.* New York: Academic Press, 127–141.

Schwartz, Shalom, H., 1970b. "Elicitation of moral obligation and self-sacrificing behavior: an experimental study of volunteering to be a bone marrow donor." *Journal of Personality and Social Psychology* 15, 283–293.

Schwartz, Shalom H., 1977. "Normative influences on altruism." In: Leonard Berkowitz (ed.), *Advances in experimental social psychology,* vol. 10. New York: Academic Press, 221–270.

Sherif, Carolyn W., Muzafter Sherif, and Roger E. Nebergall, 1965. *Attitude and attitude change.* Philadelphia, PA: Saunders.

Sills, David S., 1957. *The volunteers: means and ends in a national organization.* New York: Free Press.

Simon, Herbert, 1976. *Administrative behavior: a study of decision making processes in administrative organization,* 3rd ed. New York: Free Press.

Simmons, Roberta G., Susan D. Klein and Robert L. Simmons, 1977. *Gift of life: the social and psychological impact of organ transplantation.* New York: Wiley.

Sjoberg, Lennart, 1980. "Volition problems in carrying through a difficult decision." *Acta Psychologica* 45, 123–132.

Slovic, Paul and Sarah Lichtenstein, 1982. "Facts versus fears: understanding perceived risk." In: D. Kahneman, Paul Slovic and A. Tversky (eds.), *Judgement under uncertainty.* New York: Cambridge University Press, 463–489.

Soelberg, P., 1967. "Unprogrammed decision making: job choice." *Industrial Management Review* 9, 1–12.

Steiner, Ivan D., 1980. "Attribution of choice." In Martin Fishbein (ed.), *Progress in social psychology.* Hillsdale, NJ: Erlbaum.

Stigler, George J. and Gary S. Becker, 1977. "De gustibus non est disputandum." *American Economic Review* 67, 2, 76–90.

Toda, Masanao, 1980. "Emotion in decision-making." *Acta Psychologica* 45, 133–155.

Torrance, E. Paul, 1954. "The behavior of small groups under the stress conditions of 'survival'." *American Sociological Review* 19, 751–755.

Van Raaij, W. Fred, 1985. "Attribution of causality to economic actions and events." *Kyklos* 38, 3–19.

Walzer, Michael, 1983. *Spheres of justice.* New York: Basic Books.

Watson, J.G. and Sam Barone, 1976. "The self concept, personal values, and motivational orientations of black and white managers." *Academy of Management Journal* 19, 442–451.

Weber, Max, 1921–22/1968. *Economy and society.* Edited by Gunther Roth and Claus Wittich. New York: Bedminster Press.

Williams, Edward E. and Findlay M. Chapman III, 1981. "A reconsideration of the rationality postulate." *American Journal of Economics and Sociology* 40, 18–19.

Wolosin, R.J., S.J. Sherman, and A. Till, 1973. "Effects of cooperation and competition on responsibility attribution after success and failure." *Journal of Experimental Social Psychology* 9, 220–235.

Wright, W.F. and G.H. Bower, 1981. *Mood effects on subjective probability assessment.* Unpublished manuscript.

Zajonc, R.B., 1980. "Feeling and thinking: preferences need no inferences." *American Psychologist* 35, 151–175.

Zajonc, R.B., and H. Markus, 1984. "Affect and cognition: the hard interface." In: C.E. Izard, J. Kagan, and R.B. Zajonc (eds.), *Emotion, cognition and behavior.* Cambridge, MA: Cambridge University Press, 73–102.

4

The Responsive Community: Author's Note

One of the most interesting observations about the social sciences is that what seems elementary, even "obvious," to members of one discipline often seems unacceptable and inconceivable to members of others. One such contested assumption or phenomenon is the role of collectivities, groups, or communities in influencing individual behavior, values, emotions, and thinking. For many sociologists and social psychologists, the role of collectivities is "obviously" significant and constitutive; communities are not merely environments to which an actor adjusts as he or she would to a new climate, but they also influence to a great extent the person's most inner desires, preferences and moral commitments. This is not to suggest that there is no free will or choice but to recognize that individuality is honed out of social, collective (communal) backgrounds. On the other hand, many economists ignore collective or community factors (as well as cultural, historical, societal-structural, and political factors) or treat them as environmental constraints to which individuals adjust according to prior preferences that they somehow gained, again, extrasocietally. The essay on "Liberals and Communitarians" traces the social philosophical foundations of these two approaches and points to a synthesis.

125

For every one who finds the essays' conclusions and its direction elementary, there are two who seem to find them unfathomable, the price—and merit—of crossing interdisciplinary borders.

While the essay on "Liberals and Communitarians" attempts to build a bridge between two major camps, the essay on "Basic Human Needs, Alienation, and Inauthenticity" represents the viewpoint of a very small minority. The issue, which could not be more important, is whether human beings can be "socialized" down to their deepest, most inner commitments. Most social scientists who deal with this question assume this socialization, which then feeds into moral relativism. My position, however, is that there is a basic, underlying human nature that cannot be altered. Moreover, the basis of this universal humanness is neither genetic nor god-given. It is the product of one basic form of socialization that we all undergo. If we did not share this experience, we would not acquire human features. "To be," in the human sense— to walk erect, communicate with symbols, and so on—is to be socialized. It is this socialization that implants, willy-nilly, the same basic human needs in all of us. This essay spells out the reasons and evidence for the position I hold. Let me stress here the normative implication. One can determine that one society is more responsive to human nature than another only if one assumes a basic underlying human nature. If full socialization were possible, people in a Nazi society should be able to be made as content as those in a democratic one. This is neither the case nor a normatively sound position.

Liberals and Communitarians

Toward the I and We

Communitarians charge contemporary liberal philosophers (CLP) with an excessive focus on individual rights and neglect of obligations to the community, to shared virtues and common purposes. CLPs evolve a measure of commitment to a moderate vision of community; however, they contend that communitarians provide an insufficient basis for individual rights. Communitarians, in turn, indirectly acknowledge the need to ensure these rights in order to avoid collectivism. Out of these charges and counter-charges, a synthesis begins to suggest itself. This section highlights the key points of the debate to indicate the direction of this synthesis.

Less Individualism

In *A Theory of Justice,* Rawls founded a conception of justice on respect for the individual. Individual persons and their self-chosen ends are primary; the common good or general welfare subordinate:

> Each person possesses an inviolability founded on justice that even the welfare of society as a whole cannot override. For this reason justice denies that the loss of freedom for some is made right by a greater good shared by others (1971, p. 3).

Rawls arrives at his notion of justice by considering what individuals in the "original position," a reformulation of the state

Note: This essay was originally published in *Partisan Review,* 1990, 57(2) 215–227. It is reprinted with permission. I am indebted to Brandt Goldstein for extensive research assistance and to Kyle Hoffman and John Duvivier for editorial comments.

of nature, would choose as "principles of a justice for the basic structure of society" (1971, p. 11). Individuals in this hypothetical "original position" are "rational persons concerned to advance their interests," stripped of all particular attributes as social beings. They debate behind a "veil of ignorance" which prevents them from knowing their future position in society. Because of such uncertainty, these rational individuals cannot but choose a just order. For example, no one in the original position would rationally argue for a system that favors men, because that person might "end up" a woman. Rawls's philosophy thus emphasizes the primacy of the individual, and derives social attributes mainly from the aggregation of individuals' rational choices. Whatever concept of community or substantive good Rawls's theory allows for, is based on these being the preferred choices of individuals. The CLP's conception of the self traces back to the Kantian transcendental ego. Kant asserts that as we cannot grasp this fundamental self empirically, we must infer its existence if we are to be capable "of self-knowledge and of freedom" (Sandel, 1982, p. 9). In his theory of justice, Rawls reformulates the Kantian subject, stripping away its metaphysical trappings, recasting it within "the canons of reasonable empiricism" (Rawls, 1977, p. 165). However, the basic concept of the Kantian ego remains intact: the native of the Rawlsian original position, the abstract self, "is prior to the ends which are affirmed by it . . ." (Rawls, 1971, p. 560).

Rawls's theory, as advanced in his book, has been subject to a considerable range of interpretations, including his own, in subsequent writings. Certain of these views find him somewhat more concerned with community than hereto stated. Without engaging into this extensive interpretative discourse, we suggest that (1) Rawls's position remains *basically* a rights-oriented, individual-choice liberalism and that (2) his work has become *somewhat* more communitarian over the years, a point to which we return below.

The rights-based ethic of liberalism, as articulated by Rawls and by other noted CLPs, including Dworkin (*Taking Rights Seriously*, 1977) and Nozick (*Anarchy, State, and Utopia*, 1974), has faced a recent, growing challenge from the communitarian critics. Concerned with "the presence of moral chaos and the absence of common purposes" (Thigpen and Downing, 1987, p. 638) in contemporary society, and determined to give "fuller expression to the claims of citizenship and community than liberalism allows" (Sandel, 1984, p. 5), these critics fault liberal theory both for its conception of a freely-choosing, autonomous self, cut off from all social moorings, and for its lifeless, impoverished conception of community and the common good.[1]

MacIntyre, for example, rejects the possibility of theorizing about justice with an abstract self as the subject:

> [P]articularity can never be simply left behind or obliterated. The notion of escaping from it into a realm of entirely universal maxims which belong to man as such, whether in its eighteenth-century Kantian form or in the presentation of some modern analytical moral philosophies is an illusion (1984, p. 221).

Sandel (1982) argues that Rawls's representative rational agent "fails plausibly to account for certain indispensable aspects of our moral experience" (1982, p. 179). In Sandel's view, we are not, indeed, cannot be, entirely autonomous agents, "independent in the sense that our identity is never tied to our aims and attachments" (ibid.). Persons as we know them, Sandel maintains, are always "situated" or "embedded" in a social context, they are "encumbered" by ties of community: ". . . we cannot conceive of our personhood without reference to our roles as citizens, and as participants in a common life" (Sandel, 1984, p. 5).

Communitarians are further troubled by what they see as a weak conception of community and common good, or shared moral values. They point out that the "strong" CLP (or libertarian) position holds that individuals' ends are either competing or independent, "but not in any case complementary . . . [no] one takes account of the good of others" (Rawls, 1971, p. 521). To libertarians (among them, Nozick), social arrangements are essentially "a necessary burden," and "the good of community consists solely in the advantages individuals derive from co-operating in pursuit of their egoistic ends" (Sandel, 1982, p. 148).

For moderate CLPs, the community is far more than a "necessary burden." Indeed, Rawls contends that a "well-ordered society" founded on the principles of justice possesses "shared final ends and common activities valued for themselves" (1971, p. 525). The entire society finds "satisfaction" in this achievement. Rawls sees just institutions as "good in themselves" because they provide each individual's life with "a more ample and rich structure than it would otherwise have" (1971, p. 528). That is, individuals may seek and indeed benefit from a just society, but it is they who change it, for their individual purposes. Attempts to impose any preferred way of life are illegitimate (Dworkin, 1978, pp. 127–29).

In sum, moderate formulations of contemporary liberal philosophy allow for some vision of community beyond a mere aggregation of self-interested individuals; however, CLPs, including Rawls and Dworkin, hold the community to be secondary, derivative, and reflecting a rational choice of the individual—with whom all basic rights rest. Yet CLPs have shown some flexibility: recently, both Rawls and Dworkin have modified their positions in response to communitarian criticisms. In his 1985 essay, "Justice as Fairness," Rawls concedes that the basic values of the representative moral agent—now called the "citizen"—derive not from intuitions but from "an 'overlapping consensus' that undergirds the modern state" (Wallach, 1987 p. 584). Further, Rawls contextualizes his theory, acknowledging social and historical particulars—namely, the "democratic society reflected in contemporary, advanced, Western, industrialized nations" (ibid., p. 583)—that implicitly inform A Theory of Justice: "justice as fairness is framed to apply to what I have called the 'basic structure' of a modern constitutional democracy" (Rawls, 1985, p. 224).[2] In kind, Dworkin now considers his fundamental concept of "equal concern and respect" to be historically and politically embedded (Wallach, 1987, p. 608, n16). Wallach observes:

> Contrary to communitarians who fault Rawls and Dworkin for not paying attention to the "shared meanings and understandings" of historical societies, each claims that the

ideas he previously called intuitive presuppose them (1987,
p. 584).

It seems that CLPs, both through their critics and their
advocates, have made motions toward recognizing an important sphere beyond the individual. However, despite these
steps, CLPs remain committed to principles that must be
modified and supplemented if the middle ground is to be
evolved. As Wallach notes, to claim that "the debate between
liberals and communitarians has collapsed . . . overstates the
distance Rawls has traveled since 1971" (ibid., p. 584). First,
liberals continue to hold that individual liberty, protected by
individual rights, takes priority over any and all common
good, rather than treating (as we will attempt to) individual
and community as moral equals. Selznick writes: ". . . welfare
liberalism[3] strains toward a communitarian perspective. But it
is held back by an irrepressible commitment to the idea that
individuals must decide for themselves what it means to be
free and what ends should be pursued" (1987, p. 447). Second, the liberal concept of the individual remains atomistic
at least in that liberals do not recognize community as a constitutive element of the self.

Moderate Communitarianism

While CLPs maintain the primacy of the rights-bearing individual, communitarians seek to establish moral coherence
within society, the moral foundations of a common good. For
communitarians, the shared moral values, "virtues," and traditions of the community, rather than the rational choices of
abstract individuals, are the bedrock of moral-philosophic discourse. They see persons as "implicated" or "embedded," or
as "citizens" who share a set of moral values by virtue of their
membership in a community. Sandel insists that

> [If] we are partly defined by the communities we inhabit,
> then we must also be implicated in the common purposes
> and ends characteristic of those communities (Sandel, 1984,
> p. 6).

MacIntyre states:

> [W]e all approach our own circumstances as bearers of a
> particular social identity. . . . I am a member of this or that
> guild or profession. . . . I belong to . . . this clan, that tribe,
> this nation. Hence what is good for me has to be the good
> for one who inhabits these roles (1984, p. 220).

Moreover, this notion of common good has a dynamic element: communitarians see the community and individuals as working toward a telos, a common purpose or goal, not fulfilled in society today.

Because CLPs affirm a plurality of individual ends "equally ultimate" (Isaiah Berlin), they look to *procedural* justice—such as Rawls's theory—to adjudicative frameworks that do not presuppose a particular conception of the good. On the other hand, because of their concern with community and the common good, communitarians tend to focus on systems or institutions, substantive entities that embody their moral values. An examination of two leading communitarians, MacIntyre and Walzer, highlights the communitarian approach—and points toward the need for developing a principled basis for individual rights.

In *After Virtue*, MacIntyre (1984) articulates a "strong" communitarian vision of a moral community, premised on the suggestion that the moral foundations of modern society are incoherent, fragmented; he contends that "we have—very largely, if not entirely—lost our comprehension, both theoretical and practical, of morality" (1984, p. 2). MacIntyre's conception of the exemplary moral community derives from the Aristotelian tradition of civic virtue. In this "classical moral tradition," persons are understood to have an end or highest aim—a telos—which they achieve by exercising virtues (particular "acquired human qualities") to attain the intrinsic goods of "practices"—complex and coherent, "socially established," shared activities. The "range of practices is wide: arts, sciences, games, politics, . . . the making and sustaining of family life" (1984, p. 188). Communities that function through this involved scheme find their moral basis (in other words, conceive their moral discourse and exercise their moral judgement) in the "shared understandings," the common assumptions, of what particular human activities are virtuous and of virtue in general (Wallach, 1987, p. 593).

Individuals in such a community do not (as CLPs would have it) choose their own good; they find a common good as members of a distinct moral order. MacIntyre writes:

> An Aristotelian theory of the virtues does therefore presuppose a crucial distinction between what any particular time takes to be good for him and what is really good for him as a man (1984, p. 150).

Each person seeks to learn and exercise the virtues and achieve the internal goods of practices, to discover and achieve their *telos* (what Aristotle called *eudamonia*, loosely translated, human well-being); and in this "education," each finds that "my good as a man [or woman] is one and the same as the good of those others with whom I am bound up in human community" (1984, p. 229). Nor can the *search* for the good be an individual enterprise—the community provides the only legitimate context: "I am never able to seek the good or exercise the relevant virtues *qua* individual" (1984, p. 220).

In *Spheres of Justice,* Walzer, a moderate communitarian, formulates a system of distributive justice based on shared moral values. Each community confers particular meanings and values on goods, and from these common values, Walzer maintains, distributive justice derives.

> If we understand what a good is, what it means to those for whom it is a good [i.e., to the members of a certain community], we understand how, by whom and for what reasons it ought to be distributed. All distributions are just or unjust relative to the social meanings of the goods at stake (1983, p. 9).

The members of a community share these meanings, hence Walzer interprets injustice not as violations of individual rights, but as situations in which membership is not complete, and values and understandings are not shared by the community—whether in lower caste Indian villagers' dissatisfaction with grain distribution ("perhaps we should doubt that the understandings governing village life were really shared," 1983, p. 313) or in the case of slavery ("Slaves and Masters do not inhabit a world of shared meanings," 1983, p. 250n).

Walzer casts these shared meanings and values within a pluralistic framework to create his notion of "complex equality," the central concept of his book. Since different goods have different social meanings (and thus, different principles of distribution), these "spheres" of goods ought to be kept autonomous.

> No social good x should be distributed to men and women
> who possess some other good y merely because they possess
> y and without regard to the meaning of x (1983, p. 20).

Complex equality arises, then, when a good in one sphere, such as political office, cannot be "converted" into the good of another sphere, such as entrepreneurial opportunities.

Walzer's defense of plural social meanings and values leads by implication to the idea of plural sub-communities that flourish within a broader, latent community—clearly, he represents a more moderate communitarian stance than MacIntyre, who talks of "the pluralism which threatens to submerge us all" (1984, p. 226). Further, Walzer develops his notion of community against a "background" of rights, asserting that individuals have the right to "life and liberty," and other rights "beyond" those. But he forgoes

> the advantages that might derive to my argument from
> the idea of personal—that is, human or natural—
> rights. . . [rights] won't take us very far into the substance
> of my argument (1983, p. xv).

Moreover, while he acknowledges certain rights, Walzer does not make clear whether individuals can choose freely among the autonomous values of various sub-communities. He seems more intent upon drawing out the latent meanings of the community as a whole.

While the notions of shared moral values and of community are firmly grounded in these works, critics contend that the status of the individual is precarious in the communitarian vision. Communitarians do not establish effective boundaries against collectivism; and they do not provide a sound basis for the self to transcend social roles and assume a critical stance against society. Sandel's position illustrates the problem:

> As a self-interpreting being, I am able to reflect on my history and in this sense distance myself from it, but the distance is *always* precarious and provisional, the point of reflection never finally secured outside the history itself (1982, p. 170).

MacIntyre does not provide a clear separation of the self from its social roles and corresponding ends. We recall MacIntyre's claim that "what is good for me *has to be* the good for one who inhabits these roles" (1984, p. 220, italics added). Such a separation is necessary if individuals are to evaluate the moral status of practices; indeed, MacIntyre concedes that, by his interpretation of a practice, "there may be practices . . . which simply *are* evil," for example, "torture" (1984, p. 200). But in MacIntyre's world persons could not criticize evil practices, for they would not be able to transcend the social roles tied to these practices.

Affirming some measure of individual rights guarantees autonomy. But MacIntyre claims that "[n]atural or human rights . . . are fictions" (1984, p. 70). There are, he insists, "no such [universal] rights . . . every attempt to give good reasons for believing that there *are* such rights has failed" (1984, p. 69). Rights presuppose "the existence of a socially established set of rules . . . [in] particular historical periods under particular social circumstances" (1984, p. 67). MacIntyre's project is thus one of duties, of the obligations of membership.

Individual rights are not soundly protected in Walzer's philosophy either, as Walzer's treatment of personal autonomy (representing one segment of the range of human rights) demonstrates. "Justice," Walzer contends, "is relative to social meanings. . . . Every substantive account of distributive justice is a local account" (1983, p. 312). Bound to the particular social meanings of the community, individuals may be unable to evaluate the moral standing of their community, i.e., be autonomous and critical. True, Walzer does write that:

> When people disagree about the meaning of social goods, when understandings are controversial, then justice requires that society be faithful to the disagreements, providing institutional channels for their expression, adjudicative mechanisms, and alternative distributions (1983, p. 313).

Yet, as Fishkin (1984, p. 757) declares: "[In Walzer's work, we] lack shared understandings about how to interpret whatever shared understandings actually exist among us in our culture." In short, in *Spheres of Justice*, Walzer establishes no sure footing for the autonomous individual, no map for how to disagree, or to challenge shared meanings.

Individual rights, then, are not secured in these communitarian visions. Communitarians have indirectly acknowledged this difficulty; indeed, in their attempts to avoid the collectivistic implications of their work, they generate momentum for those who seek to develop a synthetic position. MacIntyre, for example, writes that exercising the virtues does *not* entail ". . . the liquidation of the self into a set of demarcated areas of role-playing" (1984, p. 205). Sandel talks of the "enduring attachments and commitments which taken together *partly* define the person I am" (1982, p. 179; italics added). Walzer allows (although vaguely) that individual persons may not be entirely subjected to "shared meanings" when he refers to "those deeper opinions that are the reflections in individual minds, *shaped also by individual thought,* of the social meanings that constitute our common life" (1983, p. 320; italics added). For communitarians, then, the moral force of community is a central, perhaps *the* central constituent of the individual, but they maintain that it is only *a* constituent, and not the entire self.

Selznick (1987) provides another impetus to synthesis, arguing that there is room for individual rights within a communitarian morality. He contends that communitarian philosophy's central value is "*belonging,*" and he interprets this claim to mean that "personhood is best served in and through social participation" (1987, p. 454). The result in communitarianism is the priority of duty over right; "duty is what roles are about and what membership is about" (1987, p. 454). Thus, as he points out, when we accept membership in, for example, the academic community, we think first of our responsibilities, not our rights. Contrary to MacIntyre, however, Selznick contends that *rights-claims can be legitimate:* "A duty-based community is not . . . insensitive to claims of right. . . . A moral community must recognize . . . natural rights . . . which derive from our understanding of what personhood requires" (1987, p. 455). Yet rights are not central to the communitarian project, for "rights do not define the community," nor do they provide reasons for acting. Duties, to the contrary, "summon us to action."

The I and We

The synthetic position prefigured by nuances and contours within both philosophies is the I and We paradigm, the idea that both individual and community have a basic moral standing; neither is secondary or derivative. To stress the interlocking, mutually dependent relationship of individual and community, and to acknowledge my mentor, Martin Buber, I refer to this synthetic position as the I and We paradigm (the We signifies social, cultural and political, hence historical and institutional forces, which shape the collective factor—the community; see Etzioni, 1988).

A reviewer of a previous draft of this essay wrote: "The author suggests that theorists need to consider both the individual and the community. What news!" This is indeed the crux of the issue. First, while several philosophers do "consider" both, by no means all do. Bentham wrote that "community is a fiction." Large bodies of psychological and neoclassical economic literature and significant segments of other social science disciplines are reductionist, that is, maintain that the explanatory factors are individual, and either deny the need for collective or macro concepts or depict them as the result of aggregations of individual transactions.

Typical is the argument that there is no public interest, only interests of specialized groups. Still others, from Sartre to Nozick, consider the "community" (or at least the claims of other) a burden if not "hell." And, of course, collectivists— both totalitarian and dogmatic religious—ignore the role and rights of individuals. The author is hardly the only one to observe the pressure to dichotomies. Mandelbaum (1987, p. 6), writing about the "myth" of the community and of the "self," adds, "When the first two myths compete, they often appear to drive out any tepid alternatives."

Second, even those CLPs who "consider" community, or communitarians who "consider" the individual, do not, as we have just shown in considerable detail, accord both elements an *equal,* primary moral status. CLPs, at best, grant community a secondary status, in the sense that they do not override individual rights, and at most overlay claims when these do not conflict with individual rights. Communitarians, on the other hand, tend to grant individual rights a secondary position. Indeed, work by both sides reads as if prizes were awarded to those able to build their whole moral position upon *one* primary moral building stone.

In contrast, the position advanced here is that both the individual and the community have the *same basic primary* moral standing. Hence, all specific positions—whether on the rights and duties of AIDS patients, pornography dealers, or the press (versus national security)—must be worked out with careful attention to both. One cannot use the needs of society—or individual rights—to shut out the other considerations, as for instance, do First Amendment absolutists.

If metaphors help, instead of building on one corner stone, we start with a human arch: the constituent units and the combined pattern shape and sustain one another. Without the arch, the stones are but a pile of rubble; without the stones the arch is but an ephemeral concept. In short, the position that the individual and the community, the I and the We, require one another, and hence have the same basic standing, is far from self-evident; it is a position avoided by many, although as we have seen, strains evident in their work, point to the synthesis, the I and We paradigm.

Three considerations, empirical, moral-philosophical and pragmatic, support the I and We paradigm. First, while it is possible to theorize about abstract individuals apart from a community, if individuals were actually without community, they would have very few of the attributes commonly associated with the notion of the autonomous person. A basic observation of sociology and psychology is that *the individual and the community "make" one another*, and that individuals are not able to function effectively without deep links to others, to community. House et. al. (1988, p. 540) conclude that a lack of social relationships heightens a person's susceptibility to illness: "Prospective studies, which control for baseline health status, consistently show increased risk of death among persons with a low quantity, and sometimes low quality, of social relations." The ability of social relations to moderate or buffer the effects of psychological stress on health is especially important (1988, p. 541). Berelson and Steiner (1964, p. 252), in their overview of more than 1000 social science studies, remark: "total isolation is virtually always an intolerable situation for the human adult—even when physical needs are provided for." The experiences of American POWs in isolation during the Korean War (Kinkead, 1959) and of solitary explorers and voyagers (for example, Byrd, 1938) and the results of numerous laboratory experiments (for example, Frisch, 1964, and Appley and Trumbull, 1967) all point to the conclusion that to remain viable, psychologically "sound," the individual needs deep bonds with others.

A significant strand of the sociology literature has long contended that community has weakened within modern society, adversely affecting individuals. Fromm (1941) argues that individuals won excessive autonomy as industrialization, or, more precisely, urbanization transformed society. He believes that this extreme autonomy was gained at the cost of weakened social bonds in both the family and the community. This excessive independence left the individual highly anxious, even hysterical, looking despairingly for synthetic affiliations to replace the lost bonds. Totalitarian political movements appeal to this malaise because they provide a proxy for such bonds. Similar to urbanization, the decline of religion and "traditional values" left people yearning for firm direction; and demagogues and dictators provide the strong leadership that fills this void. (Riesman, 1950, also follows this line of reasoning, arguing that people have become other-directed, seek excessively to conform, have lost inner orientation.)

Not all sociologists agree on the adverse effects of modern society. For example, Gans (1962), in *The Urban Villagers,* argues contrary to Fromm that there is village-like life in modern cities. Still, the consensus of sociological and psychological work supports the basic notion that isolation— whether the product of urbanization, mass society or other phenomena—erodes the mental stability necessary for individuals to form their own judgments and resist undue external pressure and influence. Thus, individuals require community; without it, they are diminished if not incapacitated.

Second, the I and We position finds support in that, taken alone, its constituent elements—radical individualism or collectivism—lead to policy conclusions that even their own advocates are often uncomfortable with. As discussed above, those who recognize only the primacy of the community, and consider individual rights either secondary and derivative or assert simply that "there are no such rights" (MacIntyre, 1984, p. 69), open the door to the intolerance, or worse, the tyranny found not only in totalitarian ideologies but also in absolutist theology and authoritarian political philosophies. Thigpen and Downing (1987, p. 642, 643) observe of MacIntyre's work that:

> Without a source of moral authority outside role requirements, roles are simply *vehicles for the societal imposition of values . . .* MacIntyre shrinks from this implication of his theory. However, MacIntyre fails to provide a theory of the self which can account for a critical stance against society.

Equally unacceptable are positions that focus exclusively on individual rights, particularly the extreme libertarian stand; few endorse policy ideas such as those that allow individuals the right to choose whether or not they wish to defend their country (Nozick, 1974). It may leave few to defend a country, and such a policy is patently unfair if some opt out, because those who do not serve reap the benefits of protection provided by those who fight. The same challenge to the libertarian position holds for other common goals very widely endorsed, from concern for future generations to the condition of the environment.

Finally, there are pragmatic considerations: will the I and We paradigm facilitate the development of both public policy and norms of behavior that members of relevant communities will consider compatible with their principles? Janowitz (1983) captured the issue in a very elementary form when he reported that young Americans seek to have the right to be tried before a jury of their peers, but not the obligation to serve as juror.

A more complex application is found in examining the insight the I and We could bring to the pornography debate. Elshtain (1984) explores the philosophic underpinnings of the opposing positions taken by feminists and civil libertarians (as well as neo-conservatives) in the debate over the distribution and use of pornography. Feminists have chosen to fight pornography with the same conceptual tool that libertarians use to defend it—the language of individual rights. Feminists argue that pornography violates the civil rights of (individual) women; libertarians respond that limiting pornography violates the right to free speech. Elshtain (1984, p. 18) remarks that "the idea of [individual] 'rights' cannot bear all the weight being placed upon it. But without reference to rights, how can someone press the case for cultural change in a *liberal* society?" She approaches the problem partly from a communitarian perspective, suggesting that "[c]ommunities should have the power to regulate and to curb open and visible assaults on human dignity" (1984, p. 20). Thus, Elshtain implicitly confers upon the community a prerogative to determine the boundaries of a particular *substantive* good—human dignity. She limits this prerogative, however, by warning that communities "should not seek, as groups avowedly do, to eradicate or condemn either sexual fantasies or erotic representations as such."

Similarly, Gutmann's (1987, 1988) project is clearly devoted to the philosophy of the middle ground. She seeks to formulate a position recognizing both individual rights and a substantive good, in pursuit of a "society dedicated to both freedom and civic virtue" (1988, p. 1). In *Democratic Education*, her study of democratic educational theory and policy, Gutmann develops what might be called "overriding" principles for the I and We paradigm. Such principles are necessary for guiding policy, for while the recognition of the difficulties of emphatic liberal or communitarian positions narrows the range of ethically acceptable policies, it still leaves room for further guidance.

Gutmann's position rests on the belief that the democratic society, broadly conceived, is a "good" society, and thus worth preserving. (In all societies, institutions shape members; only in a democratic society do members have an effective voice in shaping those institutions.) Given that individual perspectives differ in any one society or community, rational public deliberation of alternative views is necessary to ensure democracy. Such deliberation allows the community to determine which issues they shall reconcile, which they shall reject, and which shall remain contested (they will agree to disagree).

Gutmann thus argues that each generation must be educated "to deliberate critically among a range of good lives and good societies" (1987, p. 44). Two principles secure this deliberation against the possibility that democratic communities may undermine themselves, consensuating policies that harm democracy. The first, non-discrimination, requires that *all* members of the community acquire the capacity to deliberate, for otherwise, the participation necessary to democracy will be endangered. The second principle, non-repression, prevents the state and any group within it from restricting access to alternative views, enabling "rational consideration of different ways of life." In Gutmann's terms, non-repression thus maintains that "nobody be *required* not to be exposed to alternative viewpoints" (private communication).

Gutmann's approach is usefully applied in situations such as a Tennessee court decision to exempt Fundamentalist Christian children from reading books that their parents found offensive. The court held that the parents had "drawn a line" based on their religious beliefs, and that the court could not call this line "unreasonable." Gutmann's principle of non-repression suggests that the court erred: the children will not be exposed at home to alternative viewpoints, and the state cannot require the parents to teach such viewpoints. Hence, the public schools provide the only occasion to expose students to a range of different beliefs, a necessary process if they are going to deliberate rationally about alternative ways of life. In disputing the court's ruling, Gutmann reiterates her substantive conception of the good: the "content of public schooling *cannot be neutral* among competing conceptions of the good life" (1988, p. 11); rather, democratic education must "prepare future citizens for participating intelligently in the political processes that shape their society."

It remains for another occasion to show that other public policies based on the I and We position are more plausible and acceptable than those derived from strictly individualistic or collectivist positions. Among the numerous areas in which this position arises are the market (should it be regulated at all?); balance between AIDS patients' rights (to privacy) and obligation to community (to disclose sexual contacts); "mandatory" seat belts; due process for disruptive students in high schools; and the balance between the First Amendment and national security.

In Focus: Which Community?

While the basic issues of the CLP-communitarian debate discussed to this point indicate the theoretical orientation that the I and We seizes and seeks to develop and amplify, this next issue is more a matter of clarifying the focus; no answer seems readily apparent. We suggest that this philosophical dialogue would benefit significantly if the participants would, when they use the term "community," indicate *which* community they mean. In his most concrete description of community in *Liberalism and the Limits of Justice,* for example, Sandel (1982, p. 172–173) alludes to "a common vocabulary of discourse and a background of implicit practices and understandings." By this criterion, a football game, an undergraduate study group and an annual lumberjacking convention would all qualify. In search of a sharper focus, we now explore various communitarian notions of community, using three basic criteria: scope (hundreds, thousands or millions of people? Small group or mass society?); substance or "content" (is the community fundamentally a moral, political, religious or cultural entity, or a complex combination of these or other elements?); and perhaps most significant, patterns of "dominance," that is, how the community expresses or affirms its moral values, common interests, commitments, and ends.

Scope

When the debate focuses on concrete political issues, writers most often refer to a small, "local" community—a town, city or country. Sandel (1984, p. 6), for example, espouses "laws regulating plant closings, to protect . . . communities from the disruptive effects of capital mobility and sudden industrial change," and suggests further that communitarians would be "more likely than liberals to allow a town to ban pornographic bookstores, on the grounds that pornography offends its way of life and the values that sustain it" (1984, p. 6). Gutmann considers an "important contribution" of communitarianism to be "the explicit concern for preventing the disruption of local communities . . ." (1985, p. 320). Elsewhere, Sandel (1988) calls for the revitalization of community, local *and* national. Several of his respondents (*The New Republic,* May 9, 1988, pp. 21–23), both communitarian and liberal, took the small, local community as the subject of debate, whether agreeing on the need to revitalize it (Elshtain, lamenting "city and community powerlessness," talks of "recapturing civic empowerment at the peripheries") or not (Reich argues that "the liberal task at hand is not to add legitimacy to the spurious notion of geographic community").

Other communitarians envision community on a grander scale. Walzer (1983, p. 72) believes that in the real world, "independent states"—entire nations—approximate most closely his notion of community (see below); his historical examples include the Hellenistic city-states as well as the medieval Jewish community, in which "social pressure worked very much like political power." MacIntyre also conceives of a nation or city-state community: he seems to consider Athens in classical times a representative community.[4] Thus, for some communitarians, the nation or city-state is an alternative to the smaller-scale local community. Exploring yet a broader perspective, Walzer (1983, p. 29) considers a community comprised of "humanity itself . . . the entire globe. . . . But were we to take the globe as our setting, we would have to imagine what *does not yet exist:* a community that included all men and women everywhere."

Substance

Considering various notions of size leads to the more significant issue of substance, the content or nature of the community, for the concrete expressions of a community's scale—town, city-state, nation or neighborhood—may have social, political, economic, moral or other underpinnings. The difficulty here is that the communitarians do not draw on one clear substantive account of community. For example, Sandel does not say explicitly what makes a local residential area or municipal government (implied in his comments on pornography and plant closings) a community. However, Sandel's (1982, p. 172) notion (it should not be construed as a precise definition) of community as a "common vocabulary of discourse and a background of implicit practices and understandings," suggests that a town or city is a community by virtue of a latent cultural consensus. Sandel's repeated references to "moral experience" further suggest that the community has a moral dimension, expressed in persons' "constitutive attachments."

Walzer suggests, similar to Sandel, that a community is distinguished by its "shared understandings and intuitions," a common fund of meanings. Walzer explains that in its pure form, such a community is only a theoretical construct; in reality, "political communities" are

> probably the closest we can come to a world of common meanings. Language, history and culture come together (. . . more closely here than anywhere else) to produce a collective consciousness (1983, p. 28).

The implied community is, like Sandel's, essentially cultural-moral, presumably found in small locales, and sought for in more encompassing ones (nations, even worldwide, via the U.N).

While Walzer interprets the political community to indicate the presence of a latent cultural or cultural-moral consensus, Barber (1984) sees the political community as an end in itself. Barber espouses "strong" democracy, a politics of universal participation, in which "all of the people govern themselves in at least some public matters at least some of the time" (1984, p. xiv). Barber's conception of community involves not as much the substance of a particular cluster of "shared understandings" as the process of political participation. He envisions the nation as a town hall, and it is through the activity of direct participation that Barber fashions his community and the individuals within it: ". . . a political community capable of transforming dependent private individuals into free citizens and partial and private interests into public goods" (1984, p. 151). Public activity is elevated from a means to a community goal: "To participate *is* to create a community that governs itself, and to create a self-governing community *is* to participate" (1984, p. 135; Barber's italics).

The Responsive Community

Perhaps the central issue of these various interpretations of the substance of community is how the community expresses, affirms—versus imposes—its common values, ends and interests. A three-part classification is helpful here. First, values may be imposed by the state, which makes for a coercive community. Alternatively, values may be imposed by a "tight," non-pluralistic community, lacking moral alternatives—a "Salem-like" community, whose punitive force is largely psychological (fear, humiliation, isolation, degradation). Finally, values may be affirmed (here, we avoid imposed) by what we call a "responsive community," a non-coercive community that appeals to the "nobler" part of the self, and one that in turn the self finds compelling.

One important source of the reluctance to accord full moral standing to the community is the view that any and all community voices are coercive. Nineteen-sixties radicals referred to economic and psychological "coercion," for instance, arguing that there was no basic difference between a police state (Stalinist U.S.S.R.) and a capitalist society that forces farm hands (and many other workers) to labor at demeaning jobs for low pay, and subjects its citizens to media and junk-culture "rape." Libertarians often take a similar position, most often by simply not recognizing a difference between a state and a community; both are viewed as "making" people behave in the name of the collectivity, without regard to differences in means. Libertarians assume that both intrude unduly on decisions that autonomous individuals (conceived as independent of community) are to make. CLPs, Elshtain (1984, p. 18) explains, see the individual as free not only from state coercion but from a "public morality he may not share, and free as well from the intrusions of his neighbors into his 'private' affairs." She adds that

> Civil libertarians cannot get beyond a picture of isolated individuals, bound up in their "freedom from," going through the world en garde against possible constraints from concerned and potentially "repressive" communities (1984, p. 19).

Social conservatives construe the issues in equally extreme terms when they argue that those opposed (as liberals are) to state imposition of religion (say, prayer in schools) or a ban on abortion, are simply "against" religion or "for" abortion. The possibility that one may favor certain values but seek for them to be supported via the *moral* appeal of the community—and not forced by the state—is lost.

While the concept of community may harbor the threat of coercion, it is not necessarily the coercion of the state, but the moral compulsion of a Salem-like community. Sandel does not describe the institutions that would sustain the moral community he envisions, but, as we have seen, the individual is subject to the shared understandings, the collective consensus of the community. In MacIntyre's project, the potential for moral pressure by a monolithic community is more tangible—and threatening. "Practices," interpreted within the context of "traditions," are the institutions that structure individual lives; the societal "virtues" are the "acquired qualities" that enable individuals to achieve the intrinsic goods of a collectivity. We can infer that MacIntyre's community expects individuals to pursue practices (ideally, of course, individuals recognize such pursuit as a noble duty that is for the greater good of both self and community) as the only legitimate form of moral, productive human behavior. And we have seen that MacIntyre does not provide a sound basis for the individual who criticizes the socially fostered practices. MacIntyre's community, then, is morally domineering because human activity is sharply defined by and limited to a distinct constellation of practices—and these endeavors are the only means through which an individual can find moral meaning and worth in the community. The person who does not succeed in practices, or does not seek to follow them, is necessarily an outcast, for the community lacks in its moral vocabulary legitimate alternatives and the capacity to allow, respond to and benefit from critical and innovative individuals.

The I and We paradigm builds on the concept of *responsive* community, one that appeals to values that members already possess ("only you can prevent forest fires!") and encourages them to internalize values they currently do not command (before an appeal to litter will be effective, individuals are called upon to concern themselves with the environment). This type of voluntary moral affirmation and education provides solid foundations for a non-coercive community. When people act to express a value they have truly acquired within a pluralistic community (internalized rather than accepted as a social pressure to which they had "better" conform), they are not, nor do they feel, coerced, even in a psychological sense. Rather, they feel affirmed when they uphold what have become *their* values. There is nothing morally objectionable about such an act; on the contrary, without the expression of internalized values, there would be no social coherence or community—or for that matter, viable individuals (as functioning persons).

Notes

1. We are here concerned with only one albeit fundamental aspect of this debate, namely, the relationship between the individual and the community, and we therefore restrict our discussion to a few representative views on this specific issue. For a broader account of this debate, see, among others, Gutmann (1985), Thigpen and Downing (1987) and Wallach (1987).

2. Rawls thus acknowledges, although only partly and indirectly, MacIntyre's recent (1988) argument that the type of rationality that informs Rawls's social and historical situation "covertly presupposes one particular partisan type of account of justice, that of liberal individualism" (MacIntyre, 1988, p. 4).

3. Selznick describes both Rawls and Dworkin as exponents of "welfare liberalism"—"welfare liberals differ from their laissez-faire forebears in that they seek a richer meaning of autonomy and rationality, one more generous in spirit and more faithful to psychological and social reality" (1987, p. 446).

4. MacIntyre, however, does not limit himself to the city-state; he also considers very small communities—even a "school, a hospital or an art gallery" (1984, p. 151). In

fact, in his conclusion he calls for "the construction of *local forms of community*" (1984, p. 263), presumably because that is all we shall be capable of creating in the contemporary world—"the new dark ages which are already upon us" (1984, p. 263).

References

Appley, Mortimer H. and Richard Trumbull, eds. *Psychological Stress: Issues in Research.* New York: Appleton-Century-Crofts, 1967.

Barber, Benjamin. *Strong Democracy: Participatory Politics for a New Age.* Berkeley: University of California Press, 1984.

Berelson, Bernard and Gary A. Steiner. *Human Behavior: An Inventory of Scientific Findings.* Orlando, Fla.: Harcourt Brace Jovanovich, 1964.

Berlin, Isaiah. "Two Concepts of Liberty." In Michael Sandel, ed., *Liberalism and Its Critics.* New York: New York University Press, 1984.

Byrd, Richard E. *Alone.* New York: Putnam, 1938.

Dworkin, Ronald. "Liberalism." In Stuart Hampshire, ed., *Public and Private Morality.* New York: Cambridge University Press, 1978, pp. 113–143.

———. *Taking Rights Seriously.* Cambridge: Harvard University Press, 1977.

Elshtain, Jean Bethke. "The New Porn Wars: The Indecent Choice Between Censorship and Civil Libertarianism." *The New Republic.* Vol. 190, June 25, 1984, pp. 15–20.

Etzioni, Amitai. *The Moral Dimension: Toward a New Economics.* New York: Free Press, 1988.

Fishkin, James S. "Defending Equality: A View from the Cave." *Michigan Law Review.* Vol. 82, No. 4, 1984, pp. 755–760.

Frisch, Bruce H. "Solitude: Who Can Take It and Who Can't." *Science Digest.* March 1964, pp. 12–18.

Fromm, Erich. *Escape from Freedom.* New York: Farrar and Rinehart, Inc., 1941.

Gans, Herbert J. *The Urban Villagers.* New York: Free Press, 1962.

Granovetter, Mark. "Economic Action and Social Structure: A Theory of Embeddedness." *American Journal of Sociology.* Vol. 91, No. 3, 1985, pp. 481–510.

Gutmann, Amy. "Communitarian Critics of Liberalism." *Philosophy and Public Affairs.* Vol. 14, No. 3, 1985, pp. 308–22.

————. *Democratic Education.* Princeton, New Jersey: Princeton University Press, 1987.

————. "Freedom or Virtue?: Conflicting Aims of Educational Policy." Paper presented at the Policy Values Workshop, October 20, 1988. Kennedy School of Government, Harvard University, Cambridge, Massachusetts.

House, James S., Karl R. Landis and Debra Umberson. "Social Relationship and Health." *Science.* Vol. 241, No. 4865, July 29, 1988, pp. 540–545.

Janowitz, Morris. *The Reconstruction of Patriotism: Education for Civic Consciousness.* Chicago: University of Chicago Press, 1983.

Kinkead, Eugene. *In Every War but One.* New York: Norton, 1959.

MacIntyre, Alisdair. *After Virtue* (2nd ed.). Notre Dame, Indiana: Notre Dame University Press, 1984.

————. *Whose Justice? Which Rationality?* Notre Dame, Indiana: Notre Dame University Press, 1988.

Mandelbaum, Seymour. "Open Moral Communities." Paper presented at conference "A New Look at Planning Theory and Practice" sponsored by the Center for Urban Policy Research of Rutgers University, Washington, D.C., March 31–April 1, 1987, p. 6.

Nozick, Robert. *Anarchy, State, and Utopia.* New York: Basic Books, 1974.

Rawls, John. "The Basic Structure as Subject." *American Philosophical Quarterly.* Vol. 14, 1977, pp. 159–165.

————. "Justice as Fairness: Political Not Metaphysical." *Philosophy and Public Affairs.* Vol. 14, No. 3, 1985, pp. 223–251.

————. *A Theory of Justice.* Cambridge: Harvard University Press, 1971.

Riesman, David. *The Lonely Crowd.* New Haven: Yale University Press, 1950.

Rosenblum, Nancy L. "Moral Membership in a Postliberal State." *World Politics.* Vol. 36, No. 4, 1984, pp. 581–596.

Sandel, Michael J. "Democrats and Community." The New Republic. Vol. 198, Feb. 22, 1988, pp. 20–23.

———. ed. *Liberalism and Its Critics.* New York: New York University Press, 1984.

———. *Liberalism and the Limits of Justice.* Cambridge: Cambridge University Press, 1982.

Selznick, Philip. "The Idea of a Communitarian Morality." *California Law Review.* Vol. 75, No. 1, 1987, pp. 445–463.

Thigpen, Robert B. and Lyle A. Downing. "Liberalism and the Communitarian Critique." *American Journal of Political Science.* Vol. 31, No. 3, 1987, pp. 637–655.

Wallach, John R. "Liberals, Communitarians, and the Tasks of Political Theory." *Political Theory.* Vol. 15, No. 4, 1987, pp. 581–611.

Walzer, Michael. *Interpretation and Social Criticism.* Cambridge: Harvard University Press, 1987.

———. *Spheres of Justice.* New York: Basic Books, 1983.

Basic Human Needs, Alienation, and Inauthenticity

Most sociologists consider the concept of basic human needs as unproductive. Cohen accurately reflects the prevailing view:

> [N]obody has ever been able to formulate an inventory of original or unsocialized tendencies that has commanded more than scattered and temporary agreement. In the second place, the very meaning of "original human nature," in any other sense than a range of possibilities, each of them dependent upon specific experiences for its development or maturation, has always proved exceedingly elusive and obscure (Cohen, 1966:60).

In this conceptual discussion I indicate the reasons the concept seems useful *and* the ways the propositions advanced using it could be tested empirically. The restoration of the concept of "basic human needs" to full membership in sociological theory, I shall attempt to show, serves (a) to correct an "over-socialized" conception of man, which prevails in mainstreams of modern sociology, (b) to conceptualize a central distinction between the modern industrial society and the post-modern one, which seems to be emerging now, and (c) to bridge two main sociological traditions which have been growing apart: that of structural-functional analysis, and that of alienation, although, curiously, both rejected the concept.

As far as verification of the propositions advanced is concerned, I assume here a division of labor between those

Note: This essay was originally published in A*merican Sociological Review,* 1968, *33*(6), 870–884. It is reprinted with permission. In working on this essay, I benefited from a 1967–68 Social Science Research Council faculty fellowship. I am indebted to Albert K. Cohen and Martin Wenglinsky for their comments.

who specialize in theory-building and those who specialize in
verification (Levy, 1966:167–172). I attempt to outline a perspective, spell out propositions which are derived from it, and
indicate the ways they may be refuted or verified. I am fully
aware that they must submit to the test of empirical evidence
like all propositions.

Basic Human Needs

By "need" I simply mean that the person can be denied a
specified kind of experience only at the cost of an intra-per-
sonal tension. Our attention here is focused not on basic
needs man clearly shares with the animal world—such as
those for nourishment and sleep—but those believed to be
more distinctly human, such as the need for affection and for
recognition. With regard to these needs, three main points
of agreement seem to prevail: (1) There is no one-to-one connection between any specific need and any specific "answer";
on the contrary, the needs can be satisfied in a very large
variety of ways.[1] A great diversity of cultural patterns and institutional arrangements are both conceivable on theoretical
grounds and empirically found. (2) Whether human needs
are "universal" or not is basically immaterial because the malleability of the needs is held to be so high that they cannot
be used to explain any specific social institution we encounter, even if they were "particularistic." In accounting for differences in social institutions, explanations have focused on
the needs of the social system (in functional analysis), on historical forces (in Marxism), and on environmental factors (in
ecological analysis). (3) Classifications of human needs are
viewed as a-empirical. That is, they cannot be tested because
we never encounter the needs in pure form, outside a specific social mold. The unsocialized infant does not have these
needs, and socialized men, by definition, have internalized
social norms and patterns. Many lists of basic human needs
have been provided (Davies, 1963) but none have had more
than a fleeting hold over the sociological imagination; they
did not prove to be productive.

Sociologists are, of course, aware that some major schools of thought, especially psychoanalytical and anthropological ones, rely heavily on the concept of "basic human needs" (or "human nature").[2] But, since works in these traditions command at best the support of qualitative data, and are often presented in rather vague, abstract, or ideological language—frequently statements are couched in terms which make the statements not only unsupported but untestable—these works have added more to the rejection of these concepts by most sociologists than to their acceptance.[3] Suggestions that the notion of "basic human needs" may advance sociology as a science encounter such resistance that it seems necessary at this point to reassure the reader that the author shares the desire to keep sociology a logical and empirical enterprise, however critical such an endeavor may be.

Specifically, I suggest that it is fruitful to assume that there is a universal set of basic human needs *which have attributes of their own which are not determined by the social structure, cultural patterns, or socialization processes.* If this postulate is made, it follows that, since human needs are universal but societies differ in their cultural patterns, stratification structure, polity, and role-specifications, societies also differ in the extent to which their membership is able to satisfy their needs. That is, if we could find indicators of the membership's satisfaction with each one of the major facets of their society and build an index for those, or an indicator for the general level of affection or disaffection with a particular society, and assess this indicator for a society-wide sample of the members, we would expect to find systematic differences in the scores various societies would attain. Since such measures of satisfaction have been designed (Bradburn and Caplovitz, 1965; Almond and Verba, 1963:46–61), we can hold that the proposition concerning inter-societal *differences* in terms of the satisfaction of the members is a testable proposition. The fact that human beings can adapt and are adapting to a very large variety of societal structures and cultural patterns is not sufficient evidence that their needs are highly malleable, as long as the frustrations they suffer or satisfactions they gain also co-vary. That people *live* both in Athens and in Sparta is not proof that they find the two kinds of societies equally responsive to their needs. Adaptation may have quite different costs in the two societies.

We turn next to discuss (a) a methodological aspect of the issue; (b) the empirical indicators of the concepts and tests for the propositions outlined; (c) implications of these propositions—if further verified—for sociological theory; (d) the bridge that the conception of basic human needs provides for the functionalist and the alienation schools; and (e) a central difference between modern and post-modern (post-1945) societies with regard to their responsiveness to basic human needs.

Survival Versus Effectiveness

The pervading sociological positions, as stated above, are formulated with what I described in an earlier publication as *survival models* (Etzioni, 1964:19). The models attempt to state under what conditions a social system could survive, suggesting a set of "functional prerequisites" (Aberle et al., 1950). These prerequisites are satisfied under a very large variety of social and cultural conditions. While this seems a valid statement, in the sense that, when these conditions are met, social systems do survive, its fruitfulness is limited because it cannot account for the very large differences among social systems which do survive. It is particularly unproductive for the study of societies because very few of these social systems ever violate the "survivalist" functional prerequisites, i.e., very few cease to exist.

In studying complex organizations as social units, it is useful to analyze them in a different perspective, one of effectiveness, which asks not whether an organization survives but to what extent it realizes its goal or goals. Effectiveness models are more subtle than survival ones, if only because the latter recognize only two possibilities, while the effectiveness model recognizes numerous ones, i.e., varying degrees of relative effectiveness. To state the same basic point in the language of functional analysis: we distinguish between functional *alternatives* and functional *equivalents*. Alternatives which allow the system to survive are numerous but rarely are they equivalent in terms of the effectiveness of the system. Thus a "survivalist" model of automobiles informs us that water is not an "alternative" for gasoline; we still may be interested in the relative effectiveness of various kinds of gasoline, diesel oil, and electric current.

We add now that societies (and for that matter all other social units) may also be studied with an "effectiveness" perspective in mind. First, societies often set some goals for their members (frequently by the use of organizations—such as state agencies—as sub systems). Secondly, societies' effectiveness in satisfying their members may be used as a base to compare them with each other and over time. Societies which all score in the same way from a survivalist viewpoint, because they exist and persist, will score differently in terms of the relative level of disaffection or happiness they generate. How is one to explain such differences except by differences in the societies' respective responsiveness to their members' needs? If all could mold human needs to their specifications, no systematic difference could be expected, that is, other than those resulting from conflicting specifications. One may argue that the source of differences in the level of members' satisfaction a society generates is intra-societal, e.g., socialization to conflicting social norms generates frustration rather than the discrepancy between the norms the society prescribes and the underlying human needs. But this suggestion too assumes a human need, one for consistency, one which finds conflicting demands frustrating. If human nature was as malleable as it is often argued, why can it not be molded to find satisfaction in the variety and tensions afforded by conflicting demands? That there are some "limit" conditions under which societal demands become very frustrating to the members has been widely recognized. But the conception usually is one of a very large "box" in the confines of which more or less anything "goes" as long as the boundaries are not challenged. My position on this point is as different from the "box" image as a continuum is from a dichotomy. Any two social patterns, roles, or structures that differ significantly from each other intrinsically in social terms also differ from each other in terms of their responsiveness to basic human needs. The "box" is full of gradations leading up to and away from the "limits." Actually it is the very gradation—which can be empirically verified—which demonstrates best the *existence* and *specificity*, i.e., limited malleability, of basic human needs.

One additional clarification seems necessary before we can turn to questions raised by the need for operationalization: we hold that there are basic *human* needs which are universal but whose foundation is not biological. I am not referring to the needs for shelter or food but to needs such as those for affection and recognition. Those may exist in the animal world in some very primitive way but are, as I see it, central to the human being, and much more symbolic than in the animal world, to the extent that they are found there at all. The question must be answered, how can such needs be universal but not biological or biologically derived? What else is there which is universal but not socially shaped? The answer, it seems to me, is that these are the functional prerequisites of *human* beings. That is, unless these needs are satisfied, the animal-like newborn infant will not become a human being; extending affection, and recognition of achievements are two main ones. While these needs are answered socially, i.e., by other human beings in a social relationship, the need for them is not socially *determined* in the sense that no society can opt to do without them. Their at least partial satisfaction is a prerequisite for the *human* phenomenon—hence their universality. There is little sense in asking where do they "come from" (although a psychic-genetic or cultural-genetic answer can be given), since the frame of analysis is functional and not historical. To stay with the automobile analogy, we state that the car would not function (or be a moving vehicle) without certain kinds of fuel; who designed the car this way or where the fuel comes from is a very different set of questions, belonging to a different explanatory frame of reference.

Empirical Indicators and Tests

The methodological discussion is limited here to that of two basic human needs often listed as such: affection and recognition (Parsons, 1951:186ff.; Etzioni, 1968:624 ff.). These are both very significant ones, they are quite representative of others, and suffice for the purposes of this methodological analysis. (For discussion of other needs, see Etzioni, 1968:Chapter 21.) I focus, for the purposes of this presentation, on one attribute of these needs: a built-in, universal preference for frequent satisfaction (or release) over an infrequent one.[4] The preference is expected to hold for all but very frequent satisfactions, which are so high that there is no chance for an "appetite" to build up. Also, we expect that a balanced distribution in the frequency of satisfactions *among* various needs is preferred over frequent satisfaction of some, coupled with infrequent satisfaction of others. But these qualifications and elaborations should not detain us here; our main task is to suggest ways it could be empirically demonstrated that there is a preference for frequent over infrequent satisfaction, and that this preference is not culturally or socially determined.

Our main answer is that the proposition can be tested by checking if *both socialization costs and those of social control are higher for persons who have been socialized into roles in which their needs for affection and recognition are infrequently satisfied than for roles which offer more frequent satisfaction of these needs.* That is, we expect that, if one takes a random sample of persons of a given society or sub-society, (1) more time, resources, attention, and manpower will be required to *socialize* persons into roles which provide less frequent opportunities for affection and recognition; (2) that more time, resources, attention, and manpower will have to be devoted to *social control,* i.e., to keep people adhering to the expectations of these roles once they have acquired them, so as to prevent them from seeking roles which are more satisfying, or from attempting to change the prescriptions of these roles to be more satisfying; (3) that the direction of the *pressure to change* will not be randomly distributed but will be indicative of the patterns which are more responsive. *And we expect these relationships to hold in whatever culture, society, or sub-unit of these one chooses to study.*

I am not aware of existing studies which directly test these propositions, or the data of which have a direct bearing on them. Let us, hence, illustrate these propositions on an informal basis. Our impression is that it is more difficult to socialize people to roles which demand submerging the identity of one's efforts in a collective enterprise, i.e., a structure which inhibits individual recognition, than to socialize people to roles which allow for ample individual recognition. The impression one gains from observing children in *kibbutzim* or Soviet sport teams is that, despite strong ideological and social pressures to seek group rather than personal recognition, the symptoms of craving for personal recognition are evident. *Kibbutz* children refer to group toys as "mine"; Soviet football players are not immune from the temptation to play "solo." Over the years, collectivistic cultures seem to gravitate toward a relative increase in tolerance for individual recognition. The opposite trends are much less in evidence. There seem to be few signs that American children seek to insist on collective identities where an individual one is fostered, or that American football players object to "star" performance, when this is legitimated. More generally, we would expect that where collectivism is predominant, the rate of individualist deviance will be much higher than collectivist deviance in individualistic systems. (I discuss below the counter-argument, that these observations, although valid, are due to residues of prior individualistic socialization of citizens of collectivistic societies and not to basic human preferences. It suffices to say here that, in experimental situations, we can randomly assign persons of the same general background to roles we expect to be more responsive and to those less so, and thus control for this factor.) It should be noted that to confirm our proposition it must only be demonstrated that in collectivistic systems there is a "demand" for individual recognition and not for an individualistic *system;* such recognition can be found within a collective system. What seems frustrating and "inherently" unstable is an exclusively or very highly collectivistic system. The Soviet Union seems to have found a place for recognition of individual achievements within the content of a collective culture. China still seems to be trying for more or less complete submersion of individuality (Townsend, 1967; Schurmann, 1966).

For reasons I have discussed elsewhere, socialization costs are inversely related to the extent of selection which precedes and accompanies socialization. Hence, if recruitment to one kind of role must be more selective than to the other, i.e., more persons must be screened before "suitable" ones are found, and if the criterion of selection is not special skill but ease-of-socialization or search for abnormal personalities, this is also indicative of the "unnatural" quality of the particular kinds of roles, sub-structure, or sub-culture. (For additional discussion of the effects of selectivity, see Etzioni, 1961:155.)

In addition to differences in socialization costs, social control costs, and the direction of the pressure to change, we expect to find differences in the extent and intensity of personal "costs" charged against persons who carry out roles which are less suited to satisfaction of basic human needs as compared to those more suited. *Personal costs* are those inflicted on the actor who performs a given role, while those of socialization and social control are borne by others, such as his tutors or the police. Personal costs vary a great deal in degree and nature, including various forms of mental disorganization, psychosomatic illness, and psychological tensions.

Having dealt previously with recognition, let us draw now for illustrative purposes on the second need, that for affection. If our central propositions are valid, an average isolated person, in all cultures and societies, will be more frustrated than one who has one or more regular sources of affection. Thus, for instance, spinsters and divorcées, who are not integrated into a primary group such as a social movement "cell" or army unit, are depicted universally to be more frustrated than married ones. This may be explained by social pressures against such statuses. But even where those are minimal, as in the oft-cited anonymous city, these statuses seem to be highly frustrating (Srole et al., 1962:185ff.). Studies of the effect of isolation in prison camps ("brainwashing" studies) seem to lend some additional empirical support to this proposition (Schein, 1961; Lifton, 1966). Not all the limited data we have point to the same conclusion; for example, a study of highly homogeneous Hutterite communities shows basically the same prevalence of several kinds of mental illness as found in New York State (Eaton and Weil, 1955). While this finding alerts us that the isolation proposition is not without challenge, it suggests that our proposition can be tested in cross-cultural and societal contexts. We cannot account for the reason "deviant" data were found without conducting a new study of the Hutterite communities. It seems correct though to state that most of the available data support the proposition as stated here (Berelson and Steiner, 1964:332ff.).

While all statements made here pose some difficulties for the construction of empirical indicators of the concepts used and for the test of the relationships suggested, the concept of personal "costs" raises particular difficulties. First, socialization and social control costs are at least in part "external" while personal costs tend to be "internal" and hence harder to measure. Thus, it is obviously easier to determine whether it takes longer to socialize a person to a life of celibacy as compared to a priesthood which allows conjugal life than to measure his relative degree of mental health or even "happiness."

Secondly, the fact that our propositions do not lead us to expect a one-to-one relationship between a frustrating attribute of a given role and any specific kind of personal cost aggravates the measuring problem because all main costs must be assessed. For instance, the Japanese, in their traditional culture, are said to have been afforded fewer opportunities for affection than traditional Mexicans. It is also said that ulcers were more common among the Japanese. Now this "operationalization" of one of our key propositions (less affection—more personal costs) is of limited interest because, even if the statement is proven correct, i.e., the Japanese ulcer rate was significantly higher and affection intake lower, the Mexicans may still be said to have paid higher personal costs of some other kind. Hence, if we follow this approach, at least all the major personal costs and gains must be measured—a very difficult if not impossible task.

Still the psychological proposition may be tested: (a) if one could construct a "global" (Lazarsfeld and Menzel, 1961) score of internal satisfaction or personal costs, rather than attempting to measure each cost, e.g., frequency of ulcers, suicides, etc., and total them, one would seek to establish the general level of a person's psychic condition. (Industrial sociologists, faced with the fact that the satisfaction with one's job has many aspects, ask—in addition to questions about pay, work conditions, style of supervision—"global" questions, e.g., all said and done, how do you like your job?) (b) Instead of, or in addition to, attempting to construct a global measure one might compare a few major costs, such as rates of main types of mental illness and the main kinds of psychosomatic afflictions among role-holders. Thus, if those in role x (or society x) are found to be less frequently psychotic and neurotic, suicidal and homicidal, ulcer ridden and asthmatic, than in role y (or society y)—and we are not aware of any affliction which is distributed in the opposite way—this is of interest from the viewpoint of the question at hand, even though there still might be some affliction we did not cover, which is so heavily stressed in the opposite direction as to countervail all those we did measure. (c) Finally, and maybe most interesting, while we expect no one-to-one relation, we do expect some association between the kind of frustration and the kind of personal cost inflicted. For instance, we expect the "costs" of lack of affection to be "charged" differently than lack of recognition. While there are no studies which directly test this proposition, the kind of research we have in mind is illustrated by studies of the correlation between specific kinds of personal strains and prevalence of coronaries (Friedman and Rosenman, 1959).

One major complication which must be taken into account in testing our core proposition, whatever measure is used, is the "rigidities" revealed by the personalities of those already socialized to a given role, societal structure, and culture. The proposition ought not to be considered weakened if a person socialized to a lowly satisfying role does not immediately prefer a more satisfying one when it is offered. On the contrary, where men socialized to one kind of role are introduced to a different one without anticipatory socialization, e.g., soldiers discharged suddenly when a war ends unexpectedly, we expect some time lag before social and personal costs will decline, even if the new roles are more responsive to basic human needs. Let us illustrate this point. An oft-cited study shows that children are more responsive to democratic than to authoritarian or *laissez-faire* leadership (Lippitt and White, 1952:340–355). This would suggest that participatory systems (which is what these researchers call "democracy") are more responsive to basic human needs than exclusive or non-participatory ones. But a fact which is rarely noted when this study is cited is that the children who participated in the experiments were recruited mainly from "democratic" families and neighborhoods of the American middle class. (One child, from a different background, the son of an army man, did not prefer democratic leadership (Lippitt and White, 1952:345).) That is, it may be argued that these children preferred participatory systems not because they were more responsive to their basic needs but because the children were "socialized" to them. Moreover, if the same experiments were to be conducted in an authoritarian culture and the children proved to prefer authoritarian leadership, this would not weaken the proposition that democratic leadership is more responsive so long as, after a given period of exposure, the children would come to prefer participatory leadership. Even if, in such a transition period, the social and personal costs would *increase*, e.g., the children would find the democratic system bewildering, lacking in direction, and anxiety-provoking, theory at hand would not be contradicted so long as, after such a period, they would come to prefer the participatory system, while the opposite experiment—exposing to authoritarian leadership children accustomed to democracy—would show *continued* higher social and personal costs.

The scope, intensity, and duration of the exposure to more responsive roles before social and personal costs decline are of course key variables in further specifying our core proposition. The problem would be simpler if we expected a unilinear progression, so that we could detect some decrease in costs after an initial period of exposure to a more responsive role. However, the dynamic involved may well take a dialectic or curvilinear form, or progress may be latent until a specific level of momentum (a "critical mass") is reached. What would be "sufficient" exposure to test our proposition is a question which we cannot answer in abstraction from a specific setting and human need, and the extent and length of time it was suppressed. But we may posit that when a new generation (the second in the societal "experiment") is raised in the new socio-cultural environment, e.g., in a *kibbutz,* and it reveals still higher rather than lower costs, the "new world"—until proven otherwise—is to be considered less responsive than the old one. The generational succession is the stage at which many Utopian colonies and movements have been tested. Austerity, for instance, including severe restrictions on the expression of affection, tends to "wash out" in systems as different as the *kibbutzim,* the Soviet Union, and Catholic orders, after no more than three decades, especially as second-generation members reach adulthood.

It may be suggested that the generational "wash-out" has the kind of causes emphasized in church-sect literature: the first generation "sect" is selective; the second generation, which the first incorporates with much less selection—the fathers being unwilling to "screen out" their sons—causes the diluting "church" effect. Or, the inter-generation struggle may be said to account for the second generation's search for a different "line" to follow. While these factors are at work, we hold that the pressure toward more rewarding roles has an independent effect. This can be tested when two generations are compared in societal units whose culture is unresponsive vs. those whose culture is responsive, e.g., one whose taboos sharply limit sexual intercourse vs. one which fully legitimates lax standards. We expect some second-generation effects to set in, in both cultures, but to focus either on unresponsive elements which both may have, or be much more accentuated in the culture which is in general less responsive.

While waiting for a second generation socialized from inception to the new system (often not by the parents who are said to carry the "distortions" of the old regime but by a select group of educators who are believed to carry effectively the "new world") is the "ultimate" test, it is a rather demanding and long-run one. In many circumstances, comparative research provides a more practical approach, that is, comparing persons of the same backgrounds recruited into roles which differ in the opportunities for satisfaction they provide. Ideally, one may wish to assign men randomly to divergent roles under experimental conditions and compare their responses. For instance, we could randomly assign 100 students from lower-class background to training for coding, and 100 to essay writing about a topic of their choosing, and then repeat the same for 200 students of middle-class background. Other factors, especially early educational experience, would also have to be "controlled." The comparison of the findings should indicate, after background factors (as factors affecting prior socialization) are held constant, whether all groups still show a preference for one kind of role. Such roles may be said to be more responsive.

The basic proposition may be further tested by cross-cultural studies. Unlike comparisons within one society and culture, here observations of groups more independent of each other may be made (although the increased world-wide contacts and flows make such comparisons increasingly difficult). If, for instance, the multiple nations study Inkeles is now completing would show that men in similar roles in six divergent and separated cultures all show similar preferences, these might be indicative of a basic human nature (Inkeles, 1974).

Implications for Sociological Theory

Assuming for a moment that a variety of studies would show that there is an "absolute" anchoring—that basic human needs have some given attributes and are not endlessly malleable—what revisions would this require in sociological theory, let us say of the Meadian or Parsonian gender?

Such findings would question the analytic focus on socialization and social control and the related assumptions that persons can be shaped to find satisfaction in most any role, and that those who do not are deviant. The findings would support those who view social action as affected by an interaction between basic human needs, their specific attributes, and the particular "outlets" society provides (or tolerates). A *person may be deviant, but so may be a society,* i.e., one which sets up and reinforces a network of roles which are highly frustrating and "in the long run" (as against only for a transition period). When we observe a measure of consumption of non-toxic tranquilizing items (such as alcohol or marijuana), adultery, homosexuality among consenting adults, and "premature" retirement from work, the question will no longer automatically be "Why did socialization or social control fail?" but also "Why does the society not legitimate these releases?" And, rather than ask under what conditions these deviants may be transformed into conforming members, we may also ask under what conditions a society may become more responsive to these needs and cease to consider them deviance—as, for instance, Sweden seems to have come to view some modes of premarital intercourse.

Within the realm of the prevailing sociological theories, we are told to expect that the more socialized and controlled a group of men is, the more they conform and the lower their personal "costs." High levels of anxiety, mental disorganization, alcoholism, divorce, and so forth are all said to be signs of imperfect socialization or inadequate social control. By the revised view, this would hold only for roles, and more broadly social structures and cultures, responsive to human nature. In those which are not, people *less* socialized and *less* controlled are to be expected to pay a *lower* personal cost. Thus, the middle-class executive is expected to show more anxiety, neurosis, etc., than the lower-class "bum," although he too is not expected to be free of the effects of an unresponsive society (Hollingshead and Redlich, 1958:248).

Theories about societies, however formalized and "neutral" in their terminology, tend to have a normative impact on those who rely on them for their tools of social analysis. (The preceding as well as the following statements regarding the sociology of knowledge are of course given to empirical verification and are not logical or methodological in nature.) Theories without a conception of human needs (which have specific attributes of their own) are open to a conservative interpretation, of individuals and groups that are expected to adapt to the society as it is. Theories which assume autonomous human needs provide an independent basis with which to compare societies to each other, as more or less consonant with basic human needs, and they lead one to expect pressure to change existing societies and cultures toward more responsive ones. This may leave the impression that whatever theory one chooses, one is choosing on ideological grounds. But I suggest that a theory which expects pressure to change toward more responsive systems will be able to account for much more of the variance of social and personal conduct and in this technical sense is a more valid one. Moreover, it seems to us incorrect to hold that the sociological pictures— images of what societies are like and how they transform— conveyed by different ideologies are equally valid from an empirical viewpoint, although it would take us far beyond the confines of this paper to try to demonstrate which withstands better the test of evidence.

Several specific questions may find their answers in studies of the kind suggested above, questions which are central to our assessment of the quality and future of mass society, mass production, and mass culture. For instance, sociologists have argued for decades whether an abundance of consumer goods and the typical television fare is what the "average man" *really* wants, or whether it is what the mass society (or capitalist society) fosters in him. (Shils, 1957:587–608; Fromm, 1955:152–162; Berger, 1960:102). This seems to us to be a question that cannot be fully conceptualized outside the kind of framework advanced here, for, if a person has no basic needs independent of those that socialization instills in him, his only source of disaffection may be prior socialization which makes him out of step with recent cultural demands, or the result of socialization and social control efforts which are not coordinated with each other in terms of the standards they impose. This would suggest that in principle disaffection can be overcome by more and better harmonized societal efforts, which would make one expect that totalitarian regimes—at the height of their socialization efforts—will prove to be the most satisfying regimes, disregarding the substance of the socialization efforts in terms of the extent to which the norms and expectations instilled are responsive. This seems to us to fly in the face of the Chinese, Soviet, and Nazi experience.

In attempting to answer these questions, reliance on survey data, at least of the standard variety without projective or probing questions, is not satisfactory because, as practitioners of this method themselves assert, it assesses the relative, manifest, and in this sense superficial levels of the personality (Selltiz et al., 1959:280–314; Hyman, 1955:103–104). Since our proposition does not suggest that a person be either aware of or explicitly state his disaffection, we must turn to tools of social science which prod deeper—such as unfocused or stress interviews, and projective techniques—to seek if, underneath the apparent euphoria (where it is encountered), there is not a high degree of personal suffering. Keniston used TAT and intensive interviews in his study of university students (Keniston, 1965:1–206). Friedenberg used depth interviews and projective procedures in his study of high school students (Friedenberg, 1963:51–154). Actually, even survey studies that prodded beyond "Are you satisfied with your work?" and similar "straight" questions find considerable alienation (Seeman, 1966a:353–367; Nettler, 1957:670–677). Twenty-eight percent of adult Americans, over 33 million, were found to feel alienated, according to a Harris poll released on December 16, 1968. (See also Brenner, 1967.)

Ultimately, continued exposure to two kinds of sociocultural systems, at least to two roles, may be necessary to test the basic proposition. That a worker says that he prefers to work at the assembly line in order to be able to buy a second automobile and that he likes to watch 2.9 hours of TV a day proves relatively little. The question is whether or not *continued* exposure to less routine work, consumption not prodded by the mass media, and higher-brow culture, will still leave him preferring the "mass society" ones.

Basic Needs, Alienation, and Inauthenticity

Reducible Versus Irreducible Alienation

In the preceding section we asked what revisions the conception of autonomous basic human needs entails for works in the mainstreams of modern sociology, such as those of Mead and Parsons, works sometimes referred to as in the "integrationist" mode. The concept, though, is not much more popular among many members of the alienation school, especially those who subscribe to Marxist or neo-Marxist traditions. Still, the concept does provide a bridge between what are considered two alternative approaches, the integration (or functionalist) and the conflict approach.

Before this bridge can be charted, a conceptual distinction within the alienation school must be introduced, namely the difference between reducible and irreducible alienation. Alienation, in the terms of reference used here, means a social situation which is beyond the control of the actor, and hence unresponsive to his basic needs. Now our statement that some societies are more responsive to human nature than others is not to suggest that there can be a fully responsive society, one free of alienation. Only if we assume a limitless malleability of human nature can we expect a fully "happy" society, one in which each member is fully socialized *and* satisfied with his social roles.[5]

If we proceed with the assumption that there is a set of autonomous human needs, we face first an irreducible source of alienation in the tension among these needs—responding fully to one, such as the need for security, is incompatible with fully responding to others such as the need for variety and creativity. Second, because at the root of satisfaction of each single need is some deferment of gratification, some build-up of tension to be released, dissatisfaction cannot be eliminated.

Most of the alienation, however, seems to result from sources which are reducible, most directly from socio-cultural patterns which can be made much more responsive to basic human needs than they are, or reducible by changing the distribution of alienation within a system by altering its allocative and power structure. Most systems provide many more opportunities for gratification to a selected few than to the majority of the members (Lasswell, 1958). A more egalitarian allocation of resources, status-symbols, sexual freedoms, knowledge of the system, and access to its controls, can significantly reduce the total level of alienation.

Here it has been argued, following Durkheim, that needs are infinitely expandable, and that frustration is a function of the level to which a society allows them to expand, and not just the chances of satisfaction it provides. Rising expectations and relative deprivation may cause more frustrations in an egalitarian society than in a steeply stratified one. In response we would like, first, to stress the difference between alienation and a subjective sense of frustration.[6] The average member of a more egalitarian society is more able to share in shaping its structure and norms than one in a less egalitarian one because the share of assets is an important source of control. Since alienation is defined as incapacity to share in control, it follows that more egalitarian societies are less alienating, even if this is not reflected, in short order, in subjective feelings.

It should also be noted in this context that the frustrations resulting out of egalitarian relations (and the demands of participation, such as attending to more public life) must be deducted from the increase in satisfaction generated; I suggest that the *net* gain will be very considerable. Focusing on the new frustrations in disregard for the new satisfactions would thus provide a highly skewed picture, *if* the rise in frustration were taken as indicative of the total character of the change rather than one element of it.

Last but not least, the great concern with marginal increments over peers, and comparisons to remote groups, rather than attention to the extent to which one's own basic needs are responded to, are signs of the alienating (or, we shall see, inauthentic) society. They have not been reported for societies which are highly integrated, for viable communities, or for those whose central values are collective projects (such as social movements) rather than individualistic materialistic achievements. Hence what has been occasionally treated as a universal finding, i.e., that satisfaction rests more on relative rewards than on absolute level of satisfaction, may hold chiefly for the alienating societies, a result of their unstable social relations and lack of political bridges to collective life, i.e., of their unresponsive nature. And thus as these societies became more egalitarian and responsive, more participatory and collective, we would expect their members to focus more on absolute rather than relative levels of satisfaction, and on satisfaction derived from participation rather than from the possession or consumption of material objects.

It may be noted in passing that the upper classes, which tend to receive more of whatever the society allocates than other members, are not exempt from the personal costs of a highly alienating structure. If the society is a highly oppressive one, the elites are as "free" of the consequences of suppression as the guards of prisons: they are the targets of open or suppressed hate and must experience anxiety because their position, if not their lives, are never secure. If the society is a highly commercialized one, the business elites cannot but extend some of the pervading instrumental orientation to fellow-members of their elite and, ultimately, to their view of themselves. Only where men and women treat each other as members of a community, as having the status of goals—a state which cannot be fully realized but can be approximated—is the leadership itself relatively free from that alienation which is reducible.

The preceding propositions concerning the elites are as testable as, and do not involve more methodological difficulties than, most other nontrivial propositions concerning social phenomena. Bales operationalized the differences between instrumental and expressive orientations of group members and leaders; this allows one to establish empirically whether the prevailing orientation is one of means or of goals (Bales, 1953:111–161). Psychological tests of guards of high-security prisons can be compared to those of guards in prisons which run effective "therapeutic communities," or of the same guards as a prison shifts from a custodial to a therapeutic management (Gilbert and Levinson, 1957:197–208). Similarly, elites of various countries may be compared to each other, possibly over time, and to non-elites, with regard to their personal costs (Raiser, 1966). Thus the effect of alienation—of unresponsive structures—on the elites can be empirically assessed.

The concept of basic human needs, I suggest, calls attention to alienation which may be reduced, if the social structure is being made more responsive, as distinct from irreducible alienation whose sources are not structural. We see next that a whole category of structures, which appear as if they were responsive, may actually be highly alienating, with their participatory facades adding some alienating effects of their own to the underlying, unresponsive, structures.

Alienation and Inauthenticity

In asking to what extent a society is responsive to its members' needs, the differences between appearances and underlying realities must be taken into account. We find on the personality level a *surface* conformity coupled with an *underlying* rejection, e.g., when open rejection seems dangerous, under a Stalinist regime (Milosz, 1953). We find on the institutional level *appearances of participation* (or of other aspects of responsiveness)[7] covering *underlying exclusion*. For instance, workers are offered, under a human relations program, participation in managerial decision-making while actually management (following "leadership" or "sensitivity" training) is expected to lead the decision-making sessions to those conclusions favored by management. More macroscopically, the same cleavage between appearance and underlying reality is found in those democratic systems which maintain two or more political parties and regular elections—a participatory institutional shell—while in reality the parties offer only limited alternatives in terms of the differences between their policies, and the choice among leaders they offer is restricted to a choice among candidates who are all members of the same class and who represent similar viewpoints and interests.

To formalize these conceptions in the form of definitions, one may refer to a social condition as *authentic*, when the appearance and the underlying structure are both responsive to basic human needs; as *alienating*, when both the appearances and the structure are unresponsive; and as *inauthentic*, when the underlying structure is unresponsive but an institutional or symbolic front of responsiveness is maintained. (Cf. Sartre, 1960:92 ff.) (The fourth combination, of an alienating appearance covering a responsive reality, is rare and unstable. It may be referred to as a latent authentic condition.)

Since the distinction between surface (or "front") and underlying structure is essential for the concepts just defined, the development of measurements of this difference is essential for the operationalization of these concepts. When an actor is conscious of the difference between his public position and private self, operationalization is relatively easy, because he may express privately, in an anonymous questionnaire or to an interviewer he trusts, his private feelings and views. When the cleavage runs deeper, and the person's consciousness is part of that which is split off his subconscious and basic needs, we must rely on projective techniques or behavioral indicators for what he "really" prefers (Janis and Hovland, 1959:1–6, 16–26; Bettelheim and Janowitz, 1950). Institutions are easier to study from this viewpoint. Decision making can be fairly readily coded as to the degree to which it is shared with lower-ranking men, and as to the extent that the decisions shared are only the marginal or include also the central ones. The amounts spent on public relations and other facade activities, as compared to that invested in activities related to the stated goals of a given organization, are another indicator. Typically the advertising budgets of corporations producing new products which are at most marginally different from existing ones are much higher than those for corporations whose product is substantially different. Producers of the first kind depend almost entirely for their slice of the market on "image-differentiation," i.e., on persuading the consumers that the new product is much more different from existing ones than it actually is. Well known examples are the manufacturers of various brands of instant coffee, cigarettes, and toothpaste. For organizations whose goals are political, medical or educational, differences between the real goals and policies known to insiders, and the stated ones, presented to wider circles of members or outsiders, have often been ascertained (e.g., Selznick, 1960:113 ff.).

Persons in "pure" alienating conditions and those who are involved in an inauthentic relationship, e.g., a pseudo-Gemeinschaft—*neither* responsive to their needs—are expected to be "charged" different personal costs, due to differences in the management of frustration both conditions generate. The alienated person's aggression is likely to be focused and have one or more external targets, e.g., "the establishment." The aggression of a person in an inauthentic condition will be diffuse and at least in part internalized and "bottled-up." Studies of families of schizophrenic children provide empirical descriptions of both the underlying unresponsive orientation in the context of parent-child relations, i.e., where the expectation is for responsive orientation, and of the inner emotional condition of a person caught in the conflicting streams of supportive surface and rejecting substructure.

> The mothers of schizophrenics are seen as catching the child in a "double bind," wherein the mother verbalizes love and warmth but rebuffs the child's tendencies to respond to her words.
> S: Well, when my mother sometimes makes me a big meal and I won't eat it if I don't feel like it.
> F: But he wasn't always like that, you know. He's always been a good boy.
> M: That's his illness, isn't it doctor? He was never ungrateful. He was always most polite and well brought up. We've done our best by him.
> S: No, I've always been selfish and ungrateful, I've no self-respect.
> F: But you have.
> S: I could have, if you respected me. No one respects me. Everyone laughs at me. I'm the joke of the world. I'm the joker all right.
> F: But, son, I respect you, because I respect a man who respects himself. (Clausen and Kohn, 1960:305. See there also for references to other works.)

If one reads the father's last completely unresponsive response, it is easy to empathize with the son, who must feel unable to get across *and* unable to blame the father because he is (like the mother) verbally supportive. Seeman, one of the very few contemporary sociologists to draw on the concept of inauthenticity, points out (1966b) that one of the two main outcomes of a man being in an inauthentic condition is for "role-inversion" to take place, in which impulses are turned into "coolness," preventing their expression and release, e.g., among middle-class Negroes (Broyard, 1950:56–64). Seeman's own study (1956:142–153) shows that intellectuals refer to themselves as a minority (which puts them in an inauthentic state, by his definition) and his study shows that those who are less inclined to accept this self-definition are more creative, as ranked by their colleagues (Seeman, 1966b:71).

More generally, we expect that, when persons in relatively pure alienating conditions are compared to those in highly inauthentic ones, systematic differences will be found in the rates of various kinds of mental and psychosomatic illness. For instance, illness typically associated with a high level of anxiety, e.g., neurosis, is expected to be more common among those in inauthentic conditions, persons unsure of their self-identity and social position, while those who are purely alienated are more likely to exhibit the symptoms of withdrawal or excessive aggression, depending on their reaction to the forces which excluded them.

Much study is necessary if we are to establish the differences in the personality levels which are affected, the differential effects on each level, and on a person's total psychic costs, as well as the kinds he is charging others. For instance, we expect interpersonal violence to be more common in alienated relations and suicide in inauthentic ones.

I do not claim that there is sufficient evidence to hold that pre-industrial societies were less alienating than modern ones, or that modern societies have become less alienating as they moved from early to late industrial stages, but it does seem safe to conclude that large segments of the citizens of contemporary industrial societies feel powerless and excluded, and are uninformed about the societal and political processes which govern their lives (Kornhauser, Sheppard and Mayer, 1956:194). The proportion of those who feel they can influence local and national political occurrences is 44 percent in the United States, 53 percent in the United Kingdom, 55 percent in West Germany, and 29 percent in Italy (Almond and Verba, 1963:226). "About one-third of the American adult population can be characterized as politically apathetic or passive; in most cases, they are unaware, literally, of the political part of the world around them. Another 60 percent play largely spectator roles . . ." (Milbrath, 1965:21).

A Historical Trend?

The rise of alienation is often associated with the emergence of the industrialized economies, bureaucratic nation-states, and the age of rationalism and science. In short, alienation and modernization are said to go hand in hand. World War II, it may be added, may mark the initiation of a new period, post-industrial or post-modern, in which inauthentic elements are arising. While societies as far removed as ancient Egypt or China had some manipulative mechanisms to cover up naked vested interests and power relations with ideological fig leaves, we suggest that it is a mark of the post–World War II industrialized societies that they devote a major part of their endeavors to "front" activities. The numerous indications of this process include: the rise in the technologies of mass communication devoted chiefly to "escapist" communication (especially television sets, found in 8,000 households in 1946 as compared to 45,500,000 by 1959); the increased investment in mass advertising and public relations—$2,874 million in 1945 as compared to $11,117 million by 1959, on advertising alone in the United States (Machlup, 1962:251); the improved quality of social sciences used in manipulation of consumer tastes, work relations and political campaigns (Kelley, 1956); and the increased weight of "other-directed" values (Riesman et al., 1950; see also Lipset and Lowenthal, 1961).

In addition, one can make a fairly strong case that there is a trend toward less outright exclusion and more reliance on pseudo-participation through societal-managerial techniques in various specific societal institutions as divergent as work, education, and politics. For instance, workers in early industrial society were quite openly shut out of participation in the political system, and explicitly forbidden to organize themselves in the plant. While the church and the dominant culture did promote some notions of "status-acceptance," there was relatively little deliberate ideological activity to "cool out" workers and engineer "co-opting" outlets for their protest. This has changed in the inauthentic period, where workers' attention is mobilized by management or the mass media and the activities it promotes, and "co-opted unions" as well as other forms of pseudo-participation are offered (Bendix, 1956:308–318; see also Baritz, 1960). Similar analyses have been advanced of other institutional spheres. (In education, Friedenberg, 1963; in politics, Levin, 1960.)

Finally, a change in the composition of protest—one indication of needs not responded to—may also be indicative of the historical trend we "hypothesized." The left protest in capitalist societies, which is typically anti-alienation, is appealing to those who seek a share in controlling their collective fate and the transformation of society to be more responsive, at least to their needs. The bohemian (beatnik or hippie) protest, which was present in the industrializing society but seems to have been growing since World War II, adds a reaction to inauthenticity; there is more stress on society as a lie, and on a search—in part Utopian—for truth and for authentic relations, rather than merely for a share of power and of the control of allocative processes. The fact that the structure which underlies an inauthentic participatory front is an alienating one explains in part the fact that bohemian and left-wing protest are often mixed and not viewed as mutually exclusive but rather as complementary. Whether either provides a design for a society responsive to basic human needs which is able to function, is a question which need not be discussed here; but it seems clear that both do point to real unresponsive elements of the existing society. One may reject in detail or even in *toto* the diagnosis and prognosis of these positions, but they—and the conditions they point to—cannot be adequately understood and analyzed by frames of reference which exclude the concept of basic human needs.

Notes

1. "Man's *'original nature'* is seen largely in neutral terms, as neither good nor bad. It is, rather, a potential for development, and the extent to which the potential is realized depends on the time and society into which a man is born, and on his distinctive place in it. If it does not quite treat him as a 'tabula rasa,' modern sociology, nevertheless, regards man as a flexible form which can be given all manner of content.

    "Socialization, the process of learning one's culture while growing out of infant and childhood dependency,

leads to internalization of society's values and goals. People come to want to do what from the point of society they must do. Man is, therefore, seen, in his inner being, as mainly moral, by and large accepting and fulfilling the demands society makes on him" (Inkeles, 1964:50).

2. The first concept is used in the more technical writings; the second in more philosophical ones. The differences need not concern us here. Erich Fromm (1961) provides a popular overview of the philosophical issues involved, from a Freudian-Marxist perspective.

3. On the inability to test several of Sigmund Freud's key propositions, see Jerome Frank (1961).

4. I also hold that persons prefer particularistic and diffuse conduct over that which is universalistic and specific; the procedure in testing this statement would be the same as suggested here with regard to the preference for frequent over infrequent gratification.

5. Even within the context of an over-socialized conception of man (Wrong, 1961), one may hold that a society must answer a variety of *societal* needs and these cannot all be fully answered because these needs are partially incompatible. Thus a fully integrated society is not feasible, and members will be socialized to conflicting expectations, i.e., there always will be some *societal* source of alienation.

6. Robert Blauner (1964, especially chapter 4) shows such a difference in the case of textile workers.

7. The relationship between participation and responsiveness ought to be indicated: maximal societal responsiveness will be attained under the Utopian condition in which all members participate in the shaping of all aspects of their societal life. Even this condition would be expected to encounter some alienation, the result of the fact that not all members' needs are mutually complementary, and thus the compromises inevitably worked out leave each less than fully satisfied. Participation, however, provides the most effective way to reach such compromise; any other procedure, e.g., a wise and open-minded monarch, taking his or her country's needs into account,

would be expected to leave a greater residue of alienation than broadly based participation would. This is because, under such a system, upward communication of members' needs would be both more accurate and more powerful than under any other system.

References

Aberle, D., A. Cohen, A. K. Davis, M. Levy and F. Sutton.
  1950   "The Functional Prerequisites of a Society," *Ethics,* Vol. 60 (January, 1950): 100–111.
Almond, Gabriel A. and Sidney Verba.
  1963   *The Civic Culture.* Princeton, N.J.: Princeton University Press.
Bales, Robert F.
  1953   "The Equilibrium Problem in Small Groups," in Talcott Parsons, Robert F. Bales and E. A. Shils (eds.), *Working Papers in the Theory of Action.* New York: Free Press, pp. 111–161.
Baritz, Loren.
  1960   *The Servants of Power.* Middletown, Connecticut: Wesleyan University Press.
Bendix, Reinhard.
  1956 *Work and Authority in Industry.* New York: Wiley.
Berelson, Bernard and Gary A. Steiner.
  1964   *Human Behavior.* Orlando, Fla.: Harcourt Brace Jovanovich.
Berger, Bennett M.
  1960 *Working Class Suburb: A Study of Auto Workers in Suburbia.* Berkeley: University of California.
Bettelheim, Bruno and Morris Janowitz.
  1950   *Dynamics of Prejudice.* New York: Harper-Collins.
Blauner, Robert.
  1964   *Alienation and Freedom.* Chicago: Phoenix Books.
Bradburn, Norman M. and David Caplovitz.
  1965   *Reports on Happiness: A Pilot Study of Behavior Related to Mental Health.* Chicago: Aldine.

Brenner, Berthold.
1967 "Patterns of alcohol use, happiness and the satisfaction of wants," *Quarterly Journal of Studies on Alcohol,* Vol. 28(4): 667–675.
Broyard, Anatole.
1950 "Portrait of the Inauthentic Negro," *Commentary,* Vol. 10 (July 1950): 56–64.
Clausen, John A. and Melvin L. Kohn.
1960 "Social Relations and Schizophrenia: A Research Report and a Perspective," in Don D. Jackson (ed.), *The Etiology of Schizophrenia.* New York: Basic.
Cohen, Albert K.
1966 *Deviance and Control.* Englewood Cliffs, N.J.: Prentice-Hall.
Davies, James C.
1963 *Human Nature in Politics.* New York: Wiley.
Eaton, Joseph W. and Robert J. Weil.
1955 *Culture and Mental Disorders.* New York: Free Press.
Etzioni, Amitai.
1961 *A Comparative Analysis of Complex Organizations.* New York: Free Press.
1964 *Modern Organizations.* Englewood Cliffs, N.J.: Prentice-Hall.
1968 *The Active Society: A Theory of Societal and Political Processes.* New York: Free Press.
Frank, Jerome.
1961 *Persuasion and Healing.* Baltimore, Md.: Johns Hopkins University Press.
Friedenberg, Edgar Z.
1963 *Coming of Age in America.* New York: Random House.
Friedman, M. and R. H. Rosenman.
1959 "Association of Specific Overt Behavior Patterns with Blood and Cardiovascular Findings," *Journal of the American Medical Association,* Vol. 169 (1959): 1286–1296.
Fromm, Erich.
1955 *The Sane Society.* Troy, Mo.: Holt, Rinehart & Winston.

1961   *Man for Himself.* Troy, Mo.: Holt, Rinehart & Winston.

Gilbert, Doris C. and Daniel J. Levinson.
1957   "Role Performance, Ideology, and Personality in Mental Hospital Aides," in Milton Greenblatt et al. (eds.), *The Patient and the Mental Hospital.* New York: Free Press, pp. 197–208.

Hollingshead, August B. and Fredrick C. Redlich.
1958   *Social Class and Mental Illness.* New York: Wiley.

Hyman, Herbert H.
1955   *Survey Design and Analysis.* New York: Free Press.

Inkeles, Alex.
1964   *What Is Sociology?* Englewood Cliffs, N.J.: Prentice-Hall.
1974   *Becoming Modern: Individual Change in Six Developing Countries.* Cambridge, Mass.: Harvard University Press.

Janis, Irving J. and Carl I. Hovland.
1959   "An Overview of Persuasibility Research," in Irving J. Janis et al., *Personality and Persuasibility.* New Haven, Conn.: Yale University Press, pp. 1–6; 16–26.

Kelley, Stanley, Jr.
1956   *Professional Public Relations and Political Power.* Baltimore, Md.: Johns Hopkins University Press.

Keniston, Kenneth.
1965   *The Uncommitted: Alienated Youth in American Society.* Orlando, Fla.: Harcourt Brace Jovanovich.

Kornhauser, Arthur, H. Sheppard and A. Mayer.
1956   *When Labor Votes: A Study of Auto Workers.* New York: University Books.

Lasswell, Harold.
1958   *Politics: Who Gets What, When, How.* New York: Meridian Books.

Lazarsfeld, Paul F. and Herbert Menzel.
1961   "On the Relation Between Individual and Collective Properties," in Amitai Etzioni (ed.), *Complex Organizations: A Sociological Reader,* Troy, Mo.: Holt, Rinehart & Winston, pp. 422–440.

Levin, Murray B.
1960   *The Alienated Voter.* Troy, Mo.: Holt, Rinehart & Winston.

Levy, Marion, Jr.
1966   *Modernization and the Structure of Societies.* Princeton, N.J.: Princeton University Press.

Lifton, Robert J.
1966   "Thought Reform of Chinese Intellectuals," in Marie Jahoda and Neil Warren (eds.), *Attitudes.* New York: Penguin Books, pp. 196–209.

Lippitt, R. and R. K. White.
1952   "An Experimental Study of Leadership and Group Life," In G. E. Swanson et al., *Readings in Social Psychology.* New York: Holt, pp. 340–355.

Lipset, Seymour M. and Leo Lowenthal (eds.).
1961   *Culture and Social Character.* New York: Free Press.

Machlup, Fritz.
1962   *The Production and Distribution of Knowledge in the U.S.* Princeton, N.J.: Princeton University Press.

Merton, Robert K.
1957   *Social Theory and Social Structure.* New York: Free Press.

Milbrath, Lester W.
1965   *Political Participation.* Chicago: Rand McNally.

Milosz, Czeslaw.
1953   *The Closed Mind.* New York: A. Knopf.

Nettler, Gwynn.
1957   "A Measure of Alienation," *American Sociological Review,* Vol. 22 (1957): 670–677.

Parsons, Talcott.
1951   *The Social System.* New York: Free Press.

Raiser, John R.
1966   "Personal Characteristics of Political Decision-Makers," *Pure Research Society (International) Papers,* Vol. V (1966): 161–181.

Riesman, David, et al.
1950   *The Lonely Crowd.* New Haven, Conn.: Yale University Press.

Sartre, Jean-Paul.
1960   *Anti-Semite and Jew.* New York: Grove Press.
Schein, Edgar H.
1961   *Coercive Persuasion: A Socio-Psychological Analysis of the "Brainwashing" of American Civilian Prisoners by the Chinese Communists.* New York: Norton.
Schurmann, Franz.
1966   *Ideology and Organization in Communist China.* Berkeley: University of California Press.
Seeman, Melvin.
1956   "Intellectual Perspective and Adjustment to Minority Status," *Social Problems,* Vol. 3 (January 1956): 142–153.
1966a   "Alienation, Membership and Political Knowledge: A Comparative Study," *Public Opinion Quarterly,* Vol. 30 (1966): 353–367.
1966b   "Status and Identity: The Problem of Inauthenticity," *Pacific Sociological Review,* Vol. 9 (Fall 1966): 67–73.
Selltiz, Claire, et al.
1959   *Research Methods in Social Relations.* Troy, Mo.: Holt, Rinehart & Winston.
Selznick, Philip.
1960   *The Organizational Weapon.* New York: Free Press.
Shils, Edward.
1957   "Daydreams and Nightmares: Reflections on the Criticism of Mass Culture," *Sewanee Review,* Vol. 65 (Autumn 1957): 587–608.
Srole, Leo, et al.
1962   *Mental Health in the Metropolis.* New York: McGraw-Hill.
Townsend, James R.
1967   *Political Participation in Communist China.* Berkeley: University of California Press.
Wrong, Dennis.
1961   "The Oversocialized Conception of Man," *American Sociological Review,* Vol. 26 (1961): 183–192.

5

Polity and the Public Interest: Author's Note

It is commonly observed, in both intellectual and social science writings, that the American polity is pluralistic; that is, that numerous groups vie with one another over the direction of the polity. Some have explicitly argued that "this is all there is," that there are no communal bonds, shared goals, and so on. It has been further maintained that the concept of public interest is deceptive; each group claims it, but there is no way of telling what is actually in *the* public interest.

My position, explained in the essay on "Special Interest Groups Versus Constituency Representation," is that groups do indeed vie with each other. In relatively well integrated societies, however, such as the United States, these contests and give-and-take are exercised within a capsule of unity. Indeed, whenever a group threatens the national unity (for example, the threat posed by those who called for the establishment of a black nation within the U.S. or the South's attempts to secede before the Civil War), it is perceived as an illegitimate part of the plurality of groups—a direct threat to society and to the public interest.

The next essay, "The Fight Against Fraud and Abuse: Analyzing Constituent Support," suggests that it is possible to determine when a group is acting only in its own interest and when it is serving the commonweal, the shared bond and the public interest. A group that lobbies to line its members' pockets (never mind what it advertises as its noble reasons) is distinct from a group that serves only, or mainly, other members of the community. For example, Americans for Democratic Action is quite different from the white middle-class liberals from the North who endangered their lives, as freedom riders, to enhance the voting rights of blacks in the South. One of the most important differences is that while special interest groups strain the system, and in accumulation they may overload it, those that promote the public interest may help form countervailing forces that sustain the national-societal capsule. These forces are significant both in themselves and by setting a context within which special interest groups can safely vie.

The general conceptions advanced in the first essay lead to specific analytical tools in the second. While the immediate subject is the analysis of the causes and prevention of specific instances of abuse in a federal agency, the analysis follows the functionalist notion that persistent abuse is not accidental but structural. Such abuse reflects not merely the failure of human nature, socialization, or technical deficiencies of accounting and supervisory systems but the relative power of various constituencies. Once we understand those, we can analyze more deeply which forms of abuse are sustained by certain specific structural formations and how these may be modified—not by technical changes but by mobilizing new constituency bases (or political support) or forming new coalitions of existing groups.

Special Interest Groups
Versus
Constituency Representation

The age-old study of interest groups, and the even older concern with their proper role in a democracy, would benefit from three additions. First, a distinction between narrowly based *special interest groups* and broadly based *constituency-representing organizations*. Many of the statements made about "interest groups," we shall see, do not apply equally to these two main types.

Second, it would be fruitful to differentiate among the notions of a self-containing system (in which interest groups check and balance each other), a containing system (in which they are countervailed by other actors, institutions, and national bonds), and a system largely free of interest groups. The first conception, a self-containing system, represents an application of Adam Smith's "invisible hand" to politics. The second constitutes an attempt to preserve the commonweal without suppressing pluralism. The third notion is one of a utopia, a free community without interest groups—or the vision of an extremely totalitarian regime, in which they are all "leveled."

Finally, statements about interest groups would benefit from being consistently related to statements about the condition of the system in which they operate.[1] Especially, the

Note: This essay was originally published in *Research in Social Movements, Conflicts and Change*, 1985, *8*, 171–195. Copyright © 1985 by JAI Press, Greenwich, CT. Reprinted with permission. I am indebted to Mary Pockman for numerous editorial suggestions and to Paul Jargowsky for excellent research assistance. Kurt Lang made several penetrating critical comments on a previous draft. Additional evidence is included in Etzioni, A. *Capital Corruption* (Orlando, Fla.: Harcourt Brace Jovanovich, 1984).

strength of the integrating national bonds and the responsiveness of the political institutions seem to be relevant to an
assessment of the effects of changes in the number, power,
and techniques of interest groups. For example, groups that
may reduce the totalitarianism of a highly cohesive centrist
state and render its institutions more responsive may exacer-
bate the anarchy of a state that is being dismembered because of other centrifugal forces.

Reference to functional and dysfunctional, throughout
the paper, refer to the democratic polity. That is, the effects
of changes in interest groups are assessed from the viewpoint
of their contribution to maintaining and adapting (vs. undermining or ossifying) a specific polity; namely pluralistic democracy.

State of the System

It is nearly impossible to assess the role of interest groups
without an independent "reading" of the specific state of the
polity in a given period under study. Obviously their effect
would be radically different in a "balkanized," "fragmented,"
"tribalized" system than in a unitary, highly integrated, politically effective one. In the first, interest groups of either kind
would tend to add to the strains of the system (unless they
cut across its existing lines of fragmentation, and even then
they may overload the system). In the second, they would
make for more opportunities for the system to respond to
the plurality of interests, views, and values that inevitably continue to exist, but that may not be effectively represented
through electoral and party channels.

In the last two decades (1960–1980) the level of integration of the American national political system and the effectiveness of its institutions seem to have diminished. In the
same period, the power of interest groups—of all kinds—has
grown. While each of these twin developments fed into the
other, it is my hypothesis that they did not cause each other.
Each was driven by its own forces—as well as egged on by the
corollary development. The combined result is a political system much less able to contain interest groups and to "digest"

their inputs; that is, by the end of the period, interest groups had become, on balance, more dysfunctional than at its inception.

Changes in the Polity

Base Line: 1960
To suggest that the level of integration of the U.S. declined from 1960 to 1980 is not to imply that it was particularly high in 1960 or earlier. (See Etzioni, 1965:4–5; Haas, 1958:11ff.) Indeed, it was not nearly as high as, say, that of the U.K. and other well-integrated nations, for many historical, structural, and social reasons, reasons that persisted after 1960. They are thoroughly familiar and hence are only quickly listed here, as background factors.

The American society of 1960 was highly heterogeneous in racial, cultural, and demographic composition compared to Britain, West Germany, France, Italy, and many other Western nation-states. Its population was larger, and it stretched over more territory, including parts separated by thousands of miles of sea (Hawaii) and another country (Alaska). The U.S. had no national police force. The content of education, and thus the values it transmitted to the new generation, was almost exclusively subject to local decision-making, not under the influence of a unified national curriculum as, say, in Israel or France.

The federal structure (compared to the unitary structure of Britain, for example) allowed the political institutions to function relatively effectively without a high level of integration. Its responsiveness to rising social demands seems up to 1960 to have enhanced the effectiveness of the political institutions, rather than to have overloaded them. Within the electorate there was a relatively high sense of these institutions' effectiveness and legitimation. (See below for data.)

Relevant Changes from 1960 to 1980
The developments which in *toto* resulted in a lower level of national integration and political effectiveness are equally well known. They are not reported here as new research

findings, new insights, or a conceptual breakthrough. On the contrary, these often-reported observations are listed together merely so that the conclusion they jointly point to will come into focus: a diminished system.

Decline of Shared Political Beliefs. Sociologists have pointed to the difficulty the heterogeneous American people have in forming positive shared political beliefs. Americans have found it easier to share opposition to a different set of values, that of communism. In 1960 the American majority was still united by a strong shared worldview that saw expanding communism as a sinister worldwide force and the U.S. as the leading world power entrusted with the duty to contain it. Aside from providing a worldview defining "them" as hostile and depraved, "us" as carriers of positive attributes, and a rationale for specific foreign policy acts (such as U.S. support of anti-communist regimes in Greece and Turkey in 1946–47, and the CIA role in overthrowing Mossadegh in Iran in 1953), the Soviet threat provided a rationale for a host of domestic activities (such as increased national expenditures for R&D, science education, foreign language training, and space efforts).

This "anti" consensus was much weaker by 1980. There was division within the communist camp (especially between the U.S.S.R. and China) and within the West (especially between DeGaulle's France and other nations). The deliberate psychic disarmament of the United States was begun by President Kennedy's Strategy for Peace (1963), and expanded by President Nixon's opening to China, the various detentes, and the dissension about the war in Vietnam. Together, these developments resulted in a diminished ideological consensus and commitment.

The Rise of Alienation. Since 1966 pollsters have regularly published data on the trust Americans put in various institutions. Although in 1966, 43 percent said they had "a great deal of confidence" in the major institutions of American society, by 1979 only 23 percent said they felt that way. The political institutions especially lost in trust. The confidence ratings of Congress and the executive branch were a low 13 percent in 1978.[2]

Everett Carll Ladd (1981) has called attention to the difference between a sense of loyalty to America and commitment to its basic political system, and a sense of performance and competence. The public, data show, has lost little of the former but much of the latter (Ladd, 1981).

A quite different set of data is striking because, although it covers rather different matters, and the statements people were asked to agree or disagree with are particularly disaffected, it closely parallels the trust-in-institution data. As often as these data have been cited, it still seems telling to recall that the proportion of Americans who agree with the statement that in the United States "the rich get richer and the poor get poorer" increased from 45 percent in 1966 to 78 percent in 1980. Similarly, the proportion who feel that "what you think doesn't count much anymore" increased from 37 percent to 64 percent over the same time period. An index of disaffection, combining data on six such statements, shows a steady increase, from 29 percent in 1966 to 62 percent in 1980 (Harris, 1982:2).

Decline of Voter Participation. The percentage of the voting age population not voting for any candidate in presidential elections has steadily increased over the last two decades. In 1960, 37.2 percent did not vote; in 1980, 47.5 percent did not vote. Both Carter and Reagan were elected by parts of the electorate much smaller than the nonvoting "party." Carter was elected by 27.2 percent versus 45.7 percent nonvoting, Reagan by 26.8 percent vs. 47.5 percent. True, not all the decline is due to a diminished sense of political participation and civic competence, in the sense Sidney Verba and Gabriel Almond (1965) use these terms. It reflects, for instance, a reduction in the voting age from 21 to 18 in 1971, and lower registration among young voters. Nevertheless, it is widely agreed that a significant part of the rising voter apathy is due to a rising disaffection from the national polity.

Economic Trends. A rapidly expanding pie is commonly viewed as more conducive to conflict settlement within a community than one that is growing slowly or not at all. The average annual growth in real GNP (after "deducting" inflation) was 3.9 percent from 1960 to 1970. It slowed to 3.3 percent from 1970 to 1978; in 1979, it was 2.3 percent. However, even these figures are misleadingly optimistic. They disregard the fact that there were not only more Americans than before (due to population growth), but that a much higher proportion than before were working outside the household and hence required tools, equipment, and capital. Consequently, while the total GNP continued to grow a bit, GNP per employed worker increased 1.9 percent per year from 1963 to 1973 and a meager 0.1 percent per year from 1972 to 1975, and it decreased 0.9 percent per year from 1978 to 1980. The result is fewer resources to be allotted, and increasing strains between competing demands.

The 1973–1980 period saw different parts of the United States affected in radically different ways by the sharp increase in energy prices. Some states rich in energy, "the American OPEC," experienced very large increases in state revenues, income to their industries, and jobs; these states include Texas, Louisiana, Alaska, and Montana. Others—especially in the Northeast and the Midwest—experienced very sharp increases in costs. New England, for example, depends on oil to supply 85 percent of its energy needs, compared to 45 percent for the rest of the country (Schucker, 1976:13). The price increases after 1973 pushed energy costs in northeastern metropolitan areas to a level 97 percent higher than that in the rest of the country (McManus, 1976:344). The net result of such differences seems to have been an increased strain on national unity from general economic, and especially energy, sources, as reflected in the great difficulties to reach consensus on relevant public policy in the years at issue (1973–1980).

Institutional Changes. Congressional "reforms" and the decline of the political parties had a double effect particularly relevant to the issue at hand. They weakened the national political system per se, and they increased the power of the interest groups. The main relevant congressional reforms are those that resulted in increased fragmentation and decreased ability to act in unison—abolition of the seniority system in selecting committee chairmen, and the proliferation of subcommittees, which created numerous autonomous power centers.

The Other Side of the Ledger. In the face of these centrifugal forces, no major new development seems to have helped sustain national bonds or the effectiveness of political institutions in these years. The rise of television, "the electronic village," provided a shared national stage, but little of what played on it was relevant to nation-building. The great expansion of social programs and transfer payments may be seen as an accommodation of the polity to social pressures, resulting in some reduction in poverty and in the economic distance between whites and blacks and between men and women (although certainly not all, possibly not even most, of the change is due to public policy). The net effect of these changes is less clear. The social groups involved seem far from satisfied with the pace and scope of the resulting reallocations, although the fact that their protests became less violent and more muted may suggest some system success. (Others may argue that these groups despaired and withdrew into less political forms of expressing alienation.) And other groups have grown resentful over the reallocations, costing the system support.

In short, with several forces working to weaken the national bonds and political institutions, and relatively few working to sustain them, it seems safe to conclude that they diminished (see Etzioni, 1982).

The Rise in Interest Groups

While the system weakened, the number, scope, and power of interest groups rose. To reemphasize a point discussed before: it is my thesis that the interest groups grew on their own, aside from whatever "contribution" their growth drew from the weakened system.

Political Mobilization of Previously Inactive Groups. Histories of democracies have often been told in terms of expanding voting rights, introducing into the polity groups that previously did not have access to the system, such as slaves, women, and men without property. At the beginning of the era under review, universal suffrage existed as a nominal attribute of the system, but it was only during this period, especially following the 1964 Voting Rights Act, that black Americans in the South gained an effective vote, followed by a very substantial increase in black participation in elections and as elected officers. Youth voting rights were extended when the voting age was lowered from 21 to 18 in 1971.

Sociologically even more significant was the fact that large social groups, previously basically inactive politically, were mobilized and became politically aware and active. These groups include various minorities, women, environmentalists, and welfare clients, among others.

Rise of PACs as an Interest Group Tool. Especially after 1975 there was a very rapid and considerable growth in corporate interest groups and an increase in trade and industrial groups. The number of Political Action Committees sponsored by corporations and business groups rose from only 89 in 1974 to 949 in 1980. In addition, trade association PACs brought the total of all business-related PACs to 1400 in 1980, up from 450 in 1975 (Etzioni, 1984: ch. 2; Wertheimer, 1980:606).

The Weakening of the Political Parties. The identification of citizens with the political parties has diminished in recent years.[3] While the percentage of people who identified with one of the major parties fell only 3 percent between 1939 and 1964, it declined 10 percent between 1964 and 1974 (Dennis, 1975:192). As a result of this weakening, members of Congress are freer to deal with interest groups, and are under less countervailing pressure from the multiconstituency, broad-based, and wide-scope groups that the parties represent. Everett Carll Ladd (1980:67), reviewing the situation, summarized it: "As the parties withered, candidates for Congress and other elective offices were left to operate as independent entrepreneurs." He further quotes the Committee on Political Parties of the American Political Science Association:

> It must be obvious . . . that the whole development [the proliferation of interest groups] makes necessary a reinforced party system that can cope with the multiplied organized pressure (Ladd, 1980:72).

Typology of Interest Groups

Typically, reference to interest groups includes such diverse organizations as Common Cause, NOW, AFL-CIO, AMA, and the peanut growers. The logical next step is to ask if there are different types of interest groups, and if distinguishing among them in some systematic manner will sharpen our insights.

Obviously there is no one "right" typology; interest groups are best arranged according to the independent variable(s) one focuses on. Thus, the Lowi (1969) typology of distributive, regulatory, and redistributive policy areas works well to demonstrate the effects of the type of issue involved on the political consequences of interest groups. James Q. Wilson prefers to compare interest groups from the viewpoint of "whether the cost and benefits are widely distributed or narrowly concentrated from the point of view of those who bear the costs or enjoy the benefits" (1973:332).

For reasons which will become evident immediately, I find it useful to distinguish between two types: one which I shall call "special interest groups" (SIGs), and the other, "constituency-representing organizations" (CROs). Both, we shall see, are different from public interest groups (PIGs), which have received much attention in recent research.

These are analytic categories. No specific group is wholly of one kind or the other at all times. But groups can be distinguished as being more one kind or the other, in a given period. The criteria for differentiating among interest groups are the scope of the social base (narrow vs. wide), the scope of the interests and needs of the bases represented by the interest groups (pecuniary only, or pecuniary in conjunction with many other "status" symbolic issues), and the beneficiaries (members vs. nonmembers).

Special interest groups are organizations whose social base is relatively narrow, whose political presentation is limited in scope, typically to pecuniary interests, and whose beneficiaries are almost exclusively the groups' members. The sugar lobby often—though not always—acts as a SIG. It represents some 14,000 cane and beet farmers and is preoccupied almost exclusively with promoting limitations on the import of sugar and sustaining indirect subsidies for sugar farmers, so they can in effect sell their sugar to the government above free market prices.

Constituency-representing organizations are organizations whose social base is relatively broad, whose scope of political presentation is wide, typically encompassing nonpecuniary interests (e.g., social status, symbolic and value issues) in addition to pecuniary ones, and which seek to balance service to their members with a measure of concern for the community of which they are a part. The Urban League, the AFL-CIO, the Business Roundtable often—but certainly not always—act as CROs.

The three attributes used to define interest groups are to be viewed as dimensions of a continuum, not as dichotomous variables. Thus, an interest group's social base may be very small (e.g., a few hundred tugboat pilots), merely small (e.g., 14,000 sugar farmers), relatively large (e.g., 1,600,000 teachers who are members of the NEA), or quite large (e.g., 17,000,000 members of the AFL-CIO). Similarly, it may represent chiefly one narrow interest, quite a few interests, or a rather full gamut. The term SIGs refers to one extreme of this threefold continuum; CROs, to the other pole.

SIGs may combine to form "cooperative lobbying efforts" or coalitions. This will make the combined lobby more akin to CROs, although even such a combined lobby will still tend to focus on pecuniary interests, and not on value issues.

The inevitable question arises, as three attributes are used to define SIGs and CROs—*size* of social base, *scope* of interests represented, and *strength* of the balancing commitment to the commonweal—what if a group scores high on some of the attributes but low on the others? Other types of interest groups result, which we will not review here, either because they have already been discussed elsewhere at length (e.g., single issue groups) or because they are categories populated by very few instances (e.g., broad-based, narrowly pecuniary in scope, but high in commitment to the commonweal). Our main focus is on two types which are either high or low in all three dimensions and which are quite common—SIGs and CROs.

It is also necessary to point out that these variables are not intended to cover the whole range of issues regarding interest groups. Several major studies have been done regarding the origins of interest groups, particularly public interest groups, and their internal dynamics and structure. Others have studied the internal decision making of various types of interest groups. Some groups are oligarchic, while others are more democratic, and these differences affect the representational quality of the group. While these questions deserve further discussion for our purposes it suffices to see where a group falls on the threefold continuum outlined above, because it contains the three independent variables we focus on.

CROs should not be confused with constituencies. The term "constituency" refers to the social base: blacks, labor, business, ethnic group, etc. Constituencies are social categories (such as demographic, racial, ethnic, or occupational) that have some common or shared interest in the eyes of observers but not necessarily of their members. The terms "labor," "blacks," and "farmers" are often used as if they denote a series of interest groups. However, this is best viewed as a shorthand the author is using to refer to the organizations that represent these constituencies in the political realm, rather than to the social bases: labor unions, not "labor"; the NAACP or the Urban League, not "blacks."

If one does not assume this shorthand, the connotations are misleading. They imply that if a social group has a common or shared interest in the eyes of some social scientist, ipso facto it also constitutes a politically active group, which often it is not (see Olson, 1965; Olson, Salisbury and Reilly, 1969). Moreover, they may lead one to overlook the important fact that practically all the organizations that represent a constituency represent only some of its members, indeed quite often only a small and not "average" segment. For instance, labor unions' membership presently includes about one out of five American workers, and very few of those are farmhands. As Robert Michels put it so well, and many have reiterated, such representation is always interpreting, if not distorting, the social base (Michels, 1958; Lipset, Trow and Coleman, 1956). The decision to whom to channel money a corporate PAC has collected from numerous lower ranking individuals, for example, is made by a few persons, typically higher in corporate rank than the average contributor. Hence the merit of keeping apart the concept of a constituency and that of a constituency-representing organization.

Public interest groups are organizations whose social base varies, whose political presentation concerns the community at large or primarily non-members, and whose focus is typically on non-pecuniary interests.[4] While all three attributes are relevant to their definition, concern with the community is their most outstanding quality. Common Cause, Americans for Democratic Action, and Young Americans for Freedom often act as public interest groups.

Most, if not all, interest groups—not merely public interest groups—claim they serve the community or the public interest; and the social scientist, it has frequently been noted, will be hard put to tell what "the" public interest is.[5] It is easier to determine whether or not those who benefit by the groups' actions are first and foremost the groups' members. At issue are not the futuristic, hypothetical, potential pay-offs that interest groups are fond of promising to all, but those that line pockets here and now, or securely in the near future. Not the alleged benefits of stockpiling more silver by the military to the U.S. if one day it went to war, and ran out of the silver it already stockpiles, and then needed more silver than is now anticipated; but the benefits for silver speculators who bought silver and cannot get rid of it without a hefty loss unless the military increases its stockpile. In contrast, A.D.A.'s 1964 fight for the voting rights of black Americans served American democracy, not the members of A.D.A. personally and directly; there were very few blacks in its ranks in 1964. The indicator is not the content of proclamations but the distribution of benefits.

It is important to reiterate that the distinctions among the three types of interest groups are analytic in the sense that any concrete group may display all three kinds of behavior over time. For example, when a longshoremen's union refuses to load goods to be shipped to Poland in protest of the imposition of martial law in that country, the union is acting as a public interest group, although it typically acts as a special interest group.[6] When foundations fight for tax exemption, special postal rates, and deduction of contributions to themselves from taxable income, they act as SIGs, not PIGs.

It also follows that a group which acted for a given period largely as one type may over the years turn increasingly to become more another type. For instance, a group concerned with public service may become more and more preoccupied with the privileges of its members.

In the following discussion I shall use the analytic designation of SIG, CRO, or PIG as a shorthand, to suggest a group which acts *mainly,* in a given period, as the type indicated. No group ever "is" a CRO, SIG, or PIG; a concrete group at most may approximate one analytic type more than others. The discussion focuses on CROs and SIGs, because PIGs have received a relatively large amount of attention in recent research and theoretical deliberation, while the difference between SIGs and CROs is newly introduced here.

Special Interest Groups Versus
Constituency-Representing Organizations

It is my working hypothesis that practically all the statements made about "interest groups" apply much more to one type than to the other. Technically put, the indicated attributes correlate much more strongly with one of the two "ends" (high negative or high positive scores) of the three defining variables which separate SIGs from CROs. I start with the pivotal question: are interest groups "functional" for democracy? The following discussion attempts to show that contributions attributed to interest groups are frequently made by groups that tend to act as constituency-representing organizations, but not by those that tend to act as special interest groups.

Political Science "Conventional Wisdom"

For many decades, the "conventional wisdom" of political science has been to view interest groups as "benign" or "beneficial" (Ornstein and Elder, 1978:14), in opposition to the prevailing public view. Harmon Ziegler describes the popular view, under the caption "Traditional distrust and organized groups":

> From the beginnings of the American republic, the assumption has been made that pressure groups, irrespective of their goals, are evil because they conflict with the fundamental attributes of democracy (1964:33).

There follows a discussion of James Madison's often cited 10th Essay in *The Federalist*, which characterizes interest groups ("factions") as dangerous to a popular government. Zeigler then cites a series of publications over the years that define interest groups as a threat to democracy. He contrasts this popular anti-interest-group view with the sophisticated political science view. According to the latter, "the criticism exemplified in the writing cited above is based upon a concept of democracy which is both inadequate and naive" (Zeigler, 1964:35). The naive concept, Zeigler explains, is that of electoral democracy, the view that government should represent the public will and that the public will is expressed through the electoral process. Concessions to special interests are thus viewed as subverting the public will, as undemocratic.

Similarly, Norman J. Ornstein and Shirley Elder observe, "the American press has historically emphasized lobbying scandals and the insidious influence of groups over politicians" (1978:8). There follows a reference to Madison's view that interest groups "were *inherently* bad" (1978:9). This tradition is contrasted with the political science tradition evolved out of the work of Arthur F. Bentley (1967) and David B. Truman (1951) and also advanced by Lester Milbrath (1963) and many others. (I'll turn later to other political science perspectives.) This tradition "tends to portray groups in a rather favorable light" (Ornstein and Elder, 1978:12). .

The *International Encyclopedia of Social Science,* published in 1968, carries signed articles representing the authors' viewpoints, but nevertheless, because of the way the authors were selected and guided, the articles tend to reflect the consensus of the field at the time. The article on "interest groups" by Henry W. Ehrmann focuses on the "functions" of interest groups, rather than on their dysfunctions. He too observes that "liberal and radical traditions in both Great Britain and the United States were equally unsympathetic to 'special interests.'"[7] In contrast, he notes, political science has established that interest groups are "indispensable for the functioning of modern democracy,"[8] although they must be limited to the use of legitimate means.

The "Functions" of Interest Groups

Specifically, political scientists have often identified the following contributions of interest groups to pluralistic democratic politics:

1. *Interest groups provide a mechanism for political representation which "supplements" the electoral process.* Elections are

infrequent and each voter has but one vote to cast. A high and, at least until 1980, growing proportion of decisions has been made in the public realm. Many voters' interests and concerns are deeply affected by public policy, and hence citizens seek to represent their views more frequently and on more issues than the electoral process can accommodate. Interest groups provide for such representation. In that sense, the more voluminous and encompassing the public business, the greater the "need" for interest groups.

2. *Interest groups bridge social-economic power concentrations and the polity.* Translated, that means that in the electoral process, the one person/one vote system, which is highly egalitarian, does not well reflect the social and economic power concentrations in the body of society (although they do find some expression in the electoral process, e.g., by being able to mobilize voters better than those with less such power). Interest groups allow the political process to be more responsive than the electoral process alone to the "realities" of social and economic power differences, and thus protect the government from forming policies detached from what the society will support.

3. *Interest groups provide a bridge between the administrative and legislative branches of government,* especially needed when the executive and the legislative branches check and balance each other to the point that they find it difficult to work in tandem. Some observers have pointed to the "stalemate" of government (a viewpoint popular particularly during the Carter Administration). Others have expressed fear that an "imperial" presidency would result from the search for extra-constitutional ways to make Congress collaborate with the executive, as constitutional means seem not to suffice (one interpretation of the abuse of presidential powers by Nixon and other presidents).

Interest groups are said to alleviate the excessive separation of the legislative and executive branches by approaching both with the same advocacy, the more readily because they are not confined by the same institutionalized strictures which limit the maneuverability of the legislative branch and the federal agencies.

4. *Interest groups constitute one major source of "mediating structures"* which stand between the state and the individual, protecting the individual from undue control, if not subjugation, by the state.

5. *Interest groups contribute to political socialization and political culture* by keeping their members informed, politically aware, and active, and by providing them the opportunity to learn and exercise political skills, an opportunity that is necessary if these skills are not to be monopolized by a limited social stratum but are to be widely spread through society.

A core assumption underlying all these specific "functions" of interest groups is that the political process of a pluralistic democracy is—and ought to be— based to a large extent on group processes, not individual action. This contrasts with the notion that democracy works by individuals' casting votes they personally choose to cast.

A second underlying assumption is that if all the interest groups, or at least the main ones, are involved in the formation of public policy, a "consensual" policy can be evolved, because these interest groups represent the major segments of the society, their needs and values as well as their power. Thus, in forming economic policy, if big business, small business, labor, farmers, and consumer representatives are involved, the resulting policy will be sanctioned by consensus. Or, in religious matters, at least the three main groups, Protestants, Catholics, and Jews, are to be consulted. It is not suggested that such a system provides a precise, all-encompassing, or egalitarian representation of the public, but—it is said—neither does the electoral process. Moreover, interest groups do not replace the electoral process, but supplement it.

A Critique

To examine critically the line of analysis of Bentley, Truman, et al., the functional theory of the contributions of interest groups to pluralistic democracy, I look first at the two core assumptions, then review the five specific functions.

Existing data suggest that some of the functions attributed to interest groups are actually discharged to a large extent by social groups, not interest groups, or at least that political presentation is not the relevant feature. That is, while it is correct to assume that groups play a cardinal role in the American polity, as they do in the American society, these are not one and the same group. Thus the data which show that most people consult their kin, friends, neighbors, members of the local community, and voluntary associations when they decide for whom to vote (Lazarsfeld, Berelson, and Gaudet, 1948:137–158; Berelson, Lazarsfeld, and McPhee, 1954; Katz and Lazarsfeld, 1955) are a measure of the significance of *social* groups for the electoral process, not of interest groups. True, some of these groups, especially voluntary associations, may act as interest groups, but this is not necessary for their role as a source of interpersonal consultation.

Similarly, social groups are quite adequate to protect individuals from "mass" demagogic appeal, as suggested by the fact that people absorb communications in line with what their social groups approve (e.g., read newspapers the group favors) and interpret the communications received in line with the social group's precepts and values.

Turning to the second core assumption, I hypothesize that much of what has been said about the role of interest groups in a pluralistic democracy applies, in varying degrees, to groups which are closer to the definition of CROs than to that of SIGs. Indeed, groups which exhibit a high degree of SIG behavior may undermine rather than serve pluralistic democracies.

The main point at issue is that the wide base, broad scope, and commonweal involvement of CROs make them much more suitable building blocks for consensus formation than SIGs, which are narrowly-based, limited, and focused on pecuniary gains. The main reasons in support of this hypothesis concern system overload, resource/issue ratios, scope of satisfaction, and inflation of payoffs.

Overload. All other things being equal, I hypothesize that it is much easier to work out a consensual policy with a handful of interest groups than with scores, let alone hundreds of groups.

Thus, a new consensus for major items of an economic policy can be worked out relatively readily by dealing with groups which tend to behave as CROs, such as the Business Roundtable (representing some 192 of the largest U.S. corporations, producing about half of the GNP), the Chamber of Commerce (representing 230,000 companies and some 1,400 trade associations), the AFL-CIO, and key farm groups and consumer groups. The same political processes would be overloaded if they needed to deal with the lobbies of scores of corporations, trade associations, splinter labor unions, and lobbies for each farm product from milk to peanuts.

This is first of all a matter of sheer size. Since SIGs by definition are narrow in base, they represent only fragments of society, not large segments. Second, SIGs are, by definition, more self-interested and less involved in the commonweal; this tends to make it harder to formulate a shared policy based on SIGs.

"Cooperative lobbying" (Hall, 1969) efforts among several groups which function as SIGs can widen their base, and in this way reduce their tendency to overload the system. Since the members of a coalition must, of necessity, weigh the effects of their demands on each other, a moderated position is likely to result. An American labor union of shoe industry employees may see no harm in a high tariff on imported shoes, but a coalition of unions associated with a wide range of products would have to consider the economic impact on all its members if other countries were, in retaliation, to impose tariffs on some other product America exports. Therefore, a coalition of SIGs will tend to behave less extremely than a single SIG, i.e., will lean somewhat toward acting as a CRO. However, even a wide-based SIG—or coalition of SIGs—will, by definition, deal largely with pecuniary matters and not seek to serve a broad set of human needs and values. Hence even such a SIG-coalition typically does not a CRO make.

Resource/Issue Ratios. Many interest groups are able to commit very large amounts of resources to advancing their positions, but SIGs can commit all their available resources to promotion of a single interest, while CROs must distribute theirs among a wide array of issues they, by definition, must represent. Hence one would expect the average SIG to be more determined and detrimental than the average CRO if one compares their effects on a single item of public policy.

Also, the resources available to some interest groups have become even larger since the increase in the public sector role has made public policy-making highly consequential. For example, changing public policy on oil pricing (via decontrol) will generate an estimated $831 billion of extra revenue for the oil companies between 1980 and 1990.[9] Hence, dedicating even so much as a billion dollars to lobbying, an absurdly high figure, would pose no difficulty for the oil lobby.

Scope of Satisfaction. To the extent that CROs influence the formation of a public policy, the policy will respond to several, if not all the basic needs of those persons they represent. In contrast, because SIGs deal chiefly with one facet or area, a policy that is affected by SIGs is unlikely to respond to their members' other needs. For example, the National Parking Association may succeed in curtailing the scope of mass transportation projects or delaying the implementation of air quality standards for cities. This success may in turn improve its members' profits, but it would leave all their other needs—including transportation and environmental needs—without articulation, at least via this interest group.

Inflationary Effects. Both CROs and SIGs can cause inflation. Writing about the "revolution of entitlements," Daniel Bell, like Milton Friedman before him, has called attention to the effects of shifting allocative decisions from the market to the polity (Bell, 1975:100; Friedman, 1962:23). The market, these writers say, exercises self-discipline, as the total amount of its resources available at any one time is fixed; an increase in the allotment to one group, e.g., workers, must be accommodated by a decrease in that to another, e.g., shareholders. However, no such automatic caps or discipline are built into the polity; one can always allot more by printing money. The more groups push for more, the higher the inflation.

Although neo-conservative writers refer to interest groups in general, the examples they cite are typically the new politically aware and active constituencies and their organizations, those representing groups such as blacks, Hispanics, and women. As I see it, organizations representing the interests of other constituencies (e.g., small business) have the same effect. And I would expect SIGs to be even more demanding of pecuniary payoff than CROs, both because the SIGs respond less to symbolic payoffs (which are not inflationary) and because they have less commonweal involvement. Compare, for instance, the concessions made in the 1981 tax bill to married people who are both gainfully employed (by reducing the so-called marriage penalty) to those made to various industrial groups, such as savings and loan associations and independent oil producers.[10] Similarly, labor unions under the voluntary wage guidelines in 1979–80 and the "National Accord" showed a measure of commitment to the commonweal, reflected in their acceptance of wage increases below the rate of inflation. The AFL-CIO agreed to support President Carter's guideline of 7.5 percent to 9.5 percent wage increases, despite inflation of 11.3 percent in 1979 and 13.5 percent through 1980;[11] wages of all union workers actually rose less than inflation: 9.0 percent in 1979 and 10.9 percent in 1980 (Borum, 1981:55). SIGs—for example, the hospital lobby—showed no such restraint in the same period. Hospital room charges rose 11.4 percent in 1979 and 13.0 in 1980.

If the two core assumptions are misapplied, the five functions attributed to interest groups can hardly be on much firmer ground. For reasons already indicated, it seems that while it is true that both SIGs and CROs supplement the electoral process, SIGs, because of their large number and low commonweal involvement, go beyond supplementing it to overloading it. They provide too much of a good thing. And the more restrained interest groups, the CROs, would be enough for this function.

Likewise, both SIGs and CROs may help bridge the socio-economic and political realms. However, while CROs tend to provide bridges which in *toto* carry all the main societal segments, SIGs bring in only small fragments at a time, and satisfy at best only one facet, the pecuniary one. In short, the CROs provide broader bridges.

The same holds for the links interest groups provide between the executive and the legislative branches. Both SIGs and CROs fulfill this function, but the resulting policies are quite different, in terms of the scope and breadth of the public needs reflected.

The mediating function is more a task for social groups than for either type of interest group. Indeed, traditionally it has been credited to the family, local communities, and voluntary associations acting as social groups, not as interest groups. It is these social groups which sustain individual personalities against undue influence by the state and rally to their help when the state seeks to oppress them, e.g., by contributing funds to their legal action. True, some public interest groups, such as the A.C.L.U., may be said to play a role here when they promote the Constitution and individual and civil rights, but typically the power of mediation is not that of legal action, but that of a social fabric that countervails the state not by political representation but by limiting the effect of the psychic and economic pressures the state's agents can generate.

As for the socialization function, it is one both kinds of interest groups discharge, although I would expect CROs to be more membership organizations, and SIGs, merely lobbies. Organizations which tend toward the latter would provide fewer socialization opportunities. Moreover, one must inquire whether socialization into political action by groups with a low commonweal orientation is as functional for the polity as that into groups with a higher commonweal involvement.

In short, on the basis of a conceptual distinction between two main types of interest groups, I suggest that, for several reasons, the contributions often attributed to interest groups in general come largely either from those functioning more like CROs, or from social groups, but not from SIGs. While familiarity with specific groups that come closer to one type or the other may give this argument a measure of plausibility, it of course must be subjected to the test of comparative empirical studies.

"Leveling," Self-Contained, and Containing

If the basic power of interest groups is deemed dysfunctional, or that of one main type comparatively dysfunctional, there are at least three systematic solutions: one is to "level" the interest groups, sharply reducing their power; another is to rely on the groups to contain each other; the last is to strengthen the system and limit the means interest groups use, without seeking to eliminate or otherwise reduce their power.

The first view is attributed to several public interest groups interested in political reforms. They have been said to seek to abolish interest groups and make the electoral process the mainstay of representation and consensus-building, and public interest—as expressed by the public at large—the guide of elected representatives.

John Gardner, the founder of Common Cause, has argued that the effect of special interest groups is to immobilize government.

> Imagine a checker player confronted by a bystander who puts a thumb on one checker and says "Go ahead and play, just don't touch this one," and then another bystander puts a thumb on another checker with the same warning, and then another bystander and another. The owners of the thumbs—the interest groups—don't want to make the game unwinnable. They just don't want you to touch their particular checker.[12]

David Riesman has stated a similar view of the American political system as one in which scores of "veto groups" each have enough power to block a step forward but not to provide support for positive action, so that a stalemate results

(1953:257–8ff). More recently, Suzanne Berger has pointed
to interest groups as the source of "major new problems of
'ungovernability,' inflation and economic stagnation"
(1981:64).

Viewing interest groups in this context, public interest
groups are out to overcome them so the polity will be able to
function again. Typically, since interest groups thrive when
they can function covertly, out of public sight, Common
Cause has supported "sunshine" legislation, requiring that
bill-writing and rewriting sessions of congressional committees be open to the public (Bethell, 1980:44).

Others, from James Madison on, have criticized this
approach as naive if not dangerous. Naive, they believe, because interest groups reflect human nature and hence are
"inevitable," impossible to eliminate. Dangerous, because attempts to curb them may threaten constitutional guarantees
such as freedom of assembly, of speech, and above all, of pe-
tition. For reasons which all become evident shortly, the
elimination of all interest groups seems to me not only impractical and unconstitutional but undesirable. Sharply limiting special interest groups, while tolerating, or maybe even
encouraging, constituency-representing organizations, is
much more compatible with a pluralistic yet public-minded
democracy, we shall see.

Turning to the second response, and continuing to use
the position of public interest groups as a kind of litmus test,
it is possible to see the role of public interest groups as involving not the elimination of interest groups, but their mutual containment. If one sees the political system as resting
on a balance between unity-enhancing forces and centrifugal
forces, public interest groups may be seen as adding another
vector to those sustaining and promoting community.
Whether their leaders and ideologues aspire to eliminate all
interest groups or merely to curb them matters little from
this viewpoint. Public interest groups seem so weak compared
to the two main types of interest groups that at best they serve
as a limited corrective. There is no realistic danger, at least in

contemporary America, that they will undermine the foundations of pluralism. The various Nader groups may annoy the PACs and trade associations, but they are no match for the PACs' power; indeed PACs have grown in number, scope, and power in the years since Nader became prominent (Wertheimer, 1980:605–7; Cohen, 1980). And Common Cause may slow down the various other interest groups and force them to restrict somewhat the means they resort to, but there are no indications that Common Cause has put any of them out of business.

What about the notion that interest groups can contain each other, either through a proper system of checks and balances or through the mere existence of a multitude of interests pulling the polity and policies in divergent directions? James Madison suggested this approach in Federalist Paper 51:

> It is of great importance in a republic not only to guard against the oppression of its rulers, but also to guard one part of the society against the injustice of the other part. . . . Whilst all authority in it [the federal government] will be derived from and dependent on the society, the society itself will be broken into so many parts, interests and classes of citizens, that the rights of individuals, or of the minority, will be in little danger from interested combinations of the majority.[13]

This position is in line with Whig social philosophy, which has acquired a rising following in recent years.[14] New Whigs, as we have shown elsewhere (Etzioni, 1982), have extended to many neoeconomic areas, from community relationships to courtship, Adam Smith's notion of an invisible hand guiding the actors, each seeking his or her own well-being, to a harmonious and productive totality.

This position conflicts sharply, however, with the social science conclusion that such contests of egos or subcommunities—"actors" or units—need to be contained in a capsule or community sustained by *its own* processes and not reliant on the contesting parties. Moral commitment (e.g., to playing by the rules), sentiments (e.g., reflecting the values of the community), and shared institutions (e.g., the Constitution) are among the most often listed foundations of the unity in which wholesome diversity is possible. When the capsule is well protected, we have competition, which is bounded conflict. Without the capsule, we have unlimited conflict, catch as catch can.

Émile Durkheim's empirical and theoretical work is largely dedicated to showing that even in the economic realm, "contracting" parties (akin to the SIGs because of the limited scope of contracts) need "pre-contractual" links. Talcott Parsons' work, *The Structure of Social Action,* is devoted to elaborating the same point. And Adam Smith himself dedicated to it a volume—*The Theory of Moral Sentiments*—in which he stressed the importance of the "fellow feeling" people have for each other as the basis of human happiness. Even in *The Wealth of Nations* he argued for the government to establish and enforce the rules of the economic game, including protection of the marketplace from "monopolistic businessmen."

My own work has provided additional evidence for the view that human nature is not merely calculative-utilitarian-rationalist, but a combination of such elements with ethical commitments and sentiments.[15] A comparative study of four attempts to build union among nations illustrated the significance of the presence versus the absence of the community-capsule.[16]

One situation in which self-containment (interest groups limiting each other without outside, "system" forces) seems not to work is that in which a group acting mainly as a SIG has a decisive role in a narrow field and faces no other interest groups as it deeply, often covertly, affects legislation, regulation, public policy and programs. Nursing home owners, for example, were directly involved in writing the regulations which were to regulate them,[17] and for years they faced few countervailing groups. The same holds for the American Medical Association on many health issues, the real estate lobby on many housing matters, etc. Michael T. Hayes puts it well, in a critique of Bauer, Pool, and Dexter. He says that their "sanguine" view of interest groups is based on two unfounded assumptions, that one-sided pressure is the exception rather than the rule, and that the legislative process does not respond to groups' demands but only determines the ground rules for group struggle.[18] A similar point was made previously by Theodore J. Lowi (1964).

In areas in which several interest groups do clash, they often deflect public policy in a direction they share. This phenomenon was observed in a 1930 study of pressure groups and tariffs, which found the field dominated by domestic producers seeking different—but all increased—duties (Schattschneider, 1935); those who would have benefitted from lower duties were unrepresented. More recently, it has been observed that all the military lobbies favor hardware and "big ticket" items. While they vie with each other over who gets what, maintenance and human resources—not supported by any lobby—tend to lose out (Digby, 1977; Fallows, 1981).

If one agrees that mutual containment is not to be relied upon and sees a need to contain interest groups without abolishing them, one is ready to consider the third approach, external limitations, and ask how this might be achieved. This could be achieved if one could enhance the forces that sustain the political system and make it less vulnerable to interest group pressure, forces which range from education to shared and national values to institutions that are responsive to changing circumstances and relations within the community. However, these factors are slow to change and not highly responsive to public policy.

More immediately, specific measure can be undertaken to curb interest groups, without attempting to suppress them or to violate the constitutional rights of those involved. These measures include sharper separation of legitimate and illegitimate means (e.g., currently an interest group cannot legally pay fees to members of Congress who serve its interest, but it can pay them a very large amount—such as $10,000— for a very brief lecture); reduction of the means defined as legitimate (e.g., public financing of congressional campaigns coupled with strict prohibition of private contributions to or on behalf of the candidate); making the political institutions less vulnerable (e.g., four-year terms in the House instead of two); lobby registry, requiring a government employee to register in a publicly accessible record any calls from a lobbyist, among others.

Each one of these means has been challenged. Public financing is said to increase the number of candidates beyond reason, and promote candidates who do not have the valuable experience of having to raise funds. Longer terms may make the relations with lobbyists closer, certainly more lasting. Disclosure is said to violate the freedom of speech of the lobbyists, and so on.

Let me grant that these limiting measures may raise many problems, and that some might well be found, on additional examination, to be worse than the problem they seek to cure. My purpose here is to point to the need for such measures, not to determine which are the most suitable. However, I see no reason to accept the notion that as long as interest groups do nothing illegal, there is no need to curb them. First of all, any component may grow to the point that it unbalances a system and hence needs to be cut back, regardless of why or how it grew so disproportional. Second, the interest groups have used their power to legalize many of their practices; this does not mean that their acts have grown compatible with a viable democratic polity.

While measures such as these would curb all interest groups, they would especially curb SIGs, as there seems to be a high correlation between the attributes that define SIGs and a predisposition to act overtly. CROs, because of their wide base, can use both electoral channels and lobbying; therefore they benefit most from the overt means best suited to mobilization of the electorate. The opposite holds for SIGs: the more their acts are visible to the electorate the less they will carry the day; hence their proclivity for covert acts, at least for acts low in visibility. It follows that to the extent reforms successfully curb the use of illegal and unethical means, they will have a greater effect on organizations that typically function as SIGs, and have a smaller effect on those more like CROs. The tendency of many PIGs to rely on litigation is of interest in this context (Orren, 1976). Litigation, on the face of it, is legal and out in the open.

Strengthening the political parties is probably the single most important step to contain interest groups. Stronger parties seem to be the only force that realistically can be expected to stand up to interest groups on a continuous basis, as distinct from sporadic muckracking and reform movements.

David Cohen, a former president of Common Cause, has suggested several measures to rebuild the parties, including giving them some control over the campaign financing of candidates, issuing *party* reports on the voting records of members of Congress, and prohibiting crossovers in primaries (1979:19–22). Probably a strong revival would come only as part of a more general reconstruction of American institutions, inasmuch as the parties lost their following at the same time as other institutions, from labor unions to churches.

A renewal of the power of political parties will countervail all interest groups, but it too will curb SIGs more than CROs, because a CRO can more readily work inside political parties. Compare the role of the AFL-CIO in the Democratic Party to that of small, splinter labor groups.

Finally, it would help if the distinction between constituency-representing organizations and special interest groups gained currency in the media and the public mind, so that the public stopped treating the two as interchangeable or as equals. This would diminish the legitimacy of SIGs, or groups on the SIG end of the spectrum.

Conclusion

In sum, elimination of interest groups is neither feasible nor functional, and self-containment is not sufficient. Sustaining and building up community and containing, not suppressing, interest groups will help maintain the balance between interest groups and the polity, and it will favor CROs over SIGs, also to the benefit of this balance.

It seems that in the same period in which interest groups grew in scope, number, and power—and the narrower, more dysfunctional type, SIGs, rose more compared with broader CRO-like organizations—the political system's bonds and institutions weakened. The consequences have been variously described as a "stalemated" system, unable to form consensus on public policy; an "overloaded" system, unable to cope with the volume of decisions which must be made; a system that had lost competence and, hence, trust and legitimacy; and an inflationary system, one that had to draw down its economic assets in order to try to satisfy a great number of voracious groups with little commitment to the commonweal. Those concerned with the system's future would do well to look for ways to contain interest groups, especially SIGs, and for ways to strengthen the national bonds and institutional competence.

Notes

1. *Public Opinion,* December/January 1980, p. 42. Data represent the average confidence in nine major institutions.
2. *Public Opinion,* October/November 1979, p. 32.
3. This point is also made by Jeane Jordan Kirkpatrick, *Dismantling the Parties,* Washington, DC: American Enterprise Institute, 1978, especially p. 21.
4. Jeffrey M. Berry, *Lobbying for the People: The Political Behavior of Public Interest Groups,* Princeton, NJ: Princeton University Press, 1977. Cf. the suggestion that public interest groups are by and large anti-business, by David Vogel, "The Public Interest Movement and the American Reform Tradition," *Political Science Quarterly,* Vol. 95 (Winter 1980–81), pp. 607 ff.
5. See Berry, op. cit., p. 7. See also Irving Louis Horowitz, "Beyond Democracy: Interest Groups and the Patriotic Gore," *The Humanist,* September/October 1979, pp. 4–10. Also see Andrew S. McFarland, *Public Interest Lobbies,*

Washington, D.C.: American Enterprise Institute, 1976, pp. 25ff.

6. A case might be made that it is a CRO. To determine whether it is a CRO or a SIG may require a study of its conduct.

7. Vol. 7, p. 490.

8. Ibid.

9. *The Windfall Profits Tax: A Comparative Analysis of Two Bills*, Washington, DC: Congressional Budget Office, 1979, p. xvii.

10. Comparisons require taking into account differences in the size of the groups involved. E.g., a $37.5 billion reduction in the marriage penalty is distributed among many more people than the $11.8 billion concession to oil drillers.

11. *Business Week*, March 3, 1980.

12. John Gardner, unpublished speech, March 17, 1980.

13. Alexander Hamilton, James Madison and John Jay, *The Federalist*, Avon, CT: Heritage Press, 1945, 1973, pp. 349–50.

14. For a fine treatment of the earlier Whigs, see G. H. Guttridge, *English Whiggism and the American Revolution*, Berkeley: University of California Press, 1942.

15. This position is spelled out and documented in Amitai Etzioni, *A Comparative Analysis of Complex Organizations*, revised edition, New York: Free Press, 1975.

16. Amitai Etzioni, *Political Unification: A Comparative Study of Leaders and Forces*, Troy, Mo.: Holt, Rinehart & Winston, 1965. See also, especially, the discussion of self-encapsulation in *The Active Society: A Theory of Societal and Political Processes*, New York: Free Press, 1968, pp. 586ff.

17. Subcommittee on Long-Term Care, Special Committee on Aging, "Nursing Home Care in the United States: Failure in Public Policy, Introductory Report," November 1974, pp. 49, 67.

18. "Semi-Sovereign Pressure Groups," *Journal of Politics*, Vol. 40 (1978), p. 139. Reference is to Raymond A. Bauer et al., *American Business and Public Policy*, 2nd ed., Chicago: Aldine-Atherton, 1972.

References

Bell, Daniel
1975   "The revolution of rising entitlements." *Fortune*
        (April):100.
Bentley, Arthur F.
1967   *The Process of Government*. Cambridge, MA: Belknap
        Press, Harvard University Press.
Berelson, Bernard, Paul F. Lazarsfeld, and William N.
        McPhee
1954   *Voting: A Study of Opinion Formation in a Presidential
        Campaign*. Chicago: University of Chicago Press.
Berger, Suzanne
1981   "Interest groups and the governability of European
        society." *Items*, SSRC 35(December):64.
Bethell, Tom
1980   "Taking a hard look at Common Cause." *New York
        Times Magazine*, (August 24):44.
Borum, Joan
1981   "Wage increases in 1980 outpaced by inflation."
        Monthly Labor Review (May):55.
Cohen, David
1979   "Reviving the political parties," *In Common* (Fall):
        19–22.
Cohen, Richard
1980   "The business lobby discovers that in unity there is
        strength." *National Journal* (June 28): 1050–1055.
Dennis, Jack
1975   "Trends in public support for the American party sys-
        tem." *British Journal of Political Science* 5:187–230.
Digby, James F.
1977   "New weapons technology and its impact on interven-
        tion." Pp. 121–135 in E. P. Stern (ed.), *The Limits of
        Military Intervention*. Beverly Hills, CA: Sage.
Etzioni, Amitai
1965   *Political Unification*. Troy, Mo.: Holt, Rinehart &
        Winston.
1982   *An Immodest Agenda*. New York: McGraw-Hill.

1984 *Capital Corruption.* Orlando, Fla.: Harcourt Brace
       Jovanovich.
Fallows, James
1981 *National Defense.* New York: Random House.
Friedman, Milton
[1962] 1982 *Capitalism and Freedom.* Chicago: University of
       Chicago Press.
Haas, E. B.
1958 *The Uniting of Europe.* Stanford, CA: Stanford Uni-
       versity Press.
Hall, D. R.
1969 *Cooperative Lobbying: The Power of Pressure.* Tucson,
       AZ: University of Arizona Press.
Harris, Louis
1982 "Alienation." *The Harris Survey,* February 18.
Katz, Elihu and Paul F. Lazarsfeld
1955 *Personal Influence.* New York: Free Press.
Ladd, Everett Carll
1980 "How to tame the special interest groups." *Fortune*
       (October 20):66–80.
1981 "205 and going strong." *Public Opinion* (June/
       July):8.
Lazarsfeld, Paul F., Bernard Berelson, and Hazel Gaudet
1948 *The People's Choice.* New York: Columbia University
       Press.
Lipset, S. M., Martin Trow, and James Coleman
1956 *Union Democracy.* New York: Free Press.
Lowi, Theodore J.
1964 "American business, public policy case studies, and
       political theory." *World Politics* 16:677–715.
1969 *The End of Liberalism.* New York: Norton.
McManus, Michael J.
1976 " . . . In the face of dire economic necessity." *Empire
       State Report* 2(9):344.
Michels, Robert
1958 *Political Parties.* New York: Free Press.
Milbrath, Lester
1963 *The Washington Lobbyists.* Chicago: Rand McNally.

Olson, Mancur, Jr.
  1965   *The Logic of Collective Action.* Cambridge, MA:
         Harvard University Press.
Olson, Mancur, Jr., Robert H. Salisbury, and Thomas A. Reilly
  1969   "An exchange theory of interest groups." *Midwest
         Journal of Political Science* 13:1–32.
Ornstein, Norman J. and Shirley Elder
  1978   *Interest Groups, Lobbying, and Policy Making.* Washing-
         ton, D.C.: Congressional Quarterly Press.
Orren, Karen
  1976   "Standing to sue: interest group conflict in the fed-
         eral courts." *American Political Science Review* 70:723–
         741.
Riesman, David, et al.
  1953   *The Lonely Crowd.* New York: Doubleday.
Schattschneider, E. E.
  1935   *Politics, Pressures and the Tariff.* New York: Atherton.
Schucker, Jill
  1976   "The energy concerns of New England." P. 13 in
         Edward J. Mitchell (ed.), *Energy: Regional Goals and
         the National Interest.* Washington, D.C.: American
         Enterprise Institute.
Truman, David B.
  1951   *The Governmental Process: Political Interests and Public
         Opinion.* New York: Knopf.
Verba, Sidney and Gabriel Almond
  1965   *The Civic Culture: Political Attitudes and Democracy in
         Five Nations.* Boston: Little, Brown.
Wertheimer, Fred
  1980   "The PAC phenomenon in American politics." *Ari-
         zona Law Review* 22:605–607.
Wilson, James Q.
  1973   *Political Organizations.* New York: Basic Books.
Zeigler, Harmon
  1964   *Interest Groups in American Society.* Englewood Cliffs,
         NJ: Prentice-Hall.

The Fight
Against Fraud and Abuse:
Analyzing Constituent Support

This is the true story of an attempt to introduce into three government agencies—including the White House—a social science perspective to abet the valiant but so far quite futile drive to combat fraud and abuse. The story is modest enough. I was quite unsuccessful in gaining acceptance for the perspective I advocated. Therein lies a lesson, actually several lessons. At issue is why fraud and abuse have both yielded so little ground to so many drives against them. What are the underlying causes of fraud and abuse?

If they are systematically overlooked, as I claim is the rule, what are the reasons? And how might these reasons be overcome?

The Theater of Reform: Nursing Homes

I was minding my own business at Columbia University in 1975 when Gus Tyler, a labor union intellectual and friend, called to say that he had recommended that I use my social science training to help a new commission about to be announced. In the preceding weeks, the *New York Times* had run a series of exposés of serious and pervasive abuses in nursing homes. Even before these appeared, a book on these problems, entitled *Tender Loving Greed*, had stirred public interest.[1] Local TV and radio stations played the story for all it

Note: This essay was originally published in *Journal of Policy Analysis and Management*, 1982, 2(1), 26–38. Copyright © 1982 by John Wiley & Sons, Inc. Reprinted with permission. I am indebted to Mary Pockman for editorial assistance and to Ann MacDonald and Paul Jargowsky for research assistance.

was worth. When a flamboyant but persistent assemblyman, Andrew Stein, drew on this wave of interest to challenge New York's Governor Hugh Carey, the governor found it wise to look into the charges against the nursing homes. He appointed a special prosecutor to study the allegations and launched a special state commission to investigate the underlying causes and suggest generic cures. (The commission was to turn over to the special prosecutor, conveniently located nearby, any specific instances of "wrong-doing" it came across, so it could concentrate on the underlying forces and correctives.)

To head the commission, the governor appointed Morris B. Abram, a trial lawyer who had served as a U.S. representative to the U.N. Commission on Human Rights and had once run unsuccessfully for the U.S. Senate. Other commissioners included another lawyer and close associate of the chairman, a black woman activist, a WASP Republican woman from Rochester, and a Jewish physician from New York City. As is customary, the commissioners were to meet occasionally, a few hours a month; but under my direction the staff was going to do much of the work.

It soon became quite evident that there were two conflicting major strategies, one favored by the commission's lawyers, the other by a lone sociologist, me. These strategies deserve attention, because similar differences of approach are often encountered, implicitly or explicitly, in drives of the sort that the commission was to undertake.

The strategy favored by the lawyers was to conduct hearings and some staff research to form recommendations as to how the laws and regulations concerning nursing homes might be changed. One problem, for instance, was with overbilling by nursing home owners. When owners were caught by the government, in the act of overbilling, restitution was expected, but it was by no means commonly achieved. Nursing home owners could tie up the state in courts for years, and they could charge their legal expenses to taxpayers by adding them to the costs of their services, to be reimbursed by the government. If convicted, nursing home owners could sometimes avoid restitution by closing in New York only to reopen in New Jersey. The commission's lawyers suggested that the appropriate law should be changed so that the state agencies involved could levy interest charges on these funds until restitution was made.

The conception underlying this approach seemed so self-evident to the lawyers that it was not often explicitly discussed: Better law enforcement would be achieved if penalties for violations were higher. Greater penalties would serve both to rehabilitate abusers and to deter other potential abusers. Most of the recommendations the commission finally made were in line with this punitive-deterrent approach.

Even less often articulated and discussed—at least at first—was how to achieve the desired changes in laws, regulations, and enforcement procedures. Some heated late-night debates elicited from the commission's lawyers the theory as to where the forces of change are, and how they can be tapped. The main torchbearer was to be the public at large, whose irate drumfire was going to be kept at high pitch during a series of dramatic hearings the commission planned, hearings during which abused patients were to be rolled out in wheelchairs, and notorious nursing home owners were to be exposed. As a result, it was expected that the public was going to "demand action" and the governor "could not but respond," "as he has repeatedly promised," by supporting the legislative reforms that the commission was to unveil at the end of its appointed nine months of labor. (At one point the commission's chairman announced publicly that "his hearing on political interference in the nursing home scandals will be so revealing that lawmakers will have to pass his ethics proposals.")[2]

From the depth of my utterly theoretical background, I could not have agreed less. I had never held public office before, never run an investigation before. I was armed with a social science perspective evolved over a decade and a half studying American society, and a theory spelled out best in my book *The Active Society*.[3]

My brief was as follows. The public is a fickle ally. About the only thing you can be sure of is that it will soon turn elsewhere. Once deserted by the public, the commission (and the governor) would be alone in facing the well-heeled nursing home lobby. The commission had to use its term to fashion not merely the reforms but also the power base to support them.

One possibility was to take a leaf from the book of the National Association for Retarded Children, which in those days was raising hell about the warehousing of retarded children in state institutions. The association was not only demanding the passage of reform bills; it was monitoring their implementation, a little matter many reformers overlook. Its persistence led ultimately to the deinstitutionalization of thousands of children to homes and community centers. The commission, I suggested, could help form an association of people whose parents were in nursing homes to fill a similar role.

On consultation with people who had long worked in the field, however, I eventually concluded that this strategy was impractical. Most people who leave their elders in nursing homes, experience suggests, seem to be insufficiently motivated to act on their behalf. A secondary consideration was that the National Association for Retarded Children was widely considered a nuisance, if not a "menace," because of its often confrontational attitude; the state bureaucrats did not exactly look forward to dealing with another association of the same ilk. After all, the commission had to have the governor's support for its conclusions.

Accordingly, my main recommendation was to rely on existing power groups with an interest or commitment on the side of nursing home reform, such as the Grey Panthers, associations of social workers, and the major ethnic religious groups. Draw them to participate in formulating the commission's recommendations, so that they would consider the recommendations theirs as well as ours. Help create a pro-reform coalition of these groups by establishing a nursing home reform advisory board composed of their representatives. Recommend the formation of a permanent commission composed of these representatives.

Although these groups are often called interest groups, this term does not characterize them well. It brings to mind groups dedicated only to the well-being of their members and preoccupied with their pocketbooks. The groups listed here, however, are often quite dedicated to a view of the public interest that is above and beyond the interest of their members. For instance, though such groups had very few black members, they were often quite active on behalf of minority rights. And they were concerned with a multiplicity of needs and values, not merely pecuniary ones. Most important from the viewpoint of the issue at hand, these groups had organized memberships, political representation in Albany (in effect their own lobbyists), and a lasting ability to support public policies they believed in.

The suggested permanent commission would be expected to issue an annual statement on the condition of nursing homes in the state. Its members and staff would have the right of unlimited visits to nursing homes, typically denied to outsiders. It would also be the guardian of last resort for incompetent patients with no next of kin, both in order to protect them from the abuses that are common when nursing home owners are made guardians and to increase the occasions for nursing home visits by representatives of the commission. Finally, long after our temporary commission had been dissolved, the permanent commission could recommend additional reforms as needed and marshal support for them among its constituent groups.

I visited informally with some representatives of these groups and found interest in the general approach, broad knowledge about the problems of the nursing homes, and many specific ideas for reforms.

After lengthy debates with the commission's lawyers about these two approaches, and after a vain attempt to follow both simultaneously, the lawyers' strategy was adopted. Feeling that the commission might do little good and probably some inadvertent harm (by dissipating the steam that had been built up in the reform drive), I resigned. The commission held to its course and after a series of dramatic hearings (including a midnight visit, with TV cameras, to a nursing home) it reported eleven recommendations. Ten of these

involved fairly innocuous changes in the law. Some were marginally useful, some irrelevant. One, for example, allowed
class actions by nursing home patients against owners. Class
actions are a useful tool for consumers but not for nursing
home residents, who are under the owners' control, often
unable to move to another home, and dependent on the
home for nursing care and even food. (Though the law was
passed, no suit has ever been brought under its provisions.)

The eleventh suggestion was a bombshell. It would
have prohibited the members of the New York legislature
from being on the payroll or receiving "retainers" from the
nursing home industry. Specifically, it would have barred legislators from representing clients before state agencies. State
legislators serve part-time in most states and they usually do
have outside work. The nursing home lobby was believed to
have many New York state legislators on retainer.

By the time the commission's recommendations
reached the governor—and through him, the legislature—
the nursing home scandal had moved from an almost daily
appearance on page one to an occasional mention in fillers
on the back pages. The investigative reporter who started it
all had left the *New York Times*. The media and the public
were deeply immersed in a new issue that was even more
breathtaking, the New York city financial crisis. The New York
state legislature passed ten of the eleven proposed reforms;
predictably, number eleven was left out.[4] Morris Abram, the
commission's head, observed that he expected another nursing home scandal would erupt within five or ten years. The
New York Times, reporting his observations, added, "Indeed,
the structure of the industry remains what it was, and the cast
of characters is only slightly different."[5] The reporter who
had helped to start it all, returning to survey the industry,
summarized his findings with the statement, "Literally, it is
business as usual in the nursing homes."[6]

Why call this and other such developments the theater
of reform? Because much of the drama is staged for the benefit of an audience, the public, and much thought and effort
go into keeping it engrossing ("newsworthy"), but it results in
few if any real changes in the world behind the stage sets.

The Deaf in Dialogue

In the years that followed the nursing home drama, I had another opportunity to try to gain support for real change, based on social science considerations, in the approach to fraud and abuse, first at the General Accounting Office (GAO), an arm of Congress, and then at the Office of Management and Budget (OMB), part of the White House. With variations on the theme, I took the same fundamental position I had taken in the nursing homes case. The outcomes too proved similar.

At GAO

When people from two different academic or intellectual disciplines attempt to engage in dialogue, they must reconcile themselves to the fact that each discipline makes its own distinctive assumptions about the nature of the universe it deals with and how it functions. These assumptions are so "basic" to the members of the discipline, so firmly built into their concepts, that they are either unaware of them in daily intercourse or unwilling to deal with them explicitly. Economists, for instance, tend to assume that people are basically rational in their behavior, which is not what psychoanalysts assume.

When I tried to suggest to the senior members of the GAO, an agency set up by Congress to investigate "all matters relating to the receipt, disbursement, and application of public funds,"[7] that they use systems analysis to ferret out the root causes of fraud and abuse and to build preventive systems, I ran into just such a difference in perspective, rooted in what Veblen termed "trained incapacity." The accountants and investigators who dominate GAO, as well as the efficiency experts and economists who back them up, are expertly trained to look at the world through their particular lenses, which makes it more difficult for them than for a lay person to see it the way a political scientist or sociologist or social psychologist would see it.

The first reaction to my suggestion to use systems analysis was an open puzzle. That, I was told, had already been done. One of the GAO's main achievements over the last years, according to the agency's heads, had been to shift from transaction-by-transaction auditing to a systems analysis of the subject agencies' control and verification procedures, and beyond that to program evaluation and analysis.[8] This was the reason investigators were supplemented with auditors, and auditors with economists and efficiency experts— indeed the reason a whole division, Program Analysis, was created. Moreover, it was made clear to me that I did not appreciate how difficult it was for systems analysis to gain acceptance in a world of investigators and transaction-by-transaction auditors; indeed, the shift was still far from fully legitimated or embraced.

After considerable discussion, it gradually became clear that while we were all talking about systems analysis, we had rather different kinds of systems analysis in mind. The most progressive thinkers in GAO were thinking in terms of *administrative* systems, composed of management procedures, control mechanisms, and verification overlays. I was thinking about *constituency* systems (or power constellations) and their dynamics. Thus, a GAO person proudly pointed to their idea of using social security information to locate runaway fathers, a step that promises to reduce the cost of welfare, inasmuch as the largest item of the welfare budget was aid to families with dependent children. I had no trouble with the technical validity of the idea, but I wondered if it took into account the very strong commitment of most Americans against such use of data banks. One of the few themes shared by liberals and conservatives is a commitment to the privacy of information that a citizen voluntarily provides the government; to use social security information against a citizen in a welfare program might amount to self-incrimination. In the case at hand, I wondered if it was practical to ignore these feelings.

OMB and the IGs

The GAO did not appear particularly keen to take on a second line of systems analysis before it had completed adopting the first. Nobody denied my arguments about the need to back up the first line of analysis with the second, but neither did anybody seem eager to add to their existing load. The newly appointed Inspectors General (IGs) seemed a more promising audience. In each of the twelve federal agencies, an IG was charged, under legislation passed by Congress in 1978, with conducting and supervising audits and investigations in order to "promote economy, efficiency, and effectiveness" and, specifically, "to prevent and detect fraud and abuse."

The IGs were to report to two higher authorities: the Department of Justice and OMB. I assumed Justice would be the more deeply attuned to the punish-and-deter view, so I turned to OMB. There I had several amicable discussions with the assistant director charged with management improvement and evaluation, as well as with members of his staff. The meetings were followed by memos explicating the concept of constituency analysis, which elicited responses that would flatter the uninitiated. The ideas, it seemed, were "worthwhile," "interesting," and "valuable," but there were reasons why OMB would not, could not, act on the matter. There was a rivalry between OMB and Justice, especially the FBI, over who would control how much of the drive against fraud and abuse. And OMB's leaders were not sure the president was really very keen to do much in this area. Constituency analysis, as seen through the eyes of the professional bureaucrat, appeared "too political," more than a career civil servant could be expected to handle.

A perusal of the IG's semiannual reports provided no evidence of any concern with constituency analysis. Apart from organizational matters, the reports were dedicated largely to accounts of punish-and-deter drives; these usually had yielded relatively little.

For instance, the much touted Project Integrity, a computerized search for dishonest Medicaid doctors and druggists, "yielded 25 indictments, 8 convictions, and nearly $3 million in claims for restitution of government funds, plus other savings."[9] The sum of $3 million could hardly be noticed in the multibillion dollar program, and the possibility that a considerable part of even that sum would actually be collected appeared slight. Two observers concluded simply: "Recent Justice Department figures indicate that referrals for fraud prosecution have not increased, despite the existence of the 12 new Inspectors General."[10]

The next port of call was the Inspectors General themselves. Three of the twelve were reputed to be particularly able. One of them, with powers of inspection over the Department of Health, Education and Welfare (HEW), had at his command 1,024 positions, most filled with accountants and investigators trained—like their counterparts at GAO—in a perspective quite different from that of social science. Of all the positions, 24 were set aside for "systems analysts"; 14 of these were actually staffed. The small number of posts assigned to the function suggested something of its perceived importance. The composition of the staff was even more revealing. It included one physician, two lawyers, some accountants, several business school graduates, and an operations analyst.

The position profile does not do full justice to the issue, though. Some of those not assigned to systems analysis might actually do it. Indeed, as one accountant put it, "accountants are expected, by the tenets of their profession, to do systems analysis." Asked "But do they do it?" his response—"well . . ."—was far from reassuring. Moreover, whatever systems analysis they do tends to be of the administrative, not the constituency, type. And their organizational culture, as my accountant agreed, tends to promote "head hunting and dollar hunting."

An Inspector General further explained to me that the IGs were aware of the constituency problem but did not see it as their responsibility. He cited the IG statute as saying they should act "without regard to political affiliation," and he capped it all by observing: "We are not Common Cause."

The IG assigned to the Labor Department was quick to grasp the significance of constituency analysis and hoped to use it in the future. It was at Labor that I came upon yet another affirmation of the need for that approach, in an exploration of the forces behind the continued fraud and abuse in the program on pneumoconiosis (black lung disease). The Department of Labor determines what benefits are due to coal miners afflicted by black lung disease. Benefits are due to coal miners who are found to be totally disabled by the illness as a result of employment in the coal mines. Prior to 1977, few claims were approved and paid, because of strict requirements for the evidence needed to establish "total disability," "pneumoconiosis," and the status of "coal miner." During the period 1973–1978, only 7% of the claims were approved and a total of $78 million was paid in benefits.[11]

In 1977, Congress amended the law to relax the standard. In doing so it was prodded by members of Congress who represented states where coal mining is a big and growing business. Under the amendments, the status of "coal miner" was extended to include people who did not actually work in a coal mine but "around" one, such as truck drivers and construction workers. Most telling, physicians specially trained to interpret X-rays for the presence of black lung were prohibited from performing that function, except to determine acceptable film quality.[12]

Following these amendments the approval rate jumped to 40%, and $718 million was paid out in one year alone, fiscal year 1980. (The figure reflects both new claims and the reprocessing of some previously denied ones.) This led to outcries in Congress and the media about abuses of the program and eventually to some tightening of the standards.

The underlying force in the relaxation of standards was the pressure by the miners' union, many of whose members had come to claim black lung benefits as a part of their retirement rights, whether they had black lung or not. The root of the problem was clearly not poor enforcement of the law by Labor, or even congressionally "mandated waste," but the pressure of the coal miner constituency.

Obviously, there were ways to approach the black lung problem other than simply increasing the efforts to root out fraud, an approach that constituent groups were almost certain to block. One possibility was to consider increasing retirement benefits for all miners based on the risks of working underground. But that possibility, though reasonable on its face, has not been fully explored.

We did not do much better at Agriculture in exploring with its Inspector General what to do about school lunches. The school lunch program, which dished out more than $3 billion a year before the Reagan administration cut it, provides meals to some 27 million pupils a year, in 94,000 schools and institutions.[13] Lunches are either free, or are available at reduced prices, depending on the income of the parents. To establish children's eligibility, they or their parents must fill out forms indicating family income. There tends to be a great deal of fudging and inaccuracy in the income reports. Government audits estimate that more than 25% of the applications misrepresented families' incomes enough to result in their receiving more benefits than they were entitled to. Another 8.2% of those declared eligible for free meals or meals at reduced prices had no applications on file or provided information on their applications that was manifestly contradictory or that disqualified the applicant.[14]

Schools are reluctant to verify the applications, preferring instead to serve free lunches to "ineligible" children. "School principals," notes a representative of the American Association of School Administrators, "are not suited to make welfare determinations by either training or temperament. The nature of their professional inclinations causes them to err on the side of leniency."[15] In addition, schools found it attractive to divert some of the lunch funds for other purposes. Audits found that nearly half (45.5%) of the schools reported inaccurate meal counts. Some schools claimed the maximum number of free lunches served every day, despite any absences, so that they were paid federal funds for meals that students not in the program had already paid for.[16] Other sources of inflated meal counts include meals prepared but not served, meals served to teachers, and *a la carte* meals, none of which qualify for federal reimbursement. There followed wave upon wave of local audits and investigations, finding high "error rates" and abuses, leading the media and Congress to cry for greater school scrutiny.

Various administrative fixes have been suggested. In October 1979, the Assessment, Improvement and Monitoring System (AIMS) was proposed, which would require state agencies to monitor food programs more closely, through regular periodic reviews. This proposal met with widespread opposition from state agencies, the "Child Nutrition Coalition," food service firms, and others. Leading the many complaints was the suggestion that AIMS would create much more paperwork.

Working with the IG at Agriculture, I tried to chart the major constituencies involved. They turned out to include a surprisingly large and complicated array of groups, but four stood out.

First and foremost was the food industry, especially the food processors and the manufacturers of frozen foods, the "producers" of the lunches.

Second, the farm lobby was obviously keenly interested. The school lunch program was enacted in 1946 as a way of helping to dispose of surplus agricultural production. It is estimated that in one year alone, 1975, over $2 billion worth of food was used by the program.[17] The farm lobby was concerned mainly with maintaining the flow of products—much less with who exactly used them. But that did not stop the members of Congress representing farming districts from beating on the Department of Agriculture bureaucrats for their failure to prevent fraud and abuse in the program.

Equally predictable was the position of liberal, urban, and minority groups, which favored the program as a way to channel food to their constituents and fought attempts at extensive policing ("so what if some *near*-poor get a free lunch?").

Much less in the public eye, but not far behind the others in power, was the American School Food Service Association, whose members for a quarter of a century had run the school-lunch program and protected the regime of laxity surrounding it. They were one of those narrow-focus interest groups with good contacts in the state capitols, and among governors and congressional delegations. They were not seeking to line their own pockets but to use school lunch monies for other school expenditures, such as buying uniforms and balls for the schools' basketball teams. They also saw in the imposition of a stronger accounting scheme high administrative costs for them, invasion of the privacy of pupils and their families, and a demand to label some kids as poor.

Some obvious alternatives to the tightening of the regulations commended themselves, alternatives that were much more sensitive to the constituency problem. For example, using census data on the Standard Metropolitan Statistical Areas (SMSAs) in which schools were located, and whatever other data were available, schools could be scored according to the composite economic status of their pupils rather than "scoring" the pupils individually. Each school could then be given a lump sum for school lunches based on the proportion of students deemed entitled to free and reduced-price lunches. The rest—how much they wished to collect from whom—would be up to each school, including their use of funds they saved. There would be no opportunity to falsify the data in order to enhance the school's allotments, as the data to be used would not be under the control or influence of the school. And the federal government would save the costs of compliance, auditing, and investigation, as there would no longer be individual applications or even school expenditure audits. The school administrators could be expected to support such a reform strongly, because it would give them greater flexibility in the use of the funds and reduce the paperwork involved. The farm lobby could live with it, because it would require no cut in the use of commodities. The urban groups would probably be least sanguine about it, because it would leave local authorities much freedom to determine the allocation of the funds, while they felt national determinations would be better for their followers.

Before the details of the proposal were worked out, let alone formally recommended and tried, the elections brought a new president who, despite the previous notion that the Inspectors General were nonpolitical appointees, fired them all in one day. I left the White House to return to academe. In the months that followed, fighting fraud and abuse was not given a high priority.

A Social Science Perspective

Among the most valuable contributions of the social sciences are ways of thinking and acting in the social and personal realms that are more realistic and more effective than those provided by religion, secular ideologies, or natural science, let alone "common sense."

Systems Theory as a Perspective

With New York's investigative commission on nursing homes and with GAO and OMB, the idea that I urged on the government, elementary to social scientists, has at its root the insight provided by systems theory. The essence of systems theory is that changes introduced in one factor, the " independent" variable, cannot "predict" the consequences, the effects on another factor (the "dependent" variable), at least not in the way that cause and effect appear to be related by common sense, or by historians who belong to the school of challenge and response, or by the psychologists of stimulus and response. The social and personal worlds are governed by multiple factors that all relate to each other, making up the system. Hence, to understand what effect changes in one factor will have on another requires understanding the "place" of the two factors in the system, their relationships to the other factors that also are members of the system. What to the uninitiated are "unanticipated consequences" of initiatives are typically the work of other factors that have been overlooked by tunnel vision but that have a chance of being seen by the systems analyst.

After the nursing home drama in New York, I had not thought much about the use of systems theory to combat fraud and abuse, until I read about the legislation (Public Law 95-452) that set up the Offices of Inspector General. The bill contains not a hint of why fraud and abuse exist in the first place, or why they persist in the face of numerous attempts to go after them. Its implied foundation, confirmed by interviews with the congressional staff members who helped draft the bill, was the assumption that sending more auditors and investigators after the malefactors would reduce the problem.

The Limits of the Enforcer Approach

The enforcer approach relies on two closely linked conceptions: punishment and deterrence. It seeks to ferret out and punish those who engage in fraud and abuse, on the somewhat simple notion that if there are more crooks in jail, there will be fewer loose. The catch is that the government's work involves billions of transactions each month. Criminals and other abusers obviously have a high incentive to conceal their acts, which further swells the work of the enforcers. Moreover, the transgressors are entitled to due process in court or in administrative hearings.

Hence to catch them one by one and dispose of each case is a monumental and thankless task. It is safe to assume that even with a beefed-up force of auditors and investigators the net number of transgressions may be reduced very little. This is a lesson implied in the fact that for a long period, as more people were sent to jail, crime rates refused to fall.

Enter deterrence, the other half of the catch-and-punish-them approach. It assumes that for every one caught and punished, there will be scores of others who will take heed.

There is a well-known reason this approach often does not work: the smallness of the penalty and the low probability of having to face it. In many fields of law enforcement—nursing homes, drug traffic, white collar crime—the abuser is unlikely to be caught; if caught he is often not convicted, and if convicted, he often does not serve the sentence imposed or pay the fine. FBI statistics on violent crimes in 1977, for instance, show that in the 1,847 cities studied 39.4% of the reported offenses resulted in an arrest, 37.6% in a criminal charge. Conviction rates are lower: of the total number of offenses reported, 11.5% resulted in convictions on the original charge; another 2.9% in convictions on lesser charges; 6.3% in referrals to juvenile court.[18] In other words, the effect of "deterrence" is often the opposite of what was intended: it does not deter but encourages.

Those who fashioned the bill setting up inspectors general did not ask what level of penalties would deter, what degree of enforcement would generate a deterrent rather than an inducement effect, or under what conditions the needed penalties and enforcers would be available. It was implicitly assumed that "more" enforcement was better, but there was no concept of a threshold below which insufficient punishment ceases to deter crime.

The punishment-deterrence approach may make sense in the abstract when sufficient resources are available and other conditions, such as community acceptance, are met. The catch, to reiterate, is that typically it is applied in practice without anywhere near the needed resources or public support. Moreover, even when it is well supported, extensive reliance on it (as distinct from using it as a second line of defense) is inferior to preventive methods, because it is costly in human and economic terms.

In the attack on fraud and abuse, social science perspectives favor prevention over *post hoc* penalties, the basis of the punitive-deterrent approach, on grounds of efficiency and motivation. Reducing opportunities for fraud and abuse before the fact will tend to be much more cost efficient than dealing with the malefactors only after the fact (although prevention can be stretched to the point that it becomes overly costly and unproductive). Furthermore, as various studies show, it is much less alienating because, if successful, it often removes the motivation to engage in fraud and abuse, rather than frustrating the perpetrators.[19] And the first step in fashioning a program of prevention is to understand the constituencies involved.

Notes

1. Mendelson, Mary Adelaide, *Tender Loving Greed* (New York: Vintage, 1974).
2. *New York Post*, July 8, 1975.
3. Etzioni, Amitai, *The Active Society* (New York: Free Press, 1968). A more accessible summary is included in Etzioni, Amitai, *Social Problems* (Englewood Cliffs, NJ: Prentice-Hall, 1976).
4. *New York Times*, January 12, 1976.
5. *Ibid.*
6. *New York Times*, March 7, 1976.
7. See Rourke, John T., "The GAO: An Evolving Role." *Public Administration Review* (September/October 1978): 453.
8. For reports on this transition, see Rourke, John T., *ibid.*, and Mosher, Frederick C., *The GAO* (Boulder, CO: Westview, 1979), especially Chap. 7.
9. Remarks of Joseph A. Califano, Jr., then Secretary of Health, Education and Welfare, to the Conference on Fraud, Abuse, and Error, Washington, D.C., December 14, 1978.
10. Hopkins, Kevin, and Banhow, Douglas, "To Control Fraud." *New York Times*, April 28, 1980.
11. Private communication with Jean Peterson, Office of the Inspector General, U.S. Department of Labor, January 5, 1982.
12. Communication from Peterson, cited earlier.
13. U.S. Department of Agriculture, Food and Nutrition Service, *Assessment, Improvement and Monitoring System (AIMS) Briefing*, 1979, p. 1.
14. U.S. General Accounting Office, Community and Economic Development Division, *Analysis of a Department of Agriculture Report on Fraud and Abuse in Child Nutrition Programs (CED-81-81)*, Report to House Committee on Education and Labor, March 9, 1981, pp. 3, 5.
15. Private communication from a representative of the American Association of School Administrators.

16. *AIMS Briefing, op. cit.*, p. 3.

17. U.S. General Accounting Office, Comptroller General of the U.S., *The National School Lunch Program—Is It Working?* Report to the Congress PAD-77-6, July 26, 1977, p. 57.

18. *Statistical Abstract of the United States: 1980* (Washington, DC: U.S. GPO, 1980), p. 189.

19. For additional discussion see Etzioni, Amitai, *A Comparative Analysis of Complex Organizations*, rev. ed. (Troy, MO: Holt, Rinehart & Winston, 1975).

Part Three

THE STRUCTURE OF SOCIAL CHANGE

6

Encapsulation and Self-Sustaining Systems: Author's Note

Neoclassical economists tend to view the economy or the market as complete unto itself, as a self-sustaining system to be studied in isolation. If they consider societies, cultures and polities at all, they view them as independent entities that may interact with the market in the way, say, that the United States and Britain do. We join those who, from Polanyi on, have pointed out that it is much more productive to view the economy as a sub-system within a societal, cultural, and political context or capsule. The first essay in this chapter, "Encapsulated Competition," explores the factors that make up a capsule.

The specific ramifications of this general position are spelled out in "On Solving Social Problems: Inducements or Coercion?" through a comparison of two ways to serve social goals (or "public goods")—via command and control systems (the government) and via "the market." As one would expect from the overarching position, the difference turns out to be one of degree rather than of wholly different methods. For example, the government relies on economic factors (fines and subsidies), while the particular markets at issue, as we shall see, are heavily affected by political give-and-take. An approach that combines economic and political analysis seems to be more productive than one that treats these as wholly separate realms.

Encapsulated Competition

Introduction

While economists have made perfect competition the corner-stone of modern economic theory, dissatisfaction with the concept has led to many quests for "second best" concepts, including such notions as "workable competition," "monopolistic competition," and "contestable markets." These endeavors have focused upon modifying the intraeconomic specifications of the concept. The present effort attempts to modify the concept by concentrating upon the interface between economic and social conditions. It assumes that competition is not self-sustaining; hence, its very existence, as well as the scope of transactions organized by it, depends upon contextual factors, the "capsule," within which competition takes place. Both the capsule and competition are treated as variables in the sense that, unlike perfect competition, which either exists or is absent, encapsulated competition exists—in varying degrees and forms. To explicate this socioeconomic concept the factors that constitute the capsule are examined, as well as the effects of power concentration among the competing units on the capsule and, hence, on the working of the entire system.

Why Search for "Second Bests"?

Economists, from the early work of Walras to the later accomplishments of Debreu, have been concerned about specifying the prerequisites of perfect competition. Although lists vary about what is required, the following elements are often

Note: This essay was originally published in *Journal of Post Keynesian Economics,* 1985, 7(3), 287–302. It is reprinted with permission. I am indebted to Joseph Cordes for comments on an earlier draft.

247

included: the largest firm in any given industry is to make no more than a small fraction of the industry's sales (or purchases). The firms are to act independently of one another. Actors have complete knowledge of offers to buy or sell. The commodity (sold and bought in the market) is divisible, and the resources are moveable among users (Stigler, 1968, pp. 181–182). (For a formal discussion of the Walras model and related points see Malinvaud, 1972, pp. 138–143; Bohn, 1973, pp. 128–142.)

Behind these attempts at precise specification, there is a well-known idea: Adam Smith's notion that, as each actor in the free market pursues his own goal, the result will be not conflict but, on the contrary, an automatically harmonious self-perpetuating system; moreover, it will organize the use of resources in a maximally efficient manner without outside intervention.

Economists long have recognized that the prerequisites of perfect competition may never be satisfied *and* that, when even one of them is missing, the benefits of perfect competition will not be available. The point has been highlighted by an often-cited, masterful article by Lipsey and Lancaster (1956). The ability of a market to achieve perfect competition is dependent upon its meeting all of the conditions of the Paretian optimum. And, "it is well known that the attainment of a Paretian optimum requires the simultaneous fulfillment of all optimum conditions" (ibid., p. 11). Lipsey and Lancaster also indicate that, if one of the conditions cannot be met, "the other Paretian conditions, although still attainable, are, in general, no longer desirable" (ibid.). A different pattern or model is then necessary. For example, when an economy moves *toward* perfect competition, as the result of deregulating one industry, one *cannot* assume that one will gain some of the benefits of perfect competition. Advocates of free trade argue that if some trade barriers are reduced this would lead to improvement in the world economy. However, studies by Viner (1950) have shown the opposite effect. This finding was further substantiated by Ozga (1955). Others have shown the same effect for various economic activities, including public finance and monopolistic competition (Chamberlin, 1948, pp. 214–215). Recent work has further supported the same thesis (Newbery and Stiglitz, 1984).

Lipsey, Lancaster, and others concluded that it is not possible to derive from the perfect competition model the attributes of "second-best" systems; they are not simply composed of "less" of the constituting elements that result in a perfect system; they have their own inner logic and states of equilibrium. It follows that "second-best" systems must be found or formulated in some other way.

Encapsulated Competition Introduced

One approach followed here is to search for "second best" economic systems by making use of macro-sociology, which, in turn, draws on system theory. Here, too, behind formal terms and theorems lies a core idea, namely, that competition is nothing but contained conflict. In contrast with Adam Smith's assumption, macro-sociology assumes that people's divergent interests and pursuits do not mesh together automatically to form a harmonious whole. Hence, specific mechanisms are needed to keep conflicts within limits, and to protect competition from escalating to the point of self-destruction.

Furthermore, social systems are assumed to be neither fully competitive nor uncompetitive, but to vary in the *scope* of behavior organized by competitive rules. For example, the rules govern more relations among strangers than among kin; society considers competition more appropriate for commerce and sports than for relations among siblings. It is stronger in the American restaurant industry than among electrical utilities. Social systems also vary in the effectiveness of the mechanisms that limit competitive behavior.

One must move beyond the conceptual opposition between "free competition" and "government intervention," which implies that all interventions are by a government, that all interventions are injurious, and that unshackled competition is sustainable. A counter hypothesis advanced here is that competition can be preserved only within some socially set limits. This is true not only for the totality of social relations (avoiding societal strife) but also for economic relations *per se* (e.g., prohibiting the use of violent means; avoiding ruinous competition). The mechanisms limiting competition, thus preventing self-destruction, are explored shortly.

At the same time one must also establish the conditions under which the very same factors whose purpose is to sustain competition by keeping it within bounds themselves penetrate the realm defined by society as the proper arena for competition, violate its autonomy, and undermine its ability to function properly. In short, like a nuclear reaction, properly bounded competition is viewed as a major constructive force; unleashed—as highly destructive; suppressed—as likely to lose its power, even to be extinguished.

The Mechanisms

The principal mechanisms that constitute the competition-sustaining capsule are ethical, social, and governmental. Each of these mechanisms contains numerous specific processes that interact with the two others in complex ways. The principal mechanisms are discussed before their interactions are explored. They have been analyzed frequently and are reviewed here only to present a model of encapsulated competition as a conceptual effort, not as a report of new findings.

Ethical Precepts and Continuing Competition

All societies have beliefs that define what members consider proper and improper conduct. These include general ethical principles governing the propriety of engaging in commerce, manual labor, entrepreneurship ("making money"), and applied research (in contrast to "scholarship"). In addition, there are specific norms and attitudes ranging from those defining the level of interest that is considered usury to those concerning the assessment of multi-national corporations.

The most important contribution that general ethical principles provide to the competitive system is the legitimacy they offer to a sphere of activities relatively free of external considerations. An inner logic can be followed, allowing competition rather than political power, moral standing, or social status to determine the outcomes. Max Weber's well-known work applies here if one interprets it to mean that certain religions provided an ethical basis more supportive to economic competition than others. (Most of his arguments lead elsewhere, demonstrating that certain religions favored *other* capitalist features such as the work ethic, initiative, and saving.) Obviously, capitalist societies favor competition not only in comparison to feudal, traditional, and communist societies, but also in comparison to "mixed" social democratic societies such as Israel and Scandinavia. America's own acceptance of competition has changed significantly from one generation to another.

Undoubtedly, some general ethical principles, exogenous to competition, directly sustain it. Primary is the belief in the moral virtues of competition in general; Americans, for instance, believe that it builds character. There is also the belief in the virtue of economic competition, of the "free market," not merely among philosophers and economists, but also among the overwhelming majority of the political leaders, voters, and public. Americans tend to endow "the market" with numerous virtues, from efficiency, to protection against tyranny, to a source of welfare for all ("when the tide rises, all the ships rise") (Novak, 1982; Lipset and Schneider, 1983, pp. 286ff).

As laissez-faire conservatism provides ethical justifications for competition, so a number of socialist ideologies, humanist psychology (e.g., the works of Abraham Maslow), and many counter-culture writers provided rationales in the 1960s and 1970s in the United States for either greatly narrowing the scope of behavior governed by competition (e.g., justifying various regulations that limit its scope, for example, by introducing automatic promotion into schools) or by justifying outcomes via mechanisms other than participation in competition (e.g., affirmative action) or by questioning the whole merit of the competitive spirit and system. (See, for example, Hirsch, 1976; Hirschman, 1982, pp. 1463–1484.)

The sociological point is not *whether* these familiar ethical precepts exist, but to what extent they are endorsed and followed. Thus, for instance, during the height of the counter-culture, small-is-beautiful, less-is-more social movement, competition lost legitimacy in the United States. This was also roughly the period in which regulation of the economy for social purposes (social justice; consumer, worker, and environmental protection; and scores of others) was greatly expanded. (The proportion of Americans agreeing that "government should limit profits" of corporations rose from 25 percent in 1962 to 55 percent by 1976 and to 60 percent by 1979—*Public Opinion,* 1980.) That is, loss in legitimacy of competition was accompanied by political penetration of the competitive arena to set outcomes by exogenous criteria.

Beyond these general positions, there are specific norms and attitudes that help to either sustain or undermine encapsulated competition. An obvious example is the endorsement of competing fairly, "by the rules"—"it does not matter whether you win or lose but *how* you play" versus the notion that "winning is not the important thing; it is the only thing," immortalized by Vince Lombardi and embraced by Richard Nixon, among others. There are numerous other norms, characterizing this or that form of competition (e.g., "cut throat") or means of competition (e.g., price wars, industrial spying) as "unfair" or "immoral." Together, they either provide a specific underpinning of competition, or undermine it—in varying degrees.

Aside from periodic changes in acceptance of these norms, there are differences in the extent to which they are followed by different segments of the economy. Such differences are expected to deeply affect the nature of competition within the respective industries. While the author is not aware of a systematic study of the matter, common knowledge of American society suggests that competition is less contained ethically among most illegal dealers in controlled substances than among most computer sales personnel; is less contained among such sales personnel than among most professionals; and is less contained among marginal doctors (or lawyers) than among core members of these professions.

These ethical norms are expected to help avoid violent or otherwise ruinous competition and to keep transaction costs down. If dealers in contraband do not trust one another, they must have bodyguards, armored cars, and so on; transactions must be paid for in cash rather than with checks or financed with credit; long-run planning is difficult. Most transactions among business persons are based upon trust; few are recorded, the rest based upon oral communications; and only a fraction of what is recorded is scrutinized by lawyers. But trust is a continuous and not a dichotomous variable; it is higher in some industries (and countries) than in others. The lower the level of morality and, hence, trust, the higher the transaction costs. In the area of labor relations, Denison reports that theft by employees is a significant factor affecting the productivity of American corporations (1979, pp. 73–74 passim.). High costs of bribery are known to increase the costs of conducting business in many countries. Economists recognize the significance of these ethical norms but tend to explain them in intraeconomic terms. "Economic theory in this, as well as in some other fields, tends to suggest that people are honest *only* to the extent that they have economic incentive for being so" (Johansen cited by Sen, 1977, p. 332). This position is further illustrated by the following conclusion of Cloninger: "The possibility of reducing business risk by the acceptance of smaller amounts of moral risk could provide a rationale for the use of certain unorthodox business practices" (1982, p. 33).

If this were the case, the capsule, or at least its ethical element, would be explainable by transactions among the actors; ethics would be sustained because ethical conduct is good business. One would not need to go outside the realm of competition to explain the ethical forces that sustain it.

The alternative hypothesis is *not* that ethical principles and norms are immune to economic factors and considerations, but that they have a significant measure of autonomy and that they are partially formed by other factors, including

developments within the ethical realm itself (e.g., the rise of
new charismatic leaders and religious or moral-social movements, as in post-Shah Iran). Moreover, although it is expected that economic factors will affect ethical behavior (e.g.,
norms that exact high costs are less likely to be adhered to
than those that do not), the effects also run the other way:
economic activities condemned by ethical precepts are likely
to be less common and more costly than those extolled by
them. Without further discussion of the interaction effects
between ethical and economic factors, as long as one accepts
the idea that ethical factors have a significant measure of autonomy, one can understand why they could constitute part
of the capsule that contains and, hence, sustains competition,
but does not violate or unduly constrict it, as long as the ethical factors are properly formulated. More precisely, because
these factors are viewed as continuous and not dichotomous
variables, the content and power of the ethical factors are key
factors in determining the extent to which competition is sustained, erupts into excessive (or all-out) conflicts, or is curtailed if not completely suppressed.

Social Bonds: The Hidden Bases of Competition

The perfect competition model entails impersonal relations
among actors moving independently of one another in an
anonymous market. "The fortunes of any one firm are independent of what happens to any other firm: one farmer is
not benefited if his neighbor's crop is destroyed" (Stigler,
1968, p. 181). One might add: or, if his neighbor's crop
thrives. Their orientation to one another is one of exchange
characterized as follows: "The rational thing to do is to try to
gain as much value as I can while giving up as little value as I
can" (Dyke, 1981, p. 29). This orientation is not problematic
in the perfect competition world because it is assumed that
self-interest will sustain the system. However, in other worlds,
which acknowledge conflict, positive mutually supportive *social* bonds are found to directly sustain the continuity of *economic* relations. Much has been written about this role of so-

cial bonds in the conflict-rich U.S. Senate. Here, members are supposed to be aware that they are members of one "club," that although they are in conflict concerning some issues they soon will have to work together concerning others. Hence, they limit their conflicts; for instance, personal attacks are considered highly improper.

Similarly, among traders in the market, there are social bonds that help to sustain the trust relations described earlier (by and large, people trust those they know much more than they do strangers) and limit conflicts, for instance, by making minor concessions in the name of investing in the relationships (imagine if all differences had to be settled through litigation). This finding often has been referred to as the pre-contractual base of contracts.

While this is a point sociologists emphasized at least since Durkheim, economist Phelps put it especially well. He first states that "altruistic phenomena are equally crucial to the functioning of markets" (1976, p. 3). He then elaborates: people do not behave in the maximizing way the perfect competition model implies; many corporations do not deceive in their advertising, pay fair wage rates, keep their word and so on (ibid., p. 5). This, he adds, "contributes to economic efficiency. Certainly it reduces the risks and anxieties of being cheated or exploited. Beyond that, it tends to improve market resource allocations by lowering the transaction costs" (ibid.).

Although social bonds and ethical norms frequently are mutually supportive, they are independent factors and are not to be viewed as one variable. Social bonds tend to unite people through positive mutual feelings, because of compatibility of background (bonds tend to be stronger among people of similar social and educational background than among those of highly divergent ones), compatible or complementary personalities, and shared social activities (from golf to bowling). They are not inherently ethical; they as readily bind a group of thieves as they bind police officers sharing a beat (Etzioni, 1975, Ch. 8).

Social bonds exist on both micro, one-to-one or small group, and macro, society-wide, levels. Micro bonds help brokers and their clients, sales representatives and their customers, and suppliers and manufacturers to conduct their transactions (compare trade among strangers to that among members of the same community or those who deal extensively with one another). The existence and nature of social bonds are often reported to be significant factors in the relationships between supervisors and workers (and between other ranks), affecting productivity, quality of work, costs, and satisfaction from work. In the organizational literature this is often referred to as the addition of human relations (or Mayonian) considerations to those of "scientific management" (or Taylorism).

On the societal level, social bonds exist among regions (in the United States they were quite weak between the South and the North, but strengthened after the Civil War and the Reconstruction Era), races, classes, and generations. Historically, workers, minorities, and women resented not being included in major social networks, which unfavorably affected their economic opportunities. Growing social acceptance frequently is cited as one reason that American labor is much less radical, and more accepting of the political *and* the competitive economic system, than its European counterpart. Strikes and violence are reported to be less common.

Both micro and macro social bonds are to be considered as a continuous variable (or set of variables), not as a dichotomous one. It is too elementary to argue that such bonds exist; at issue is their relative strength and scope.

The relevance of these observations (often made, but also often overlooked) is as follows: the measurement of these attributes of the social bonds has to be tied (or correlated) to the scope (and other attributes) of competition. A *curvilinear* relationship can be hypothesized to exist between social bonds and competition. All things being equal, when the bonds are absent or very weak, the capsule that contains competition can be expected to be insufficient, with competition showing signs of threatening to break down the containing capsule, leading to all-out conflict. In labor relations, long and destructive strikes, shut-outs, wild-cat strikes, acts of sabotage and violence, and use of strike breakers would be indications of such a tendency. However, when various ranks of the employees consider themselves a community, if not an extended family (as they are said to do at Delta Airlines), labor relations are expected to be more harmonious (this is not to suggest that conflict will be caused only by weak social bonds, but that the latter is a contributing factor).

At the opposite extreme, where social bonds are very powerful, encompassing, and tight, economic competition is likely to be restrained, if not suppressed. For example, members of a close knit family are expected not to charge one another for services rendered. This is one reason market economics tends to be limited, if not absent, in primitive tribal societies.

Accordingly, competition is expected to thrive not in the impersonal, calculative system of independent actors unbound by social relations, implied by the perfect competition model, nor in the socially tight world of traditional societies, but in the middle range, where social bonds are strong enough to sustain mutual trust and low transaction costs but not to suppress exchange orientations. Aside from being of middle strength (more than between total strangers but less than between kin and close friends), social bonds favor competition when they distinguish between matters that bonds preclude (cheating) and those they endorse or at least tolerate (trading). This is the point at which social bonds and ethics are intertwined. But, before such points of articulation are considered, the third mechanism is to be introduced.

The Competition-Building Role of Government

In the perfect competition model, the government is a distorting factor because the economic system is assumed to be self-regulating. Whatever government does here is properly termed "distorting" or "intervention" because it pulls the system away from its pure, "natural," Paretian-optimal state. On the other hand, it is sufficient to observe that all societies have some measure of government to conclude that a second-best competition model must be found. Laissez-faire conservatives, who are philosophically attuned to Adam Smith's economics, tend to argue that the government could be limited to noneconomic functions, especially to defense. However, defense requires a revenue-raising mechanism. And however it is constituted, even if it taxes only consumption and only individuals (not capital nor firms), it still "distorts" the system, breaks the Paretian mold.

In contrast, the model of encapsulated competition *requires* some governmental activities, while it defines some other governmental activities as undermining the proper balance between activities organized by the rules of competition and those that constitute the capsule. Government is required to sustain the capsule because conflicts are assumed to be endemic to the system, and gaining resolutions cannot rely only upon voluntary ethical commitments and social bonds because an actor can violate them at will. It follows that an institution that commands coercive power must be the ultimate arbiter of conflicts (e.g., by jailing violators of a court decree to force compliance). Moreover, the fact that the competitors themselves might resort to violence necessitates an institution able to disarm or at least deter the competitors from using their resources in violent clashes.

On the other hand, the government undermines encapsulated competition when it goes beyond sustaining the capsule to trying to affect the outcome of competition, by favoring some competitors. This might be justified by other values, such as social justice. In addition, to the extent that the government helps formerly excluded competitors to participate on an equal footing, such help legitimizes the system. Nevertheless, when these values are achieved by externally determining competition results, instead of improving the ability to participate in the competition, the balance between the capsule and the autonomous realm of competition is tilted against competition.

While analytically the competition-sustaining and the competition-undermining roles of government are clearly distinct, research on the effects of various government actions is often required before they can be appropriately classified. For instance, laws that prohibit shops' opening on Sundays, or after agreed hours, or laws prohibiting stores that sell the same items from being situated too close to one another may be used to sustain the capsule (by avoiding ruinous competition) or to favor white Christian shopkeepers over racial and ethnic minorities. A compelling argument has been made in favor of "income policies" which will use wage and price moderation; this would preempt the argument in favor of recessionary blood baths (Appelbaum, 1982; Davidson, 1982; Rapping, 1979; and Weintraub, 1978). Others argue that such programs would "distort" the economy and are effective only for short periods. Some government acts, such as laws that protect private property and the currency, or prohibit fraud and violence, are clearly supportive. Other acts obviously have other primary purposes: for instance, regulations on the quality of billboards to achieve "highway beautification."

Interaction Effects

Although the three mechanisms that constitute the capsule have been discussed individually, in the working of encapsulated competition they are present simultaneously and affect one another as they affect the scope of competition (the range of areas of behavior governed by competition versus those in which it is deemed inappropriate) (Arrow, 1974). For instance, the stronger the ethical prohibitions against violence and the tighter the social bonds, the less need there is for government action. And, the more effective the government deterrence, the more likely it is that parallel ethical prohibitions will hold. A particularly significant area of interaction between the government and the ethical mechanisms is that of maintaining trust (e.g., in banks, in the currency, in the government itself). The capsule is, therefore, best considered an intertwined set of ethical, social, and governmental mechanisms whose relative strength and effects upon one another must be studied before the extent to which a capsule is effective can be ascertained.

Power Relations

The perfect competition model assumes that actors have no power over one another. This point is usually expressed by saying that no firm has an ability to affect the market. As Stigler puts it: "The essence of perfect competition, therefore, is in the utter dispersion of power" (1968, p. 181). He adds that in this way power is "annihilated . . . just as a gallon of water is effectively annihilated if it is spread over a thousand acres" (ibid.).

Disregarding the second-best insight, numerous economists have favored nudging, and policy makers have attempted to nudge, the economy toward such a model, for instance by favoring anti-trust policies. The fact is, though, that in numerous industries there are at least some power differences among the actors. Most of the economic analysis of this behavior relates it to the perfect competition model. When the numerous studies are pieced together, they are reported to show that (a) there are factors in the market that keep prices "substantially above competitive levels for extended periods of time" (Scherer, 1980, p. 266), however, (b) at a level closer *to full competition* (or cost) than one would expect from the small number of sellers and other such competition-limiting factors, and that, hence, (c) all said and done the "pricing performance in modern industrial markets has on the whole been fairly satisfactory despite significant departures from *the structural ideal of pure economic theory*" (ibid., italics provided). Several attempts to develop second-best models of less than perfect competition have not yielded widely accepted alternatives to the "first-best" model.

Encapsulated competition introduces a major new dimension to the issue at hand: actors are assumed to vary not merely in their economic power (ability to affect the state of the market), but also in their political power (ability to affect the government which is part of the capsule). Concentrated economic power may be converted into political power and exercised *either* to thwart the neutrality of the capsule-sustaining mechanisms or to use the government to favor one actor (or group of actors) over others (for instance, favoring big business over small business).

It follows that the power prerequisites of encapsulated competition include, first of all, dispersion of economic power. This requirement is not absolute, as it is in the perfect competition model. Everyday experience suggests that encapsulated competition can work despite some power concentration. (How much can be tolerated and what ill side effects are caused by various degrees of concentration is far from clear.) However, high concentration of economic power will undermine encapsulated competition not only because it will reduce the number of competitors (a point emphasized by economic theory of competition) but also because the higher the concentration of economic power the more likely it is to be a source of political power, which, in turn, undermines the capsule (a factor familiar to economists but not encompassed in economic theory).

Second, encapsulated competition requires segregation of political from economic power whatever its degrees of concentration (e.g., abolishing property-weighted franchises and poll taxes; prohibiting campaign contributions by corporations and labor unions) (Etzioni, 1984, pp. 131ff). The more effective the segregation of political and economic power, the more encapsulated competition can withstand concentration of economic power, although even under complete segregation (difficult to imagine) high economic power concentration would have some debilitating effects. Finally, encapsulation requires maintaining an ethical prohibition built into codes and traditions of the executive branch, enforced by the courts and legislatures, against the use of the capsule-sustaining power to affect the outcomes of the competition.

These prerequisites are to be viewed as variables in that they are rarely, if ever, perfectly met or completely absent and in that whatever their specific "readings" (or scores) they affect the various attributes of encapsulated competition. A weak government will permit a relatively high degree of monopolistic behavior and a high level of political corruption (in the sense of political power captured by some economic actors). Such behavior will tend to undermine the capsule because some participants in the competition will be able to neutralize, deflect, or specify the mechanisms that are supposed to be applied evenly to all participants. This, in turn, will tend to weaken the legitimization and power of the capsule. A powerful government will tend to apply its powers to areas in which it was not granted control (or legitimized) and, hence, constrict the scope of activities set aside for competition. Many details of these relationships have yet to be clarified and empirically validated.

Conclusion

The search for "second best" competition models might draw on a core idea; actors are not necessarily in harmony with one another; competition is actually a form of limited conflict. The limiting capsule, within which competition is free to range, is composed of interacting ethical, social, and government mechanisms. Their power varies from being too weak to discharge their mission to too powerful, going beyond limiting conflicts to suppressing competition. Empirically determining the status of the capsule will help to explain the scope of the competition, in varying historical situations, without assuming one "perfect" model. Such a "perfect model," once violated, as it invariably is, explains little about the economic systems one actually studies or for which one must prescribe policy.

References

Appelbaum, Eileen. "The Incomplete Incomes Policy Vision." *Journal of Post Keynesian Economics,* Summer 1982, 4(4), 546–557.

Arrow, Kenneth, *The Limits of Organization.* New York: Norton, 1974.

Bohn, Peter. "Necessary Conditions for Pareto Optimality." *Social Efficiency;* Appendix 1, 128–142. New York: Macmillan, 1973.

Chamberlin, E. H. *The Theory of Monopolistic Competition.* 6th ed. Cambridge, Mass.: Harvard University Press, 1948.

Cloninger, Dale O. "Moral and Systematic Risk: A Rationale for Unfair Business Practice," *Journal of Behavioral Economics,* Winter 1982, *11*(2), 33–49.

Davidson, Paul. *International Money and the Real World.* New York: Wiley, 1982.

Denison, Edward F. *Accounting for Slower Economic Growth.* Washington, D.C.: Brookings, 1979.

Dyke, C. *Philosophy of Economics.* Englewood Cliffs, N.J.: Prentice-Hall, 1981.

Etzioni, Amitai. *Capital Corruption.* Orlando, Fla.: Harcourt Brace Jovanovich, 1984.

———. *A Comparative Analysis of Complex Organizations.* Rev. ed. New York: Free Press, 1975.

Hirsch, Fred. *The Social Limits of Growth.* Cambridge, Mass.: Harvard University Press, 1976

Hirschman, Albert. "Rival Interpretations of Market Society: Civilizing, Destructive, or Feeble?" *Journal of Economic Literature,* December 1982, *20,* 1463–1484.

Lipset, S. M., and Schneider, William. *The Confidence Gap.* New York: Free Press, 1983.

Lipsey, R. G., and Lancaster, Kelvin. "The General Theory of Second Best." *Review of Economic Studies,* 1956, *24,* 11–32.

Malinvaud, E. *Lectures on Microeconomic Theory.* Amsterdam: North Holland Publishing Company, 1972.

Newbery, David M. G., and Stiglitz, Joseph E. "Pareto Inferior Trade." *Review of Economic Studies,* 1984, *51,* 1–12.

Novak, Michael. *The Spirit of Democratic Capitalism.* New York: American Enterprise Institute/Simon & Schuster, 1982.

Ozga, S. A. "An Essay in the Theory of Tariffs." *Journal of Political Economy,* December 1955, 489–499.

Phelps, Edmund S. "Introduction." In his *Altruism, Morality and Economic Theory.* New York: Russell Sage, 1976, 1–9.

Public Opinion, June/July 1980, p. 33.

Rapping, Leonard A. "The Domestic and International Aspects of Structural Inflation." In *Essays in Post-Keynesian Inflation.* Ed. by James Gapinski and Charles E. Rockwood. Cambridge, Mass.: Ballinger, 1979, 31–54.

Scherer, F. M. *Industrial Market Structure and Economic Performance.* 2nd ed. Boston: Houghton Mifflin, 1980.

Sen, Amartya K. "Rational Fools." *Philosophy and Public Affairs,* 1977, *6*(4), 317–344.

Stigler, George. "Competition." *International Encyclopedia of Social Science.* Vol. 3. New York: Macmillan, 1968, 181–182.

Viner, Jacob. *The Custom Union Issue.* New York: Carnegie Endowment for International Peace, 1950.

Weintraub, Sidney. *Capitalism's Inflation and Unemployment Crisis.* Reading, Mass.: Addison-Wesley, 1978.

On Solving Social Problems:
Inducements or Coercion?

The case for using economic incentives to solve social problems has acquired some ideological overtones. Frequently, the incentive approach is characterized as advancing core values of the American society, such as freedom, individual dignity, and economic welfare, while "command and control" techniques (C&C) are said to entail oppression, coercion, and waste. Adjectives attached to C&C systems in such writings are typically negative; for example, William J. Baumol and Edwin S. Mills, in "Incentives for Solving Social Problems" (*Challenge*, November/December 1984) refer to them as "clumsy." In contrast, while many terms have been used to refer to the preferred approach, including "charges," "effluent fees," and "prices as a regulatory mechanism," the most often used term—"incentives"—is the one that has the most favorable connotation.

Most importantly, incentives are often discussed in an idealized form, as a purely conceptual scheme, with relatively little attention to implementation and other "practical" problems. For instance, Baumol and Mills, along with Edwin G. West (in "The Demise of 'Free' Education," *Challenge*, January/February 1985), refer to the merit of using subsidies without discussing the serious problems caused by this economic tool—for instance, in the farm sector of the American as well as many other economies. When C&C systems are depicted, they are often not idealized ones but implemented ones. A hypothetical incentive scheme is compared to excessive and inane regulations introduced by OSHA, for example, rather

Note: This essay was originally published in *Challenge*, 1985, *28*(3), 35–40. It is reprinted with permission of M.E. Sharpe, Inc. 80 Business Park Drive, Armonk, NY 10504.

than to a hypothetical, idealized system of regulation, one in which the administering agency is well designed and effectively run. There are deep reasons to expect that implemented systems, which must satisfy multiple and partially incompatible needs, will compare unfavorably to theoretical conceptions or models, in which a single principle can be logically followed. I do not argue that advocates of incentives have deliberately tilted their comparisons in this manner; only that comparing ideals of one system to the realities of another results in an ideologization of the comparison.

My attempt to reduce the ideological tint begins with the question of what is the precise referent and the best term for the "incentive" approach. Here a bit of history is useful. In 1977, it was still common to refer to the approach at issue as one that would rely on "effluent charges" and be used largely to control pollution. Since then, the concept has been greatly expanded in terms of the means to be employed (to include tax exemptions, outright government payments, credit below market rates, and so on) as well as in terms of the social problems the approach might be applied to (from crime to traffic congestion, from voter apathy to littering). The danger is that if the concept continues to be diluted, soon all economic policies that attempt to correct for any market imperfections will be encompassed. For example, an across-the-board tax cut might be said to help reduce unemployment by creating incentives to work. The criterion of correcting for social costs (or externalities) not reflected in market prices is insufficient; practically every activity has some such externality. It seems best to limit the concept to *indirect government economic activities targeted to solve one or more social problems.* The concern with indirect action, "via the market," rather than direct impingement on economic actors, is the characteristic that best distinguishes this approach from the C&C one.

The focus on government is crucial because "incentives" can be introduced by other agents—for example, by private, not-for-profit foundations. However, for reasons that will become evident, such private incentives systems would be quite different from those discussed in the sizable literature on the subject, which properly deals with government schemes.

Targeting is essential to the definition as well, because otherwise, macro-policies, such as increasing the money supply, might be included and the subject at hand will lose its distinction from general economic theory.

In short, the correct technical term is I.G.A.T.S.S.P., for Indirect Government Activities Targeted at Solutions of Social Problems. To spare the reader, I will substitute the term "government inducements" (GIs). The term correctly implies that those affected do not simply follow their free will, their unadulterated predisposition; "incentives" is somehow too voluntary, too sanguine. At the same time, the term "inducement" correctly indicates that no coercion is entailed.

The Government/Market Continuum

When one compares C&C and inducement schemes it is wrong to consider them as two opposite types, one governmental, one free-market; *both* are forms of government action.

From a psychological viewpoint, it is common to refer to C&C as "coercive" and hence alienating and to GIs as working like a free market, hence self-motivating. Coercion, however, has two major meanings. One is the use and threat of use of physical force involved in jailing or executing people. In this sense, most C&C systems are not coercive. For instance, violation of many regulations results, at most, in the imposition of a fine. The situation then is akin to the one many readers are familiar with when they consider parking illegally in a non-tow-away zone when the fines are low, ticketing is known to be infrequent, and parking lots' fees are high. People then "estimate" whether or not it is cheaper to park illegally. This response is not significantly different from the reaction to a via-the-market "signal" that, say, the cost of polluting has been increased by a new government charge. Even when the regulation (or law) reads "$2,500 fine and/or a year in jail" it is common knowledge that the prohibited activity is only irregularly scrutinized and that those caught are often not charged, those charged are quite often not convicted, and those convicted as a rule fined rather than jailed; individuals subject to such regulation will not feel coerced and will act as if they face a market-like situation. (Indeed, several major studies of crime have indicated that even criminals engaged in acts of violence, including murder, act in this way.) I can weaken my point considerably and it still holds: as long as the main tool for enforcing C&C techniques is economic, there is no reason to expect them to be significantly more alienating than GIs. GIs are not, psychologically speaking, much more efficient; in both systems, people sense that they have a choice.

What about economic efficiency? C&C schemes mandate specific responses (such as pollution-control device x), while GIs leave it to the private decision-maker to choose the most efficient response. This is a compelling point in favor of GIs, although the less enforced the "mandated" response is, the closer C&C moves to GIs; businesses act as if they have a choice—to ignore the directives.

But is there no difference between making a choice that is illegal (under C&C) and making one that is legal (under GIs)? There is, but it is smaller than it may seem, because when a mandated requirement is not perceived as legitimate (and most regulations are not considered legitimate by those they seek to constrain), it does not pack much moral persuasion. I do not argue that there are no significant differences between the two schemes; only that they are less stark than has often been suggested.

Along the same lines, GI schemes are not without enforcement, and hence coercive elements. To avoid charges, polluters may try to hide their emissions. Union Carbide did not report scores of toxic emissions at its plant in Institute, West Virginia, farmers will collect fees to idle land and cultivate it anyhow, and so on. The enforcement systems to keep a GI honest, so to speak, are generally backed up with the same means C&C schemes use: typically, economic sanctions (fines) and only very rarely coercion (jail sentences).

C&C is coercive in the second sense of the term, of foisting a direction on individuals who would not have followed it on their own, voluntarily. Such coercion occurs whether the source of the pressure is economic, psychic (for example, severe expressions of disapproval), or physical. However, in this sense GIs are also coercive. Say John Doe is dumping toxic waste into the river and the local government announces that while he may continue to do as he wishes, he'll be charged $5,000 a day from here on. Doe will feel pressure that is not radically different from that confronting a person who faces a $5,000 fine for dumping. Similarly, while a business person told he "must" introduce technology *x* will feel more coerced than one who is told he can use any one he wishes as long as it produces a required result, the second person will also feel imposed upon, "intervened with." Note that GI schemes are not exactly popular in the industries into which they have been introduced, though they may well be preferred to C&C schemes.

All said and done, it seems fruitful to view C&C and GI schemes as points on a continuum between two extreme poles. At one extreme are pure intra-market voluntary acts (transactions among buyers and sellers who have no market power and equal "urgency"); at the opposite end are pure coercive (forced) relations, at the point of a gun. In between are various GI and C&C schemes. GIs still come out ahead, but only as a matter of degree.

There are also government programs that combine the C&C and GI approaches, and others that would be easy to conceive. These include law enforcement that combines a mandatory sentencing period with one of probation; government contracts that offer universities a choice between a fixed and an adjustable rate for calculating indirect costs; and several "prospective payment" Medicare schemes.

Inducements and "Rent"

The government that fashions both C&C and GI schemes is not the minimal, neutral government that laissez-faire economists prefer, nor is it the representative of the public interest that liberals used to assume. It is, in part, "political" in the sense that all significant governmental acts are, in part, shaped by the give and take among various power groups in the society. In recent years a theory has arisen that in effect says that laissez-faire economists, always leery of government, are not leery enough. The theory, which calls itself "neoclassical political economy" (NPE), argues that in addition to whatever waste the government generates by intervening in the economy, it fosters a second waste, referred to as "rent," by leading economic actors to invest in activities that do not increase economic welfare, yet produce profits—the result of political manipulation of the government. For instance, tariffs, aside from undermining the economic benefits of free trade, also cause exporters and importers to waste resources when they lobby to modify the tariffs.

This approach can be extended to the comparison of C&Cs and GIs. The government that sets up both is not viewed as a benign servant of the public, merely dedicated to eradicating poverty, pollution, or crime, but in part as captured by various power groups, including those who benefit from nonresolution of the social problems and those who draw substantial profits from the specific format C&C or GI programs take. Thus a new cost, imposed either by a government standard or by a new charge, on those who do not reduce pollution, will pose more difficulties for companies near bankruptcy (say, Chrysler a few years back) than on their stronger competitors (especially GM). If major outlays are involved, companies with strong balance sheets will find it easier and less costly than weaker ones to meet the new standards or to avoid the new charges, say by installing a new technology.

While extending the rent theory, my analysis differs from the NPE approach in two nontrivial ways. First, it rejects the NPE core assumption that the rent-seeking actors (typically special-interest groups acting on the government) abide by the rules of perfect competition and rational utility maximization. As we shall see, competition in politics is restricted. As a result, political action provides "monopolistic" profits to power groups that gain an upper hand, and neoclassical models of perfect competition cannot be used to explicate rent-seeking. A genuine political theory is needed. Second, factors other than political ones, especially values, also play a significant role in these matters. I use the term "socio-economics" to flag these differences from the NPE approach.

The Partial "Capture" of C&C and GI Programs

The ways in which both C&C and GI programs are designed and implemented are subject to political give and take. Political actors may be numerous, but they include mainly those who favor a solution to the social problem via tighter standards, higher charges, and so on (e.g., environmental groups); those who oppose *both* C&C and GIs (e.g., polluters); and the public at large (under most circumstances, a relatively weak and mercurial power base). The various politically active groups tug and pull as the programs are being prepared and carried out. Some have gone as far as to suggest such programs are completely captured—are, in effect, worse than public-relation fronts for those who ignore social costs, because they provide them with *benefits,* say by blocking entry of competitors into their markets. I expect that, under most circumstances, capture will be but partial, because the pro-solution groups will to some extent counter the "anti" groups and because the public at large also plays a role. The capture discussed from here on is assumed to be partial. Note, though, that partial capture may suffice to generate rent that exceeds social returns.

Efforts to capture C&C programs take the form of opposition to the introduction of any regulation or other forms of governmental controls (often in the name of the danger they pose to a free market) or pressure to delay initiation dates (often in the name of the need for more research, for example on air bags), to set less stringent standards (for example, requirements that auto bumpers withstand, without damage, a collision at 2–1/2 miles per hour instead of 5), to adopt less-encompassing coverage (for example, primary but

not secondary treatment of waste), or to relegate enforcement to weaker and easier-to-"capture" agencies (many state
and local agencies, for example, instead of federal ones).

The design and implementation of GI programs are
also subject to political give and take and to capture. Decisions on the levels of charges, effluent fees, subsidies, the
price of permits, who will be eligible and for what levels of
performance, and so on, are not made in a political vacuum;
they are not merely expressions of the public interest or of
an economic theory as to where the proper "price" should be
set. These decisions are subject to political pressures both
with regard to what the relevant facts are and what the
proper inducements are.

Political pressures enter into the determination of the
facts because the full scientific knowledge needed for rational design and implementation is often not available, and its
interpretation is subject to considerable license. And even if
the relevant scientific facts were perfectly known, the attempt
to mimic the market would run into limits of economic
theory and modeling. Baumol concluded that the difficulties
in establishing the "correct" level of charges are so great they
will have to be set by trial and error.

Beyond matters of knowledge, there is the motivation
to modify the schemes. It is a grievous error to suggest that
when the government introduces, say, a new charge on
dumping toxic waste, producers will find it is to their benefit
to cease to dump (as long as the charge is higher than the
costs of transporting the waste to the proper disposal location) "just as if the costs of a production factor have risen."
When GI-imposed costs rise, the rational response is, as the
rent-school points out, to *lobby to reduce the charge*.

Other forms of GIs are similarly subject to politics and
to capture. For example, subsidies, loan guarantees, or fees
offered as inducements place considerable pressure on eligi-
bility criteria, both in terms of actors entitled to receive the
inducements and in terms of actions that would qualify to get
them. A quick illustration of how such politics works: before
1977, few claims were paid out to coal miners for black lung

because the law strictly defined the illness (pneumoconiosis) and those eligible ("coal miners" who were totally disabled). Between 1973 and 1978, only seven percent of the claims were approved, and a total of $70 million was paid. In 1977, "coal miner" was redefined to include people who do not work in a mine but are "around" it, such as truck drivers and construction workers. Moreover, physicians who specialize in reading X-rays were explicitly barred from passing judgments on claims! Payments on claims approved rose to $718 million in fiscal year 1980 alone.

The question of whether C&C or GIs are more open to capture cannot be answered on this level of generality because of great differences among various C&Cs and among various GIs. Classifying the major kinds of GIs will allow a better approximation of an answer.

A Classification of GIs

There are three main kinds of GIs, analytically speaking (and numerous concrete combinations): cost-enhancing, neutral, and revenue-enhancing. (The terms profit-suppressing and profit-enhancing might be more accurate, because the first type may also work by reducing revenue and the last one by reducing costs. However, practically, most GIs either increase costs or increase revenues rather than decrease either.) Reference is to the total system, not to the result for any one economic actor affected by them.

Cost-enhancing GIs attempt to modify the decisions of the economic actors subject to them by increasing their costs—by introducing new charges, permits that must be bought if pollution is not corrected, and so on. Simple example: Singapore's method of reducing rush-hour downtown congestion, by selling entry licenses for cars with fewer than four people. An important feature of pure cost-enhancing GIs is that the revenue they generate is turned over to a government's treasury; it is not paid out to any economic actors or used to finance any specific government service from which they may benefit.

Revenue-enhancing GIs attempt to modify private decision making by offering new sources of revenue. Simple example: incentive payments to those who bring their toxic wastes in for disposal (rather than dumping them), or, in Baumol and Mills' words, "subsidies to reduce emission of ordinary pollutants." An important feature of pure revenue-enhancing GIs is that they are financed from general government revenues and not from charges on particular economic actors; nor do they entail a reduction in any other specific government service from which these actors benefit.

Neutral GIs are those that create a new market by a balanced system of costs and revenues, with all the costs (including the indirect ones of administering the system) borne by the economic participants and all the revenue dedicated to them. In other words, the system is wholly self-financing. A pollution-abatement system that imposed charges on those who pollute above a given level, but provided fees to those who reduce it below this level (with charges and fees properly balanced), would be a case in point.

While, as far as I can determine, the different kinds of GIs have not been studied as to which is more prone to produce rent, I would expect that revenue-enhancing GIs will produce most, and neutral GIs—not the cost-enhancing ones—the least. The reason for this is that those who might gain rent from the revenue-enhancing GIs are in effect rewarded the more they are able to modify the system to pay them more and to alter their behavior less, with no established ceiling on how much they can get out of the system. Cost-enhancing GIs can also be corrupted by reducing the costs they impose, limiting the conditions under which they must be incurred, and so on. But since costs cannot be reduced below zero, there is a built-in limit to the rent-generating capacity of such GIs.

I expect neutral GIs to resist corruption most readily because, once in place, they will tend to divide would-be capturers into two groups: those who would seek to increase their revenues and those who would seek to reduce their costs.

While there seems to be no direct experience with such a GI, the National Labor Relations Board provides an analogue. It is considered a less-captured regulatory agency than most because business groups pull it one way and labor unions in the opposite way, keeping it relatively straight. Other regulatory agencies are pushed on the one side by organized industries (e.g., securities) but often face on the other side only an unorganized, politically weak public at large.

Similar differences exist among C&C schemes, ranging from those that impose only requirements and penalties, to those that provide only direct payments, to those that combine the two approaches. That is, the extent of rent that might be generated depends mainly on the kind of GI or C&C scheme that is being introduced, not on the fact that it is a GI or C&C scheme.

The NPE approach suggests that rent-seeking is rational in the sense that a firm or individual will increase expenditures on lobbying, bribes, etc., until the marginal costs will match the marginal revenues resulting from political manipulation. If this were true, it would be an argument against the use of GIs when the response costs (to be incurred by those who must modify their behavior) are sizable and as a result the rent (and waste) potential would be correspondingly sizable.

However, politics is a restricted business. In 1984, more than ninety percent of incumbent members of Congress, of *both* parties, succeeded in "blocking the entry" of their challengers and winning re-election. Many private actors limit their political activities because of moral considerations, self-image, and concern for reputation. (For example, many firms refuse to pay bribes, set up PACs—even lobby). Others do not have the "contacts" that can be only slowly cultivated and for which there is no ready market. Evidence shows that expenditures on rent-seeking are surprisingly low compared to potential and actual returns. Hence, from this viewpoint the polity is more favorable to GIs than the NPE would lead one to assume.

Values and Other Factors

I have argued so far that political factors deeply affect the ability to design and implement both C&C and GIs. Other societal factors are important as well. Some of these have been explored in an important study by Thomas C. Schelling and his associates (*Incentives for Environmental Protection*, 1983, MIT Press). Others, especially the role of community bonds, remain to be studied. Here, I will explore the role of only one other factor: societal values. Each society has one or more sets (and often numerous subsets) of values that define what its members (or segments of them) consider to be morally right and wrong. To the extent that these values are shared in the relevant community (town, region, nation), social scientists refer to the existence of consensus.

Clearly, the ability to introduce either a C&C or a GI system rests not merely on the determination by economists that a market has "failed" and that an externality is ignored, but also on whether the community has formed a consensus on the existence of a social problem, its severity, its likeliness of responding to treatment, and the extent to which other values may have to be set back to advance the favored solution (the lack of consensus on the last point, for example, undermines affirmative action).

The effect of the scope and depth of consensus on the C&C approach is obvious and has been often discussed; its role in advancing GIs is rarely mentioned. In effect, it is quite similar. Assume that there is a social problem (say, corruption in Congress) the relevant public considers relatively insignificant and unresponsive to reform efforts; it is unwilling to endorse large expenditures to deal with the problem (in this case, by providing candidates for congressional office with the option of public campaign financing if they will forego private contributions), and it feels strongly about other values on which the solution impinges (limiting the use of public monies); under such conditions it will be difficult to introduce GIs, not merely C&C systems. The government action that is entailed will not be supported by the public and reform groups with enough clout to overcome the opposition of those who benefit from the problem's continuation.

Holding constant the scope and depth of the consensus on all the matters discussed so far, the question arises: which type of scheme requires more consensus for its introduction? It may seem at first blush that the C&C does, but this is not necessarily the case. The answer depends in part on the specific historical period and the particular social problem. For example, in recent years in the United States, not only the federal government's involvement in solving social problems, but its use of inducements—especially revenue-enhancing ones, those that entail government expenditures—have been generally out of favor. However, the consensus in the early 1960s was obviously quite different.

Moreover, in some areas introduction of GIs tends to backfire, creating a consensus against them. For instance, after the first experiments with education vouchers (however flawed their design was from the viewpoint of a "model" GI scheme) they were out of favor, though they have acquired a new following quite recently. In still other areas there are taboos on GIs that would make their successful introduction at least difficult. Consider, for example, allowing people to buy their way out of the draft, although that system was in place in 1863.

The point is not that public consensus is "right," or that it should be the main criterion in evaluating the merits of C&C and GIs or in comparing various kinds. The point is that the prevailing consensus (to the extent that it exists) is likely to affect a program's relative costs, its ability to resist capture, and the social benefits to result from both schemes. While GIs have had the advantage here in recent years, this has not always been true. Their greater acceptability is conditional—not generic.

7

Unification and Integration of Systems: Author's Note

Many systems in which members interact in a closed loop are not well integrated in the sense that they lack effective bonding mechanisms, shared values, social bonds, and a central government with which to form capsules. This lack of integration is found especially in international systems, though it is also the case in some nations. Some of the most interesting sociological phenomena are historical situations in which two or more entities interacting in a slightly integrated system create a higher form of integration. This is particularly captivating when, in the process, they shift from a reliance on violence, to resolution of differences by peaceful means (say, representation in a joint parliament). Switzerland, which until 1848 experienced a thousand years of tribal wars, provides a prime case in point. Other examples, as well as the ways in which interunit violent conflicts are transformed into intracapsule, nonviolent conflicts and resolutions, are discussed in the first essay in this chapter, "On Self-Encapsulating Conflicts." (My book *Political Unification*, recently reissued, includes much more detail and discussion.)

Needless to say, not all or even most international systems or poorly integrated national societies evolve to higher levels of integration. The factors that determine their level of integration are spelled out in a theoretical discussion that draws on four extensive case studies, presented in the next two essays, "A Paradigm for the Study of Political Unification" and "The Epigenesis of Political Communities at the International Level". These include a study of the rather successful European Common Market, the stagnant Nordic Council, and the failures of the Federation of the West Indies and the United Arab Republic. Even those with little interest in these particular cases may find some illumination here of other situations, from Canada's secessionist problems, to the rising wave of ethnic quests for greater independence worldwide.

The final essay in this chapter, "European Unification: A Strategy of Change," deals with the European Community's efforts to build a United States of Europe. This essay, originally published more than twenty-five years ago, is presented deliberately unmodified as an example of an often maligned social science at work. Many of the hindrances expected on the basis of the analysis of the European approach indeed slowed down the development of EUROPA in the years since. And while these lines are written early in 1990, with predictions running fast and furious about political unification and a high level of integration in 1992, the analysis in that essay suggests that these expectations are excessive, explains why, and points to alternative approaches.

On Self-Encapsulating Conflicts

Encapsulation refers to the process by which conflicts are modified in such a way that they become limited by rules (the "capsule"). The rules exclude some modes of conflict that were practiced earlier (or at least not ruled out), while they legitimize other modes. Conflicts that are "encapsulated" are not solved in the sense that the parties become pacified. But the use of arms, or some usages of arms, are effectively ruled out. Hence the special interest of this process to the student of international affairs. Most observers do not expect the Communist and the capitalist views to become reconciled and hence suggest that the political basis for disarmament is lacking. They see only two alternatives: two (or more) powers that are basically either hostile or friendly. Encapsulated conflicts point to a third kind of relationship. Here feelings of hostility, differences of belief or interests, and a mutually aggressive orientation might well continue, only the sides rule out some means and some modes of conflict. In this sense encapsulation is less demanding than pacification, since it does not require that the conflict be resolved or extinguished but only that the range of its expression be curbed; hostile parties are more readily "encapsulated" than pacified.

At the same time encapsulation tends to provide a more lasting solution than does pacification. When pacified, the parties remain independent units that, after a period of time, might again find their differences of viewpoint or interest provoked, leading to new conflicts or renewal of the old one. Once encapsulated, the parties lose some of their

Note: This essay was originally published in *Journal of Conflict Resolution,* 1964, *8*(3), 242–255. Copyright © 1969 by Sage Publications, Inc. Reprinted with permission. I am indebted to D.B. Brennan and David Riesman for comments on an earlier version. The thesis presented here is elaborated in Etzioni, A. *Winning Without War* (Garden City, N.Y.: Doubleday, 1964).

independence by being tied and limited by the capsule that has evolved; it is this capsule that limits future conflicts, though the possibility of breaking a capsule—i.e., undermining the rules and bonds formed—can by no means be ruled out.

Capsules differ considerably in their scope and hence in their strength. Some minimal rules govern even the most unrestrained conflicts, such as the use of the white flag, the avoidance of poison gas, and the treatment of prisoners of war. In the present context these minimal capsules are of little interest since by themselves they obviously do not provide a basis on which an international community capable of significantly curbing interbloc conflict can grow. The following discussion is concerned not with capsules strong enough to rule out certain kinds of wars (e.g., all-out nuclear wars), the concern of strategists of limited war (Halperin, 1963), but with capsules that might be able to rule out war altogether—the disarmer's hope.[1]

The most difficult requirement the disarmer's prescription has to meet is for the process of encapsulation to be *self-propelling*. Once a third superior authority is assumed, the rabbit is put into the hat and all the fascination that remains is limited to the particular way it is going to be pulled out. Once a world government or a powerful United Nations police force is introduced, an authority is assumed that can impose rules on the contending parties and thus keep their conflicts limited to those expressions allowed by the particular capsule. But the unavoidable fact is that such universal superior authority is not available, and hence the analysis must turn to *conflicts that curb themselves*, in which, through the very process of conflict, the participants, without assuming neutral referees, work out a self-imposed limitation on the means and modes of strife.

Imperfect Cases

Combing history for a precedent, scanning the sociological treasures for an illustration, the patient disarmer finds several *imperfect* cases: three are imperfect in that encapsulation was not fully self-propelled, and the fourth was not fully encapsulated. Still, they do provide some insight into the dynamics of self-encapsulation. It is not our purpose here to do justice to any of these cases, but to describe their basic features for illustrative purposes.

Shortly after Uruguay gained its independence in 1830, the country was torn by civil strife between two gaucho armies, named after the color of their insignia Colorado (red) and Blanco (white). The first president of Uruguay was Rivera, the head of Colorado; his army-party held the upper hand for most of the years that followed. But the Colorado was never able to defeat decisively the Blanco; this kept the country in the torment of war that flared up sporadically over the next two generations, as the two neighboring powers of Argentina and Brazil were feeding the fire. Various limitations on warring were introduced over the years, such as limiting the arena (excepting the cities) and the means of war, under the pressure of business groups, professional groups, and ranchers, whose losses were heavy and who were tired of the continuous strife. At the turn of the century the government turned civilian and, pressed by a dissenting Colorado wing, allowed the Blanco to participate in the elections. These were initially quite fraudulent and led to a short but bloody clash between the sides in 1904. Though the election was won by the Colorado, it was followed by several reforms that allowed more genuine participation in political life for all sides and much advanced the shift of the conflict between various societal groups to political-constitutional channels. Armed confrontation between the sides disappeared. Now the Colorado and the Blanco (renamed Nationals) are two parties which fight each other with ballots, leaflets, campaign promises, and the like, but not with arms. Encapsulation first limited the warfare and now rules it out (Fitzgibbon, 1954).

Labor-management relations in most modern capitalist societies knew an earlier period of considerable violence which was gradually ruled out and is today practically excluded. In the United States, for instance, in the first half of the nineteenth century, labor organizations were viewed as conspiracies and fought with all the instruments management could marshal, including the local police, militia, armed strike-breakers, professional spies, and the like. The workers, in turn, did not refrain from resorting to dynamite and other means of sabotage nor from beating the strike-breakers. The Haymarket riot of 1886 and the Homestead strike of 1892 are probably the most often cited battlegrounds of American management and labor. At the end of the 19th century labor gradually won some rights of organization and collective bargaining, though the process of ruling out violence, on both sides, continued well into the 1930s. While sporadic violence still erupts, by and large the power of the sides in a conflict is assessed without resort to force, and the means of conflict are largely limited to peaceful strikes, public relations campaigns, appeals to government agencies, and so on. The typical representative of the side is a lawyer or someone coached by a lawyer, not a strongarm man or an agitator. While there never was a state of all-out war between American labor and management, there is no question but that over the last two generations their means and modes of conflict have become much more institutionalized and constitutional, and violence as a means of conflict has largely been excluded (Perlman, 1957).

These two cases, different in practically every aspect, have one characteristic in common: both occurred within a national society, and hence could to some degree draw on it; in both, the sides were under some pressure from the society to curb their conflict. In this sense encapsulation was not self-propelling and provides a poor analogue for the study of intersocietal conflicts. Actually the limitation is not as severe as it might first seem, since initially labor was not a recognized part of society; the relations between the industrial and the working classes were referred to as those between "two nations." Part of the process of encapsulation was indeed the integration of labor into the American society, and the relationship between management and labor in the industrial context benefited from the evolution of the bond between them as classes in the realm of the national society. For instance, it made it possible for both sides to work out some of their differences by turning to the legislature, which was initially responsive only to one of them.

The same point can be made about Uruguay. It is not as if a full-fledged national society existed to begin with; actually it evolved in part out of the process of encapsulation and in the effort to contain the conflict between the Whites and the Reds. In this sense encapsulation here was more self-propelling than in the case of labor-management relations. In capitalist societies it was a question of admitting into the national community a new social group; in the case of Uruguay it was more a question of creating such a community.

The encapsulation case most often cited is that of the religious wars, which seems more relevant since it was "international," transgressing the boundaries of any one society. The history of the religious wars, waged in Europe between the Catholics and Protestants in the sixteenth and seventeenth centuries, is a highly complex one. Its main feature, though, is that somehow the contest was transformed from a war of armies to a competition between churches. Missionaries replaced knights, orders replaced the columns of warriors, and persuasion replaced violence. The transition, to be sure, was gradual. First, some areas were excepted; Richelieu, for instance, allowed the Huguenots to pursue their Protestant religion in their part of Catholic France. The rule of *cuius regio eius religio* also limited the extent of violence for a while, though a fuller limitation of the conflict followed only when tolerance evolved for both religions in each territory.

Encapsulation here was self-propelling, since there was hardly an encompassing society that could impose limitations on conflict between Catholic and Protestant states; initially the conflict was universal, in terms of the then relevant universe, and the limitations on it—whose evolutions (in particular the role of nationalism) have yet to be studied—must have grown largely out of the conflict itself. Still, even this analogue is less than completely satisfying, not only because it took many years of violence to tire the parties to the extent that they became ready for encapsulation, but also because their mutual tolerance seems to have grown only as secular conflicts, those of nationalism, replaced the religious ones. The parties were rearranged and war continued under different flags. In this sense, the European encapsulation did not advance enough to provide a helpful analogue.

Price Wars As an Analogue

To close this long quest for a model, I find by far the most rewarding analogue in quite a different area; namely, in the avoidance of price wars in certain industries. To obviate the necessity of discussing a multitude of irrelevant details, a hypothetical case will have to suffice. Imagine two superfirms competing over the car market; one firm seeks to capture a larger and larger share of the market; the other firm is trying to hold on to its share. The competition is waged (let us assume, in order not to complicate matters unnecessarily) through changes in quality and in prices; that is, the expanding company attempts to cut into the market of the other one by offering automobiles of higher quality for lower prices. The defensive firm counters by matching the offers of the expanding firm. Both companies realize that an all-out price war might well be ruinous for both sides, and the small price markdowns might easily lead one side or the other to offer larger ones, soon passing the point at which cars are sold above cost and thereby undermining the economic viability of both firms. Quality contests, in which each firm tries to excel over the other, are also expensive; but for reasons that are not completely clear, quality contests are much more self-limiting and much less likely to ruin the companies.

For these reasons it is more "rational" all around to limit the interfirm competition to quality contests; indeed, years pass without a price war; the companies seem to have implicitly "agreed" not to resort to this devastating means of conflict. But any day a price war might erupt. The expansionist firm, set on gaining a larger share of the market, any day might turn to a price war if it finds that it is making no progress in the quality contests. The defensive firm, on the other hand, attempting to make the other firm accept a duopolistic sharing of the market, feels it must not allow even a small fraction of the market to shift to the other one; even a small encroachment would reward and thus encourage expansionist efforts. The defensive firm, it is hard to deny, might have to initiate a price war to counter encroachments on its share of the market. Both firms realize that by resorting to price war they might undermine their own viability, but both hope that the price war will be limited and that they will be able to use it to show their determined commitment to whatever policy they favor, be it expansionist or duopolistic. Theoretically there are several ways out of this tense and potentially ruinous situation; in practice it seems the range is much more limited.

The solution advocated by the defensive firm is to formalize and legalize the existing allocation of the market; each firm will hold on to its part, and thus *both price* and *quality* contests, the conflict in *toto,* would be stopped once and for all. The expansionist firm finds it difficult to accept this duopolistic solution; such freezing of markets provides no outlet for its ambition and it feels that some buyers, given a free choice, would prefer its product. Whether its ambitions are justified or its feelings valid does not matter; in either event it refuses to accept the duopolistic settlement and there is danger that the implicit curbs on the conflict will be eroded.

The tension thus generated—either firm might suddenly find that a price war has begun—has led several executives on both sides to consider an all-out price war to drive the other firm to bankruptcy; but this, the cooler heads on both sides point out, requires taking some rather forbidding risks, actually endangering the very survival of the firm. Economics is not enough of a science, and the information about the resources of the other firm is not adequate, to provide any assurance about the outcome of such a showdown. In short, while this alternative is constantly considered, it has been avoided so far because it is believed to be too risky.

Still another approach, favored only by a few, is to form a monopoly by merging the two superfirms. But practically everybody realizes that the two firms could never agree who the president of the merged corporation should be, what it should produce, how to share the profits, etc. This solution may not be dangerous but it seems unfeasible.

Finally, the existing precarious "encapsulation" might be extended not by imposing new arrangements but by building an extension of existing relations between the two firms. This would involve making an explicit *agreement* to avoid price wars and setting up limited *machinery* to enforce the agreement, while allowing—within very broad limits—*free competition* through quality. The goal here would be to formalize an implicit accommodation toward which the firms have moved by themselves; to provide both sides with reliable assurances that there will be no regressions; to relieve the psychological strains and the economic cost of fear. Unlike the duopolistic approach, encapsulation does not rule out continuation of the competition: while some means of conflict (price wars) are ruled out, others (quality improvements) are legitimized. *It should be emphasized that this conflict-under-rules, or competition, is not far removed from the existing relationship between the firms,* which was in effect limited to quality contests and avoidance of price wars but which involved no explicit agreement. The question is not whether the conflict is or is not imposing limits on itself, i.e. encapsulating, but whether the capsule formed is to remain implicit or to be further strengthened by being made explicit.

Among the conditions under which the firms are likely to be willing to shift to explicit curbs on conflict are the following: both firms have to realize that (a) their chances of driving the other into bankruptcy (winning a total victory) are minimal; (b) unless explicitly and effectively ruled out, price wars may occur and would very probably be ruinous to both—that is, implicit encapsulation is too weak; (c) the expansionist firm has to accept the limited outlet for its ambition provided by competition in quality, on the assumption that trying to satisfy greater ambitions is too dangerous and that the only other alternative offered is a duopoly in which there would be no safe outlet at all; (d) the defensive firm has to be willing to forgo its desire to frustrate completely the drive of the other firm, because it realizes that in the long run such an effort is unlikely to succeed, if only because buyers like to shift; and the other firm would probably not agree to pacification through a duopolistic division of the market. At the same time, the defensive firm has to feel able and *be* able to compete in quality; to feel that losses of buyers will be at worst limited, probably temporary, with some real possibility of regaining customers lost earlier. Thus competition will jeopardize the defensive firm's control of its present share of the market, but it will also open the door to potential gains.

Validation

The international analogues to the interfirm model are too obvious to need spelling out. The Western response to the Communist challenge is largely dominated by the sharp distinction between parties in conflict and parties in peace. East and West are in conflict; resolution through the formation of a world government or all-out war are seen as either unfeasible or immoral, or both. The main Western approaches are "protracted conflict" and a search for pacification. The first approach foresees no accommodation with the Communist system and hence prepares for many years of conflict. The other approach implies a hope of full resolution as the Communist system mellows. A third alternative—open competition in some spheres coupled with a prohibition of conflict in others, through effective international machinery—is not now being viewed as a realistic goal or as the direction in which East-West relations are actually shifting.

The fusion of containment and deterrence, policies that still form the essence of contemporary American strategy, reflects this conception. For the advocates of "protracted conflict" it means holding the line, buying time, though it is never quite clear for what this time is to be used. For the advocates of pacification, this strategy offers a solution reminiscent of the stalemate of the Anglo-French conflict over

Africa in the 1890s. It suggests, in effect, a duopoly dividing the world into two spheres of influence along the containment line; each side is deterred from challenging the other's sphere by nuclear, conventional, and subconventional arms. If such an arrangement were acceptable to the expansionist camp, according to this view, then both sides could live happily ever after in a state of peaceful coexistence.

Duopoly, in this as in other cases, is a stance favored by the challenged side which seeks to preserve its sphere of influence; it is one of the least attractive alternatives for the expansionist side, requiring it to give up its ambitions and its drive and settle for whatever it had gained before the agreement. The central question is whether there is any other approach which the United States could advocate that would be more attractive to the U.S.S.R. and still be in line with the basic values and objectives of the West. The disarmer's answer is encapsulation of the interbloc conflict so as to allow full and open competition in unarmed capabilities and effectively to rule out armed competition.

There is an important psychological difference between duopoly and encapsulation. Duopoly seeks to extinguish the expansionist drive by frustration: if the Soviets are confronted with an "unalterable counterforce at every point where they show signs of encroaching upon the interests of a peaceful and stable world" (Kennan, 1947), they will gain nothing and sooner or later stop trying. Encapsulation, by contrast, draws upon both negative sanctions and positive rewards. Violations of the rules must be frustrated, but the use of "allowed" means of conflict is rewarded. This approach provides a legitimate outlet for ambition. In this sense encapsulation builds on sublimation, not on extinction.

This difference in psychological quality has some significance for the West, too. The combination of containment and deterrence is not only hindering the Communist efforts but also frustrating the West. Ever since Korea this policy has faced domestic political difficulties because it offers no accommodation except protracted conflict or because the expected accommodation— peaceful coexistence—has not yet been achieved, half a generation after the policy was initiated. Our state of continuous half-mobilization is alien to democracies in general and to the American tradition in particular; the psychological pressure is toward either a rush strike or appeasement, though effective leadership has so far countered both. Encapsulation would allow an end to the psychological state of war and, in peaceful competition, provide an outlet for Western drives as well, since unarmed efforts would have no geographical limits. Trade with Poland, cultural exchange with Outer Mongolia, etc., might be forerunners of broader efforts.

Encapsulation requires drawing a sharp line between permissible and nonpermissible means, but *where* the line is to be drawn is a different question altogether. Theoretically it can be drawn between all-out and limited wars, nuclear and conventional wars, inner and outer space, and the like. There are considerations of political feasibility, inspection technology, and the assessment of the dangers of escalation of permissible into nonpermissible conflicts. Such questions cannot be explored within the limits of this article. Here we will explore the characteristics of an encapsulated conflict where the line falls between armed and unarmed means, where war is tabooed but competition in aid, trade, and ideas is fully accepted. One may ask whether the East and the West do not already, in effect, rule out nuclear war and most other kinds, and focus their sparring on a space race and a development race, i.e., unarmed competition.

In effect they do, but the analogue of the two rival firms highlights the difference between an implicit and unenforced limitation on conflict and an explicit and enforced one. The present interbloc accommodation is of the first type. Whatever limitations have been introduced are based on expedient and probably transient considerations. There is little in the present system to prevent either party from exploiting some major technological breakthrough (e.g., in the field of anti-missile defense) by means of an all-out blow against the other. Secondly, since the existing limitations on the conflict are self-imposed and have never been explicitly negotiated and agreed upon, they are vague and ambiguous. Khrushchev, for instance, may not have anticipated the American reaction to his Cuban missiles; yet the U.S. saw them as a major violation of the status quo which it thought the U.S.S.R. had gradually come to accept. Thus violations *might* be quite unintentional and still trigger the spiral of responses and counter-responses that would split open the capsule of implicit limitations.

Thirdly, since there is no *effective machinery for adjusting* the implicit curbs on conflict, the main way of seeking to reduce or extend their scope is to commit violations; these efforts are highly volatile and endanger the whole capsule. The lack of effective machinery also means that arbitration procedures are worked out each time on an *ad hoc* basis. Lastly, practically *no machinery is evolved for validation and enforcement* of the rules. The sides rely almost completely on their partisan reporting for validation and on the threat of retaliation for enforcement. Thus they always hover only one step away from unlimited conflict. (Among the exceptions are the mutual inspection privileges included in the Antarctica agreement and the 1963 treaty for partial cessation of nuclear tests.)

New World

There are two factors, one obvious and one less obvious, that exert pressure on both the U.S. and the U.S.S.R. to move toward a higher international order, toward a more explicit and enforceable limitation of interbloc conflict. One lies in the technology of weapons, the other in the change in bloc solidarity.

When the basis of our current "duopolistic" strategy was formulated in 1946–47 there were only four atomic devices in the world, while by 1964 the United States alone commanded more than 40,000 atomic and nuclear weapons. Their dangers have often been listed, including unintentional nuclear war growing out of mechanical accident, unauthorized behavior, miscalculation, escalation, technological breakthrough, and the spread of nuclear capabilities to other countries (Kahn, 1960). These dangers weigh heavily on both the American and the Soviet leadership. In themselves they do not suffice to produce a movement toward a new international system, but they do constitute a background factor that keeps alive—if not active—an interest in ways of curbing the conflict.

Less often discussed in this context is the impact of the disarray of the two camps, which is still often viewed as transient. Actually it seems that neither the U.S.S.R. nor the U.S. will reestablish in the foreseeable future the kind of superpower hegemony they enjoyed during the 1950s. The rising power and foreign-policy independence of France, of Communist China (which makes up with resolve for part of its lack of resources), of Britain to a degree, and soon of West Germany make for changes in the basic international constellation, and these changes tend *to favor more effective and far-reaching encapsulation.* In the more nearly bipolar world of the 1950s the rules of the game could be left implicit and much reliance could be placed on the fact that the blocs were stalemating each other. As long as there were only two camps the room for maneuvering was small and the moves highly predictable.

The rebellion of bloc-lieutenants opens the international arena to many new combinations. The Germans, French, and Chinese fear an American-Russian deal at their expense; the U.S. fears a German, or French, or German-French deal with Russia. France recognized Communist China; Britain was refused a hookup on the American-Soviet "hot line"; Canada and Britain broke the policy of economic isolation of Cuba, etc.

Both superpowers are now challenged by junior competitors and threatened by the prospect of nuclear anarchy. Unable to solve these problems on their own, they resort increasingly to the joint imposition of universal rules. The direct communication line between the White House and the Kremlin, completed in September 1963, is one measure. Its heralded function is to prevent accidental war, but it may also allow the U.S. or the U.S.S.R. to dissociate itself from a provocation by one of its allies. Thus it warns the other powers to heed the big two and respect the order they establish—or else be left out on a limb. The limited ban on nuclear testing is another rule set by the big two for global adherence. If this trend continues, the order-by-blocs may be *in part* replaced by regulation through universal rules backed by the two superpowers (and smaller powers). American and Russian support of India against China, U.S. curbs on Cuban exiles, and Russian curbs on Castro agents in Latin America—all these fit the new mold.

Next Steps

If both sides should continue to seek joint or coordinated acts and encapsulation continued to advance, to what areas might the attention of the superpowers turn next? The disarmer's way of putting the same question would be this: assuming an "optimistic scenario"—that is, under the best circumstances that can realistically be expected—in what ways might the presently limited encapsulation be extended? There seem to be three major areas: (a) the reduction of armed capacities, without which little credence can be given to conflict curbs in other areas; (b) expansion of unarmed capacities as these become, even more than before, the center of the global competition; and (c) strengthening the line that separates the unarmed conflicts from the armed ones, thus making unarmed competition less volatile.

The following discussion spells out some of these possibilities. It may seem very much like a trip into a never-never land unless the reader keeps in mind that it represents the optimistic limit of the range of possible developments and that measures which seem impossible one day are often implemented the next day.

Reduction of Arms

In the last decade and a half, both sides have tried to increase their strategic force by qualitative and quantitative improvements. Each side has responded to the achievements of the other by fresh efforts of its own. But as both sides acquire fully protected second-strike (retaliatory) forces, which will make any additional build-up unjustifiable, this upward arms spiral is expected to slow down and even halt (McNamara, 1963). American production of nuclear bombs and long-range bombers has slowed down already; the production of missiles is expected to be curtailed later on (*ibid.*). If the U.S.S.R. does likewise, once having protected its strategic forces, the strategic arms race may for the first time find a plateau—especially if there is no major technological break-through.

An effective ban on deployment of weapons in outer space, which can be comparatively readily verified, would be a natural correlate; it would prevent the arms race from spilling over into a virtually limitless area.[2]

Many experts believe that some reduction of strategic forces could be initiated at this stage, to be verified without inspection—through intelligence, destruction of weapons at a neutral spot, and other devices (Institute for Defense Analyses, 1962). Additional reductions would require considerable inspection of the member countries by outsiders and are, in my judgment, not to be expected in the near future. But reduced forces geared for retaliation would suffice to provide a much more congenial environment for encapsulation. The need to reduce conventional and subconventional forces (those used for subversion and counter-subversion) is usually underplayed, but it seems to me of the utmost importance. All the armed clashes in the last fifteen years involved conventional arms and took place in the large underdeveloped territory, or "third world," which has become the focus of the interbloc contest. It is here that the pattern for unarmed competition is molded, as both the U.S. and the U.S.S.R. are sending aid, technical assistance, cultural missions, and the like to the same group of countries (e.g. Indonesia, India, Egypt). Claims of superiority for their respective technologies, economies, methods of administration, industrialization, etc., can thus be tested according to the degree and quality of help offered to the underdeveloped nations. This is the kind of competition that any fair-minded observer cannot help but bless. The problem is, though, that the limits of this unarmed contest are neither fixed nor guarded; it constantly threatens to spill over into limited armed confrontations, brush-fire wars, that both hinder encapsulation and threaten to escalate.

A step toward understanding between the two camps would be to treat the whole underdeveloped world as a big Austria out of which both sides would keep their armed forces, both overt and covert. Such a multicontinental embargo on the shipment of forces and arms, if it could be effected, would have the following virtues: (a) it would avoid the dangers of escalation by keeping the superpowers out of local conflicts; (b) it would enhance encapsulation by providing a large arena in which the two blocs could compete peacefully to their heart's desire; (c) it would allow revolutionary forces in these countries to run their course without big-power intervention—in other words, the fate of governments would be decided by the people of those countries rather than by "big brothers." There is good reason to believe that this would encourage governments that are more development-oriented and responsive to their people than are the present ones; and this in turn is probably the best way to forward their commitment to freedom and social justice.

Under most circumstances, such an extension of the "Austrian" system to scores of countries will not be feasible. It is likely only if the dangers of unintentional war and nuclear anarchy are more fully recognized, if the rebellion of the bloc-lieutenants continues, and if the U.S.-U.S.S.R. experience with limited agreements continues to be positive. Even under these favorable circumstances, certain safeguards will be required.

Such safeguards might include *remote deterrence forces* against armed intervention in the third area. As both sides withdrew their forces, as they did from Austria in 1955, they could be expected to hold these forces in high readiness outside the area to deter or counter any violation by the other side. Furthermore, some *machinery* would be necessary to investigate alleged violations of the embargo. The Communist bloc has often provided indigenous troops with arms, as was the case in Greece in 1946–47 and in Indochina in 1953–54, without initially arousing much public attention. On the other hand the Western press has often accused indigenous forces, such as the Moslem rebels in Lebanon in 1958, of receiving armed help from the Communist bloc when this was not the case. All this is hardly avoidable in the Cold War context but it could be highly detrimental to the "arms-out" agreement.

The task of validating the embargo rules might well turn out to be less forbidding than is generally expected. While it is almost impossible to prevent the actual flow of arms across borders, practically all secret shipments of arms in significant quantities have become known within weeks after they occurred, whether it was to Egypt, Cuba, Guatemala, or Palestine.

The presence of a *United Nations observer force* on the boundaries of the third area, ready to move to places where violations are reported or anticipated, could also assist in validating the embargo. Such a force would be equipped, not with weapons, but with inspection tools such as searchlights, infrared instruments, helicopters, and jeeps. The embargo agreement should entitle each side to ask for the deployment of this force without any right of veto. A refusal to admit the UN observer force to take positions on a border—say, between the U.S.S.R. and Afghanistan—would in itself constitute sufficient evidence that the embargo had been violated, and would leave the other side free to take counter-measures. It is not implied that such an observer force would be completely reliable, but it would serve as an important addition to the remote deterrence forces and partisan sources of information (e.g., intelligence reports). All together—under the favorable conditions of our "optimistic scenario"—these measures might suffice.

Unarmed Capacities

The willingness of the sides to limit their confrontation to an unarmed contest is determined only in part by their fears of an armed one; in part it is determined by their confidence in their nonmilitary capacities. From this view, by far the most encouraging sign for the disarmer is the secular trend, in both camps, to build up these capacities. The Soviets increased their foreign aid from $13 million in 1955 to $403 million in 1959; their number of technical assistants from 4,500 in 1958 to 8,400 by 1962; their propaganda effort was also greatly expanded. At the same time, they reduced the ratio of foreign aid devoted to military assistance by two-thirds and increased accordingly that devoted to economic aid. In a long struggle within the Communist parties of Malaya, Indonesia, India, Japan, the Philippines, and scores of other countries, the new Soviet line that favors progress through nonviolent means over those of terror and insurrection has won, according to Western observers (Morris, 1962). Some observers are quick to add that this is merely a change of tactics, and that the Soviets believe that such constitutional means will serve their expansionist goals better than the violent ones. This is quite true, and for those who seek a full pacification of the interbloc conflict, such a change of tactics might seem of little value. But for encapsulation it is of much interest, since here the continuation of Soviet ambitions is fully expected and accepted, and the question of means used to forward these goals is all-important. No extinction of Soviet goals is hoped for, demanded, or necessary for this form of accommodation. If the Soviets are willing to limit their campaign to peaceful means, this satisfies the conditions under which encapsulation can progress. The Western stand in the limited conflict will then depend on its unarmed capacities.

The West seems increasingly ready to engage fully in such a contest; it has built up unarmed capacities over recent years. The ratio of economic over military foreign aid was greatly increased, the Peace Corps was added, technical assistance was extended, efficacy of information services was improved, association with anti-colonial causes increased, and the Alliance for Progress was initiated. While there are many imperfections in most of these efforts, it must also be pointed out that the claims made about the efficacy of the opponent's efforts are often grossly exaggerated. There is little doubt that if the Western concern and effort in this area were intensified, it could fully compete in the unarmed area.

It is here that the mistaken zero-sum notion often comes to haunt the strategist. Either East or West is likely to have the upper hand in the development race, it is said, and the loser will be under much pressure to broaden the means of conflict employed in an effort to restore its position. Thus any limitation of the conflict, it is said, will be temporary. This view overlooks the important consequence of the vagueness of the measuring rods of the development race. For the last fifteen years, each side claims to be doing better in developing countries in its sphere of influence; in Asia, for instance, both China and India have been watched for more than a decade as test cases for the Communist and the democratic ways of modernization, but no evidence of a "victory" is in sight. Who is doing better, India or China?

Second, the nonaligned countries tend more and more to receive aid from both sides; they trade with both sides, invite their technical assistance, visit their capitals, without joining either bloc; gains in the "sympathies" of these countries are transient, with Pakistan one day more inclined to the West, the next day flirting with Communist China; Egypt, Iraq, Guinea, and many other nonaligned countries "move" somewhat to the East and somewhat to the West, but the total stock of floating votes, which both blocs court, is not depleted. Gradually the two blocs may realize that neither will be victorious in this race, but both will benefit as the "have-not" countries' standard of living rises, as their prospects brighten, and as their stakes in world order are enhanced.

Machinery

The need for a more potent international machinery has often been spelled out. Its value in providing peaceful channels for settlement of differences of interest and viewpoint has often been indicated; its neutralizing role in conflict, its arbitrator function, its service as a neutral meeting ground, have all been told. Much less often discussed are the conditions under which this machinery is likely to evolve. This is a major subject in itself, but in the present context the following points stand out:

(1) The international machinery—be it the UN, the International Court, or a new world disarmament agency—is most likely to evolve significantly if the major powers see it as enhancing their interests. The rebellion of the bloc-lieutenants and the threat of nuclear anarchy seem to involve such interests. In 1964, for the first time, the Soviets recognized a need for a supranational government as an element in disarmament, and the U.S. State Department initiated motions aimed at strengthening the UN.

(2) The need to service the encapsulation process, for instance with an observer force, is another factor that makes the expansion of international machinery more determined by than determining interbloc relations.

(3) In the short run, no major strengthening of international institutions can be expected; the veto in the Security Council is likely to continue and no effective UN police force is likely to be charged with global security. Yet such developments are not necessary for a significant extension of the encapsulation process, for a considerable broadening of interbloc accommodation. If events do follow our "optimistic scenario" of arms reductions, increased reliance on unarmed capacities, and some extension of the power and use of international institutions, a whole vista of new modes of accommodation and world order will open up—modes which can hardly be realistically assessed at this initial stage.

The utopias of a totally disarmed world have been worked out in great detail; now the paths that lead there need to be charted, explored, and cautiously but persistently travelled. The disarmer's best case rests on identifying and enhancing the forces that advance encapsulation.

Notes

1. The relationship between the reduction of armed conflicts and the growth of global community is explored in Part III of Etzioni, 1962.

2. This has been recommended by the UN but still needs to be backed up by the sides, a point elaborated in Chapter 7 of Etzioni, 1964a.

References

Etzioni, Amitai. *The Hard Way to Peace: A New Strategy.* New York: Macmillan, 1962.

————. *The Moon-Doggle: The Domestic and International Implications of the Space Race.* Garden City, N.Y.: Doubleday, 1964a.

————. *Winning Without War.* Garden City, N.Y.: Doubleday, 1964b.

Fitzgibbon, Russell H. *Uruguay, Portrait of a Democracy.* New Brunswick, N.J.: Rutgers University Press, 1954.

Halperin, Morton H. *Limited War in the Nuclear Age.* New York: John Wiley, 1963.

Institute for Defense Analyses. *Verification and Response in Disarmament Agreements.* Woods Hole Summer Study, Washington, D.C., 1962.

Kahn, Herman. *On Thermonuclear War.* Princeton, N.J.: Princeton University Press, 1960.

Kennan, George F. ("X" as pseudonym). "Sources of Soviet Conduct," *Foreign Affairs,* 25 (July 1947), 566–82.

McNamara, Robert S. Testimony before the House Armed Services Committee, January 30, 1963.

Morris, Bernard S. "Recent Shifts in Communist Strategy: India and Southeast Asia." In John H. Kautsky (ed.), *Political Change in Underdeveloped Countries.* New York: Wiley, 1962.

Perlman, S. *A History of Trade Unionism in the United States.* New York: Macmillan, 1957.

A Paradigm for the Study of
Political Unification

A paradigm is more than a perspective but less than a theory. It provides a set of interrelated questions, but no hypothetical answers or account of validated propositions. It provides a "language," a net of variables, but it does not specify the relationships among the parameters of these variables. It is less vague than a mere perspective, providing an ordered, specific, and often logically exhaustive and tightly ordered focus for research and speculation. A paradigm is often a stage on the way from an old perspective to a new theory.[1]

The test of a paradigm is not only the validity of the theories constructed with its help, but also its fruitfulness in terms of the spectrum of significant problems whose study benefits from it. First we turn to delineating the subject matter of our paradigm and then we present the paradigm itself. The major body of this article is devoted to an indication of the kinds of problems that can be handled by this instrument; at the same time, we hope to point out some of the issues that are essential to an understanding of political unification.

Delineation of the Subject and Concepts

Our paradigm provides a set of dimensions for the study of a process—specifically, the formation of political communities out of units that previously shared no or only a few political

Note: This essay was originally published in *World Politics,* 1962, *15*(1), 44–47. It is reprinted with permission. It was written while I was a research associate at the Institute of War and Peace Studies, Columbia University. I am indebted to Ernst B. Haas for valuable comments on an earlier version.

bonds. This process is referred to as *unification*. We are particularly interested in the unification of already existing nations. But the paradigm applies also to the formation of other political communities, such as national communities, out of tribal, village, or feudal societies.

A community is fully established only when it has self-sufficient integrative mechanisms—that is, the continuation of its existence and form[2] is provided by its own processes and not dependent upon those of external systems or member-units. A *political community* is a community that possesses three kinds of integration: (1) it has a monopoly over the legitimate use of means of violence (though it may "delegate" some of this monopoly to member-units); (2) it has a center of decision making that is able to affect the allocation of resources and rewards throughout the community; and (3) it is the superior focus of political identification for the large majority of the politically aware citizens.

The degree of integration is the main characteristic that distinguishes political communities, whose member-units are nations, from other international systems. *International system* is the more encompassing concept, indicating that changes in the action of one nation affect actions in others *and* that these changes, in turn, have repercussions on the unit or units in which or from which the change was initiated.[3] While the parts of a system are, by definition, interrelated, its level of integration—on each of the three counts specified above—may be high or low, and its interdependence may be self-maintained or sustained by the component units (e.g., nations), or be a product of the external environment (e.g., forced by a superior power, not a member of the system). One cannot, for instance, deduce from the fact that the U.S.S.R. and the United States have become part of one global system—that they affect each other—anything about the integrative level of this relationship.[4] Even countries engaged in war are parts of one system. In short, parts of systems are interdependent; members of communities are integrated.

Several of the most frequently used terms in international studies, usually defined inductively and eclectically, can be viewed as applying to international systems that differ consistently in their degree of integration. International organizations, blocs, and empires are all international systems that are more integrated than *mere* international systems but less integrated than political communities. They can be fruitfully ordered according to their relative position on the three dimensions of integration. First let us consider monopoly of the legitimate use of means of violence. *International organizations* command no such means,[5] let alone a monopoly over their legitimate use. Members of *blocs* (and alliances) often coordinate their military efforts (as did the Allied Forces in World War II) but the forces remain chiefly under the control of the member-units, the nations. *Empires* have armed forces of their own, but their claim to legitimate monopoly is frequently challenged by member-units. Only political communities are international systems that have well-established, legitimate monopolies.

All of these types of international systems have some common decision-making center, but they differ greatly in the capacity and scope of this center. *International organizations* are consultative bodies, whose decision-making scope is limited to one or a few spheres (e.g., postal services, or health, or labor, etc.), and to functions that are not essential to the survival of the member-units, nor do these functions have a significant bearing on their ability to pursue their national interests. The decision-making of *blocs* (and alliances) tends to be consultative, like that of international organizations, but their scope is larger. They are often multi-functional (e.g., political and military; cultural and economic), and the functions affected are more highly valued by the member-societies than those involved in typical international organizations. *Empires* have a considerable amount of decision-making power that binds member-units—i.e., their decisions are enforceable. Their scope is larger than that of blocs, frequently encompassing political, military, and economic functions as well as those of communication, culture, education, and the like. The decision-making centers of empires are not as encompassing as those of political communities, not in regard to their power but in the legitimation of the decisions made. Since membership in empires is not voluntary, and responsiveness to member-units is not high, it might well be said that empires have "supranational" power, but only limited "supranational" authority.[6]

Finally, international organizations rarely serve as a focus of political identification. *Blocs,* historically, have been lacking in this value, though since World War I blocs have acquired some ideological meaning (as the contemporary "Free World" has). *Empires,* on the whole, are not much more integrated on this score than blocs, but they usually have at least one core unit (Rome, Britain) that strongly identifies with the empire, a commitment only approximated but not matched by bloc leaders. There was a paternalistic element in the orientation of the core-country of empires to those subordinated to it; the orientation of bloc "superpowers" to other bloc members tends to be governed more by expediency. The core-countries used to view the empire as an extension of their own polities; they often attempted to assimilate the subordinate units into the superordinating one. They even granted citizenship to the indigenous populations. The bloc superpower, on the other hand, usually views the bloc as a limited partnership with outsiders. (The Soviet system comes closer to an empire than a bloc from this viewpoint.[7]) At least some local elites in the subordinate countries responded by identifying with the empire, a phenomenon less intensively reproduced in the attitude of members of blocs to the superpower (e.g., it seems that there were more Romanophiles in Greece than there are U.S.-philes in England). In short, empires drew more identification than blocs but neither attracted the kind of encompassing and intensive identification that political communities command.

Thus, in sum, on these three counts, international organizations are less integrated than blocs, blocs less than empires, and empires less than political communities.[8]

The concepts of international organization, bloc, empire, and political community are used in the literature of international relations only approximately as defined here.

Since these concepts were originally employed by historians and journalists, they do not constitute part of a formal language or theory. Hence it is not surprising that when they are defined deductively and viewed as positions in a multidimensional space, some discrepancies between their definition and their traditional usage occur. By our definition the Soviet bloc, between 1945 and 1953—at least some parts of it—was not a "bloc," but an empire; parts of the Roman Empire, at least in its heyday, were not an "empire," but a political community. It would be futile to search for deductive definitions that will exactly fit concrete cases or inductive concepts. Actually it is a point in favor of our approach that it calls attention to the fact that behind the commonly used labels lie analytically different phenomena. We gain from this distinction by being able to note that since 1953 the Eastern European part of the Soviet system (with the exception of Albania) has changed from an empire system to a system somewhat closer to that of a political community, rather than stating that the Soviet system—all of it—was and is a bloc, just as, let us say, the Free World is. Similarly, it might be useful to state that the Roman system, during its heyday, at least for the countries other than those at its periphery, came much closer to a political community than, let us say, the Ottoman system, which was chiefly an empire. Such statements require keeping our definition analytically pure, and viewing reality as being composed of various configurations of our analytical concepts.

Our paradigm serves not so much to study this or that state of integration but the process of unification, a process through which integration is increased. Since systems that are moving toward a community—that is, a high level of integration—are often confused with those that have *reached* such a state—as when one refers to the present European or Scandinavian system as a supranational community—we introduce a concept to avoid this ambiguity. We use the term *unions* to refer to potential political communities, systems that are in the process of increasing their integration. *Political communities* is used to refer strictly to highly integrated systems.

A Unification Paradigm

Four major questions have to be asked about every process: Under what conditions is it initiated? What forces direct its development? What path does it take? What is the state of the system affected by the process once that process is terminated? We use this paradigm of processes to construct one for the study of political unification, especially for the study of unification of nations. We ask first, what is the state of the international relations and the various political units when the increase in integration is initiated? Which factors enhance, and which hinder, unification? Once unification has been initiated, we ask what forces are applied to control the process, and how are these forces distributed among the various participants? What pattern does unification itself follow? Do all societal sectors unify simultaneously or successively and, if successively, in what order? Which sector comes first, which later? Finally, we ask, once unification is interrupted or has ceased, what degree of integration has the system reached, how encompassing has it become, and what function does it serve?

Whatever the independent variable—background conditions, integrating forces, retarding factors—we turn to the same dependent variables: the degree and scope of unification; that is, we wish to outline the problems involved in determining the effect these various factors have on the success or failure of unification.

More specifically, our paradigm includes the following dimensions:[9]

1. The Pre-Unification State
   i. Unit properties
      a. individual properties
      b. analytical properties
   ii. Environment properties
      a. non-social (ecological) properties
      b. social properties
   iii. System properties

      a. pre-unification integration and scope
      b. shared properties (other than integration)
2. The Unification Process: Integrating Forces
    i. Effective configurations
   ii. Effective distributions
      a. degree of elitism
      b. degree of internalization
3. The Unification Process: Integrating Sectors
    i. The first stage: Take-Off
      a. determinants of take-off
      b. the take-off sector
   ii. Expansion of the union's scope
      a. a stable scope
      b. sequences of unification
4. The Termination State
    i. Degree and scope
   ii. The dominant function

In the following pages we briefly discuss some of the conceptual problems involved in applying our paradigm, devoting the main body of this article to a discussion of the specific researchable questions that the paradigm raises for those who study political unification.

The Paradigm: Conceptualization and Illustrations

The Pre-Unification State

The question of under what condition the process of unification is initiated must be answered from four viewpoints. First, what is the state of each societal unit that is to become a member of a particular union? Is it likely to resist unification or is it willing and able? Second, what is the aggregate of these units like: are most or all units "ready" for unification, or only a few? Third, what are the units like that do not participate—that is, are environmental factors favorable for unification? Finally, to what degree was there international independence and integration before the process of unification (i.e., of build-up in the degree and scope of integration) had occurred? Many specific questions have to be answered before any such general questions can be tackled. In the following pages no attempt is made to examine specific problems or provide any inventory of all or most of the issues involved. We will only illustrate each of the four basic perspectives by discussing one or two of the questions raised by an effort to establish the conditions that existed before or during a unification process.

Unit Properties
Individual Properties: Integration and Resistance to Unification. The unification process is one in which control of the means of violence, resources, and rewards and identification are transferred from member-units to the system in which they are members. This obviously involves at least some reduction of the integration of the member-units (they become more dependent on the system). It is, therefore, clear that the degree to which these units have been initially integrated greatly affects their potential resistance to unification. The question is, what level or levels of unit-integration are most conducive to unification? One possibility is low-level integration. Haas, for instance, showed that the internal fragmentation of European societies (e.g., sharp cleavages between labor and management) enhanced the development of the ECSC and the EEC.[10] Another possibility is high integration. Countries that fall apart, like the Republic of the Congo, can hardly form a union with other countries. The efforts of Ghana to unify its tribes impede its effort to give substance to the Union of African States that it founded with Guinea and Mali. Actually, most developing countries are less integrated than developed ones, and less often engage in successful inter-country unifications.[11] Thus lack of unit-integration might hinder super-unit integration.

Other possibilities also have to be entertained until research answers these questions: A medium level of unit-integration might be optimal for unification. Or, medium unit-integration might be conducive to the first stage of unification; low unit-integration, to later stages. Or, unit-integration might be high in countries supporting unification, and low in those resisting it.

Further specification of the study of the effects of unit-integration might proceed by studying the effects of differences in the degree of integration on the three dimensions spelled out above. For instance, we may need to know how much control over means of violence the government of a member-nation has, how responsive the national center of decision-making is to various groups of the population, and how legitimate the government is. What is the nature of the unit-legitimation: is it chiefly religious or secular? In either case, is it national (like the tradition of the English Church or the American "heritage") or cosmopolitan (as Catholicism and communism are)? What effect do these differences have on unification?

The reader may have noticed by now that we studiously avoid the term "supranational communities," which is often used in referring to regional political communities. This term should be avoided because it turns one possible parameter of a variable into part of the definition of a concept. In supranational communities the legitimation of the unit-members is high, and it is of the secular-historical type called "nationalism." But many historical *and* contemporary unions have been initiated among units that either were expressing their nationalism by creating the union (e.g., Germany, Italy) or took place before nationalism significantly affected either the units or the system (e.g., the federation of Nigeria). In short, unification might be initiated in a prenationalist period, in a post-nationalist one, or be, itself, an expression of nationalism. It would seem that post-nationalist unifications would be more difficult to attain than the other two kinds, and that unification that expresses nationalism would be the easiest to accomplish. But, so far, the fact is that the two most successful contemporary unions—the Scandinavian one and the EEC—are post-nationalist. Thus, this question, too, must be left open for further research.

Analytical Properties: Heterogeneity and Unification. Analytical properties are not the property of any single unit but are derived from a study of the distribution of unit-attributes.[12] Unlike unit-properties and relational properties, analytical properties cannot be observed. They are "second order" abstractions.

The most important analytical property for the study of prerequisites of unification seems to be the degree of heterogeneity of the merging units. It is commonly assumed that the less homogeneous a group, whether it is a small group, community, or nation, the less likely it is to be highly integrated. It would seem that this is also the case on the international level. Differences in income per capita (or, national wealth) have been one of the factors that hindered or undermined unions. The higher income per capita of Nigeria and of the Ivory Coast was one reason they did not join the Ghana-Guinea-Mali union; it affected Jamaica's vote against the constitution of the Federation of the West Indies (September 1961); it contributed to the secession of Syria from the UAR, and to the Katanga secession from the Republic of the Congo. Richer Senegal broke a union—the Federation of Mali—with poorer Mali. In all these cases, unification would or did entail some "leveling" before the citizens of the unit to be adversely affected were committed to the evolving union. In Syria, for instance, many army officers, politicians, and journalists lost their jobs as the result of the union, and foreign trade privileges, important to the large Syrian merchant class, were concentrated in Cairo.

Most contemporary unification efforts have been made among countries that have not only a similar level of income per capita but also a similar level of literacy, civilization, and culture, and a similar degree of industrialization. This holds for the Central American Union, the two West European unions, two West African unions, and the East European one (all to be discussed below).

Political homogeneity is given as one of the necessary prerequisites for unification,[13] and as one of the reasons why the European Economic Community (EEC)—which includes only democratic countries—was more successful than the European Free Trade Association (EFTA) and NATO, which include both democratic and nondemocratic countries (e.g., Portugal).

It would, however, not be safe to conclude that heterogeneity necessarily hinders unification. Because nationalism initially tended to unify people with a common ethnic background, a shared cultural tradition and language, the impression was created that these were necessary prerequisites for unification. Actually, an increasing number of nations, like Switzerland and Canada, are highly different on all these counts. Nigeria, for example, holds 250 different tribes. When the Nigerian government issued pamphlets to explain its new constitution to its citizens, it had to publish them in twelve languages in addition to English. Many nation-unions are multilingual, including Benelux, the EEC, the Scandinavian union, and the East European union.

Moreover, there is at least one major type of heterogeneity that enhances rather than hinders unification. Differences in economic specialization of countries, such as between agrarian and industrial countries, or light and heavy industrial concentrations, are supportive to unification. Thus, the question as to whether heterogeneity indeed hinders unification, or under what conditions it does or does not, has yet to be answered. Nor has the question been solved as to how various properties differ with regard to the degree of homogeneity necessary for unification: Is economic heterogeneity as detrimental as cultural heterogeneity? Is political homogeneity as necessary as similarity in income per capita?

While we are interested here only in these properties as prerequisites, it might be worth while to note in passing that, once unification is launched, it is not only affected by but also affects the degree of heterogeneity. For instance, linguistic heterogeneity is reduced when one language becomes the common *second* language of the participant countries (like Russian in East Europe, and English in those Commonwealth countries for which it is not the primary one). Cultural heterogeneity is somewhat reduced by developing shared educational institutions such as the *College de l'Europe* in Bruges, the new European University of Florence, the Scandinavian Academy (both now planned) as well as increased communication, tourism, and cultural exchange programs. Economic compatibility among the East European countries is promoted by a twenty-year plan of the Council for Economic Mutual Assistance.[14] The Agreement on the Regime for Central American Integrated Industries and the Multilateral Treaty on Central American Free Trade Area and Economic Integration, both signed in June 1958 by the five Central American countries, spell out an inter-country specialization program, according to which new industry developed in one country will not be developed in the others.[15] Finally, political homogeneity was maintained in an earlier Central American union by dropping Guatemala during the period it was under the rule of the left-wing Arbenz government.[16] Thus, the study of the effects of heterogeneity on the success of efforts to initiate unification has to take into account not only that heterogeneity may not necessarily hinder unification, but that when it does, part of the effort to initiate a union might be channeled toward a reduction of the heterogeneity. The degree to which such effort is successful depends, in part, like that of other unification efforts, on the environment in which the effort is made.

Environment Properties: Ecological and Social
Environmental properties include ecological factors, such as the physical environment in which the union is initiated and by which it is surrounded, and social factors—properties of nonmember units that effect unification.

Nonsocial (Ecological) Properties: Union of Nonadjacent Territories. Many ecological factors affect the probability that a union will be initiated, including the morphology of the region, the distribution of natural resources in it, the existence (or nonexistence) of a natural border that marks the area. High mountain ranges, for example, have been an important barrier to unifications of Central America and South America; the recent development of a Pan-American Highway is reported to improve chances that the new unions will be successfully initiated.[17]

Territorial unity of political communities seems to be so important that there is a question as to whether a union of nonadjacent territories—that is, one in which the ecological base of the union is broken up by a "no man's land" (e.g., seas) or by nonmember countries—can be successfully formed at all.

Lack of adjacency is an unsettling, tension-provoking factor even for national political communities. West Germany and West Berlin, and West and East Pakistan are two well-known cases. The separation of a small Israeli enclave on Mt. Scopus in the Palestinian part of Jordan is similarly a source of tension. Adjacency of all member countries seems to be one factor in favor of the EEC, and lack of it seems to be one factor undermining EFTA, in which Austria and Switzerland share a union with Portugal, Britain, and the Scandinavian countries. (Interestingly, the three adjacent members of the EFTA constitute a stronger union, the Scandinavian community.) The United Arab Republic was adversely affected by the lack of a shared border between Syria and Egypt. Albania's low integration into the East European Communist union is in part explained by the lack of a shared border between it and other member countries. (It was much better integrated with the union as long as Yugoslavia was also a member.) Mexico is the only country of the seven members of the Latin American Free Trade Area that shares no borders with the others; it remains to be seen if Mexico will be a viable member. The nonadjacent Ghana-Guinea-Mali union has so far acquired little substance. The stretches of the Caribbean Sea that separate Jamaica from Trinidad and from other islands of the Federation of the West Indies certainly hinder the Federation's development. Rebellions against the national government of Indonesia invariably are initiated on another island than Java, the seat of the government.

It would be hasty, though, to conclude that political unification is impossible without territorial unity. The island groups of both Japan and New Zealand are well integrated; so seem the Philippines; the union of England with Eire disintegrated in 1949, but England maintained its ties with North Ireland; Canada's union with Newfoundland is viable. Denmark is an integral part of a union with Norway and Sweden. One might suspect that these unions maintain themselves because the water stretches that separate their parts are fairly small, but the United States seems to have no difficulties in bridging the 2,000 miles that separate Hawaii from the mainland. Moreover, the British Commonwealth includes countries on five continents, only two of which share a border, and the union now has lasted more than four decades.[18]

The study of the effect of territorial continuity on unification will have to proceed by examining the underlying sociological and political variables that are affected by lack of adjacency in order to determine what compensating mechanisms are used to overcome its negative impact. The most often cited of such factors is hindrance to *transportation of goods and people*, which in turn hinders the integration of the societal units and cultural interactions.

Second, integration is negatively affected by the lack of freedom of *movement for military units*. Nasser might have suppressed the 1961 Syrian secession, or it might not have occurred, if the Egyptian army had been free to interfere from its home bases, unhindered by the intervening states, Jordan and Israel. This seems also to account, in part, for the ability of small Albania to be the only pro-China country of the Eastern European Communist union.

Third, because of the long association with statehood and nationalism, territorial unity has become a *symbol of political unity*, and its lack has therefore become an expression and symbol of division, as is the case in the West Indies, where the islands, rather than their federation, are the major frame of political identification. It would be of interest to establish to what degree being on a separate island bolstered the distinct social identity of Ireland, or of the various islands of Indonesia. To what degree command over modern means of communication and transportation, which these countries are gradually acquiring, will allow them to overcome differences in cultural tradition, language, and historical experiences created by the lack of such means in earlier generations is a question that has to be answered before the impact of lack of adjacency on unification can be determined.

Social Properties: Enemies, Partners, and Diffusion. The threat of a common enemy is probably the factor most often credited with initiating a union of countries. But Deutsch and his associates have already pointed out that this is much less common than is believed, and when a union is initiated to counter an enemy, it tends to disintegrate as the threat passes.[19] The question is, of course, why a defensive alliance sometimes does mature into a more encompassing and lasting union, while in other cases its life is as short, if not shorter, than that of a real or conceived threat. We will return to this question below when the development of unions is discussed; suffice it to say here that the study of "initiation under threat" will have to take account of the predisposition toward unification of sectors *other* than the military, to determine the chances for such a union to succeed.

While the importance of common enemies may well be overemphasized, the desire to unite in order to avail against an overwhelming partner is underplayed for obvious reasons. This seems to be a central factor in *accelerated subregional* unification. We find frequently that when a region is uniting, one subarea is uniting more rapidly than the rest, and that this subarea includes the weaker members of the region. This holds for the Scandinavian countries in the EFTA,[20] for the Benelux countries in the EEC,[21] and for the South in the United States.[22]

But since in each of these cases stronger ties already existed among the subarea units than among the others before regional unification was initiated, the desire to countervail an overwhelming partner—England in EFTA; West Germany and France in the EEC; and the Northeast in the United States—has yet to be established. This would require demonstrating that these subareas continue to maintain a higher level of integration than the rest of the union, and that they are more integrated, the more "overwhelming" the superior partner or partners are.

A third way in which social units that are not a member of a specific union (or subunion) can affect it is through diffusion or imitation, a process often studied by anthropologists but rarely by students of international relations. There seems to be such a thing as "fashion" in international relations, in which institutions that function in one region are transferred to another. The Marshall Plan directly affected the formulation of the Molotov Plan; the formation of the Organization of European Economic Cooperation, in West Europe, under the initiative of the United States, affected the foundation of the Council for Economic Mutual Assistance (CEMA), in East Europe, by the U.S.S.R. The EFTA, created three years after the EEC, often imitated it. For instance, when the EEC accelerated cuts in customs for its members, the EFTA did the same for its members. Even the rates of cuts were similar.[23] While the formation of economic unions in Latin America and Africa was discussed and planned before the development of the EEC, the particular treaties finally signed by LAFTA, the Central American Union, and the *Conseil de l'Entente* were affected by the text of the Treaty of Rome, and the institutions created for its implementation.[24]

While the present vogue is for common markets, the earlier one was for regional commissions. The South Pacific Commission (est. 1947), for instance, "took its model" from the Caribbean Commission (est. 1946). An Economic Commission for Europe was founded in 1947, and one for Latin America in 1948.[25]

The question arises whenever social patterns or political institutions (e.g., the American Constitution) are transferred from one region to another: Are the conditions that allowed for the functioning of the pattern in region x available or reproducible in region y? When this is not the case, one of two things is bound to happen: (a) the vogue for unification, like other fashions, follows its own dynamics—a rapid rise in popularity is succeeded by an equally rapid extinction. The imitation fails because of the different conditions, and the new institutions are rejected. Or (b) the imported institutions survive, maintaining the same formal structure, but actually fulfilling different functions. For example, EEC-type institutions in Central America might enhance development by reducing inter-country competition and coordinating development plans without much increase in the small inter-country trade. Thus, while the EEC serves chiefly to enhance the welfare of the participant countries through large inter-country trade, the Latin American unions will enhance industrialization through inter-country cooperation and coordination. If implemented, they will form development alliances, while called, in deference to the source of the vogue, "common markets" or "free trade areas." [26] To what degree these unions are hampered by the use of an instrument originally forged for different purposes and to what degree the same international treaty can be used without negative repercussions to serve different functions—and which functions—are further questions that this paradigm raises but cannot answer.

System Properties

Theoretically a unification process might start among countries that have had no previous relationship or were not interdependent and did not constitute an international system. Actually all the unification movements that we are aware of were initiated among countries that were previously interdependent. In any case, the study of the pre-unification stage is not complete unless the relationships among the potential participants in a union are investigated, even if the finding is that no such relationships existed. Both the pre-unification level of integration and its scope have to be assessed and other relevant properties (see below) of the system have to be determined. These properties will be remeasured when the unification process is terminated, and a comparison of the two sets of measures will inform us of the extent of the process.

Pre-Unification Integration and Scope. Unification is a process in which the integration of a system is increased, a process that tends to be accompanied by expansion in the scope of the system in terms of the sectors that are "internationalized." This means that pre-unification integration and scope can be very low (just sharing a few international organizations), low (sharing membership in a bloc), or medium (as in empires); it is pre-unification as long as both do not grow, whatever the parameters happen to be (unless, of course, they are already maximal).[27]

Shared Properties: The Example of Culture. The pre-unification system may have many shared properties; which one or ones we chose to study before and after unification depends on the specific problem at hand. Let us examine briefly the effect of culture[28] shared by the participants upon the initiation of unification.

According to widely held opinion, shared culture is an essential prerequisite for unification. It is pointed out that, under the impact of nationalism, old political units broke up (especially empires) or formed larger unions (Germany, Italy) in an effort to bring units that shared a culture and political unions in balance. Deutsch, for instance, shows in his important study, *Backgrounds for Community*, that sharing cultural symbols, ethnic origin, a language, a religion, a sense of identity, etc., preceded the formation of a union in practically every case he studied.[29]

On the other hand, many unions do not have most or all of these elements of shared culture. This holds true for Canada, the Union of South Africa, Switzerland, Belgium, Nigeria, India, and, of course, for most of the supranational unions from the EEC to the Eastern European one and from the British Commonwealth to the Union of African States.

One might view these two positions as completely con-
tradictory and await additional findings and reexamination
of earlier ones to determine which position is valid. It is possible, however, to view this contradiction as more apparent
than real. Each of the following interpretations could resolve
the contradiction, but which one does, if any, has to be determined empirically.

First one might claim that most cultural values are politically irrelevant. Information can be exchanged, aesthetic
values be held in common, religious beliefs draw similar commitments—and the countries so disposed still may not share
a sense of political identity or have the necessary foundation
for a shared legitimate government. All Russian scientists
might subscribe to American journals and all American scholars read Russian ones, and all Russians see *My Fair Lady* (and
like it) and all Americans appreciate the Moscow ballet, etc.,
and the two countries might still go to war the next day, not
to mention failing to form a union. After all, the European
societies shared culture and civilization during many hundreds of years and scores of wars. This position suggests that
sharing culture is not required for unification, nor does the
lack of a shared culture prevent it; it simply has little effect
on political unification.

True, there is a limited set of values and symbols directly related to all unification, including legitimation of the
new power center, a sense of national or supranational identity, shared political rituals, and the like. But it is the emergence of these shared political values that the study of unification has to explain; their existence is part of our definition
of integration. If we view the same factors as our dependent
variable (integration) and as our independent one (culture),
we are spinning tautologies.

Another possible way to resolve the apparent contradiction is to claim that unions whose members do not share a
culture may be initiated but will not develop successfully, at
least not until their culture becomes shared. Thus, the Union
of African States may well have little shared culture, and the

British Commonwealth come to have less and less as non-Western societies join it, but the first union has yet to become a political-social reality, and the Commonwealth shows a parallel decrease of integration as the degree to which culture is shared is declining. Similarly, the success of the union of Nigeria and India is certainly not guaranteed; and to the extent that they increase their integration, they also increase their shared culture.

This view suggests that shared culture is not a prerequisite for unification but a requirement that has to be fulfilled before the process can be completed. No union, one might suggest, is safely integrated unless a shared culture has evolved. This would also imply that while cultural exchange programs can hardly trigger a unification process when other factors are missing, once unification is progressing—let us say, owing to economic, military, or political factors—cultural integration fulfills an independent role in an "advanced" stage of the unification process.

We would like to point out in passing that there may well be other such *solidifiers*—that is, factors that can operate effectively only in a later stage of a process. Shared scientific projects, international professional associations and conventions, increased tourism, international television networks, sister-cities movements, supranational holidays, and multi-country universities may all then be able to play a role in those unions where they originally seemed "unnecessary" or impossible.

The Unification Process: Integrating Forces

Socio-political processes such as unification do not proceed in a trial-and-error fashion. Once initiated, they tend to follow one of a limited number of patterns (to be discussed in the subsequent section), according to the direction given to them by the integrating forces. This raises the question as to what kinds of integrating forces are applied in the unification process and who is applying them.

A Classification of International Forces:
A Conceptual Digression

To decide which integrating force is the most effective in launching a successful unification endeavor requires clear conception of the kinds of integrating forces that exist. The following threefold classification seems to be satisfactory; integrating forces, we suggest, are either coercive (e.g., military forces), or utilitarian (e.g., economic sanctions), or normative (e.g., propaganda). The classification is exhaustive; each concrete power is either one of the three or is composed of their various combinations.[30] The classification covers both "real" (coercive and utilitarian) and "ideal" (normative) elements. It directly represents the three major sociological schools: the Italian school of Pareto and Mosca, which was especially concerned with force; the economic-Marxist one; and the Weber-Durkheim tradition, which emphasized sentiments and ideas. However, it avoids a flaw common to all three: their tendency to see one set of factors— means of violence, ownership, or sentiments and ideas—as *the* major determinant of history and hence also of international relations.

On the most general level, one might state that international relations are characterized by the frequent use of coercion by one unit against another as compared with the interaction of other social units, and by less frequent and less effective exercise of normative power. Utilitarian powers are frequently used in international as well as intranational relations. Unification processes are directed by all three kinds of powers. Some unions are largely forced, as is the Federation of Rhodesia and Nyasaland. Some are "encouraged" mainly by economic means, as

European unification in the OEEC initially was. In order to receive American reconstruction funds under the Marshall Plan, a country had to commit itself to cooperate with other European countries. Still other unions are initiated chiefly by propaganda pressures, as was the United Arab Republic. Other unifications were directed initially by a more balanced combination of various powers: Prussia, for instance, used them all—in good measure—to force, bribe, and persuade the German states to unite. Nor are all "subordinate" countries necessarily treated in the same way. Certainly the larger and more powerful Chile is more coddled and less subjected to pressure by the Latin American leaders, Argentina and Brazil, than is the small, weak, and highly dependent Paraguay.

Effective Configurations
The question of which configuration of forces is most effective for unification has no one answer. It is quite evident that different kinds of unions (e.g., military only, economic only)[31] develop effectively when different kinds of forces are used. Each stage of unification, of the same kind of union, might well require also a change in the forces applied to maximize the development of the union. Does one, perhaps, best start with coercion and gradually increase normative pressures as the member-countries become more responsive to normative appeals, or does one best apply normative forces initially and resort to others only if the normative ones are not effective? What role do economic forces play in the different types of unions?

One question deserves special attention in view of its high political, ideological, and moral nature: does the use of coercion in the initial stage of unification necessarily undermine its long-run success?[32] If this is not the case in general, under what conditions is coercion detrimental and under what conditions is it not? Is the extent of coercion a major determinant, so that limited coercion (as used by Prussia to unify Germany) will not undermine the emerging union, but extensive use of force (as in Hungary in 1956) will undermine it? Does extensive use of coercion become less ineffective when combined with extensive propaganda (normative) efforts? Is there a "cut-off" point at which reliance on extensive coercion can be stopped? Can, for instance, the Soviet Union keep its Red Army out of orthodox Communist Czechoslovakia without risking its loss to the union?

There could hardly be more significant questions to the architects of unions—or to those who wish to undermine them—but there are few systematic answers available.

Effective Distributions

Whatever the forces employed to initiate and bring about a union, the way these forces are distributed among various units—i.e, the relative power the units have over each other—is of much consequence to the unification process. Two major dimensions have to be taken into account: (1) the degree of elitism—that is, the degree to which power is concentrated in the hands of one or a few units, as against a more or less even distribution among many—and (2) the nature of the unit (or units) that have more power than others (if any), in terms of membership in the emerging union. Is the elite unit (the powerholder) a member or does it impose unification from the outside?

Degree of Elitism. Many unification processes are carried out under the leadership of one elite. In most of the historical cases studied by Deutsch and his associates, one unit was by far superior to the others, both in its interest in and preparedness for unification, in terms of resources as well as communicative and administrative capacities, and thus was able to bring about a union.[33] England played such a role in the union with Wales and with Scotland; Britain played this role in the formation of the EFTA as well as in its disbanding;

Egypt was the dominant partner of the UAR; the U.S.S.R. obviously has this position in Eastern Europe; Guatemala was the central force in first building and later disintegrating the Central American Federation (1823–1839). In several other cases, two countries appear to hold an elite position: Argentina and Brazil seem to be the two prime powers in the LAFTA; and West Germany and France seem to be the major powers in the EEC.[34]

Other unification efforts, while not completely egalitarian, seem to come considerably closer to an even power distribution. The major participants of the Scandinavian union—Sweden, Norway, and Denmark—have similar power positions (though Sweden may have a little more than the others); the same holds for the members of the present Central American Union, and the two main members of Benelux. It seems safe, however, to generalize that equalitarian or near-equalitarian unions are considerably less frequent than elitist ones.

The most frequently found pattern is not necessarily the most effective one, though when a process is at least partially planned, and effectiveness constantly assessed, frequency and effectiveness tend to be associated. The question is whether hegemony is a better way to unification than dual leadership, and dual leadership more effective than lack of any clearly superior unit. Is hegemony the most effective power distribution when the member-countries are quite willing to unify, or is it effective only when some or most potential participants are unwilling or at least reluctant to join a union or stay in it?[35]

A closely related question concerns the association between the configuration of forces applied and the power distribution. It would seem that when power is relatively concentrated in the hands of one or two units, coercion is more likely to be used; when it is fairly evenly distributed, normative appeals are more common; and economic sanctions are frequently used in both elitist and comparatively egalitarian power-distributions, but are more frequent in the elitist type.

Whether this is really the case or whether these are the most effective combinations are open questions.

Degree of Internalization. The second dimension for examination of the effect of various power-distributions on unification is the membership status of the elites (equalitarian unifications are of members only). Membership has to be viewed as a continuum; there are partial members in varying degrees, full-fledged members, and nonmembers. The United States, for instance, for a number of years has supported many unifications (and other forms of international cooperation) of non-Communist countries, participating in some (e.g., NATO, OAS), being an "informal member" in others (e.g., CENTO), and not a member in still others (EEC, EFTA). Similarly, Britain is a member of the Commonwealth but not of the Federation of Nigeria that it engineered and launched. France is a member of the EEC, but not of the Conseil de l'Entente, though it has much influence over each of the four members (Ivory Coast, Upper Volta, Niger, and Dahomey) and their collective action.[36] The question is, what difference does the membership status of the elite make? Does effective leadership require membership? Do outside elites tend to be rejected after the initiation period, and to be replaced by member-elites—i.e., is the elite role internalized? Are outside elites limited in the kind of power they can effectively exercise; in particular, is effective use of normative power chiefly limited to member-elites?

An interesting phenomenon that deserves further exploration from this viewpoint is that some external elites become themselves "internalized," to varying degrees, in the process of unification. The United States, for instance, had no intention of becoming involved in the Baghdad Pact when it was originally formed in 1955 (it became CENTO after Iraq's withdrawal in 1959), but since then there has been a growing pressure on the United States to deepen its participation, a pressure it only partially resists. By 1960 the United States had signed bilateral agreements with each of the members—a procedure frequently used to join a union without formally joining—in which it pledged itself to take "appropriate action, including the use of armed forces," to help each country to resist aggression. In 1961 it committed itself to appoint a permanent military staff commander for CENTO.[37] Similarly, France not only did not intend to become an informal leader of the *Entente* (Ivory Coast is the semi-official, on-the-scene leader), but resisted its original formation.[38] Finally, the United States—when it supported the formation of the EEC in 1957, and later the inclusion of the non-neutral EFTA countries—did not fully realize the heavy pressures that the success of this union would put on it to create a larger union—sometimes referred to as the Atlantic Community— in which the United States is expected to be a member. It is far from clear why this "sucking-in" process occurs, why it remains "unanticipated," why elite countries become involved in more unions, and to a larger degree, than they intended to. The central question remains: does internalization of elites make them more responsive to non-elite members, and does this increased responsiveness enhance unification?

The Unification Process: Integrating Sectors

When the prerequisites are present and integrative forces are operative, and the level of integration of the international system grows, its scope tends also to expand. That is, more and more functional needs of the member-units are fulfilled through collective actions, more and more sectors of the member-units are unified, and the process of unification develops momentum of its own. In the following section, problems concerned with how the process is initiated are outlined first, then various reasons why it picks up momentum and the directions in which it might continue to grow on its own are discussed; and finally, an exhaustive list of the functional spheres that can be shared is presented and questions are raised concerning the order in which unification spreads into these spheres.

The First Stage: Take-Off

Take-Off: A Conceptual Digression
Most social scientists, until recently, when studying the beginning of a process or the formation of
a polity, focused on the initiation period. The
granting of a charter, the signing or ratification of
a treaty, the founding convention, and similar
events were considered the birthday of organizations, societies, and political movements. The
concept of take-off, first used by students of aerodynamics, then economics, and recently introduced into political sciences by Rostow, Deutsch,
and Haas,[39] calls attention to a second point in
the "beginning" of a process that is in many ways
more important than its formal initiation. Takeoff
occurs when a process has accumulated enough
momentum to continue on its own, without support of non-system units. This is not to suggest
that the initiation point is irrelevant; on the contrary, the virtue of the concept of take-off is that
it calls attention to the fact that for many processes the initiation stage and the take-off stage
are not identical. A plane starts rolling, but only
after it accumulates a certain speed can it continue without the support of the runway. Economic development is often initiated by contacts
with Western civilization, but it "takes off" only
after the production capacity of a country has increased to a degree that it can answer the increasing current needs and still show a significant
balance to be invested in the build-up of production means. In this way, self-sustained growth is
ensured.

Unification at the initiation stage is dependent on external units or member-units; it has no
momentum of its own. Any significant change in
the position of these units can bring the initiated

union to an abrupt end. We know that at some later stage elements of community-authority develop (e.g., the High Authority of ECSC; the Economic Commission of the EEC), that the process gains speed (e.g., EEC cut tariffs ahead of schedule), and that unification seems to become a force in itself, one that counters attempts to halt the evolving union. It is then that unification has taken off.

Determinants of Take-Off. What actually happens, what factors change, is far from clear. At least two changes in the nature of the process seem to occur that might account, at least in part, for the take-off phenomenon. One change is that the flow of people, goods, and communications across the national boundaries is increased. Some of such increases, though by no means all of them, require an increase in the amount of international decision-making. Increased *shared* activities—like running a common defense line—seems to increase the need for common decision-making even more than increases in intercountry flows. The intergovernmental procedure is cumbersome for a large volume of decisions. Hence the tendency is to form a "supranational" bureaucracy to make secondary decisions, leaving policy decisions to a superior, intergovernmental body. This was the case in the ECSC, EEC, LAFTA, NATO, and other unions. Once a supranational bureaucracy is formed, its evolution tends to follow that of other bureaucracies: it strives to increase its functions, power, and legitimation and to resist attempts to reduce them.

The other factor accounting for take-off is secondary priming; that is, unification in one sector of society tends to trigger unification in others.[40] For instance, a steel and coal customs union (ECSC) created the need for supranational cooperation on matters concerning transportation of those goods and on sources of energy other than coal (which led, among other things, to the formation of the Western European atomic energy agency, Euratom).[41]

Cooperation on these matters created the need for co-ordination on working conditions and finance in the affected industries. Cooperation on a large number of specific economic issues led to the Treaty of Rome, which covers the economies of the six in general. Generalized economic unification, in turn, produced considerable pressure toward political unification, though up to date it has not gone much beyond electing a powerless but symbolically important European Parliament, holding frequent meetings of the Prime Ministers of the six countries, and attending talks about a European federation or confederation. Economic and political unifications have affected some cultural cooperation (e.g., the formation of a European University, to be opened in Florence, Italy). The main point about this expansion of the original unification effort, or "spill-over," as Haas called it,[42] is that it is based on secondary priming. Unification in one sector triggers a similar process in others, rather than any external force doing the triggering. Hence, the significance of the study of secondary priming for take-off. Once secondary priming sets in, it might continue up to complete unification of the countries involved, even if the external powers that initiated the process have ceased to exist or are now trying to hinder its evolution.

In sum, the foundation of supranational bureaucracies and secondary priming accounts for the take-off of unions. This raises two questions: what patterns does unification follow once it has taken off; and what is the optimal sector in which to initiate unification?

The Take-Off Sector. Unions may be initiated in many ways, including military alliances, economic unions, political coalitions, and normative communities (sense of shared norms and values). The question is, which one of these unifications provides the optimal base for take-off? Almost all possible functional spheres have been considered as optimal from this viewpoint by one authority or another. Deutsch points to the importance of the existence of a community of consent (or normative union) at the first stage.[43] Kissinger sees in military alliances an effective way of binding nations together; he believes, for instance, that NATO could serve as an effective base for unification of the fifteen member countries.[44] Haas finds that economic unification (common markets) has the highest spill-over value, and therefore is obviously the best take-off base.[45] "Functional" organizations, increases in tourism, and cultural exchange have been viewed as effective ways to increase international integration and unification.[46] The effort to establish which sector (or sectors) is the optimal take off base will have to draw on an analysis of the internal structure of the societies that participate in the unification process. Various societal sectors seem to differ in the degree that they are interrelated. The more articulated they are, obviously the more spill-over will occur. What is far from obvious is whether there is one "most articulated" sector in each society, if it is the same in all societies, and which one (or ones) it is.

Expansion of the Union's Scope
A Stable Scope: Alternative Propositions. Once the first stage has been completed and a union has taken off, the question arises as to what elements are needed to form a stable union; more specifically, is high integration and unification of all sectors required, or will a lower level of integration and a less inclusive union be the most stable one (i.e., persist in time)?

A stable union is formed, we suggest, only when a full-fledged political community is established—that is, when integration on all three dimensions (monopoly of violence, center of decision-making, focus for identification) is high, and unification has penetrated all major societal sectors. Unification might stop short of high integration and full scope, and the resulting union might exist for considerable periods of time. Moreover, high integration and full scope might be more difficult to attain, and more risky to aim at, than some less integrated and less encompassing form of international association. All that we hypothetically suggest is that in the long run, once attained, unions that have become highly integrated and have a broad scope are more stable than those that are less integrated or less inclusive.

The opposite view is represented by Deutsch and his associates. They found that the less integrated "pluralistic security communities" were more stable than the "amalgamated" ones. Only one of the former failed, while seven of the latter did.[47] Since the Princeton authors have a mountain of data to support their position, it is incumbent on us to explain why we hold to the alternative proposition. The reason lies in the different conceptions of integration. Deutsch and his associates see a union as amalgamated (integrated, in our terms)[48] once a common government has been established. The United States in 1789 became an amalgamated community; the Empire—and, for that matter, all empires by the definition introduced above—was an amalgamated community. From our viewpoint, these are partially integrated unions. They lack at least one central element of integration, that of being the focus of political identification of the citizens. Second, their scope is rather limited. It seems to us, then, that what Deutsch and his colleagues are suggesting is that low-integration, low-scope unions are more stable than *medium*-integrated, low-scope ones; this does not preclude the possibility that highly integrated, broad-scope unions will be the most stable type. In other words, we suggest that future research will still have to decide which unions are more stable—low-integration, low-scope ones, or those that matured into political communities.[49]

Sequences of Unification. Naturally, the next question is: In what order, if any, are the various sectors unified? Do they have to be "assembled" in a specific order? If one is skipped, will this disintegrate the union, merely retard it, or allow it to continue in a limping way until the missing link is added (though in the "wrong" order)? Here, more than with any of the other questions raised, we are in the realm of speculation rather than knowledge. Following the Parsonian model, one would expect the more functional sequence to be the one that starts with military or economic unification and introduces political and normative unification later.[50] It is of interest to note that the attempts to start with European unification politically, by electing a European Parliament and "government" in the late 1940's and early 1950's, got virtually nowhere,[51] while the economic unification of the ECSC "spilled over" effectively into the EEC, which in turn seems to point in the direction of political unification.

Deutsch and his associates present an alternative hypothesis. Discussing the "assembly line of history," they state: "Generally speaking we found that substantial rewards for cooperation or progress toward amalgamation had to be timed so as to come before the imposition of burdens resulting from such progress towards amalgamation (union). We found that as with rewards before burdens, consent has to come before compliance if amalgamation is to have lasting success."[52] If we may extend the right of interpretation to its limits, we would read the Princeton authors as suggesting, in Parsons' terms, that allocation (of rewards) ought to precede adaptation to the environment (burdens), and that normative unification (consent) ought to come before a political one (compliance).

This of course does not exhaust the possible sequences; the four sectors might be assembled in twenty-four different ways, and other scholars may find it fruitful to distinguish between more than four sectors. Moreover, we should be open to the possibility that there is, in fact, no one optimal sequence for unification but that each kind of union is "assembled" best in a different fashion. And this brings us to the last tier of our paradigm.

The Termination State

A union has "taken off," "spilled over," following one sequence or another, until it reaches a "termination" state. That is, for a period of time—before additional unification or regression sets in—the union remains basically unchanged.[53] Unions differ greatly in the level of unification at

which they stabilize—i.e., stop increasing their integration
and expanding their scope. These "termination" states provide a fruitful base for the classification of unions not only
because they provide a relatively fixed frame of reference
(unlike the fluid state of the unions in other phases), but
also because differences in termination states might associate
significantly with variables examined so far; that is, unions
that differ in the state at which they stabilize might differ also
in the conditions under which they are initiated, in the forces
that integrate them, in the sequence they develop, etc.[54]

Degree and Scope
The state at which unification is terminated or interrupted
can be measured in terms of the closeness of such a state to
that of a political community. The preceding discussion suggests the following criteria:

(a) *The degree of integration is terminated on the basis of the
degree of integration of each one of the three dimensions.* Unions
integrate gradually; hence, when unification stops, a union
might be only partially integrated. Part of the means of violence, but not all, might be under the control of the new
collectivity (as is the case in NATO); some, but not all, parts
of the economy might be controlled by the supranational authority (agriculture was until 1962 largely exempted from the
Treaty of Rome and hence the authority of the European
Commission); and identification with the new collectivity
might be partial, both in terms of the percentage of the citizens whose identification has been transferred to the new
polity and the intensity of the identification of those who did
make the transfer.

(b) *The number of sectors in which unification has taken
place and their nature in terms of the secondary priming potential of
the sector.* The higher the secondary priming potential, the
more likely the union is to continue to grow or to regress
after a period of stabilization; the lower this potential, the
more likely the union will be to continue in its "stable" state,
unless outside forces interfere.

(c) *The degree of unification in each sector, e.g., the ratio of international versus intranational trade.* It should be noted that even political communities whose scope of integration and unification is high—i.e., they possess all three kinds of integration and their unification has penetrated into all four sectors—may differ as to how high their integration is and how encompassing their scope. While all political communities have, by definition, a center of decision making—i.e., "supranational" government—they differ in the scope of the decisions of their governments. In this connection, a distinction is sometimes made between communities with a federal government (high decision score) and those which have a unitary government (even higher decision scope). Actually, federal structures may themselves become more centralized (as the United States has over the last three decades) or less centralized (as the Soviet Union has since 1953), and unitary governments may be either highly centralized (e.g., France) or comparatively less centralized (e.g., Britain). Similar, more "subtle" distinctions can be made on the other dimensions (subtle in the sense that high scores are compared with very high ones instead of merely high to medium and low ones). While previously we advanced the hypothesis that highly integrated unions are more stable than ones with medium or low integration, this does not necessarily hold for the *most* highly integrated ones. It is quite possible that a less centralized structure will prove more stable, since it allows for more expression of the ex-national powers and loyalties. By the same token, though, it leaves more power in potentially secessionist units. An hypothesis suggests itself: namely, that the more integrated a community is (by other standards), the more political decentralization it can tolerate.

The Dominant Function

Another major difference among various termination-states is the dominant function that the new collectivity serves. This criterion not only differentiates unions (e.g., military, economic, normative unions), but also political communities.

True, a political community encompasses all major societal sectors and in this sense serves all major functions, but communities can be characterized according to the function in which they invest more resources, manpower, and energy, and which they value higher as compared with other communities. While this dominant function changes over time, it is usually possible to point to one that dominates a given historical period. Thus, it has been suggested that the United States, viewed as a model of a political community that emerged from earlier autonomous units, stressed adaptation in the industrialization period (1875–1930); that concern with welfare and consumption took the place of the production emphasis after 1930; and that this was superseded in the late 1940s and early 1950s by "other-directedness"[55] and concern with ideological positions. At that same time, the cold war with communism intensified and the struggle with radicals at home reached a peak.[56] Renewed emphasis on adaptation marked 1958, when the Russian space probes and long-range missiles provided a strong environmental challenge to the United States. Unlike the earlier production concern, the present one is focused on means of violence rather than on consumption, and on service to the national collectivity rather than directly to the individual.[57] The scientist, the space-technologist, and to a degree the executive, but not the merchant or entrepreneur, are the new cultural heroes. Similar statements can be made about the changing focus of other unions. Yet many may have a "persistent" function that is stressed in the long run (though not necessarily "forever") despite short-run ups and downs—e.g., expansionism (adaptation) in the case of the Soviet Union.[58]

Before statements about the dominant function of a society or larger political collectivity at a given period can be formulated with proper precision and responsibility, much more theoretical work and empirical research are required. But it should be pointed out that it seems quite evident even now that the nature of the dominant function is an important variable for the study of unions and political communities. Some functions—especially the political, social, and ideological ones—require higher integration and broader scope than others (e.g., individual-oriented consumption). Hence, the level and scope at which the unification process terminates are crucial variables that both are affected by and affect the dominant function of the new political unions.

No paradigm is ever complete, in the sense that additional work in the area, whether theoretical or empirical, continues to add dimensions to its structure. It can be exhaustive only in the sense that all additional dimensions will find a place in one of the categories already included. The only way to assure this is by deriving the categories instead of inducing them. This we did when we used as our major three tiers the beginning (initiation state), middle (the process), and end (termination) states of unification. Similar procedures were used in arriving at the other dimensions—for instance, at the distinction between the take-off stage and expansion (i.e., between the first and later stages) of unification. Other distinctions—e.g., between integration and scope—are derived not from simple logic but from substantive sociological theories. Like all other distinctions that are derived, their test is in the fruitfulness of the questions raised. The major effort remains, of course, to determine through empirical research the validity of the various alternative answers that one could give to the questions raised by the paradigm.

Notes

1. Two paradigms that had a lasting impact on sociology have been constructed by Robert K. Merton, one for functional analysis and one for the study of sociology of knowledge. See his *Social Theory and Social Structure* (rev. ed., Glencoe, Ill., 1957).

2. Most functional models deal only with the conditions under which a collectivity survives. I spelled out elsewhere the need to study the conditions under which a collectivity maintains its form or structure (or, in the case of an organization, its level of effectiveness). See Etzioni, "Two Approaches to Organizational Analysis: A Critique and a

Suggestion," *Administrative Science Quarterly*, V (September 1960), 257–78.

3. See Morton A. Kaplan, *System and Process in International Politics* (New York, 1957), 4.

4. Cf. Talcott Parsons, "Polarization and the Problem of International Order," *Berkeley Journal of Sociology*, VI (Spring 1961), 130ff.

5. The League of Nations and the UN differ from most international organizations on so many counts that they should be treated as a distinct category.

6. Following Max Weber, "authority" is defined as legitimate power.

7. See Zbigniew K. Brzezinski, "The Organization of the Communist Camp," *World Politics* XIII (January 1961), 175–209, and *The Soviet Bloc* (Cambridge, Mass., 1960).

8. An hypothesis emerges from this comparison: the broader the scope of an international system in terms of the number of sectors (e.g., economic, cultural) included, and the more significant they are to its survival and goals, the more integrated the system is on all three counts of integration (monopoly, decision-making, and focusing of identification). I return to this point below.

9. This should not be viewed as a table of contents, since conceptual digressions are not included.

10. Ernst B. Haas, *The Uniting of Europe: Political, Social, and Economic Forces*, 1950–1957 (Stanford, 1958), passim.

11. Lincoln Gordon, "Economic Regionalism Reconsidered," *World Politics*, XIII (January 1961), 235–36.

12. Paul F. Lazarfeld and Herbert Menzel, "On the Relation Between Individual and Collective Properties," in Amitai Etzioni, ed., *Complex Organizations: A Sociological Reader* (New York, 1961), 422–40, esp. 427.

13. On this property, see Karl W. Deutsch and others, *Political Community and the North Atlantic Area* (Princeton 1957), 62, 66ff.; Ernst B. Haas, "International Integration: The European and the Universal Process," *International Organizations*, XV (Summer 1961), 374–378.

14. See Margaret Dewar, "Economic Cooperation in the Soviet Orbit," *Yearbook of World Affairs* (London, 1959), 45–61.
15. "The Emerging Common Markets in Latin America," *Monthly Review* (Federal Reserve Bank of New York) (September 1960), 156.
16. Norman J. Padelford, "Cooperation in the Central American Region: The Organization of Central American States," *International Organization*, XI (Winter 1957), 46.
17. Ibid., 50.
18. For a fine study of this rather exceptional form of international association, see J. D. B. Miller, *The Commonwealth in the World* (Cambridge, Mass., 1958).
19. Deutsch and others, 44–46.
20. On the pre-EFTA period, see Frantz Wendt, *The Nordic Council and Co-operation in Scandinavia* (Copenhagen 1959).
21. See F. Gunther Eyck, The Benelux Countries: An Historical Survey (Princeton, 1959), 87ff.
22. W.J. Cash, *Mind of the South* (New York, 1960).
23. Miriam Camps, *Division in Europe*, Policy Memorandum No. 21 (Center of International Studies, Princeton University, 1960), 50.
24. The Arab League was sufficiently affected by the vogue to review twice the suggestion to form an Arabic common market. *New York Times*, October 12, 1858; *Arab News and Views*, July 1, 1961.
25. This is not an instance of pure diffusion, since all commissions are UN organs, but without a "vogue"—based on diffusion—they would hardly be so acceptable to the various countries represented. For another instance of diffusion, see Paddelford, 43.
26. See Gordon, 245–50.
27. For additional comments on the integration of the international systems in this stage, see the delineation of the subject above.

28. Culture being viewed in the broadest sense of the term, including religion, secular ideologies, civilization, language arts, etc.

29. Karl W. Deutsch and others, *Nerves of Government: Models of Communication and Control* (London: Free Press, 1963).

30. This classification is extensively discussed in my *Comparative Analysis of Complex Organizations* (Glencoe, Ill., 1961).

31. Types of union are discussed in the last section of this article.

32. The answer depends in part on the criterion of success that one chooses to use. A union can be maintained, at least in the short run, by extensive use of force. How effective it is, in terms of the level of integration attained, the scope of the unification, or resistance to external hostile powers, are different questions altogether.

33. Deutsch and others, *Political Community*, 50ff. See also Karl W. Deutsch, *Nationalism and Social Communication* (New York, 1953).

34. Up to now neither of these countries appears to have used its superior power to gain special concessions from the EEC authorities.

35. The frequency of forced integrations as distinct from voluntary ones has been pointed out by Crane Brinton in *From Many One* (Cambridge, Mass., 1948). See also Harold D. Lasswell, "The Interrelations of World Organization and Society," *Yale Law Review*, LV (August 1946), 889–909.

36. See Immanuel Wallerstein, *Africa: The Politics of Independence* (New York, 1961), 108, 116.

37. *New York Times*, April 29 and 30, 1961; and *The Reporter*, July 20, 1961.

38. Immanuel Wallerstein, "Background to Page Paper II," *West Africa*, August 5, 1961, 861.

39. W. W. Rostow, *The Stages of Economic Growth* (Cambridge, Mass., 1960), chap. 4; Deutsch and others, *Political Community*, 83–85; and Haas, "The Challenge of Regionalism," *International Organization*, XII (Autumn 1958), 440–58.

40. See Rostow, 52, on "derived-growth sectors."
41. William Diebold, Jr., "The Changed Economic Position of Western Europe," *International Organization*, XIV (Winter 1960), 12ff.
42. Haas provides a most stimulating and insightful analysis of this process in *Uniting of Europe*, esp. chap. 8.
43. Deutsch and others, *Political Community*, 71.
44. Henry A. Kissinger, "For an Atlantic Confederacy," *The Reporter*, February 2, 1961, 16–21. See also his *Necessity for Choice* (New York, 1960), 165–68.
45. "International Integration," 372ff.
46. For a review of this approach, see Stephen S. Goodspeed, *The Nature and Functions of International Organization* (New York, 1959), 595–6.
47. Deutsch and others, *Political Community*, 30.
48. Deutsch and his associates use "integration" to refer to the relationship among countries that no longer consider engaging in war with each other (ibid., 31). This is of course a different definition, one that has a lower threshold, than ours. Haas uses "political integration" to refer to "the process whereby political actors in several distinct national settings are persuaded to shift their loyalties, expectations and political activities toward a new center, whose institutions possess or demand jurisdiction over the pre-existing national states" (*Uniting of Europe*, 16). The threshold of this definition is much higher than that of Deutsch, almost as high as ours. Cf. Haas's discussion of "political community" in ibid., 4–11.
49. We defined "political communities" above as systems that have reached a high level of integration on three dimensions (monopolization, decision-making, identification). Since the discussion suggests that such integration tends to exist in unions that penetrate all the major societal sectors, the question arises as to what these sectors are. Following Parsons, we suggest that a full collectivity is one that solves autonomously its four basic functional problems: it adapts to its ecological and social environment, allocates means and rewards among its

subunits, integrates its subunits into one polity, and establishes as well as reinforces the normative commitments of its members. A union that matured into a political community would thus include "supranational" activities of all four types.

50. This point is considerably elaborated in my "Epigenesis of Political Communities at the International Level," *American Journal of Sociology*, LXVIII (January 1963), 407–21.

51. Goodspeed, 591.

52. *Political Community*, 71.

53. The length of the period is, like all such "cut-off" points, largely an arbitrary decision of the researcher, affected more by the scope of his study and problem than by "reality."

54. One reason such a relation is expected is that actors in earlier stages sometimes view the termination stage as the goal toward which their efforts are directed.

55. This is, of course, the central thesis of David Riesman and others, *The Lonely Crowd* (New Haven, 1950).

56. Underlying this statement is the idea that over the last seventy-five years, the United States moved from the adaptive to the allocative, social integrative, and normative integrative phase. It is derived from Talcott Parsons' treatment of the subject "A Revised Analytical Approach to the Theory of Social Stratification," in Reinhard Bendix and Seymour M. Lipset, eds., *Class, Status, and Power* (Glencoe, Ill., 1953), 92–129. See also Parsons, "'McCarthyism' and American Social Tension: A Sociologists View," *Yale Review*, XLIV (December 1954), 226–45.

57. The stress on the need to shift resources from private to collective consumption is championed by J. K. Galbraith in *American Capitalism* (Boston, 1952) and *The Affluent Society* (Boston, 1958).

58. This is a central thesis of George Kennan's *The Sources of Soviet Conduct: American Diplomacy, 1900–1950* (Chicago, 1951).

The Epigenesis of Political Communities at the International Level

A Model for the Study of Political Unification

Historical and Contemporary Unifications

So long as international relations are governed by highly calculative orientations, or by the exercise of force, there is relatively little that sociology can contribute to their study. However, during recent decades international relations seem to have changed. Ideology became a major force; non-rational ties among nations were more common; and, recently, institutional bridges became more numerous. Thus, international relations gradually have become more amenable to sociological analysis. Of these trends, probably the most interesting to the sociologist is the formation of new unions whose members are nations (e.g., the European Economic Community [EEC]).

The EEC is by no means an extreme case. There have been many "historical" unions in which units that were previously autonomous merged to such a degree that today they are considered as one unit (e.g., Switzerland, the United States, Italy, Germany); and there are quite a few contemporary unifications where the new community is just emerging and is far from complete (e.g., the Scandinavian community; East European one), exists as a treaty and formal organization

Note: This essay was written while the author was on the staff of the Institute of War and Peace Studies at Columbia University. It was originally published in *American Journal of Sociology,* 1963, *68*(4), 407–421. Copyright © 1963 by the University of Chicago.

rather than as a full-fledged sociological entity (e.g., the Ghana-Guinea-Mali union, the Latin American Free Trade Area), or is so tenuous that it is more likely to collapse than to reach fuller integration (e.g., the Federation of Nyasaland, Rhodesia).

The emerging communities are frequently referred to as supranational communities, a term that is misleading since it implies that the merging units are nations. Actually, many of the historical unifications occurred before the units were sanctified by nationalism (e.g., the Italian cities; the American colonies), and even contemporary unions are not necessarily unions of nations (e.g., the federation of Eritrea with Ethiopia, the formation of the Federation of Nigeria, and the merger of Southern Cameroon with the Cameroon Republic). Moreover, analytically the emergence of a nation state from several tribes, villages, or feudal states—let us say in contemporary Ghana, India, or late medieval France—is in many ways similar to supranational unification. Hence, our concern is with unification of political units that previously shared few or no political bonds. The degree to which these units have been foci of identification for their populations and the degree to which the normative substance of this identification was secular-historical of the kind that marks nationalism are two variables of our analysis, not part of the definition of the concept. Therefore, we refer to the emerging entities simply as political communities and to the process as one of unification. The term "unions" refers to entities that seem to develop in the direction of a political community but have not reached such a high level of integration.

Epigenesis Versus Preformism

A strategy often used in sociological studies of international relations is to draw on theories developed in the study of interaction among other social units, bearing in mind the special nature of the subject to which they are applied, and checking whether additional variables have to be introduced or whether the theories require revision in view of the new data. Here we draw on a sociological theory of change.

Most studies of social change presuppose the existence of a unit, and ask: How does it change, why, and in what direction? The analytical framework frequently used for this analysis of social dynamics is the *differentiation model*,[1] which assumes that the "primitive" social unit contains, in embryonic form, fused together, all the basic modes of social relations that later become structurally differentiated. While relations originally fused gain their own subunits, no new functions are served or new modes of interaction are molded. There are, for instance, some universalistic relations in the most primitive tribes. According to this viewpoint, every social unit, if it is to exist, must fulfill a given set of functions; those of adaptation, allocation, social and normative integration. On the individual level, the evolution from infancy to maturity can be analyzed in terms of the differentiation of the personality.[2] On the societal level, the evolution of a primitive society, from a traditional into a modern one, is also seen as a differentiation process. All societal functions are fulfilled by the primitive tribe; they merely become structurally differentiated; that is, they gain personnel, social units, and organizational structures of their own. Religious institutions gain churches, educational institutions gain schools, economic institutions gain corporations, and so forth.

Philosophers and biologists have long pointed out that there is an alternative model for the study of change. While Bonnet, Haller, and Malpighi represented the differentiation (or preformism) approach, according to which the first unit or seed possesses in miniature all the patterns of the mature plant, Harvey, Wolff, and Goethe advanced the accumulation (or epigenesis) approach, according to which "adult" units emerge through a process in which parts that carry out new functions are added to existing ones, until the entire unit is assembled. Earlier parts do not include the "representation" of later ones.

The two processes are mutually exclusive in the sense that new units are either institutional "embodiments" of old functions or serve new ones. They may occur at different times in the same social unit: for example, a unit may first follow a preformistic model of development, then shift to an epigenetic model (or the other way around); or it may simultaneously develop some subunits following one model and some following the other. But unlike the particle and wave theories, which are used to explain the same light phenomena, the change pattern of all sociological units of which we are aware follows at any given period either a differentiation or an accumulation model.

Until now sociology focused almost exclusively on differentiation models. There are, however, several social units whose development cannot be adequately accounted for by a preformistic model. This article presents an outline of an alternative model, drawing for illustration on the formation of various social units, in particular, international unions. The following questions are asked: (1) Where is the power located that controls the accumulation process? (2) What form does the process itself take? (3) What sector is introduced first? (4) How does this affect subsequent development of sectors? (5) What sequences does the entire process follow? (6) What kinds of "products" do different accumulation (or epigenesis) processes produce? It is essential to bear in mind constantly the peculiar system reference of this analysis; it is a system that does not exist but which the potential members are gradually building up. It is like studying the effect of social relations among students in their postgraduate life before they have graduated.

Power and Epigenesis

Locus of Power: Elitism and Internalization

The main distinction between preformism and epigenesis is the function that new subunits serve; that is, old functions versus new ones. Determining the structural location of the power that controls the development of a social unit, especially that of new subunits, is essential both for distinguishing between units whose development follows one model and for differentiating between those of one model and those of the other. We need to know whether or not any one, two, or more elite units specialize in control functions;

that is, whether or not control is equally distributed among all or most units. This will be called the *degree of elitism*. To the degree that there are elites, the question arises whether they operate from within or from without the emerging union. This dimension will be the *degree of internalization* (of control).[3]

Degree of Elitism. Organizational analysis shows that there are two major ways of forming a new corporate body: An elite unit may construct the performance units, or several existing organizations that have both elite and performance units may merge. On the international level, a new community is formed in the first way when a nation more powerful than the other potential members "guides" the unification process. Prussia played such a role in the unification of Germany; Ghana, in the formation of the Ghana-Guinea-Mali union; Egypt, in the late UAR. The cases in which one nation played a central role are so numerous that Deutsch et al. suggest that unification requires the existence of one "core" unit.[4]

While many organizations and communities are established by one or a few elite units, the control center of others is formed through a merger of many units, each contributing a more or less equal part. The power center of the emerging community is a new unit rather than an existing unit subordinating the others. One might refer to the first as elitist, to the second as egalitarian, unification. A study of the Northern Baptist Convention in the United States provides a fine illustration of egalitarian unification.[5] The development of the Scandinavian union appears to follow an egalitarian pattern also. While Norway was initially less supportive of the union than Sweden and Denmark, the differences in their support to, and in their control of, the emerging union (and the Nordic Council, its formal instrument) come close to the egalitarian ideal type.[6]

The degree of elitism (or egalitarianism) should be treated as a continuum. In some nation unions one unit clearly plays a superior role (England in the early Commonwealth); in some, two or more countries are superior (Brazil, Argentina, and to a degree Chile, of the seven members in the Latin America Free Trade Area); in others, participation, contribution, and power are almost evenly distributed among all participants (as in the Scandinavian union).

The degree to which one or more units control the unification process versus the degree to which it is an effort of all participants is closely related to the means of control used. At the elitist end of this continuum we find mergers in which one country coerces the others to "unify." It seems that on the international level cases of elitist and coerced unification are much more frequent than egalitarian, voluntary unions, especially if we regard the extensive use of economic sanctions, not just military force, as resulting in a non-voluntary unification.[7] At the egalitarian end, use of normative means, such as appeal to common sentiments, traditions, and symbols, plays a much more central role than coercive means or economic sanctions. Economic factors operate here more in the form of mutual benefits derived from increased intercountry trade than sanctions or rewards given by one country to the others.

This raises an empirical question: How effective are the various means of unification? One is inclined to expect that unification that begins with coercion ends with disintegration. But the Roman empire, despite its coercive techniques, lasted for about five centuries before it finally collapsed. Nor was the German union weak or ineffective because of the methods employed by Bismarck to bring it about. Quite possibly the line that distinguishes effective from ineffective unification efforts lies not between coercion and non-coercion but between high coercion (of the kind used to keep Hungary in the Communist bloc in 1956 or to hold the Federation of Rhodesia and Nyasaland together in 1961) and lesser coercion.[8] Effectiveness seems also to be highly determined by the degree to which coercion is coupled with other means—for instance, with propaganda.

Degree of Internalization. Collectivities whose developments follow an epigenesis model can be effectively ordered by a second dimension, namely, the degree to which the elite unit (or units, if they exist) controls the emerging union from the outside or from the inside. This is not a dichotomous variable, for there are various degrees to which an elite unit can be "in" or "out." An elite might be completely "out," encouraging or forcing the merger of two or more units into a union which it does not join, sometimes relinquishing control once unification is initiated. Colonial powers brought together, frequently unwittingly, subordinated units, only to have to withdraw once their union was cemented: For example, resisting the British control was a major force in bringing together the thirteen American colonies, the various tribes in the Gold Coast that became Ghana, and the Jewish colonies in Palestine that formed the Israeli society. On the international level, the United States required some degree of intra-European economic co-operation as a condition for receiving funds under the Marshall Plan; it encouraged the union of the six countries that formed the European Economic Community, and is now encouraging the EEC to include Britain, without having joined these unions. Britain was the major force behind the efforts to launch a Federation of the West Indies and the formation of the Federation of Nigeria. In all these cases the center of power was with a non-member, external unit.

In other cases, the elites that initiate and support unification do not stay entirely out of the emerging community, nor are they a fully integral part of it. The United States, for instance, is an "informal but powerful" member of CENTO. It signed bilateral pacts with Iran, Turkey, and Pakistan, the three members of CENTO, which in 1961 showed signs of becoming more than just a treaty.[9] Similarly France, while not a member of the *Conseil de l'Entente* (a loose West African custom, communication, and, to a degree, military union of Ivory Coast, Upper Volta, Niger, and Dahomey), still is an active participant in this union through various treaties.[10]

Finally, in still other cases, the elite is a full-fledged member of the union as Britain was in the European Free Trade Area and Prussia in the unification of Germany.

Power, Capability, and Responsiveness. The units that control the epigenesis of political communities differ not only in their degree of elitism and internalization but also in their communication capabilities and degree of responsiveness to the needs and demands of participant units.[11] Deutsch pointed out that when all other conditions are satisfactory a unification process might fail because the *communication capabilities* of an elite are underdeveloped. This was probably a major reason why empires in medieval Europe were doomed to fail; they were too large and complex to be run from one center given the existing communication facilities.[12] Sociologists have concerned themselves extensively with communication gaps, but studies frequently focus on the interpersonal and small-group level (even in many of the so-called organizational studies of communication). Sociologists are often concerned with the structure of communication networks (two-step communication systems,[13] as against chain systems[14]) rather than with the articulation of these networks with the power structure.[15] For students of political systems and of complex organization, ideas such as "overloading" of the elite (presenting it with more communication than it is able to digest; requiring more decisions per time unit than it is able to make) is an interesting new perspective that connects communication studies with power analysis much more closely than the widespread human-relations type of communication analysis.

The concept of *responsiveness* further ties communication analysis to the study of power by asking to what degree does the power center act upon communication received and digested in terms of reallocating resources and rewarding the compliance of sectors.[16]

Thus to analyze epigenesis effectively, we must know not only who has how much power over the process but also what are the communication capabilities and what is the degree of responsiveness of the various power centers.

Performance and Control: Dynamic Perspective

The performance, power, and communication elements of a social unit developing epigenetically do not always develop at the same rate. As the limbs of an infant develop before he has control over them so new performances might be taken over by the accumulating unit before its power center gains control over them. Frequently, part of the performances of an accumulating unit are controlled by another unit, at least temporarily. The industrial capacity of colonies often developed before they gained political control over industry.

New communities, whose development follows the pattern suggested by epigenesis rather than that of preformism, tend to develop new performance abilities first and to internalize control over these activities later.[17] Just as a child first learns to walk, then gains the right to decide when and where to walk, or as military units in basic training first learn to act as units under the control of the training ("parent") unit's instructors and sanction system before acquiring their own command, so some countries engage in some collective activity under the control of a superior, non-member power.[18] Later, control is internalized by the evolving supranational system, and a supranational authority is formed, which regulates collective activities previously controlled by the superior external power.

It is the existence of a supranational authority—at first limited, then more encompassing—that distinguishes *unions of nations* from *international organizations*. Unions have at least a limited power center of their own, whose decisions bind the members and are enforceable; they have internalized at least some control. International organizations, on the other hand, are run by intergovernmental bodies, whose "decisions" are merely recommendations to the members and are not enforceable.[19] They have, in this sense, no power of their own. The special importance of the High Authority, a governing body of the European Coal and Steel Community (ECSC) is that its decisions directly bind the steel and coal industries of the six member nations and it can levy fines on industries that do not conform to its rulings (though national police forces would have to collect the fines, if they were not paid). Moreover, individuals, corporations, and states have the same status before the Court of Justice of the ECSC; they all can sue each other, an individual suing a state, or the High Authority suing a member state.[20]

Until the ECSC was formed in 1952, almost all European cooperation, such as the Organization for European Economic Cooperation (OEEC) and NATO, was intergovernmental. In 1952 the High Authority was formed; this was the first major step toward self-control of the evolving supranational community. (Interestingly, this is also the year NATO developed a supranational authority with the formation of SHAPE, which provided a supranational headquarters for the multination armies.)[21] In the following years functions and powers of the High Authority gradually increased. In 1957 the more encompassing common market (EEC) was established, which has its equivalent of the High Authority, the Economic Commission, except that its supranational powers cover more "performances"—much of the intercountry economic actions—than does the High Authority, which is limited to matters related to steel and coal.[22]

Attempts to develop supranational control over shared political activities, in which the members of the EEC do engage, have not yet succeeded. Whatever collective political action the Six take is based on intergovernment consultations of these countries, not supranational direction. *Thus, in the development of this union of nations, as in the epigenesis of many other social units, collective performances expand more rapidly than collective control.* (It should be noted that while frequently performance accumulation occurs before power internalization, the reversed sequence might occur, too. Power *capabilities* can be built up before performance. Modern armies, for instance, train groups of officers in headquarters work before they are given command of military units.)

We saw that communities are built up by accumulation of *new* performances (e.g., military ones) and control over them. We now turn to the dynamics of accumulation, recognizing three problems as basic to the analysis of all accumulation processes: (1) Under what conditions does the process start? (2) What factors contribute to its expansion and pace? (3) What is the sequence in which the functional sectors that make a complete community are assembled? The rest of this article is devoted to these problems.

Initiation, Take-Off, and Spill-Over

Between Initiation and Take-Off

The concept of take-off, borrowed from aerodynamics, is applied to the first stage of epigenesis to distinguish the initiation point from that where the continuation of the process becomes self-sustained. The image is one of a plane that first starts its engines and begins rolling, still supported by the runway, until it accumulates enough momentum to "take off," to continue in motion "on its own," generating the forces that carry it to higher altitudes and greater speeds. The analogue is that through accumulation, while relying on external support, the necessary condition for autonomous action is produced. Also during "take-off" the pilot, released from airport tower control, gains control of his plane. (This control take-off might occur before or after the performance take-off.)

Economists use this concept in the study of industrialization, especially in reference to foreign aid. An underdeveloped country requires a certain amount of investment before its economy reaches the level at which it produces a national income large enough to provide for current consumption and for increased investment which, in turn, provides for additional growth of the economy.[23] An economy has taken off when additional growth is self-sustained; when no external investment or externally induced changes in saving, spending, or work habits are needed.

The concept of take-off can also be used in studying political, communication, and other social processes. A group of leaders, some labor unions, or "reform" clubs, join to initiate a new political party. Again, "to initiate" has two meanings, to which the concept of take-off calls attention: There is the day the leaders decide to launch the new party, a day that, if the launching is successful, will be known as the party's birthday. However, the new party initially draws its funds, staff, and political power from the founding leaders and groups. Gradually, as the party grows, it accumulates

followers and contributors directly committed to it, and if it
is successful, it eventually reaches the stage at which it can do
without the support of its initiators and continue growing "on
its own." While this point is far from being sharply defined,
obviously it rarely coincides with the actual birth date. Much
insight can be gained by comparing different polities with
regard to the lapse between their initiation and their take-off
points. For instance, the greater the lapse the more difficult
it is for small or new groups to gain political representation.
On the other hand, if the lapse is very small, entering the
political competition becomes too easy, and it will be difficult
to find a majority to establish a stable government.

In many countries there is a formal barrier that has to
be surmounted before political take-off. Parties that poll less
than a certain percentage of the votes are denied parliamentary representation. Frequently founders' support is given
until the election day; then the party either gains representation and becomes a political factor in its own right or it floun-
ders; it either takes off or crashes. One of the special characteristics of the American political system is that the take-off
point for participation in national politics is remote from the
initiation point. Many "third-party" movements that polled
many hundreds of thousands of votes still could not continue
to grow and to become permanent participants on the federal level.[24]

Take-off is especially important for the study of social
units that are initiated by charter, enactment of a law, or signing of a treaty. While sometimes these "paper" units might
be an expression of an already existing social unit, often the
formal structure precedes the development of a social one.
While it has been often pointed out that an informal
structure is likely to evolve, turning the formal one into a
full-fledged social unit, we do not know under what conditions these informal processes take off, as against those
conditions under which they never reach such a point.
Clearly not all formal structures become functioning social
units. This applies in particular to international relations

where the supranational take-off, that is, the transition from a formal, intergovernmental structure to self-sustained growth toward a political community, is quite infrequent.[25] Under what conditions, then, does take-off occur?

While these problems still require much research, there appears to be one central factor bringing unification movements to take-off: the amount of decision making called for by intercountry *flows* (e.g., of goods) and by *shared performance* (e.g., holding a common defense line) that, in turn, is determined by the scope of tasks carried out internationally. If the amount is large, intergovernment decision making will prove cumbersome and inadequate and pressure will be generated either to reduce the need for international decision making— by reducing the international tasks—or to build a supranational decision-making *structure*, which is a more effective decision-making body than are intergovernmental ones.

The central variable for the "take-off" of supranational authority is the amount of international decision making required. This, in turn, is determined largely by the amounts and kinds of flows that cross the international borders (e.g., tourists, mail) and the amounts and kinds of shared international activities (e.g., maintaining an early warning system). It should be stressed, however, that each flow or shared activity has its own decision-making logarithm. Some flows can increase a great deal and still require only a little increase in international decision making; others require much more.[26] Moreover, the relationship seems not to be linear; that is, some increases in a particular flow (or shared activity) can be handled by the old decision-making system, but once a certain threshold is passed, some supranational authority is almost inevitable.

It seems also that expanding the power and scope of a supranational authority is easier than to form the first element of such an authority. Initially a supranational authority is often accepted on the grounds that it will limit itself strictly to technical, bureaucratic, or secondary matters, and that the major policy decisions will be left in the hands of a superior,

intergovernment body. This was the initial relationship between the High Authority and the Council of Ministers of the
ECSC; between the Economic Commission and the Council
of Ministers of the EEC; and between NATO's SHAPE and
NATO's conferences of ministers.

Once such a bureaucratic structure is established, a
process often sets in whereby full-time, professional bureaucrats tend to usurp functions and authority from the part-
time, political, "amateur" superior bodies, thereby expanding
the scope of the supranational authority. At the same time,
the very existence of supranational control in one area tends
to promote such control in others. The concept of spill-over,
or secondary priming, which is used here to study the epigenesis of nation unions, is applicable to the study of accumulation processes in general.

Secondary Priming of Change

"Spill-over" refers to expansion of supranational performances and control from one sphere of international behavior to another. It was introduced by Haas to refer to expan-
sions within the sector in which unification originally started
(e.g., from coal and steel industries to transportation) and
from sector to sector (e.g., from the economic to the political).[27] Spill-over refers only to secondary priming; that is, to
processes—in our case, unifications—that have been initiated
or have taken off because of epigenesis in *other* social sectors.
NATO, for instance, unifies the military organizations of fifteen nations, and the EEC integrates the economies of six of
the NATO countries. While these processes probably support
each other, only a little spill-over has taken place. Basically
the military unification did not initiate the economic one or
vice versa.[28] There was original priming in each area. Both
unifications may have had certain common sources (e.g., the
conflicts between the United States and Soviet Russia) and
may be mutually supportive, but they did not trigger each
other. On the other hand, the integration of the economies
of the Six generates pressures toward integration of their gov-

ernments, though so far political unification is mainly a "grand design."[29]

It follows that one can hardly understand supranational spill-over without studying the internal structure and dynamics of the participating societies. This must be done from a dynamic perspective, for spill-over raises the following questions: Under what conditions and at what level of change does unification of one sector lead to the exhausting of its "degrees of freedom" and trigger unification in other sectors?[30] Which sector is likely to be affected first, second, and nth? Which sector will be affected most, second, and nth?

The Sequence of Epigensis

Clockwise and Counterwise Sequences

The concept of take-off suggests that epigenesis has to gain a certain momentum before it becomes self-sustaining. However, it does not suggest in what sector accumulation takes off, or what the effects of the selection of a particular take-off sector are on the probability that general unification will ensue. Similarly, the study of spill-over traces the relation between sectors once take-off in one sector has occurred, but it does not specify either in which sector accumulation is likely to start or in what order other supranational sectors are likely to be built up (since it does not account for primary, simultaneous, or successive priming). To put it in terms of the accumulation model, we still have to determine: Which part is assembled first, which ones later?[31]

A hypothesis defining the sequences most functional for the epigenesis of nation unions can be derived from an application of the Parsonian phase model.[32] Parsons suggests that the most functional cyclical fluctuations in the investment of resources, personnel, and time follow one of two patterns: either a clockwise sequence (adaptive, allocative, socially integrative, and normative integrative), or a counterclockwise sequence.[33] The two patterns can be applied to the study of epigenesis. They suggest that it is most functional for a new community to assemble its subunits and its self-control from the adaptive to the normative, or the other way around; and that all other sequences are less functional.[34]

Before we turn to express this hypothesis in more substantive terms the difference between the application of the Parsonian phase model to preformism and its application to epigenesis should be pointed out. The phase model, as such, concerns the movement of an existing system, not its pattern of growth or change in its structure. Unless other processes take place, after a full round of the phase movement the system is the same as it started. Moreover, while each system is once accumulated or differentiated, the phase movement can continue ad libitum.[35]

Parsons also suggested a pattern for the analysis of social change, that of differentiation, according to which fused units bifurcate first into expressive and instrumental elements; then, each of these splits. Expressive elements are divided into social and normative ones; instrumental into adaptive and allocative ones. This, like all preformism models, is a pattern according to which functions that were served by one, fused structure, become structurally differentiated; that is, they gain their own subunits.[36] The accumulation model, on the other hand, knows no bifurcation, but suggests an order in which new structures serving new functions are conjoined. For example, countries that shared only a common market also establish a common defense line; that is, the union acquires a new function, not just a structural wing. The order we expect to be functional for unification movements to follow is either from the adaptive to the normative or the other way around.

In more substantive terms, the major question raised by the hypothesis concerning the sequence of accumulation is this: Is unification initiated in a particular sector more likely to lead to complete unification (to a political community)? If so, which is it: the military, economic, political, or ideological? Is the probability of success higher if accumulation follows a certain sequence? Which sequence (if any)? And is the most effective sequence the same for all types of unifications? (See below.)

On the basis of the study of ten historical cases Deutsch and his associates reached the following conclusion:

> It appears to us from our cases that they [conditions of integration] may be assembled in almost any sequence, so long only as all of them come into being and take effect. Toward this end, almost any pathway will suffice.[37]

They added, however, that:

> In this assembly-line process of history, and particularly in the transition between background and process, timing is important. Generally speaking, we found that substantial rewards for cooperation or progress toward amalgamation had to be timed so as to come before the imposition of burdens resulting from such progress toward amalgamation (union). We found that, as with rewards before burdens, consent has to come before compliance if the amalgamation is to have lasting success.[38]

Deutsch's distinction between sequence and order in time seems unnecessary for our purposes. Especially after examining his important book, *Backgrounds for Community*, in which his historical material is analyzed in great detail and potency, we conclude that Deutsch suggests—if we push the freedom of interpretation to its limit—that the allocative phase tends to come before the adaptive one (rewards before burdens); and that the normative phase (consent) tends to come before the social-integrative phase (compliance). In other words, interpreting liberally, we find Deutsch suggesting that a counterclockwise sequence from normative to adaptive is most common.

Haas compares the findings of his study of a modern unification with the findings of Deutsch *et al.* on historical cases from this viewpoint.[39] He distinguishes between identical expectations (or aims) and converging expectations that make actors cooperate in pursuing their non-identical aims. The distinction comes close to Durkheim's dichotomy of mechanic and organic solidarity and is similar to the dichotomy of expressive and instrumental elements.[40] Haas reports that the ECSC has followed a clockwise sequence in which convergent (or instrumental) expectations preceded the identical (or expressive) ones.[41] Interpreting Haas liberally, one could state that in the case of the ECSC adaptive integration (custom union) came first, followed by allocative integration of economic policies (regarding coal and steel and later the formation of a common market). The union is now on the verge of political integration (election of a European parliament; planning group for federal or confederal institutions) and at the beginning of normative integration. Actually by the time Haas completed his study in 1957, there was hardly any supranational merger of normative institutions, and even attitudes only started to change from convergent to identical.

Any effort to codify Deutsch's and Haas's findings for the benefit of further research on the question of the relative effectiveness of various sequences will have to take into account (1) the nature of the merging units, (2) the nature of the emerging unit (i.e., the kind of union established), and (3) the nature of functional statements.

Merging Units

One might expect that supranational unification of societies that differ in their internal structure will proceed in a different sequence. If, for instance, the merging units are three newly independent states such as Ghana, Guinea, and Mali—states that in themselves are still in the process of building up their "expressive" foundations—the emphasis on normative and social integration on the supranational level might well be higher than when long-established and well-integrated states unify, as in the Scandinavian union, where the instrumental elements of the unification are stressed. These observations support the far from earth-shaking hypothesis that sector integration most responsive to the functional needs of the individual societies that are merging will come first in the unification sequence. After take-off, however, unification is expected to *proceed more and more in accord with the intrinsic needs of the emerging political union, less and less in accord with the internal needs of the merging units.*

The preceding statements should not be read to imply that "political communities develop differently in different historical context"; that, for instance, one can account for the difference between Deutsch's findings and those of Haas by pointing to the fact that Deutsch deals with historical cases while Haas is concerned with a contemporary one. Such statements are frequently made by historians who believe that each context is unique, hence what needs explanation is not diversity but uniformity—if ever found. For the sociologist the "historical context" is a shorthand phrase referring to the values of a myriad variables; unless these are specified, little is explained by the statement that "the context is different." In our case the question is: Which contextual variables account for the difference in sequences and for how much of the difference? (Often numerous factors have an effect but a small number accounts for most of the variance.)

"Historical cases," for instance, are often preindustrial societies; hence it comes to mind that the level of industrialization might account for part of the difference; industrialized societies might tend to merge in an adaptive-first, normative-last sequence; non-industrial ones, in a normative-first, adaptive-last sequence. This formulation seems suggestive because, if valid, it points to the direction in which these findings can be generalized. We would expect, for instance, contemporary non-industrialized societies to unify in the "historical," not in the "contemporary," fashion. The hypothesis also calls attention to the special importance of historical cases in which unification came after industrialization. If these unifications followed a "contemporary" sequence, the hypothesis on the relation of industrialization to the sequence of unification would be strengthened.

Another variable to be teased out of the undifferentiated phrase, "historical context," is the degree of nationalism. There seem to be three major kinds of unions: pre-nationalist (e.g., the Roman Empire); post-nationalist (e.g., the EEC); and unions that are themselves an expression of rising nationalism (e.g., the unification of Italy). All other things being equal, we would expect the initial phases of pre- and post-nationalist unions to stress the adaptive aspect and follow the clockwise pattern; and those unions that express nationalism to be initiated on the normative side, following the counterclockwise sequence.

Kinds of Union

The sequence of unification is determined not only by the *initial* needs of the merging units (e.g., industrialization) and the "period" (e.g., advent of nationalism) but also by the function the union fulfils for the various participant units as it is *completed*. Unions of nations differ greatly on this score. The most familiar type is that of custom unions, which keep up the level of international trade among member countries. The new Central American Union, formed in 1959, and the Latin America Free Trade Area, ratified in 1961,[42] are actually oriented at economic development, international division of labor, sharing of information, and even of capital rather than increased regional trade.[43] Wallerstein points to still a different function of unions: Some serve as instruments of subordination, while others serve to bolster independence.[44] Thus the whites, who are stronger in Southern Rhodesia than in Northern Rhodesia and Nyasaland, use the federation of the three regions to hold the regions in which they are weak.

Functional analysis of social units that develop epigenetically is more complex than such an analysis of existing social units, for here we deal with functional analysis of change where the system itself is changing. Thus, as unification evolves, it comes to fulfill different (either additional or substitute) functions for the participant units and the emerging union. The West European unification might have been initiated in 1947 as a way to gain capital aid from the United States to reconstruct the postwar economies; soon it acquired the additional function of countering Soviet military expansion; then it came to serve economic welfare and, with the "rebellion" of France since De Gaulle has returned to office, it even serves, to a degree, to countervail United States influence in the Western bloc.[45] (It should be mentioned in passing that at a given stage of development the same union may have different functions for different participants. Thus, Germany supported the EEC partially to overcome its "second" citizen status in the community of nations; allied control of German steel industry, for instance, was abolished when Germany entered the ECSC.[46] France supported the formation of NATO in part to gain some control over a rebuilt and rearmed Germany.)

All functional needs—those of individual members, those common to all members, and those of the evolving community—vary with the various stages of the unification process; and they all seem to affect the sequence in which the "parts" are assembled. It remains for future studies to relate differences in sequence to these functional variations, to validate two hypotheses: (1) the higher the degree of unification the more its pattern of accumulation can be accounted for by common (identical or complementary) needs, rather than by the individual needs of member states, and by needs of the union rather than by common needs of the members; (2) accumulation sequences, whatever their take-off sector, are most likely to complete the process of unification if they follow the clockwise or counterclockwise sequence than any other.

Functional and "Real" Sequences

An important difference between the statements about sequences made, on the one hand, by Deutsch and by Haas and the statements made, on the other, by Parsons, his associates, and in the preceding discussion is that the former refer to actual occurrences (the ECSC followed this and that pattern) and empirical frequencies (nine out of ten historical cases followed this sequence), while the latter refer to functional sequences. Functional statements suggest that if epigenesis proceeds in a certain sequence, it will be most effectively completed; if it follows another sequence, certain dysfunctions will occur. The nature of the dysfunctions can be derived from the nature of the stages which are skipped (e.g., high social strain is expected if the expressive elements are not introduced), or incorporated in a "wrong" order (e.g., high strain is expected when allocation of resources is attempted before adaptation has been built up). The fact that a particular unification follows a sequence other than the one suggested by the epigenesis model does not invalidate the latter so long as it is demonstrated that the "deviation" from the model caused dysfunctions. In short, the test of the model lies in its ability to predict which course of action is functional and which one is not, rather than to predict the course of action likely to be followed.[47]

In the construction of epigenesis models for the various kinds of nation unions, the use of two types of functional models must be distinguished: The crude *survival* model and the more sophisticated and demanding *effectiveness* model. The first specifies the conditions under which a structure exists or ceases to exist; the second also takes into account differences in the degree of success. In the case of nation unions, then, while many are likely to continue in existence, some will stagnate on a low level of integration while others will continue to grow in scope, function, and authority.

Conclusion

Sociological theories of change tend to be preformist; they provide differentiation models for the analysis of the structural development of existing social units. We presented some elements of an alternative, epigenesis model, which suggests that some social units acquire new subunits that fulfill new functions, do not just provide new subunits for functions served before in a less specialized manner. Since these new elements are incorporated from the environment, epigenesis (or accumulation) models are much more concerned with input from, and articulation with, external units than preformism (or differentiated) models. Hence the first question we asked was: Where does the power lie that controls the process—is it evenly distributed among the participant units or is it concentrated in the hands of elites? Are the power-holders members of the new emerging communities or outsiders? Does increase in self-control of the union precede, follow, or coincide with the growth in its performances?

Turning from the powers that control accumulation to the pattern of accumulation itself, we asked: Where does the process start, what subunit is built up first? Which follows? What effect does the construction of one part have on that of the others? The concepts of take-off and secondary priming proved to be useful in understanding the initiation and progress of accumulating processes. An application of Parsons' phase model served us in formulating a hypothesis concerning the functional sequence of accumulation.

The distinctness of accumulation models should be emphasized: While differentiation models focus our attention on internal processes, accumulation models are concerned with boundary processes; while differentiation models are interested in internal elites, accumulation models ask about the changing power distribution between external and internal ones and their respective impacts on accumulation. Analytically speaking, preformist models see their subject units— even when undifferentiated—as functionally complete, whereas epigenesis models view their units as either partial (to varying degrees) or complete.

We emphasized the need to treat social units and their change as multilayer phenomena, including at least a performance, a power (or control), and a communication layer.[48] If we deal with a phase, differentiation, or accumulation model, we need not assume that changes on one layer are automatically concomitant with changes on the others.

Although the epigenesis model can be applied to many social phenomena, we are interested here primarily in using it to study international unification. There is hardly a subject less frequently studied by sociologists and more given to sociological analysis than the development of political communities whose members are nations. Since the evolution of these communities is likely to be supportive of both the short-run armed truce and the development of the social conditions for lasting peace,[49] and since the processes of social change involved in forming supranational communities are comparatively highly planned, deliberately and frequently drawing on expert advice, the study of supranational unification carries the extra reward of not just better understanding of human society but also of understanding how to better it.

Notes

1. This model is applied to the study of small groups by Robert F. Bales and Philip E. Slater, "Role Differentiation in Small Decision-Making Groups," in Talcott Parsons, Robert F. Bales, and Edward A. Shils, *Working Papers in the Theory of Action* (New York: Free Press, 1953); to socialization process by Parsons, Bales, *et al.*, *Family, Socialization and Interaction Process* (New York: Free Press, 1953), chap. iv; to industrialization by Neil Smelser, *Social Change in the Industrial Revolution* (Chicago: University of Chicago Press, 1959); to the study of the family by Morris Zelditch, Jr., "Role Differentiation in the Nuclear Family: A Comparative Study," in *Family, Socialization . . . , op. cit.*, pp. 307–51, and by Smelser, *op. cit.*, chaps. viii–x; to the study of elites by Amitai Etzioni, "The Functional Differentiation of Elites in the *Kibbutz,*" *American Journal of Sociology*, LXIX (1959), 476–87; and to the study of underdeveloped countries by Neil Smelser, "Toward a Theory of Modernization," in Amitai and Eva Etzioni (eds.), *Social Change: Sources, Patterns and Consequences* (New York: Harper-Collins, 1963).
2. *Family, Socialization . . . , op. cit.*, chap. iv.
3. I found this dimension of much value in analyzing the relationship between specialized units and parent organizations (see "Authority Structure and Organizational Effectiveness," *Administrative Science Quarterly*, IV [1959], 62–67).
4. Karl W. Deutsch *et al.*, *Political Community and the North Atlantic Area* (Princeton, N.J.: Princeton University Press, 1957), pp. 28, 38–39.

5. Paul M. Harrison, *Authority and Power in the Free Church Tradition* (Princeton, N.J.: Princeton University Press, 1959).

6. Frantz Wendt, *The Nordic Council and Cooperation in Scandinavia* (Copenhagen: Mumsgaard, 1959), pp. 98–100 (see also Norman J. Padelford, "Regional Cooperation in Scandinavia," *International Organization,* XI [1957], 597–614).

7. The infrequency of voluntary unions is stressed in Crane Brinton, *From Many to One* (Cambridge, Mass.: Harvard University Press, 1949), pp. 49 ff.

8. For an outstanding discussion of the Soviet bloc from this viewpoint see Zbigniew K. Brzezinski, *The Soviet Bloc* (Cambridge, Mass.: Harvard University Press, 1960), chap. xii, and his "The Organization of the Communist Camp," *World Politics,* XII (1961), 175–209.

9. The Ministerial Council of CENTO decided in its meeting in Ankara in April, 1960, that a shared military command would be developed; intercountry roads and telecommunication improved; and economic and cultural ties increased (*New York Times,* April 29, 1961). Projects already completed include a new Turkish-Iranian railway, a new road linking the CENTO countries, as well as a microwave communication network (*International Organization,* XV [1961], 523).

10. Immanuel Wallerstein, "Background to Paga," *West Africa,* July 29, 1961, p. 819, and August 5, 1961, p. 861, and Walter Schwartz, "Varieties of African Nationalism," *Commentary,* XXXII (1961), 34.

11. Karl W. Deutsch, *Nationalism and Social Communication* (New York: Wiley, 1953), pp. 65, 143.

12. Karl W. Deutsch, *Political Community at the International Level* (Garden City, N.Y.: Doubleday, 1954), pp. 13–15.

13. Elihu Katz and Paul Lazarsfeld, *Personal Influence* (New York: Free Press, 1955).

14. Alex Bavelas, "Communication Patterns in Task-Oriented Groups," *Journal of the Acoustical Society of America,* XXII (1950), 725–30.

15. For one of the few studies that successfully tie the two see R. H. McCleary, *Policy Change in Prison Management* (East Lansing: Michigan State University, 1957).

16. Deutsch, *Nationalism and Social Communication,* p. 143 (see also his *Political Community at the International Level,* p. 37).

17. "Internalize" means here the transfer of power from external elites to internal elites.

18. It should be pointed out that on the international level the power of a new union is more often generalized from its constituent units—"pooling of sovereignty"—than internalized from superior power. From the present viewpoint this distinction is not relevant; the question is: Who controls the collective action—the unit itself or other units (without regard to whether they are outside or constituent units)?

19. For an outstanding discussion of the differences between intergovernment and supranational decision-making bodies, see Ernst B. Haas, *Uniting of Europe* (Stanford, Calif.: Stanford University Press, 1958), chaps. xii, xiii. The following discussion of the High Authority draws on Haas's work.

20. In March, 1961, the Economic Commission—which is roughly, to the EEC what the High Authority is to the ECSC—brought the Italian government before the court of the EEC for violation of an article of the Treaty of Rome concerning a ban on subsidies for trade in pork. This was the first such action taken since the formation of the EEC (*New York Times,* March 27, 1961).

21. See Andrew J. Godpaster, "The Development of SHAPE: 1950–1953," *International Organization,* IX (1955), 257–62, and William A. Knowlton, "Early Stages in the Organization of SHAPE," *International Organization,* XIII (1959), 1–18.

22. William Diebold, Jr., "The Changed Economic Position of Western Europe," *International Organization,* XV (1960), 1–19, esp. p. 12.

23. W. W. Rostow, *The Stages of Economic Growth* (Cambridge,

England: Cambridge University Press, 1960), pp. 4, 7–9, 36 ff.

24. Daniel Bell (ed.), *The New American Right* (New York: Criterion, 1955).

25. See Deutsch *et al., op. cit.,* pp. 85–87, on supranational take-off.

26. Hence the fact that a mere increase in flows is not related to increase in supranationalism does not reject the hypothesis that these variables are positively related. Cf. I. Richard Savage and Karl Deutsch, "A Statistical Model of the Gross Analysis of Transaction Flows," *Econometrica,* XXVIII (1960), 551–72; Deutsch, "Shifts in the Balance of Communication Flows," *Public Opinion Quarterly,* XX (1956), 143–60.

27. *Uniting of Europe, op. cit.,* chap. viii.

28. Diebold (*op. cit.*) points to the reasons why efforts to base economic integration on NATO have been unsuccessful. Kissinger, on the other hand, believes that NATO could serve as the basis of an Atlantic confederacy (*Reporter,* February 2, 1961, pp. 15–21). Deutsch *et al.* pointed out that where the initial unification efforts were based on military integration half of these efforts failed (*op. cit.,* p. 28).

29. On spill-over from the economic to the political area see essays by Paul Delouvrier and by Pierre Uri in C. Grove Haines (ed.), *European Integration* (Baltimore, Md.: Johns Hopkins Press, 1957).

30 In other words, up to a point each institutional realm changes independently, but, once that point has been reached, further change affects another institutional realm.

31. Note that though sector spin-over occurs in the member societies, it leads to expansion in the scope of the supranational community.

32. Parsons *et al., Working Papers . . . , op. cit.,* pp. 182 ff.

33. Here, as well as in an earlier work, I found it fruitful to apply Parsons' concepts with a certain amount of liberty. A long conceptual quibble seems unnecessary. The use

of allocation instead of "goal attainment" and of normative integration instead of "pattern maintenance and tension-management" may serve as a reminder to the reader concerned with such conceptual subtleties that Parsons is not responsible for my way of using his scheme.

34. This is one of those statements that sounds tautological but is not. Since there are four phases in the system, the statement suggests that two modes of movement are more functional than twenty-two possible other ones. The first pattern—adaptive to normative—is referred to as clockwise because the convention is to present the four phases in a fourfold table in which the adaptive is in the upper left-hand box, the allocative in the upper right-hand box, the social-integrative in the lower right-hand box, and the normative in the lower left-hand box.

35. Note also that there is no one-to-one relationship between the pattern in which a system is built up (whether accumulated or differentiated) and the pattern in which it is maintained; e.g., the epigenesis of a system might be counterclockwise and the system will "click" clockwise once its epigenesis is completed.

36. For a later development of this model see Talcott Parsons, "A Functional Theory of Change," in Amitai and Eva Etzioni (eds.), *op. cit.*

37. *Op. cit.*, p. 70.

38. *Ibid.*, p. 71.

39. Haas, "The Challenge of Regionalism," in Stanley Hoffman (ed.), *Contemporary Theory in International Relations* (Englewood Cliffs, N.J.: Prentice-Hall, 1960), pp. 230–31.

40. *Ibid.*, p. 229. In Haas's own words: "Converging expectations make for regional unity instrumental in nature rather than based on principle."

41. *Ibid.*, p. 230.

42. See "The Emerging Common Markets in Latin America," *Monthly Review* (Federal Reserve Bank of New York), September, 1960, pp. 154 ff.

43. This point was made by Lincoln Gordon in "Economic Regionalism Reconsidered," *World Politics*, XIII (1961), 231–53.
44. On these unions see Immanuel Wallerstein, *Africa* (New York: Random House, 1962), chap. vii.
45. Edgar S. Furniss, Jr., "De Gaulle's France and NATO: An Interpretation," *International Organization*, XV (1961), 349–65.
46. *Uniting of Europe, op. cit.*, pp. 247–48.
47. Note that the system this statement refers to is not the existing one but a future state—that of a complete unification—of a community. The use of a future-system reference might prove useful for the general development of the functional analysis of change.
48. See my *A Comparative Analysis of Complex Organizations* (New York: Free Press, 1961), chaps. v and vii.
49. These functions of nation unions are discussed in chap. viii of my *The Hard Way to Peace* (New York: Macmillan, 1962).

European Unification:
A Strategy of Change

The success of the European Economic Community often
has been hailed as the most important development of international relations in the West in the last century. Even if
the EEC does not progress beyond the point it has already
reached, it is probably the most integrated union ever to
have been formed among nation-states. Moreover, observers have been impressed by the momentum the EEC has had
until recently, leading most of them to expect that its level
of integration will continue to rise and its scope of unification to grow. Much of the credit for the success of the EEC
is often attributed to "background" factors, to the fact that
the member countries share the same European tradition,
have a sizable Catholic population, are in a similar stage of
economic development, have a similar civilization, and so
forth.

This homogeneity of background factors, it must be
noted, had existed for many generations; it did not hitherto
prevent these very countries from fighting each other. No less
striking is the fact that earlier attempts to form unions of
these same countries, in the years immediately preceding the
formation of the EEC, failed. Part of the credit must hence
be given not solely to the background conditions but to the
way they were used, to the strategy of change employed by
those who initiated and supported the EEC. These were often the same individuals and forces that participated in and

Note: This essay was originally published in *World Politics,* 1963 *16*(1), 32–
51. It is reprinted with permission. It was written while I was a research
associate at the Institute of War and Peace Studies, Columbia University. I
am indebted to Leon N. Lindberg and Robert McGeehan for comments
on an earlier version.

hence learned from the earlier failures. I am not suggesting that any group of countries that employed this strategy would inevitably succeed in forming a Common Market. But when the background conditions are favorable and similar to those present in Europe in the 1950s, an effective strategy could make the difference between success and failure.

Before we turn to an analysis of the strategy employed in the case at hand, two conceptual comments are required. First, success is measured with regard to the degree to which the goal of a given organization is realized; no value judgment by the analyst is involved. Second, while strategies are deliberately designed and employed policies, it is not a necessary assumption that those who employ them are aware *a priori* of all their consequences and ramifications. For instance, a party might follow a moderate strategy and hence succeed in a situation where a more drastic one would have led to failure, without being aware that the chosen strategy was moderate or that the alternative course—not taken— would have been a calamity. The analyst, helped by hindsight, may nevertheless conclude that the success of the endeavor was due to the use of the strategy in question.

Building Up Homogeneity

The theory has often been stated that the more homogeneous a group of countries is, the more likely they are to form a union. Homogeneity is generally viewed as a set of given background characteristics; France and Italy have many characteristics in common which they do not share with Yugoslavia, and there is little that any of them can do about it. There is, however, one strategic consideration the initiator of a union faces that greatly affects the heterogeneity of the group with which he has to work, and that is what countries he invites or allows to join an attempt at unification. The surest way to reduce the heterogeneity is not by trying to make the countries more similar to each other—a painful and slow process—but by leaving out initially or subsequently screening out some of the countries. These can be either those that are most different, or a whole subgroup of countries that are quite similar to each other but different from the other subgroup(s), or those that most strongly resist unification. The development of European unification since 1945 followed all these lines of exclusion until a group homogeneous enough for effective unification was formed.

When in 1944 the leaders of the resistance movements of countries under Nazi occupation met in Geneva to discuss the formation of a United States of Europe after World War II, many still thought of including all the European countries, including those of Eastern Europe.[1] The initial invitation to benefit from the Marshall Plan funds and to cooperate in the planning of European reconstruction was sent to the Communist countries as well. This was done in part to embarrass Russia, which was unable to match American offers of assistance to these countries, and in part because the United States did not want to bear the onus for "splitting" Europe. But following the withdrawal of the Russian delegation from the 1947 Paris negotiations, the circle was limited to non-Communist countries.[2]

The Organization for European Economic Cooperation (OEEC), the next station in the narrowing-down process, was formed in 1948, with sixteen members. The membership of the Council of Europe, another outgrowth of the postwar unification efforts formed in 1949, included fourteen countries, largely the same as those in the OEEC. Both organizations failed to "take off." That is, they made little impact on the international relations of the participant countries, and did not trigger the expected process of either economic or political unification. NATO, with many of the same members and of similar size, scored somewhat better in attaining some degree of supranationality and integration with the formation of SHAPE in 1951, but it never led to the formation of an Atlantic Community, or even to an effective integration of the military establishments of the members.

The next attempts were made among a smaller group of countries, considerably more similar in their background conditions, and more similar in their commitment to unification than those left out. Six continental countries attempted to form the European Coal and Steel Community (ECSC) in 1952, and in 1954 the European Defense Community (EDC) and the European Political Community (EPC). The latter two failed for reasons discussed below, but the ECSC succeeded, serving as the forerunner of the EEC. Left out were all neutral countries (including those that had been members of the OEEC, such as Sweden and Switzerland); all countries that were low on the scale of commitment to unification (especially the United Kingdom); all countries that did not have a sizable Catholic population (especially Norway and Denmark); and all countries that were less developed, even if they were in NATO (Turkey and Greece) or Catholic (Portugal and Spain).

Thus, the cause of European unification was pursued by a shrinking circle of participants, until a group of countries was left that was both less heterogeneous and more committed to unification than the earlier and larger groups. This might now seem an obvious course, but in the negotiations from 1955 to 1957 efforts were still made to keep a much larger number of countries in the unifying group—first, to include the United Kingdom in the Common Market, and then to form a European Free Trade Area including all or most of the OEEC members, as a substitute or supplement to the EEC. Only at this stage, as a reaction to the obstructionist position of the United Kingdom in the Council of Europe and in the OEEC, and to the support its orientation found among the Nordic countries, did the need for a smaller circle become evident to the leaders of the European integration movement.[3]

What effects the present tendency to increase the number of members of the EEC, and therefore its heterogeneity, will have on the success of the union remains to be seen. While it appears as if the trend would hamper high integration,[4] much can be said for the theory that once a union is established, its institutions molded, and its image crystallized, it can absorb more countries and withstand more heterogeneity than when it is being initiated.

Aiming High, Scoring Low; Aiming Low, Scoring High

There is a strong negative relation between the level of ambition of various postwar European organizations and their degree of success: the higher the aim, the lower the score, and vice versa. I am not suggesting that the nature of the aim was the only factor, but surely it had a great effect on the results of these earlier unification efforts. The highest aim was full political unification as the immediate goal of an inter-European effort. Political unification (the formation of a supranational parliament and executive) is "highest," since it affects all the societal sectors, from defense to education, from economy to foreign policy. Political unification hence means *ipso facto* wholistic unification. The slogans reflected the mood: "No Europe Without a Common Sovereignty" and "Federation Now" were among the popular ones. This was the goal of the 1947 International Committee for a United Europe, the 1948 Hague Congress, and the European Movement that resulted from the Congress. The Hague Congress advocated setting up a European Assembly as a federal parliament and "other measures designed to unite Western Europe."[5] The score of these efforts was quite poor. They yielded the Council of Europe, which among all the postwar European organizations was probably the most anemic one or, as Goodspeed puts it, "little more than an experiment" and "a hybrid between a very loose-unit international parliament with purely advisory powers and a dignified international forum."[6]

A similarly ambitious plan was to form a military and political union of six countries under the EDC and EPC. The EPC aimed at forming "an indissoluble supranational political community, based on the union of peoples." Its parliament was to have a federal structure, and a European Executive Council responsible to this parliament. The EDC was to have multinational ("mixed") units and a supranational command, patterned after the High Authority of the ECSC. Neither of these ambitious projects was ever launched. The EPC treaty was not signed, and the EDC not ratified. One might point out that the EDC treaty was signed by all of the six countries and ratified by all but France; had it not been for the thaw in the Cold War and the death of Stalin, the French Assembly would probably have ratified it. But one must point out that, even if ratified, there is considerable doubt whether the EDC would have taken off. Other less ambitious military efforts, such as the Western European Union or NATO, despite the latter's Article 2, even in a period of intense cold war never led to much political or economic unification or, for that matter, to extensive military integration.

An economic union is a much less ambitious goal than military or political unification. It does not require tackling the very institutional and ideological core of the nation-state: its constitution, government, parliament, its sovereignty. It is, initially, limited to one societal sector, the economy. Even if it eventually leads to wide unification, it allows the illusion of sovereignty to be maintained unharmed, at least until the economic factors have rearranged themselves to accept and support unification and until various spill-over processes have been triggered in the ideological field (e.g., increase in "European" sentiments), in the institutional field (e.g., increase in the power of the Economic Commission), and in the political sphere (e.g., the formation of supranational interest groups and political parties).

The first attempt at economic unification, the OEEC, while less ambitious than the political ones, was still aiming too high in terms of membership and tasks. Economic cooperation and integration were to be attained among sixteen countries, including some countries that were partially devastated during the war (the Netherlands and Norway), countries that suffered considerably less (Denmark and Belgium), and countries that were unharmed (Sweden and Switzerland). The scope of economic cooperation attempted was broad; the OEEC was to cover from the outset all major economic sectors in which intercountry trade was conducted. Nevertheless the OEEC, while it did not serve as a take-off

base for European unification,[7] achieved some limited economic goals, especially in the liberalization of intercountry
trade and in matters of foreign exchange.[8]

The first fairly successful unification effort came of the
less ambitious attempt to free the trade and harmonize the
policies of two industries, coal and steel, rather than whole
economies. Initially not much was expected to come out of
the Schuman Plan.[9] Still it was the ECSC, as has often been
pointed out, that served as the take-off base for the EEC.[10]
We should mention in passing not only that the aim of the
founders of the ECSC was more modest, but also that it included fewer countries than the OEEC, that the initiation of
this union was indigenous, while that of the OEEC was American—a condition for recipiency of Marshall Plan funds[11]—
and that the ECSC was initiated after much reconstruction
had taken place, while the OEEC was faced with several countries preoccupied with maintaining mere subsistence. But in
the same period, among the same countries that formed the
ECSC, the more ambitious programs of the EDC and EPC
failed. Thus, the nature of the goal chosen is clearly an important factor in determining the success of a union.

The founders of the EEC, six years later, were aiming
higher than those of the ECSC, but the situation had
changed; the EEC could benefit from the integrative forces
formed or triggered by the success of the ECSC. Moreover,
the goal of the EEC was *broken up into immediate, visible targets
that were quite low and into more remote and less visible targets that
were higher.* We cannot rerun history to prove that, had the
long-term goals of the EEC been clear to the six when the
Treaty of Rome was ratified, one or more of the six parliaments might never have ratified it. But we can point out that
those who consciously devised the strategy for the initiation
of the EEC were very much aware of a need to aim lower in
order to score higher; they had just failed in their effort to
launch the more ambitious EDC and EPC and they realized
that the idea of European integration could not survive many
more failures.[12] Here is the way one reporter depicts that

period: ". . . the European Movement had anything but clear sailing for the next several years. It suffered its worst setback in August 1954, when a proposal for a European Defense Community, aimed at integrating the armed forces of the Coal and Steel Community nations . . . was killed by the French National Assembly, which felt that to establish a common army with Germany would be going too far. After this blow—a really shattering one, since it showed how deep the old fears and prejudices still ran—the European Movement abandoned its optimistic headlong pace for a cautious step-by-step approach. . . . The problem was to avoid risking another defeat—perhaps a final one." [13]

The Gradualist Approach

The Treaty of Rome is a master example of a step-by-step or gradualist strategy. It amplifies close targets and underplays more remote (and more ambitious) ones; it breaks up, into small bits, both the adjustments the parties have to make and the loss of sovereignty they have to endure; it allows "stretch-outs"; and it follows a multi-path approach. At the same time it also provides for acceleration, a locking-in system, and the build-up of an integrative center that is stronger than the one provided in the text of the treaty itself. Each of these principles requires some elucidation.

Amplify the Close; Underplay the Remote

Now that the EEC is safely launched, its president and many of its initial designers state that its aim is political unification, not merely economic.[14] But this is not quite what the parties emphasized in 1957. The preamble of the treaty includes some vague phrases, such as "to establish the foundation of a closer union among European people," which can be interpreted to mean anything from a federation to a free trade area. It is put in a clearer context in the first articles of the treaty, which stress the economic focus of the European

Economic Community. The crucial Article 2 reads: "It shall be the aim of the community, by establishing a Common Market and progressively approximating the economic policies of Member States, to promote throughout the Community a harmonious development of economic activities, a continuous and balanced expansion, an increased stability, an accelerated raising of the standard of living and closer relations between its Member States."

The treaty goes on to spell out in hundreds of articles how these economic goals are to be obtained. No political goals are suggested, other than that hidden in one subclause at the end of a paragraph about "closer relations between the Member States." No mention is made of the method for progressing toward political unification, while the service of the economic goals is spelled out in great detail. Even in regard to organizing the shared economic activities, the use of the term "supranational" is avoided—though a supranational commission is provided for by the Treaty. In short, if the goal of the initiators and most enthusiastic supporters of the treaty was a United States of Europe, as Monnet's Action Committee title suggested, little was done to make that goal visible between the 1955 meeting in Messina, where negotiations over the EEC Treaty were initiated, and the 1957 meeting in Rome, where it was signed.

This should not be understood as implying that the European Movement conspired to enroll the governments of the six in a political union under the guise of an economic one. Politicians in Europe could not fail to recognize the goals of the European Movement and the devotion of people like Spaak, who played a crucial role in designing the treaty, or Monnet, to these goals. But the important point is that this time the "Europeans" were going to rely on spill-over effects and a gradual process rather than try to make their way by a headlong attack on the windmills of sovereignty. They did not conceal their long-range desire, but they neither emphasized it, focused their efforts on it, nor insisted on including it in the treaty.

Phasing of Adjustments

Practically all the changes, adjustments, and sacrifices that the member countries were expected to make under the treaty were broken into many small steps. Although after fifteen years no one may be able to tell the difference, it is one thing to inform a government that it will have to give up its control of international trade, flow of labor, and level of employment as of the first of next year, that it will have to form monetary, tax, investment, planning, and social policy—in short, economic policy—in harmony with six other governments, with decisions made by a weighted majority in a supranational body, and quite another thing to tell the same government that it will have to reduce its tariffs to some countries by 10 percent next year, and that similar reductions will have to be introduced in the following twelve to fifteen years, and that this will require the development of common economic policies sometime in the next half-generation.

Specifically the Treaty of Rome called for: (1) elimination of tariffs among the member countries over a period of twelve years; (2) gradual removal of qualitative trade controls (e.g., quotas) during the same period; (3) step-by-step harmonization of external tariffs over twelve years; (4) formation of a common agricultural policy at the end of the first stage (see below); (5) formation of shared economic policies on matters vaguely defined, at times not specified; (6) formation of a community organ, the Economic Commission, with power to initiate and formulate proposals, but leaving the sole power of approval in the hands of the intergovernmental Council of Ministers. That is, the commission was given, on paper, considerably less supranational power than the High Authority of the ECSC.

Phasing Supranationality

The varied and complex voting patterns of the treaty need not be explored here. Of great interest, however, is the fact that these patterns lead to more supranational decision making as the union advances from stage to stage. The treaty does not use the term, but a trend toward supranationality is implied, in that many kinds of decisions which must be reached by unanimous vote in the first stage are to be made by a qualified majority in the second stage, and by a qualified majority in the third stage. This allows for some development of community institutions, sentiments, and vested interests before supranationality is built up (though some of it is introduced from the onset by the very establishment of the Economic Commission).

"Stretch-Outs"

As a further device for easing the adjustment pains, the treaty institutionalized "stretch-outs" in which the participants can extend the period of adjustment beyond the envisioned twelve years. The treaty implementation is broken into three stages of four years each; at the end of the first stage, the member states can agree by a majority vote to extend the first stage by two years. Further extension of this stage or of the second and third ones can be obtained through a unanimous vote of the Council of Ministers, but the total adjustment period cannot be extended over more than fifteen years. While a total of three years of "stretch-out" is not very great, it still provides another measure to lure the timid into trying the Common Market way. The fact the "stretch-out" provision has not been used at the end of the first stage, and seems unlikely to be used later, supports Monnet's often quoted "theory of change"—that nothing moves governments better than having started them moving; hence the main effort should be one of initiation.

Multi-Path Approach

The Treaty of Rome goes farther than the instruments drawn up for either the Council of Europe or the European Defense Community in allowing for a large variety of institutional arrangements. Kitzinger effectively pointed out this quality of the Treaty of Rome: "The system [set up by the treaty] is neither one of centralized public planning, nor one of laissez-faire competition; it is neither one of nationalization nor one of purely private enterprise. . . . For atomic energy the system contains strong elements of public ownership and public control. For agriculture it is one of state support and quality control. For underdeveloped regions it is one of public finance and public encouragement of private capital. For transport it is one involving central plans and a mixture of European, national, and private enterprise."[15]

Provision for Acceleration

The treaty does more than ease the adjustment and lure the timid; it also provides ready-made outlets for the eventuality that a momentum evolves that is greater than was initially anticipated. Provision for acceleration ensures that the more supportive sectors will not be frustrated by cautious arrangements originally designed to get the community started. The treaty allows for the timetable of various unification processes to be accelerated. These provisions turned out to be of much use when the members found that they wanted to accelerate the build-up of the community, among other reasons because they wanted to make it irreversible in view of external pressures to dissolve the EEC in a large union; because the first steps seemed not only undisruptive, but quite beneficial to the participants; and because anticipation of a free market at a later stage led many industries to expand their production capacity and become anxious to gain full access to the larger market.[16] Thus, tariffs were twice reduced ahead of schedule, in 1961 and 1962, and quotas were abolished in four instead of twelve years.

Locking-In System

A little-emphasized provision of the treaty provides for a system that locks in integration that has been attained and

makes regression difficult. The transition from the first to the
second stage requires a unanimous agreement of the six
members; the transition from the second to third stage and
from the third to completion of the whole adjustment process requires no decision whatsoever—it is automatic. Only a
unanimous decision of all the six can delay the initiation of
stage three or the completion of the process. Thus, no one
has a veto power on progress, and everyone has a veto against
regression; any one party can prevent a legal retreat once the
first stage is completed, which it was in 1962.

Provision for Institutional Spill-Over

The Treaty of Rome was constructed to allow its institutions
to increase the scope of the subjects regulated or controlled
by them—of the power they apply in general, and, in particular, of the power they apply supranationally—without having
to return to the national parliaments for ratification of
changes or amendments of the treaty. From this viewpoint it
is of interest to compare the Treaty of Rome with that of the
ECSC. The High Authority of the ECSC is given more
supranational power than the Economic Commission, but the
usages to which this power might be applied, the goals to be
pursued, and the policy to be followed are carefully spelled
out. The Treaty of Rome, on the other hand, as Lindberg
pointed out in his keen analysis, is a permissive or framework
treaty.[17] It provides the Economic Commission with fewer
supranational powers than the High Authority, but it has
much less specific goals than the community institutions
(e.g., agricultural policy). Actually, while it specifies some
matters (e.g., amount and timetable of tariff reductions) and
leaves the implementations of some other specific goals to
the community institutions (e.g., agricultural policy), it leaves
almost completely open many questions of economic policy.
This provision for institutional spill-over turned out to be
valuable because the commission sought and acquired more
authority and more power than specifically assigned to it,
without violating or revising the Treaty.

The significance of this point should be spelled out. The commission cannot, even under a permissive rather than a prescriptive treaty, introduce proposals that are in great conflict with those which the national governments are willing to support; the governments may not only refuse to approve or even discuss proposals in the Council of Ministers, but also can refuse to reappoint the commissioners when their four-year term is up. The importance of permissive treaty structure is twofold: (1) it leaves the commission free to take the initiative in bringing about greater consensus among the national governments than they might reach without the commission's prodding; (2) there is no need to go through the cumbersome and risky process of ratifying a treaty revision when the governments or the Council of Ministers are willing to delegate more power and tasks to the commission—as they did several times, for instance, in matters concerning acceleration and agricultural policy. The Treaty of Rome leaves it largely to the discretion of the ministers when to delegate their power to the supranational commission.

No Reallocation Before Integration

While it cannot be documented here, one of the central factors that precipitated the break-up in 1961 of both the United Arabic Republic and the Federation of the West Indies was the attempt to reallocate economic assets, and the anticipation of more reallocation, among units whose community ties were not yet built up.[18] Communities, whether national or international, are composed of units whose assets are never equal. Taking from the rich and giving to the poor is a common mode of reallocation in modern communities; in national ones it is often achieved through a progressive income tax and a regressive allocation of welfare services— that is, the rich pay more taxes and the poor receive more services. Such reallocation of assets is acceptable to the richer units (e.g., New York State) only *after* they conceive of the poorer units (e.g. Mississippi) as part of the same community. In the same way, reallocation in favor of labor was not carried out as long as the British middle class saw labor as another "nation,"[19] but it became the rule once the labor force was seen as an integral part of the British national society. Attempts to use resources of the comparatively better off islands, Jamaica and Trinidad, to finance the development of the much poorer remaining eight islands of the Federation of the West Indies, before the community of the West Indian nation was firmly established, was one cause of the break-up of that union.[20] In the UAR, the 1961 acceleration of the efforts by the Egyptians to change the allocation within Syria in favor of the farming and working classes, and to transfer to Egypt the control of Syrian commerce, industry, and army—again before the sense of community had jelled—helped to precipitate that union's collapse.[21]

The EEC deliberately minimized reallocation in the first stage. Efforts were made first to build up community sentiments, institutions, and integrative forces; reallocations were to be left to later stages. The continuation of a strong prosperity, high employment (and increasing employment in Italy), accelerated economic growth (better than 5 percent per annum), and the continuous increase in intercountry trade (85 percent in the first five years) served as a general rewarding background. Whether the EEC can be credited with all these achievements is an open question; the fact remains that it did not stop prosperity and almost surely contributed to it, and that most people thought it contributed much more to prosperity than it probably did. Thus, in addition to the reward of real economic success it acquired the myth of success, which was supportive to the EEC institutions and gratifying to its supporters.

Many specific interests of national economic groups were expected to be satisfied through unification. Italian labor expected free access to other countries' employment sources; France, Italy, and the Netherlands, increased export of their agricultural products to Western Germany; Western Germany, a larger free market for its industry, etc. Labor was at first somewhat suspicious of a community to be governed by a Christian-Conservative majority, one to which business was committed, the forerunner of which appeared to be a steel and coal supercartel. But labor's support of European unification was secured through the policy of an *upward leveling* of the working conditions started by the ECSC and continued by the EEC. According to this policy, the best working conditions of each member country—the wage rate of Luxembourg, paid vacations in Belgium, equal pay to women and men in France, etc.—were to be the standard the whole community would strive to establish.

The only major sector that seemed likely to suffer was the farm sector, and there seemed to be no way to satisfy the others without depriving it. As in other modern economics, the agricultural sector in the EEC countries is inefficient, but through political pressures the farmers obtain various state subsidies and other aids, which in effect reallocates the national income in their favor. The formation of the community, dedicated to raise the standard of living of all citizens, provided both a new urge and a new opportunity to reduce the most inefficient sector of these countries. This, however, would involve considerable adjustment pains if not outright loss of income and power to the farmer. Typically, whatever effect the EEC will have on rural-urban relations was not made explicit before the treaty was signed, nor is it stated in the treaty. Despite the fact that three members, especially France, were greatly interested in including agriculture in the Common Market, it was agreed to delay the formation of a common agricultural policy until the end of the first stage— that is, until integrative powers were built up. Moreover, what was to happen at the end of the last stage was left most vague. All the treaty stated was that a common agricultural policy had to be formed, and, as one writer added, "that farmers should receive as much money as possible, and consumers get their food as cheaply as possible, and that these two desirable but conflicting objectives should be brought about by almost any known method."[22]

Since the number of farmers in each country varies, ranging from 10 percent of the active labor force in Luxembourg to 41 percent in Italy, and since the German farmers are considerably less efficient, because of their smaller holdings, than the French,[23] a major crisis occurred when the EEC came around to forming an agricultural policy. Since by now both industry and labor were solidly behind the EEC and their expectation of higher trade, continued prosperity, full employment and, to a lesser degree, upward leveling had been fulfilled, the union was hardly endangered.

As these lines are written, it is far from clear what the common agricultural policy of the Community is going to be. While it has been agreed that the Community will collect levies on imported foodstuffs and use the income to finance in part subsidies to the farmers, gradually replacing the varied national subsidies, it is not clear yet what the level of these subsidies will be. If they are high, most of the burden of adjustment will be shifted to outsiders (e.g., American farmers), who will be driven out of the German market to make room for the French and other EEC farmers' products. If they are low, the EEC farmers in general, and in particular the more inefficient ones, will have to shift to different occupations to earn their living. In one case, reallocation will be largely between outsiders and insiders; in the second, between farmers and other sectors, or farmers of one member-country vis-à-vis others. Again, one cannot rerun history, but there can hardly be any doubt that attempts to form a reallocation policy (especially an internal one) before the treaty was signed, before integration was actually initiated, and before the Economic Commission was formed, might well have prevented the initiation of the union. In at least one other case, that of the Nordic Common Market, the lack of consensus on agricultural policy was one of the major factors that prevented its establishment.[24]

It might be of interest to note in passing that when the EEC began to formulate its agricultural policy at the end of 1961, it still could not squarely face the question of reallocation; it phased it. First, it was agreed that the subsidies to farmers would be continued; second, that the subsidies would be given by the community rather than the national governments, and be under the supervision of the commission, thus taking the question out of national power centers that are subject to direct pressure from the farmers. It was decided to determine the level of support at a later date.

Cushioning

The "no reallocation before integration" principle works on two assumptions: (1) The marginal alienation of the groups from which benefits are taken is going to be greater than the marginal gratification of the groups to which benefits are given. For instance, the alienation of those farmers who will lose subsidies is greater than the gratification of the taxpayer who will pay less taxes or buy cheaper food. (2) The alienation of the deprived groups will be more concentrated and politically better articulated than that of the gratified ones. Major reallocations are hence deferred. But if unification is to be initiated, complete avoidance of adjustment by any group is impossible. For instance, although the gains to be derived from increased intercountry trade are universal for all industrial countries, some adjustments, such as the closing of the most inefficient plants and some shifting of workers, is inevitable. Actually, the EEC has faced relatively little need for such adjustment because of the high level of employment of resources and labor force that was maintained. Three devices, however, were built into the Treaty and used to cushion these adjustments, and thus to reduce their negative political repercussions.

(1) A *Social Fund* was set up. It pays for the retraining of workers and their resettlement as well as some unemployment benefits for the adjustment period. The fund is financed by the EEC budget—i.e., all members pay to ease the adjustment of some industrial workers. But unlike the major adjustment of the farm sector, here only small groups and hence small sums are involved. The total budget of the fund, for 1958–1961, was $26 million.[25]

(2) A *European Investment Bank* was set up that has a cushioning function similar to that of the Social Fund, except that it is intended to help less developed regions, like the Italian South, rather than specific occupational groups. Again the assistance was limited in time and amount. It has not smoothed major adjustments, but eased those of small sectors which were expected to be especially hard hit if left to their own devices.[26]

(3) Finally, there are the *escape clauses* built into the treaty which enabled the commission to allow an industry or country to delay the reduction of a particular tariff or other protectionist device, to stretch out the transition period. This device, on the surface, costs the community nothing in the sense that no funds need to be raised to pay for the adjustment; it is "paid" by losses to the other industries or countries whose removal of protection is not reciprocated, but those are less visible as long as this device is not employed too liberally. The EEC allowed the use of escape clauses to help the adjustment of some industries—including the Italian shipbuilders and the French paper-pulp industry—but, all in all, it was not widely applied. Thus, unlike the "stretch-out" clauses that allow the delay of the whole process, the escape clauses serve those especially injured, or those that require special concessions because of humanitarian or political considerations; in this way they help the continuation of unification rather than cause its delay.

So far we have explored strategies followed on the international level—the nature of the treaty, the role of the supranational institutions, and so forth. The question that remains to be answered is what strategy is followed within the member countries. We should like to comment on three major decisions made by the supporters of European unification and on the effects of these decisions, which are of interest to socio-political theorists and to the Federalists and participants in the minimalist-maximalist controversy.[27] The supporters of unification, a great many of whom are Federalists, faced three problems: Should they focus their efforts on winning the support of the wider publics or that of national governments? Should they seek: to advance their cause through legislation, education, and propaganda, or through "direct action"? How many societal sectors should be tackled first—all of them at once, only a few, or one at a time?—and which ones should they be if not all were included in the first round? Not all of these are mutually exclusive alternatives, but there is always a question of emphasis and arguments over relative efficacy.

The initial tendency of the European Movement, in the late 1940s, was clearly to focus on the people rather than on governments, on education and propaganda, and on wholistic unification through political integration. The Federalists are in general suspicious of governments and put their trust in the good judgment and common sense of the informed citizen. After World War II, in which many European governments showed their weakness by succumbing to Nazi Germany, a much higher value was placed on the assent of the people than on that of governments. Although the European Union idea received the blessing of heads of governments from Churchill to Adenauer, the focus of the initial unification efforts was on a popular movement, headed by citizens' "action committees," and on informing the people of the value of a united Europe. It was following the clamor of this movement, which called for a United States of Europe, that the abortive Council of Europe was set up, a high-level forum in which the Grand Debate continued.

In sharp contrast was the initiation of the successful Schuman Plan, designed in secrecy in the French Planning Office by Jean Monnet and his staff. He is reported not to have discussed it with the German authorities, or for that matter with those of any other country, although he did privately consult some American acquaintances in Paris.[28] When the draft of the plan was completed on May 3, 1950, it was brought before the French Foreign Minister, Robert Schuman, whom Monnet expected to be more willing to surrender some economic jurisdiction to a supranational body than the ministers in charge of economic affairs. Schuman informed Dean Acheson, the American Secretary of State, on May 7; the French Cabinet approved the plan on May 8; German contact and assent were obtained on May 9; and the plan was made public later that month.[29]

The drafting of the Treaty of Rome was less shrouded in secrecy, but it proceeded on the same high level of governmental planning and negotiations, with the public being informed at later stages. The central "European" figures, like Monnet and Spaak, exercised their influence largely through their governmental positions and contacts in the various administrations and parliaments. Monnet's influential Action Committee was formed on the basis of this principle; it includes some forty political leaders of the six countries of "Little Europe." The membership covers the full political spectrum with the exception of the extreme right or left; each member is there not just as an individual but as a representative of his organization.[30] The committee issues public statements from time to time, but chiefly works out of the public eye. In short, the initiators of the ECSC and the EEC focused on governments rather than on people, on national legislation rather than on public education, and on the economic sector rather than on the political one.

This is not to imply that the Federalists, and their efforts at public instruction, had no effect on the evolution of European unification. They did much to spread the European idea. which had little sociological force before World War II. They established some of the public support for the ECSC and EEC, both of which needed parliamentary ratification once they were announced. Still, it was more through the tapping of deep national interests of the six countries (e.g., Germany's desire to abolish the International Ruhr Authority, one of the institutions through which its status as an occupied country was maintained) and the economic interests of major national pressure groups (e.g., labor, through the promise of "upward leveling" of working conditions) that these plans gained support, than through the Federalists' call for supranational executives and legislators. Even today the Economic Commission studiously avoids identification with the Federalists, although it benefits from their maximalist demands in the European Parliamentary Assembly in its negotiations with the comparatively minimalist Council of Ministers. When a European Parliament is directly elected by the European people and has full control over a European executive, it will be much more an expression and result of economic, military, and political integration than their prime mover, as Federalist theory implies.

The Limits of the Strategy

The limits of this strategy are those common to all strategies; the most they can do is to make effective use of a given set of circumstances. A gradualist approach cannot be used by the Black Muslims to make the United States government grant them a state for themselves, or by the WCTU to reintroduce Prohibition, or by the United Nations to unify Israel and Egypt. It is only when the background conditions are ripe, and the goal, high or low, is in line with the basic values of the participants, that a gradualist strategy can be effectively employed.

As a typical reform orientation rather than revolutionary approach, it is geared to gradual adjustment or improvement rather than speedy change in international relations or political structure. Hence, it serves best when the political structure itself is stable and when it is not undermined by a national defeat, wild inflation, deep depression, or civil war. It serves best those who have some access to power, or are in power, as Monnet, Hallstein, Spaak, and Schuman had or were, and will not do for those who have no foothold on the power pyramid. It serves best those who have the patience and the time to wait for gradual change. Those who are in a hurry, like those who wanted a United States of Europe in 1946, will have to try more sweeping attacks. Moreover, the fact that the gradualist approach served to initiate effectively the unification of Europe does not ensure its continued success. Actually, in 1963 the EEC faces many political and economic problems that may well not be satisfactorily solved. But whatever the future of the EEC, the strategy used to launch it will remain of much interest. Further study of this strategy and the conditions under which it can be effectively used must inevitably face such questions as whether this strategy can be usefully employed in tackling greater problems, such as forming unions in communities larger than Little Europe, strengthening the United Nations, and advancing the cause of general and complete disarmament.[31]

Notes

1. Hans A. Schmitt, *The Path to European Union* (Baton Rouge, La., 1962), 16.
2. *Ibid.*, 22.
3. On British orientation to unification, see a report by Chatham House Study Group, *Britain in Western Europe* (New York, 1956). On Nordic support for the British position, see Frantz Wendt, *The Nordic Council and Cooperation in Scandinavia* (Copenhagen, 1959), 226–27.
4. For a discussion of this concept and of various levels of integration, see Etzioni, "A Paradigm for Political Unification," *World Politics*, XV (October 1962), 44–74, especially p. 70.
5. Stephen S. Goodspeed, *The Nature and Function of International Organization* (New York, 1959), 588ff.
6. *Ibid.*, 589, 591.
7. "The intimate union of economies, which had been expected on both sides of the Atlantic, had not materialized under the OEEC" (Schmitt, 30).
8. For an account of the achievements of OEEC, see M. Margaret Ball, NATO and the European Union Movement (New York, 1959), 217–52. It is important to keep in mind the criterion used here for defining an aim as "high" or "low," which is the amount of unification a given group of countries is willing and able to accept as compared with the amount aimed at by the charter of the organization in question. The goal of the OEEC, which was too high for its sixteen members, might well have been too low from some other viewpoint—for instance, for initiating a strong and wide enough spill-over process to bring about a United States of Europe.
9. Some socialists thought it was just another cartel. (Erich Strauss, *Common Sense About the Common Market* [New York, 1958], 76ff.) See also George Lichtheim, *The New Europe* (New York, 1963).

10. Ernst B. Haas, *The Uniting of Europe* (Stanford, 1958), 109ff.

11. Strauss, 19.

12. It should also be pointed out that after the failure of the EDC and before the formation of the EEC, the less ambitious and more limited EURATOM was created.

13. John Brooks, "The Common Market," *New Yorker* (September 22, 1962), 56.

14. "It is only now that the political implications of this [economic union] are beginning to appear." (Roy Pryce, *The Political Future of the European Community* [London, 1962], 9.) See also *The Spectator* (October 5, 1961), 464.

15. U. W. Kitzinger, *The Challenge of the Common Market* (Oxford, 1962), 21–22. For another example of the efficacy of the multi-approach—in this instance, to international stabilization of prices of primary commodities—see Jan Tinbergen, *Shaping the World Economy* (New York, 1962), 74ff.

16. Leon N. Lindberg, *The Political Dynamics of European Integration* (Stanford, 1963), 201ff.

17. *Ibid.*, Part 1.

18. The conditions under which these, as well as four other contemporary unions, developed is the subject of a comparative study by the author entitled *Political Unification: A Comparitive Study of Leaders and Forces* (1965).

19. Disraeli's book on the relations between the middle class and the laboring class was entitled *Sybil, or, The Two Nations* (New York, 1934).

20. David Lowenthal, ed., *The Federation of the West Indies* (New York, 1961).

21. See note 18 above.

22. Brooks, 47.

23. On the agricultural problems and policy of the EEC, see J. F. Dewhurst, J. O. Coppock, P. L. Yates, and associates, *Europe's Needs and Resources* (New York, 1961), passim.

24. Wendt, 165ff.

25. Kitzinger, 43.

26. A third fund, that for Overseas Development, is not discussed since it would require an analysis of the relations between the EEC and the African nations, which is beyond the scope of this article.

27. For a most effective review of this controversy, see Inis L. Claude, Jr., *Swords into Plowshares* (New York, 1961), 407–32. See also Etzioni, "European Unification and Perspectives on Sovereignty," *Daedalus*, LXII (Summer 1963), 502–14.

28. Schmitt, 59–61.

29. *Ibid.*

30. The Latin America Free Trade Area was initiated in a similar fashion—that is, an intercountry political pressure group was created under the leadership of Raul Prebisch. (Andrew Shonfield, *The Attack on World Poverty* [New York, 1962], 42.)

31. The value of a gradualist approach to disarmament is illustrated by the following findings. In 1961, two-thirds of the respondents in three countries, in answering the question, "For the next few years, would you give major attention to strengthening the Western deterrent or to pursuing general disarmament, as a matter of relative priority?" said that they would favor disarmament. Yet, when they were asked if they preferred stage-by-stage disarmament or a "big package," the results were:

	Stage-by-stage	Big package
U.K.	93%	6%
Germany	95%	4%
France	73%	9%

(Daniel Lerner and Morton Gordon, *European Community and Atlantic Security in the World Arena* [Cambridge, Mass., 1961], chap. V, 10.) A gradualist approach to the reduction of international tensions and arms and to the development of international organization is presented in Etzioni, *The Hard Way to Peace: A New Strategy* (New York, 1962).

Part Four

THE ETHICS
OF
SOCIAL CHANGE

8

Ethics and Change: Author's Note

Criticism of social scientists, especially neoclassical economists and those in the other social science fields (exchange sociology, public choice political science and so on) who share their utilitarian, consequentialist paradigm, has been done to perfection. There is little to be gained by extending this line of analysis. What is needed is development and synthesis of various paradigms that draw on different ethical and social philosophical—that is, normative—foundations. Deontology, much less known in the United States than utilitarianism, provides a strong alternative. It builds on binding moral duties, intentions, and values rather than on consequences, although the two approaches can be combined to some extent. The purpose here is not to contribute to the development of ethics or social philosophy but to apply their lessons to the development of social science and base the arguments on normative grounds, which I find, for reasons given below, more compelling. Concepts explored in "Toward Deontological Social Sciences," such as the multiple-self and macro-factors that form preferences, are steps in that direction.

The fruitfulness of a deontological paradigm is evident in the conceptual and normative advances that are achieved once the mono-utility concept, according to which pleasure, self-satisfaction, or self-interest is the overarching goal against which all efforts are measured, has been cast aside. When it has been, we are in a position to recognize the power of moral causes in comparison to that of others. By separating moral causes out of the myriad factors that are said to affect utility, we are able to study the historical, cultural, societal, and psychological factors that enhance or retard the role of moral factors. We gain a conception that is more empirically valid (as documented in this chapter in "The Case for Multiple-Utility Conception") and ethically ennobling at the small cost of making the paradigm somewhat but not significantly less parsimonious.

While one may argue over whether it is empirically productive to assume one overarching utility or several, there can be little doubt that multiple criteria of evaluation must be used when one engages in policy analysis. In this kind of analysis, which is directly related to action rather than merely to contemplation, to systematically leave out moral considerations seems immoral. To do so leads to such morally untenable policy suggestions as that blacks ought to be asked to sit on the sunny side of sports arenas because their lower sensitivity to skin cancer would reduce overall cancer rates. True, moral evaluation is difficult, but far from impossible, and it can be systematically combined with considerations of efficiency (as we see in "The Moral Dimension in Policy Analysis").

Toward Deontological
Social Sciences

"Is it all right to cast *one* Christian to the lions if it will provide considerable pleasure to *many* Romans?" This was a question posed to a group of students attending a seminar. Students were reassured that if they sensed that there were not enough Romans in the coliseum to justify the "trade off," they could assume the Christian/lions confrontation was broadcast on television. Those who subscribe to the utilitarian notion that distribution of resources should aim at generating the greatest happiness for the greatest number will be hard put to provide a principle that would suggest why such a trade-off is unacceptable. (In effect, much cost-benefit analysis is based on such a calculus of gains and sacrifices; Kelman, 1981). The principle of Pareto-Optimality is sometimes brought to bear to argue that one ought to increase everybody's happiness as long as it does not diminish anybody else's. However, this principle is not derivable from utilitarian ethics: why not reduce, to some extent, the happiness of one person, if this increases the happiness of many considerably? In addition, there seem to be insurmountable difficulties in operationalizing the Pareto concept. And, there is also the question of whose happiness (or preferences) is to be taken into account: Only that of this generation? Future generations? How far into the future? Minors? Mental patients? Criminals? Aliens? Members of other nations? (Whittington and MacRae, 1986). That is, whatever is deemed "optimal" reflects one's value judgments as to whom one chooses to embrace in one's community, rather than an

Note: This essay was originally published in *Philosophy of the Social Sciences,* 1989, *19*(2), 145–156. Copyright © 1989 by Sage Publications, Inc. Reprinted with permission.

objective criterion. Yet the students in the seminar, and probably most readers are searching for a principled reason to oppose the sacrifice of a single human life for the sheer pleasure of many. The reasons are to be found in another ethics, deontology, which recognizes, at least in its Kantian version, ultimate (absolute) values, categorical imperatives and the claim that people should treat one another as ends and not just as means. The discussion proceeds by briefly reviewing the deontological position before its potential for a new paradigm for economics, and more generally for social science, is indicated. The article closes with a discussion of the methodological implications of the new paradigm and its implications for the social bases of liberty, two implications that turn out to be close to one another.

Moderate Deontology

Deontological ethics is often compared with utilitarian ethics; the first focuses on intentions, the second on consequences. (The ethical trouble with casting a person to the lions stems directly not from the loss of human life, a distressing but very common occurrence, but from the deliberate, intended nature of the act.) However, there is reason to view the two ethical philosophies as if they were partially reconcilable. Moderate deontology recognizes that consequences ought to be taken into account, as a secondary criterion, just as a moderate utilitarian recognizes intentions—as a secondary consideration. While an extreme deontologist may argue that it is ethical to donate blood (if the sole intention was to help another person), even if the patient soon died and the donation had no direct beneficial consequence, at the same time, most would file with moderate deontologists who might argue that if the donor would have known ahead of time that the donation would be futile, it would be more ethical to donate blood to those who are likely to benefit rather than to those who would not. From here on this moderate version of deontology, not too remote from moderate utilitarianism, is applied.

While it is common to identify deontology as an ethics of intentions, usually the focus is on moral intentions rather than on the larger universe of all possible intentions. This is indicated in the term deontology itself, which is derived from the Greek term *deon,* meaning "binding duty." The fact that one may recognize intentions but not identify those as moral in source or form stands out when one follows Frankfurt (1971), who asked: what distinguishes a person from other beings that have mental capacities and corporeal characteristics? He finds the answer in their ability to form "second-order *desires,*" to want to be different than they are, including changing their first-order desires.

Hirschman (1984), who directly draws on Frankfurt, refers to the second-order desires as meta-preferences. He stresses that there is a continuous conflict between preferences and meta-preferences. If the preferences would prevail all the time, the meta-preferences would have little meaning; they would reflect a kind of lip service paid to values, of little importance. Similarly, if the meta-preferences would prevail all the time, there would be little point in drawing the distinction; urges would have little or no role; values would dominate.

Sen (1977) uses the term commitment in a similar manner. "Commitment," not formally defined, is contrasted with concern for others when it is based on one's own welfare. Sen gives the following example. If you see another person being tortured and it makes you sick, you act out of sympathy. But if you think such action is wrong, you act out of "commitment." Commitment is, of course, closely connected with one's morals, Sen explains (ibid., p. 329). The significance of the concept of commitment, he elaborates, is that it points to a source of preference, or value, other than being "better off."

Note, though, that none of the three authorities identifies their concept with moral duties or values. For Frankfurt, the second-order faculty is akin to the first order one; both are "desires." Hirschman's meta-preferences could be based on aesthetic considerations, or enlightened (longer run) self-interest. Sen's commitments come close but are not outright moral derivatives. Indeed, there is no reason to doubt that second-order considerations may be derived from many sources, and may be justified on many grounds. However, we suggest that moral commitments are a major, if not the major, source of second-order judgments, and a major way they are evaluated. Deontological ethics, with its preoccupation with intentions and their ethical standing, is particularly suited to explore the source and standing of these moral commitments. Above all, we suggest, adding the dimension of moral intentions, moral commitments, and duties to one's paradigm enriches the foundations of social sciences in general and of economics in particular, as we shall attempt to show next.

(Deontological ethics encompasses many positions on other issues. These are not explored here because one can draw on the basic perspective, as just outlined, without necessarily subscribing to those other positions. For example, one can be a deontologist without accepting Kant's view that only the noumenal self has a free will.)

The Significance for Human Nature and Social Order

At the core of most social science paradigms is an explicit or implicit concept of human nature and of social order. We explore first the concept of human nature. The major social science paradigm in the West is the neoclassical one, which is utilitarian both in origin and in much of its contemporary content. At the core of the neoclassical paradigm, shared by neoclassical economics, "exchange" sociology, public choice political science, and several other social science theories, is the concept of a unitary person, a well ordered bundle of self-directed urges, expressed in the actor's preferences. The actor is viewed as an autonomous individual, acting on his or her own, the well known *homo-economicus*.

What concept of human nature emerges from the deontological position? First of all, a view of the person as *divided self*. The person is in perpetual conflict between two or more internal forces. Kant distinguishes between two "men," found within each of us. One is instrumental, seeking efficient means, directly observable. The other is the seat of free will and values, the world of "reason," which leads to recognition of moral imperatives. The first "man" acts out inclinations; the second—in pursuit of what is right. The first is determined by nature, the second is free. Freud's distinction between an *id* and a *super-ego* captures the conflict between urges and socially introduced morality. (Internalized, and individually honed, morality is placed in the *ego* itself.) Schelling (1984) collected numerous examples of individuals who find themselves simultaneously subjected to conflicting preferences. Elster (1985) provides an excellent overview of various theories about the nature and dynamics of the divided self.

The question raises itself, if both urges and moral commitments reflect to a significant extent social forces (socialization and social control), and to some extent one's individual development, why do they tend to diverge? Why are the urges not "socialized" to the point they conform to morally prescribed behaviour? The observed fact is that urges and moral commitments are often in conflict (Etzioni, 1988). Indeed, most moral duties and commitments are expressed in terms of prohibiting acts individuals would be otherwise inclined to engage in (e.g., adultery, theft) or require acts they would otherwise not perform (e.g., giving to charity). Among the possible explanations is that urges are closer to the biological base of human behaviour than morality, i.e., reflect a lesser extent of socialization and internal development. Another possible explanation is that they reflect different stages of socialization (urges precede moral education, in that sense, are more infantile).

Aside from being of general interest, the concept of the divided self has significant implications for the understanding of economic behaviour. It helps explain why all items (commodities, resources, transactions) have two valuations: their economic value and their moral standing. For instance, a stolen product can be used like one that has been legitimately acquired, but its moral standing is hardly equivalent. It has been suggested that this distinction does not hold for most mundane purchases. But a moral dimension is often readily discernible and always present. It affects all purchases that are considered "sinful" but not illegal, for example alcohol and cigarettes (as reflected, for instance, in special taxes imposed on them); it is evident in illegal work (in the underground economy) and trade (e.g. in controlled substances); it is reflected in preference for American vs. "foreign" products, from "Jap" cars to Mexican lettuce; it can be discerned in the condemnation of "junk" food, food high in calories, salt, and cholesterol (considered irresponsible toward self); in the production of products that are environmentally dubious, marketing via persuasive advertising, and in the propensity to save, to conserve energy, to pay taxes, to work hard and so on. (For evidence, see Etzioni, 1988.)

In still other areas, moral commitments go beyond influencing transactions—they taboo exchange behaviour and market orientations. Various philosophers have identified numerous areas in which exchanges are "blocked" (Okun, 1975; Walzer, 1983), for example those covered by constitutional rights. Thus, First Amendment rights cannot be sold or bought and contracts to enslave are not enforceable. The recent court battle over the question whether or not contracts to "sell" babies conceived by surrogate mothers are enforceable is, in effect, on the question where the market zone ends and blocked exchanges start.

Next to drawing on a concept of human nature, social science paradigms build on a related concept, that of a social order, on the ways the individuals—given their nature—combine into sustainable wholes. Indeed, historians of science suggest that the social sciences evolved once religious conceptions of social order broke down and the quest was on for secular accounts of order in society.

At the heart of the question what accounts for order, is the question whether order must be introduced, say by force, by a powerful authority, or—does it arise naturally? Deontological social sciences find the answer, first and foremost, in the moral order. Individuals' interests are not assumed to be naturally harmonious, i.e., mutually supportive and compatible, or made to be so by an *invisible* hand. Nor is there a reason to assume order must be imposed on individuals who are, in Hobbes' term, wolf to one another. The social realm and its order are based on the assumptions that individuals have acquired a set of shared moral commitments that legitimate the social order and that lead them to treat others the way they seek to be treated themselves.

The logical next step for a deontological social science is to deal with the question: what are the sources of the moral commitments? This is a question utilitarian social scientists need not deal with because they take individual preferences as their starting point (e.g., in the concept of consumer sovereignty). The deontological answer is a dual one: in part, the sources of individual commitments are moral values shared by the community of which individuals are members; in part, they are the result of internal moral individual developments.

Regarding communities' values, the main point is that individuals *internalize* those and make them part of their inner self; they are turned from constraints (matters the community demands, one more external condition the actors take into account in their deliberations) into meta-preferences and preferences (criteria the actors use to judge the course of action or form, in part, their decision in the first place). In contrast, utilitarians, to the extent they recognize community values at all, see them as external factors. For example, according to utilitarian social psychology, an actor who faces group pressures to conform, say to donate blood, will calculate whether or not the costs of disregarding these moral expectations, of not conforming, exceeds the benefits (let's say of being socially accepted). Deontologists recognize that values are treated that way on some occasions, but also recognize that on other occasions, following internalization, individuals either see the donation of blood as the right thing to do from *their* viewpoint or something they are compelled to do. That is, *one cannot argue from the existence of expedient morality that authentic moral commitments do not exist, or are insignificant.* Moreover, to deny that internalization occurs is, in effect, to deny the existence of education. It leaves the neoclassicists with the odd implicit assumption that persons are born biologically and psychologically mature, roughly at the age of eighteen to twenty-one if not older.

While the community often accounts for a significant part of a person's moral commitments, in part these moral commitments are internally developed. One important source for such individualization, is the fact that in many societies individuals are frequently subject to conflicting societal demands (often from different social groups, such as immigrant, kin, and ethnic groups vs. the encompassing community). This leaves the individuals freer to choose which moral code to follow. Also, moral socialization and social control are often far from complete, leaving room for individuals to develop their own position (often more in the extent to adherence, than in content). Finally, exceptional individuals rise, who fashion their own codes and affect that of the community (e.g., Luther). Still, all these individual developments are best studied on the backdrop of shared social values, and the examination of the societal structures that encourage or discourage individualization, because they account for most of the variance.

What are the implications of these divergent views of moral codes for the specific views of social order? Utilitarians see individuals as autonomous, psychologically self-sufficient, as "under-socialized" (Granovetter, 1985). They see the social order as arising out of either a deliberate contract among free-standing individuals, or as a natural result of their each pursuing his or her self-interest. Groups and communities are either ignored or "reduced" to aggregations of individual choices, deemed to have no attributes of their own.

In contrast, deontological social scientists recognize that because individuals have a debased element, a "lower" self, they may be prone to war with one another, and hence there is a need to foster a social order. The question is: how and to what extent is this achieved? The notion that order may be imposed by a government, is found to be unsatisfactory because coercion leads to alienation and rebellion, and because of practical limitations on the ability to govern those opposed. There are never enough police to control a community whose members are actively opposed to an authority, and who shall police the police? are familiar arguments that apply here. That is, only a government that is viewed as legitimate by a significant part of the community, and to a significant extent of the total scope of action, can provide a social order. Legitimacy, in turn, rests on being in line with accepted moral values. Hence, ultimately the social order rests on the moral community, not on the government.

The moral community benefits from social bonds that tie people to one another. Individuals, psychic entities, are *not* self-sufficient but require one another, are in part intertwined in ways they do not relate to objects. Their sense of identity and direction, their ability to function as individuals, their sense of inner stability and self-esteem, are all anchored in other persons and in groups. They are each other's keepers. These bonds of mutuality, are the sociological bases of their treating one another as ends and not merely as means, on which the moral, and in turn the social order, build.

Opening the Preferences: Can Be Operationalized

The position outlined so far has a major methodological implication: we need to study the sources of individual preferences. Neoclassicists take these preferences as given and as stable, that is, a person's desires are taken as fixed. The extent to which a person is able to set on his or her preferences, is able to realize them, the factors that account for differences in actual behaviour, are seen as due to differences in constraints (given a particular level of income). For example, a person who desires to "buy" higher education is viewed as likely to buy less (given his or her income) the higher the price, the more requirements are imposed for obtaining each degree, the longer the commute to college, the fewer child care facilities are available and so on.

Neoclassicists have opposed "opening up" the preferences, to see whether behaviour may also change over time because preferences have changed, say because the valuations individuals accord to what they are buying, higher education, have changed. One reason given to this opposition is that neoclassicists argue that the factors that modify preferences cannot be studied empirically because they are irrational (such as value changes, impulses, eruption of social movements). Our response is that one should not confuse the irrationality of the subjects (or the actors), or their value commitments, with those of the observers. That is, we *can study* scientifically nonrational and even irrational behaviour. Thus, we may examine the effects of bright colours on people shopping, without being swayed to buy a single item ourself. We may observe that once the lead lemming jumps off a cliff others will follow, while we still remain standing at the top.

Neoclassicists also argue that values "cannot" be measured, or, that statements about them are based on "ephemeral" data, data about states of mind rather than observable behaviour, for example, attitudes and survey data. This criticism is in part correct. These data do not provide reliable predictors of behaviour, although predictions based on economic data often do not fare better. However, there is no reason in principle that the same behavioral data, of the kind used by economists, cannot be used to determine the effects of values. We need to go into this matter here in some detail because the charge of "cannot be operationalized" is a serious one. It is tantamount to stating that to study the sources and dynamics of preferences, one must leave the realm of science.

To highlight the ways economic behavioral data can be used to study values, we draw on Lancaster's idea of disaggregating the attributes of consumer goods, as long as we have repeated observations over time. Lancaster (1966) points out that if we have numerous observations about the price people are paying for a product, say, autos, that varies in several ways, such as color, design, and size, we can establish how much these people are willing to pay for each attribute, say red color, four versus two door, acceleration to 55 miles per hour in less than six seconds, and so on. We suggest that moral and other social valuations can be treated as one or more such attributes. For example in the post World War II era, it was considered unpatriotic to buy foreign cars; in some parts of America there were specially strong anti-Japanese and anti-German valuations. This should be reflected and be measurable in the price like any other attribute of a car. Furthermore, a comparison of the price of similar American and foreign cars over time would allow us to test the hypothesis that values were at work, because we know that over the years between, say, 1955 and 1970, anti-German and anti-Japanese valuations have declined significantly. (Further validation could be achieved by another form of disaggregation, by comparing groups within the U.S.A. For example, Jewish groups were in some years slower to accept German cars than other ethnic groups.)

Some neoclassicists argue that values are reflected, like many other factors, in the preferences, and there is hence no reason to single them out. They treat, as Mike McPherson put it, a "taste" for peanut butter and the taste for god as interchangeable. I provided elsewhere some arguments why it seems productive to distinguish between the utility of consumption and that of the affirmation of moral values; deontological ethics provides additional reasons for the distinction as we already outlined. Here a methodological reason comes into focus: to develop a satisfactory theory of economic behavior, indeed of behavior in general, one needs to know what "drives" preferences rather than take them as God sent or "given." Values turn out to be a major factor shaping and reshaping preferences. The next step is to ask what accounts for value changes? Here the role of the education, leadership, the mass media and social movements, all macro—not intro-individual but collective, historical, institutional factors—come to the forefront. Without a systematic understanding of these, the dynamic study of behavior is deeply lacking.

The Anchoring of Individual Freedoms

The recognition of the moral and social realm as non-reducible has another major implication: it provides for a rather different conception for understanding the conditions under which liberty will persist rather than be threatened. The reason is closely related to the methodological issue we just explored: the need to open the preferences. This is evident in two main ways: one concerns the reactive nature of the neoclassical individual versus the active one of the deontological person. The second is evident in the collective anchoring of individual freedoms.

The neoclassical paradigm, precisely because it tends to assume that the preferences are fixed, sees behavior as driven by changes in constraints, i.e., in the environment. The individual may have various wishes, dreams and aspirations, but these are of little interest to the neoclassicists; what the individuals *do,* their behavior, is *determined* by how ample vs. restrictive the environment is. Thus, if supply is abundant, prices low—people will buy more; and if tight—less. There is no room for a concept of a free will. Behavior is externally dictated.

> It is in the non-rational domain that individuals are free to identify and adopt something on the order of the Kantian or Christian (or any other) ethic. . . . It is in the non-rational domain that the individual can rightfully be characterized as *internally* directed as opposed to *externally* directed as in Becker and Skinner behaviouralism.
>
> And it is because of the non-rational domain that personal responsibility for actions has any reasonable meaning. In the externally directed world of behaviouralism, all action is a response to external forces and no act, therefore, can be accurately attributed to the individual actor. In fact,

> Skinner explicitly argues that personal responsibility is an arcane, pre-scientific concept which has no meaning in the world of the behavioral technologist. (McKenzie, 1979, p. 152)

In the deontological paradigm emphasis is put on the individual's intention. In an extreme version this may turn into a futile voluntarism, into the assumption that the individual is a god-like, omnipotent creature, able to fashion the world in his or her image. (This is reflected in some of the writings on legislation and international law that assume that passing a law or signing an international treaty or charter, will have major societal consequences. For example, those who chartered the U.N. in San Francisco after World War II believed they laid the foundation to world peace. For additional discussion of voluntarism see Etzioni, 1968.) In moderate versions, which systematically recognize consequences and hence constraints, individuals are seen as struggling to insert their will into a limiting world. They *actively* approach the world, seeking to advance their goals, but realizing the limits it imposes.

Despite the fact that the individual acts are largely or wholly dictated by the environment according to the neoclassical paradigm it sees the individuals as the decision-making unit, because it assumes that their preferences govern. This is much more than a working hypothesis; it is an article of faith grounded in a deep commitment to the value of liberty. Neoclassicists argue that if one assumes that individuals' preferences can be manipulated or changed by social forces, one undermines the foundations of liberty—the notion that each individual is able to render decisions of his or her own. In contrast, we hold that to recognize that individuals are in part socially shaped is not to argue for a government to make decisions for them, but to acknowledge the need to deal in one's theory with significant historical, cultural, and societal forces. Only when these are allowed into one's paradigm can a systematic search for the conditions under which liberty may be protected from—or enhanced by—these forces begin.

The insights and findings of psychologists and sociologists indicate that typically cut-off, isolated individuals—the actors of the neoclassical world—are unable to act freely, while they find that individuals bonded into comprehensive and stable relationships and cohesive groups and communities *are* much more able to make sensible choices, render judgment, be free. Indeed, the greatest danger for liberty arises when the social moorings of individuals are cut. The atomization of the society, the reduction of communities into aggregates of isolated individuals results in the individuals' loss of competence, capacity to reason, and self-identity and is the societal condition that has preceded the rise of totalitarian movements and governments. The best protection against totalitarianism is a pluralistic society laced with communities and voluntary associations, as observed so keenly by Alexis de Tocqueville. The I and We paradigm is as much concerned with individual liberties as the neoclassical one. However, it assumes that liberty requires a viable, albeit not over-bearing community, and seeks to study the conditions under which such a community evolves and is sustained.

The essence of Fromm's (1941) argument is that freedom has costs. Individuals won autonomy as society changed following industrialization or, more precisely, urbanization. However, Fromm shows, the gain was at the cost of reduced social bonds in the family, and community. This left the individual highly anxious, even hysterical, despairingly looking for synthetic affiliations to replace the lost bonds. Totalitarian political movements are said to appeal to such persons because they provide such bonds. Also, the decline of religion and traditional values leaves people to yearn for firm directions; demagogues and dictators provide such strong leadership. (Another offshoot of this line of reasoning is David Riesman, 1950, which argues that people become other-directed, seeking excessively to conform, without inner directions.)

The concept of the mass society points in the same direction. Reference is not to a large number of people per se, although mass relations are less likely to occur in small populations. The essence of the mass society is that it replaced the closely woven social fabric of numerous, small, direct and stable social units (villages) with aggregates of people, each on their own, somewhat like the mass in a crowded railroad station. Cities were viewed as places where masses of individuals aggregate, but tend not to favour solid social bonds. The high level of geographic mobility, constantly reshuffling individuals, is believed to further flatten ties. Religious and ethnic groups were also seen as losing their hold over people as they join large associations that may represent the interests (e.g., labor unions or political parties), but, at least in the U.S.A., often provide little social cohesion. Mass media directly speaks to individuals. Eruption of massive social movements is seen as a result (Kornhauser, 1959). Many early critics of the mass society saw it as a dangerous result of the transition from an orderly, aristocratic, to a mass-participating, democratic society. De Tocqueville (1835) served as a source for the argument that if the societal fabric is preserved, pluralism maintained, which he found in America, democracy may be preserved. (While he turned more pessimistic after the 1848 revolution in France, his earlier position was adopted by many.)

For those unfamiliar with the social science literature, it must be noted that the preceding statements and findings are challenged, as are most statements and findings in social sciences. Thus, Gans (1962), in a book entitled *The Urban Villagers*, showed that there is village-like life in cities. And Srole's (1975) work, which showed the negative effect of social isolation on mental stability, has been criticized on methodological grounds. One learns from the Gans-like studies that the statement about the effects of urbanization must be mitigated; they do not hold (or hold less) for those who can form solid social groups within cities. And, the work of Srole and others must be further verified. Still, the consensus of sociological and psychological work is to lend support to the basic notion, that isolation is incompatible with the condition necessary for mental stability needed for individuals to be able to form their own judgments and to resist undue external pressure and influence, i.e., that liberty is, to a significant extent, socially anchored.

The preceding discussion provides, at best, the barest outline and elementary rationale for deontological social sciences. Deontological social sciences still require much elaboration and testing before they can provide a full paradigm. Many hundred thousands of man and woman years were invested in evolving the neoclassical paradigm, and the social sciences build within its confines. Those who are interested in such an endeavour may take heart as they note that many scholars, including several cited above, have been doing deontological work, without the label and the suggested rationale.

References

Elster, Jon, ed. (1985) *The Multiple Self.* Cambridge.

Etzioni, Amitai (1968) *The Active Society.* New York.

———— (1988) *The Moral Dimension: Toward a New Economics.* New York.

Frankfurt, Harry G. (1971) 'Freedom of the Will and the Concept of the Person', *Journal of Philosophy,* 68, 5–20.

Fromm, Erich (1941) *Escape From Freedom.* New York.

Gans, Herbert J. (1962) *The Urban Villagers.* New York.

Granovetter, Mark (1985) 'Economic Action and Social Structure: A Theory of Embeddedness', *American Journal of Sociology,* 91, 481–510.

Hirschman, Albert O. (1984) 'Against Parsimony: Three Easy Ways of Complicating Some Categories of Economic Discourse', *Bulletin: The American Academy of Arts and Sciences,* 37, 11–28.

Kelman, Steven (1981) 'Cost-Benefit Analysis: An Ethical Critique', *Regulation,* January/February, 33–40.

Kornhauser, William (1959) *The Politics of Mass Society.* Glencoe, Ill.

Lancaster, Kelvin (1966) 'A New Approach to Consumer Theory', *Journal of Political Economy*, 74, 132–157.

McKenzie, Richard B. (1979) 'The Non-Rational Domain and the Limits of Economic Analysis', *Southern Economic Journal*, 46, 145–57.

Okun, Arthur (1975) *Equality and Efficiency: The Big Tradeoff*. Washington, D.C.

Riesman, David (1950) *The Lonely Crowd*. New Haven, Conn.

Schelling, Thomas (1984) 'Self-Command in Practice, in Policy, and in a Theory of Rational Choice', *American Economic Review*, 74, 1–11.

Sen, Amartya K. (1977) 'Rational Fools', *Philosophy and Public Affairs*, 6, 317–44.

Srole, Leo (1975) 'Measurement and Classification in Socio-Psychiatric Epidemiology: Midtown Manhattan Study (1954) and Midtown Manhattan Restudy (1974)', *Journal of Health and Social Behaviour*, 16, 347–63.

De Tocqueville, Alexis (1945 [1835–1840]) *Democracy in America*, 2 vols. New York.

Walzer, Michael (1983) *Spheres of Justice*. New York.

Whittington, D. and D. MacRae (1986) 'The Issue of Standing on Cost-Benefit Analysis', *Journal of Policy Analysis and Management*, 5, 665–82.

The Case for a
Multiple-Utility Conception

In recent decades, neoclassical economists have made heroic efforts to accommodate within the confines of the concept of rational utility maximization the fact that individual behavior is significantly affected by moral considerations. This article argues the merits of using an alternative approach: recognizing that individuals pursue at least two irreducible sources of value or "utility," pleasure and morality. The possibility that some additional utilities may have to be recognized is explored. This raises the concern that conceptual anarchy will break out, which in turn will force a search for a common denominator, and thus a return to one overarching utility. Arguments are presented to show that this concern is unfounded. The main focus of the article is a criticism of the monoutility conception and a brief for separating the sense of discharging one's moral obligations from all other satisfactions. The article first deals with general conceptual points, and then cites both everyday observations and empirical evidence in support of this position.

Monoutility: Too Parsimonious

A critic of the concept of utility used by economists is faced with the problem of shooting down a revolving target: no sooner has one idea been shot down, then a rather similar one appears, and before long, a third jumps into sight, and soon thereafter, the first one reappears. Economists use three

Note: This essay was originally published in *Economics and Philosophy*, 1986, 2(2), 159–183. It is reprinted with permission. I am grateful to Michael S. McPherson, James Childress, Charles Dyke, and Daniel M. Hausman for their comments on previous drafts.

main variations of the concept of utility. First is the original concept, that of the pleasure of the self, coined by utilitarian philosophers and loaded with their psychological assumptions. The second, a much expanded version, increasingly (although not widely) used, encompasses the satisfactions an actor gains both from his own consumption as well as that of others; i.e., it includes satisfactions derived from benevolent acts and a certain understanding of community-minded duty. This concept is sometimes referred to as the interdependent utility (Boulding, 1978, p. 191; Lipsey and Steiner, 1975, p. 143). Finally, still other economists use the term *utility* as a formal attribute, a common denominator, according to which all specific quests for satisfaction can be ranked, which is needed to allow for mathematization (and to shore up the assumption of a monoutility world) but with no substantive attributes—a grand *x*. In the following discussion, to keep the targets apart, these concepts are referred to respectively as P-utility (pleasure), I-utility (interdependent), and X-utility (formal). They are all wanting, but for different reasons. The following discussion seeks to establish logical grounds (concerning proper conceptualization), as well as substantive ones, for keeping the concept of *satisfaction* derived from doing what one likes, enjoys, and finds pleasurable, distinct from the sense of *affirmation* that accompanies living up to one's moral commitments, commitments that are often in themselves taxing rather than pleasurable. That is, for recognizing a moral "utility" above and beyond a P-, I-, or X-utility.

The Pleasure Utility

The original use of the term *utility* in modern economics was narrowly self-oriented and straightforwardly hedonistic: the gain of pleasure, the avoidance of pain. Bentham (1948, pp. 1–2) wrote, early in the nineteenth century: "Nature has placed mankind under the governance of two sovereign masters, *pain* and *pleasure*. . . . They govern us in all we do, in all we say, in all we think. . . . The *principle of utility* recognizes this subjection. . . ." Samuelson (1980, p. 48) explains, "As a customer you will buy a good because you feel it gives you satisfaction or 'utility.'"

To understand the source of this concept of utility it must be recalled that its origin and base are in utilitarian philosophy. It assumes that all means find their justification in the ends they serve; the ends give "utility" to the means. While it is possible to have a nonhedonistic utilitarian philosophy, in which the end that bestows value is not the self's pleasure, it is the hedonistic version of utilitarianism that lies at the root of modern economics. Happiness, satisfaction, and pleasure are used as synonyms (Walsh, 1970, pp. 21–26).

Pleasure is invested with moral approval; it is good while pain is evil. Bentham stressed that pain and pleasure are not only empirically our masters but also our normative guides: "It is for them *alone* to point out what we *ought* to do, as well as to determine what we shall do" (Bentham, 1948, p. 1, italics added). They, he added, set the standards of what is right and wrong. "The utilitarians suggested that actions by the self or by others whose consequences to the self are harmful (painful) are naturally deemed bad and arouse anger or punitive tendencies, and actions whose consequences are beneficial (pleasure) are naturally deemed good . . ." (Kohlberg, 1968, p. 486). Once this gross value judgment about the moral goodness of pleasure is removed, and one takes into account that numerous acts are either pleasurable or moral but often not both (see below), the monoutility world is undermined. The door is then opened to the recognition that there are at least two major, distinct, irreducible sources of value widely recognized in nonutilitarian philosophies, in culture and in language, and "revealed" in behavior.

The Interdependent Utility

When the concept of P-utility is challenged as amoral, asocial, and as counter to basic facts about human behavior, including numerous community-minded, altruistic, cooperative, and loving acts, economists tend to point to a concept of utility that is, in effect, radically different but goes under the same name; one that contains service to others and commitment to values beyond the pleasure of self. A simple conceptual device is used: making consumption by *others* a source of the actor's pleasure (hence the term *interdependent utility*). When one person acts altruistically, it is said, the other person's pleasure has become a source of the ego's pleasure, part of the ego's utility.

This I-utility notion of gaining satisfaction from others' pleasure crosses over by degrees into the more abstract X-utility notion as the range of objects that may be a source of the ego's pleasure widens. Thus, besides caring about the extent of another's satisfactions, I may care about what particular goods he consumes, or about the well-being of plants and animals, or what have you. Here, the discussion concentrates on versions of the argument that retain the notion of the ego's psychological state of satisfaction as the ultimate source of motivation; purely formal versions of utility maximization are considered under "The Great X" below.

Note that the I-utility concept remains true to the hedonistic version of utilitarianism: altruistic acts must be explained by the *ego's* pleasure; true altruistic acts, acts of self-denial or sacrifice, are incompatible with the concept. What would motivate them? is the implied question. Of course, if one assumes that only the quest for pleasure (and avoidance of pain) *can* motivate people, one must conclude that saints enjoy their sacrifices, are masochistic. However, once one breaks out of the straitjacket of one utility, and allows for other factors to drive behavior, one sees that normal people do some things because they are right, whether or not they enjoy them. Indeed, over the centuries numerous theologians and philosophers have defined the uniqueness of human beings as compared to animals as the ability to pass judgment over one's urges instead of automatically yielding to them. True, not all such judgments must be ethical; they may, for instance, be aesthetic. However, moral factors are clearly central in defining such judgments.

Moreover, the all-inclusive expansion of the concept of

utility violates the rules of sound conceptualization. Once a concept is defined so that it encompasses *all* the incidents that are members of a given category (in the case at hand, the motives for all human activities), it ceases to enhance one's ability to explain. The result is akin to that of multiplying all variables in an equation by one. As long as the ego's and the alter ego's pleasures are treated as equal in their status for the ego's utility, the concept ceases to differentiate. Thus, if someone gives me X new resources, I advance my utility when I use them to enhance my consumption, but I enhance it just as much when I give them to charity, or share them with those I love, or burn them the way the Kwakiutl do (Benedict, 1934, p. 143). Presuming I enjoy the fire, what does the concept add? It simply sprinkles whatever a person is after with the term *utility.* Sadism, a quest for a fair or an unfair return, or for mutual affection all have the same status. To the degree that this "theory" aims to shed light on motivation, it constitutes a conceptual failure, because the purpose of introducing concepts is to call attention to meaningful distinctions. The same problem arose in the psychology of instincts, when people who were hungry were said to respond to their instinct, and those who were after sex, to their instinct, and so on. (Before that, the ancient Greeks populated the world with endless gods, "explaining" each event with the working of a god assigned to produce it.)

Leading economists have recognized the unproductive and tautological nature of this approach which states that whatever one does is said to "reveal" one's pleasure. As Stigler pointed out, "a reason, we would be saying, can always be found for whatever we observe man to do" which "turn[s] utility into a tautology" (1966, p. 57). "In the classical view, each consumer is a satisfaction maximizer, i.e., he is a rational egoist. . . . This assumption is so obviously contrary to fact that economists have turned it into a tautology. Any consumer behavior is by definition an attempt to maximize satisfaction" (Bowie and Simon, 1977, pp. 194–95). The authors go on to point out that as a result, "we no longer have an empirical theory about consumer behavior" and the theory becomes "utterly trivial" (ibid.). If one commits suicide, life "must have been" worse than death. In other situations in which some of the pleasures can be measured but still do not explain the act (such as a tax deduction that does not explain a gift because the deductions as a rule are lower in value), it is assumed that some other, unmeasured factor— say reputation in this case—"must" make up the difference. From a sociologist's viewpoint it is at least as plausible to hypothesize that the difference is due to a moral commitment.

Beyond undermining its explanatory power, the all-inclusive expansion of the concept of rational utility maximization undercuts a central thesis concerning the source of order in the economic system, a thesis that economists have advanced for centuries. As Adam Smith emphasized, the market system relies on each actor's pursuing his *self*-interest.

> It is not from the benevolence of the butcher, the brewer or the baker that we expect our dinner, but from their regard to their own interest. We address ourselves not to their humanity but to their self-love, and never talk to them of our own necessities but of their advantages (Smith, 1937 [1776], p. 14).

If there is no fundamental difference between "self-love" and love for others[1] Smith's whole thesis vanishes. Indeed, if people can derive pleasure directly from serving others and the community, there is no need for an invisible hand to tie their individualistic pursuits to the common good. Moreover, problems that might arise in coordinating non-selfish actions effectively would not necessarily be handled effectively by the invisible hand. It thus seems, on grounds of sound conceptualization, that the quest for self-satisfaction and seeking to serve others (the public included) out of a sense of moral obligation are best kept apart.

The Great X

Another major attempt to shore up the monoutility paradigm is to suggest that the concept of utility, whatever its philosophical origins or the psychological "bedtime stories" it used to entail, should be treated as an abstract entity, without any content, neither pleasure nor consumption. It is merely the great common denominator, an x, into which all other values can be converted or by which all rank-ordering can be systematized. Hirshleifer put it succinctly: "What modern economists call 'utility' reflects *nothing* more than the rank ordering of preference" (1976, p. 85, italics added). Utility "need not refer to anything" (Little, 1957, p. 20).

This concept of X-utility, in its pure form, if it is taken as devoid of any content, and merely a formal factor according to which the various preferences can be ranked, must be given substantive content in order to be useful for scientific purposes. A means must be specified for determining what the preference rankings of the subjects of study actually are. A basic difficulty here is that the subjects' ranking or valuation of a set of objects will depend on the dimensions along which they are assessed. And because all empirical objects have multiple aspects such as calories, vitamins, minerals, and moral standings, their *value* or *utility* will depend on how they are viewed. Unlike mathematical symbols, objects do not have one clear value (Little, 1957, pp. 19ff.).

One way out of this dilemma would be to provide people with one or more criteria for ranking items (or "choices"); the selection of these criteria both introduces substance into the X-utility and raises the question of what it will be—merely pleasure, also morality, or some other utility—which is precisely the question the concept of X-utility seeks to avoid.

Modern economists circumvent this issue by an empiricist device; they draw on the subjects of study and observation, the consumers, the choice makers, to rank their preferences by whatever criteria are in the front or back of their minds, without asking them or otherwise seeking to establish what these criteria are. One way this is done is to ask people what they "prefer" (or which of two products or baskets of products they would rather "have" or "take"). Such questions reintroduce the pleasure utility because they evoke notions of consumption (or ownership, i.e., wealth or potential consumption). People will rank the same items quite differently if they are asked different ranking questions—say, what they value more—because this would bring to mind moral judgments. This is evident in a survey conducted by Juster. Americans were asked what they "benefit" from most. They responded in line with what they expected to be the morally approved answers, which is evident in the way their behavior diverges from their verbal rankings. Americans ranked highest, "talking with children" and seventeenth, "watching television," while it seems clear that in practice most Americans spend much more time watching TV than they ever do talking to their children (Juster, 1985).

To the extent that people are not asked but their choice-behavior is observed, or their ranking is said to be "revealed" in what they buy under various "constraints," especially of income, one runs into severe empirical difficulties. The problem is that it is not sufficient to show that at a given income level a rise in the price of coffee will lead people to buy more tea; one must deal with all the simultaneous changes in all other prices and "compensate" for the loss in across-the-board buying power. Even when this is attempted, under extremely simplified and controlled conditions of experiments with rats, the findings are extremely difficult to interpret (Kagel et al., 1975). Their applications to humans are dubious. Field experiments, such as the income maintenance and health coinsurance ones, run into very considerable, possibly unsurmounted, methodological difficulties. Several economists the author queried about this matter responded, at first, by stating that one need not know what motives "lurk" behind the preferences for the theory to be "very useful," "enormously illuminating," and for it to "allow to predict quite well people's behavior." When reminded of the difficulties listed above, they agreed that actually the predictive record "is quite weak." Indeed, they added, at best the theory predicts the direction of the change of behavior that results from changes in prices, not the magnitude.

Last but not least, the theory does not even seek to explain either the dynamics of preferences or what causes them, or how the consumers allocate their income among alternative goods to begin with. Such explanation is necessary because people change their preferences as the constraints under which they "implement" them change. Without a conception and measurement of preference dynamics, in which values play a pivotal role, a satisfactory theory of economic behavior is hard to imagine. The economist's assumption that people's preferences are "stable," ignores the most elementary observations of daily experience. The argument that absurd assumptions do not matter because the resulting theory is predicting successfully is highly questionable and, it is widely agreed, inadequate.

The suggestion that values and other factors that shape preferences are not the economists' turf is but one more major reason for a paradigm change, to combine economics with psychology and sociology, to develop a socioeconomics, which in turn may provide for a richer but not overdetermining conception.

All this is not to deny that there may be economic applications within which one or another of these simplified utility theories—P or I or X—is serviceable; the point instead is that there *are* important ranges of human behavior—including some with significant economic aspects—where a more complex theory of motivation and choice is called for.

Antecedents

The suggestion that more than one utility is at work, and that one of them is moral, has been often raised before. However, most of those who embark on this road stop before completing the journey. They typically point to many reasons and considerable evidence that one should assume two utilities but then add, sometimes quite arbitrarily, that "after all," the two utilities can, somehow, be accommodated within one overarching one. Buchanan, for example, after a strong argument in favor of distinguishing between two motivational modes, one that he calls "economic self-interest" and the other that he terms "community," adds, in passing, that what

"I label moral-ethical, can be analysed in a utility-maximization model" (1978, p. 366). Others whose work lies along this line include Harsanyi (1955), Thaler and Shefrin (1981), Margolis (1982), and Lindenberg (1983). A smaller number of authors called for recognizing two utilities (albeit not in exactly those words), but have not elaborated their reasons, provided amassed evidence, or spelled out an alternative conception. These include Sen (1977) and Hirschman (1984). We turn next to pick up where they left off. What is the nature of the moral "utility"? And once one recognizes two basic dimensions of valuations or utilities, must one open the flood gates to many more?

The Moral "Utility"

What constitutes a moral act? A visit with the relevant philosophical literature leads to the not surprising conclusion that philosophers, after being at it for many hundreds of years, have not yet produced a definitive definition of what is moral. Without attempting here to review the immense literature on the subject, the different approaches, or the difficulties each encounters, for the purposes at hand it suffices to consider moral acts those that meet four criteria, each necessary by itself but sufficient only in conjunction: moral acts reflect an imperative, a generalization, a symmetry when applied to others, and motivate intrinsically.

The *imperative* quality of moral acts is reflected in that persons who act morally feel they "must" behave that way, are obligated, duty bound. We are all familiar from personal experience or introspection with the sense that one ought to do something because it is right as distinguishable from doing it because it is enjoyable.

The notion of an imperative is close to the widely recognized fact that people set aside certain realms or spheres as important, compelling, "sacred" ones. Goodin (1980) sees people as treating moral principles as important and as doing so by setting them aside as a *differentiated,* distinct, set of considerations. Others, especially Durkheim and recently

Walzer (1983), point out that people treat certain acts and considerations as "sacred" (which, of course, need not be religious).

One characteristic of such considerations, Goodin suggests, is to repudiate the instrumental rationality of considerations of costs and benefits. A person feels obligated to save a life, make a donation, and so on, without such calculations. Mothers dash into fires to save their children without stopping to calculate. Family members asked to donate a kidney to a child or sibling tend to respond with a quick positive commitment (Simmons et al., 1977). Indeed, the "instantaneousness" of the decision at hand is used by several researchers as one indication that a nondeliberative commitment is made (Fellner and Marshall, 1968).

Only after these moral principles are violated, do people enter into a second realm of decisions, in which moral considerations are weighed against others and calculations enter. This, by the way, explains why people *sometimes* calculate how much to give, and seek to establish what giving *x* dollars will do for their reputation, or what they will get in exchange, that is, exhibit what Goodin calls prudential morality; this should not be used to argue that they do not have *other* "sacred," nonnegotiable moral commitments. Morality affects their choices in two different ways: by providing a sense of an absolute command, and as a source of preferences and a commitment to choose certain means, the moral ones, over others, but not at all costs.

People first sense an absolute command to act morally, but that does not mean that they will always heed it. That they are less likely to heed it if the costs are high does not indicate that there is no imperative; indeed, all other things being equal, it is what drives up the costs. On the other hand, if the moral commitment is not reflected in behavior but only in verbal expressions or "attitudes," then there is no imperative.

The need for additional criteria arises because there can be nonmoral imperatives; for example, obsessions with a forlorn love or even with an object, such as controlled substances or a fetish. The addition of the second and third criteria helps to segregate moral imperatives from others (Childress, 1977).

Individuals who act morally are able to *generalize* in the sense of justifying their acts to others and to themselves by general rules. Statements such as "because I want it" or "I need it badly," do not meet this criterion because no generalization is entailed. Statements that one believes one ought to act in a certain manner because "these are *all* god's children" or "all men are born equal" are examples of generalizations. (For additional discussion of "general obligations," see Fishkin, 1982.)

Symmetry is required in that there must be a willingness to accord other, comparable people under comparable circumstances, the same standing or right. Racist ideologies, which otherwise have the appearance of moral systems in that they are compelling (to their believers) and generalizable, fail to qualify by this test.

Finally, moral acts *affirm or express a commitment,* rather than involve the consumption of a good or a service. Hence, they are *intrinsically* motivated and not subject to means-end analysis. Does the fact that moral acts are affected by costs not belie this characterization? Pure moral acts ignore costs, like the mother who dashes into the fire to save *her* child, the child she feels morally responsible for. Heath (1976, pp. 1–2) points out that the notions of the pursuit of a utility, of rational choice, and exchange behavior have been much extended to apply not only to market relations but also to friendship and even love. However, he observes, "excluded from this conception of exchange is behavior which is not motivated by the return but by a sense of duty or by some other internalized value. The action of the man who believes in the rightness of his cause and is not affected by the praise or blame of others cannot be included in the category of exchange." (See also Elster, 1979, ch. 4.) As to the argument that moral acts themselves are not impulsive acts but reflect deliberations and judgments (especially evident when one must sort out what course to follow when one is subject to conflicting moral claims), these deliberations are not of the same kind as means-end considerations; they require judgments among ends. Two major studies provide ample evidence that even consumption is often an act of communication and expression rather than of a choice behavior (Douglas and Isherwood, 1979; Thompson, 1979). (These are nonmoral acts that are intrinsically motivating, but that does not invalidate this criterion. It only shows that the universe of such acts is larger than that of moral acts and hence, as was already indicated, this criterion is necessary but not sufficient.)

The significance of the preceding observations should be explicated: Economists frequently argue that moral factors may affect preferences, together with many other factors, but they need not be examined separately because they are reflected in the preferences, and hence ultimately in the price, so one need not study what lurks behind the preferences. Several objections to this approach have already been listed to which it may be added that moral factors affect not only the preferences but also the "constraints." Well, respond the economists, then they will affect the costs. However, to the extent that moral factors sanctify one line of action or set of means over all others, or heavily favor one, they must be included in the analysis because, like oligopolistic or oligopsonistic factors, they rule out options that are preferable from a P-utility maximization viewpoint. A case in point is longshoremen who refuse to load ships that carry cargoes to Poland in protest against the regime's suppression of Solidarity, even if it means they lose some pay. This might be said to be an esoteric exception which, even if not explicable by some hidden pleasure or expediency, does not matter much. However, studies of labor relations are replete with evidence of loyalty of employees to the job, to management, and to the place of employment—and of commitments by higher ranking personnel to lower ranking ones. Economists have often recognized that as a result labor "markets" do not "clear," do not behave as they are expected (Thurow, 1983, ch. 7; Solow, 1980).

Furthermore, when one contemplates the substance of the term "moral behavior," the kinds of acts the term encompasses, one finds another reason to maintain its distinctiveness: moral acts are a source of value and of motivation other than pleasure. What one feels when one lives up to one's moral obligations, discharges one's duties, does "what is right," is distinct from the sense one has when one indulges one of the senses, satisfies a need, does things because they are "fun." *Indeed, many are explicitly based on the denial of pleasure in the name of the principle(s) evoked.* Doing penance, abstention from premarital sex, and Ramadan fasting are not what most people consider sources of pleasure. True, acting in line with one's moral precepts produces a kind of satisfaction, a sense of moral worth, but it's more the kind one gets when a hard day's work is done than the pleasure of getting off work early with full pay.

While pleasure and living up to one's moral commitments are not always or necessarily in conflict, they very often are in terms of their call on resources (the time, energy, and assets dedicated to one are often required by the other as well, a major factor, say, in the life of parents who work outside the home). Quite frequently pleasure-seeking acts and moral commitments are also incompatible in terms of the behavior expected and rewarded (e.g., when managers are under great pressure to increase profits but also not violate the rules of the game; using kickbacks or bribes to get more business are cases in point).

Moral commitments, here and throughout, unless otherwise indicated, refer to moral obligations that have been internalized, that individuals feel as their own, not to those they treat as external conditions to which they merely adapt. Internalization has been defined as part of the socialization process in which a person learns to "conform to rules in situations that arouse impulses to transgress and that lack surveillance and sanctions" (Kohlberg, 1968, p. 483). Social scientists may trace the genesis of one's moral commitments to one's parents, culture, peer or reference groups; but whatever their source, once internalized they become an integral part of the self. Thus, those who feel they ought to serve their country, god, or a cause, feel strongly—sometimes despite strong protestations from spouses, friends, and peers—that such actions are in line with *their* values, are *their* duty.

Does all this mean that the pursuit of pleasure or self-interest is immoral? Obviously not. There are significant areas within which their pursuit is judged to be legitimate, especially in economic activities. This discussion focuses on areas in which the two are in conflict only because it is in these areas that the distinct quality of acts that are judged to be moral stands out most clearly.

More Than Two?

Once the monoutility model is abandoned, why limit the category of utilities to two? Envy, anger, achieving social dominance, conformism, and xenophobia have been nominated as additions (Scitovsky, 1976, would add "novelty"). Psychologists have made long lists of motives or needs. The methodological significance of this challenge should not be overlooked. It is advanced by economists who argue that the existence of myriad "utilities" shows the need for *one* utility to order them all; that to abandon the reigning order leads to anarchy.

In response, one should note first that utilities (or dimensions of valuation) are not to be equated with specific needs, motives, goals, aspirations, preferences, or predispositions; they are analytical categories that encompass numerous concrete manifestations. Just as the concept of a P-utility encompasses numerous specific pleasures, there is no separate utility for sports-car-pleasure and lawn-pleasure, so the moral "utility" encompasses numerous expressions. Moreover, myriad specific needs, motives, goals, aspirations, preferences, and predispositions can be analyzed as an expression of two utilities.

There is, however, no reason to argue that it is logically necessary, or productive, to assume that there are only two utilities (or main sources of valuation), and no others may be considered. One candidate for a third utility that has often been cited is that of affection. It is part of Adam Smith's theory of moral sentiments, in which he sees people as balancing their own conscience with the demands of positive bonds to others.

The main question, though, is not whether one can discern a third (or fourth or fifth) utility, but whether one can keep the *number small*, to preserve parsimony. And one must ask for the *criteria* for introducing into one's paradigm new utilities versus subsuming an observed motive, drive, or preference in one that is already a member of one's paradigm or theory.

The answer is, in part, *pragmatic.* Utilities are not found in nature or in locations in the brain; they are concepts we introduce to organize our thinking and the evidence we generate. The question is hence, in part, a matter of what "works," what is productive. For example, if we try to explain voting behavior in traditional utilitarian terms (as neoclassical economists have repeatedly done), voting makes no sense because it entails efforts and yields no specific return. (A voter cannot reasonably expect to affect the outcome of the elections.) Neoclassical economists deal with this "anomaly" by introducing ad hoc assumptions, suggesting that voters do "expect" to affect the elections after all, for various reasons. For example, they will turn out in larger numbers in close elections. (Actually, the correlation between turnout and closeness is weak and hence the concept of "expected" closeness is added, which is difficult to measure. And still the correlations remain weak [Hirshleifer, 1985, p. 55].) If, instead, one introduces another utility, *expressing* one's patriotic duty, one finds that there is a considerable correlation between the level of such a commitment and voting (Barry, 1978, p. 17; Godwin and Mitchell, 1982). One thus achieves higher predictive power, *without* any loss, indeed a gain, in parsimony, and the additional concept, which we shall see often "works" elsewhere, adds to our explanatory power by bringing to mind factors that the monoutility concept does not. For example, one criterion to be used in deciding whether or not a utility is to be added is whether or not it *significantly* enriches our predictive and explanatory powers without overdetermination.

Another criterion is *reducibility,* i.e., the ability to account for a phenomenon by categories already in the theory. For example, to the extent that one can show that affection is part pleasure (enjoy your friends) and part obligation (the dictum to treat others like one's self and not as a medium of exchange), the case for introducing a new category is weakened. However, if a factor, say some emotion like hatred, can be shown not to be accountable by our knowledge of people's moral predispositions and quests for pleasure, say if people's hatred drives them to do things that are both immoral and self-hurting (i.e., not pleasurable), a third category might be called for (Hirschman, 1977, pp. 38–66 traced the long history of opposition between "interests" and "passions").

How can one foretell if these criteria will lead to conceptual anarchy, the result of the introduction of ever more utilities? Observing people's choices strongly suggests that while they are often subject to numerous forces, they experience them as the sum of a limited number of factors. Typically a person may feel that x is "fun" to do but for reason y he feels he *ought* not to do it. True, in many situations a person may feel that x would be pleasurable for two, three, or more reasons (a winter vacation in the South may be relaxing and comfortably warm) while moral considerations may include conflicting obligations to spouse, children, and, say, the community. Nevertheless, people's thinking and behavior reveals that *they* reduce these numerous forces to a small number before the final choice. Most people usually feel torn in two or three ways, not umpteen ways; those that do are considered mentally ill. These summary feelings can guide us in developing the theory of utilities.

In the scope of this essay, the exercise cannot be completed by attempting to determine which exact number of summary concepts will prove to be the "right" one. This would involve exploring the cognitive and emotive organization of peoples' psyches, and the many complex issues raised by the notion of a multiple self. The question of how many facets there are is not merely a question of the convenience of "doing" science but also of the structure of what is found. Nor does it matter for the issues at hand whether the final number turns out to be three, four, or five. What have been indicated are the criteria that may be used in adding utilities or dimensions of value and why the result is expected to be a small number.

Challenging Findings and Observations

To this point, the essay has (a) argued that there are no principled reasons for insistence on adhering to the monoutility model, (b) indicated how the moral dimension of valuation can be characterized, and (c) defused the concern that the search for multiple "utilities" must eventuate in conceptual anarchy through identifying an excessive number of dimensions of valuation. The discussion has presumed that distinguishing between "moral" and "pleasurable" sources of valuation will prove fruitful through calling attention to and accounting for phenomena that strain the monoutility framework. The final verdict on this claim can only be the product of the kind of sustained research program this essay calls for. This section provides scattered evidence that suggests this program is promising. First, some evidence is cited that authentic altruistic behavior occurs and that such behavior is expressive rather than calculative. Second, the role of moral factors in *economic* behavior is illustrated. True, each of these items of behavior may be explained by some hidden rational considerations (economists have been quite ingenious in coming up with such explanations). The relative merit of these interpretations as compared to those given here is a matter of research called for but not carried out in this essay.

The second line of neoclassical defense is tackled next. Economists say in effect, "well, there may be moral imperatives but these can be explained by *economic* factors." Some evidence is presented to argue that moral acts are not reducible, that they have distinct attributes.

Moreover, the existence of irreducible moral factors, as suggested below, casts doubt about a core assumption of the choice theories that lies at the base of neoclassical economics: that people have clear preferences and can "trade off" relevant items.

Authentic Altruism and Expressive Behavior

A considerable body of experimental data supports the existence of significant amounts of authentic altruistic behavior, i.e., behavior in which there is no pleasure for the ego, directly or indirectly, or the costs (or, opportunities sacrificed) clearly outweigh the gains. Several experiments show that many people mail back "lost" wallets to strangers, cash intact (Hornstein et al., 1968). In another study, sixty-four percent of the subjects who had an opportunity to return a lost contribution to an "Institute for Research in Medicine" did so (Hornstein et al., 1971, p. 110; Hornstein, 1976, pp. 95–96). The cost involved is the cash and the postage and the trouble. The reward? Chiefly, the inner sense of having done what is right.

In some situations, many individuals who see others in distress rush to help them without calculating the consequences for themselves when they feel responsible, as mothers do for their children in houses on fire (Janis and Mann, 1977, p. 27). People who donate a kidney report doing so following an almost instantaneous decision, without deliberation of merits or costs (Fellner and Marshall, 1968). In a set of experiments designed to study "costly self-sacrificing" behavior, people were asked whether they would contribute bone marrow for strangers, not relatives (Schwartz, 1970, p. 283). Of those asked, fifty-nine percent said they would donate; an additional twenty-four percent indicated at least a 50/50 chance that they would if called upon; twelve percent indicated a less than even chance that they would make such a contribution; only five percent said they would refuse outright (ibid., p. 289). Attitudes are not a firm predictor of behavior; the proportion of actual donors is likely to be significantly smaller but not trivial.

Latane and Darley (1970) sent researchers into, of all places, the streets of New York City, requesting help. High proportions of New Yorkers did assist people they thought were in distress in a variety of situations. For example, an investigator who repeatedly fell down as drunk gained help from passersby in seventy percent of the staged episodes (Piliavin, Rodin, and Piliavin, 1969). For additional evidence and review of several of the studies cited see Rushton (1980) and Derlega and Grzelak (1982).

In many situations gifts are *not* given to elicit reciprocal gifts nor adjusted "in terms of marginal utilities to the recipients" (Wells, 1970, p. 47) but to *express* a family commitment or bond (Cheal, 1984, p. 1; Cheal, 1985), which illustrates that moral affirmations often entail no means-end analysis or choice, but, on the contrary, the one means deemed appropriate is fused to the goal. That is, the means and the goal are intrinsically linked in such a way that they cannot be separated and hence the question of the relative merit of the means at issue compared to some others simply does not apply. This is often the case in rituals. For instance, a *proper* bow is the only way to pay respect in certain South Korean relations. No other bow or mode of paying homage will do; indeed, they are perceived to show disrespect, because the proper means was not used. In the case of gifts, a variety of objects may be used but cash—even if more "efficient"—may be considered rather improper. That is, a whole different scheme of the process of action is involved than that implied in the notion of rational utility maximization.

A Factor in Economic Behavior

Commitments to moral values also affect economic activities. Consider saving behavior. Economists explain the level of saving mainly by the size of one's income (the higher one's income the more one saves), by the desire to provide for consumption in retirement, and by the level of interest rates. Together these factors explain part of the variance in the amount saved. However, there are at least three moral norms that also affect the amount saved: the extent to which one believes that it is immoral to be in debt; that one ought to save for its own sake (because "it is the right thing to do" and in order not to be dependent on the government or one's children); and that one ought to help one's children "start off in life." These moral commitments are affected in turn by the content and level of morality in society, by the norms of one's subculture (for example, these prosaving norms seem stronger in small towns than in the big cities), and by other noneconomic factors.

Economists have established that people save much more than can be explained by the desire to ensure their consumption after retirement. "At no age above sixty-five are Americans on average dis-saving" (Thurow, 1983, p. 221). Attempts have been made to explain this "excessive" saving by the need to hedge the "risk" that one will live longer than expected, but still there is a sizable unaccounted "surplus." This, in turn, is explained by older people's enjoyment of the consumption of their offspring "extending through several generations," according to one economist (Shorrocks, 1979, p. 416), and the "consumption of their [household's] descendants in all future generations," according to another (Laitner, 1979, p. 403). This seems an excessive attempt to stretch the consumption function; it is somewhat difficult to visualize how one can enjoy the consumption of one's yet-to-be-conceived offspring of offspring. Assuming a moral commitment to help one's own children seems at least as plausible.

Moral commitments reduce what economists have come to call "moral hazards." Specifically, *the stronger the moral underwriting of implicit contracts, the lower the administrative costs resulting in less of a need to buy hedge protection* (in case resources are not delivered, workers quit, and so on) *and to spend resources on legal action* (drafting explicit contracts, litigation). While reference here is to specific situations—for example, differences between those industries where one can ("usually") rely on one's word versus those where such reliance is less assured—the same point has been made about whole societies. It is common to note that because it is not possible to provide enough police, accountants, and inspectors to verify but a small segment of all the transactions that take place, economies and societies require that most of the transactions be based on voluntary compliance. This, in turn, is significantly affected by the relative *level* of morality within a given society (or subsociety), within a given historical period. To put it differently, to the extent that moral commitments enhance the resources that can be dedicated to the economic activity rather than to supervision and verification, a higher level of morality might increase productivity and even GNP. (On the role of employee thefts and other crimes in reducing productivity, see Denison, 1979.)

While economists tend to go to great lengths to explain behavior without resort to moral explanations (as just illustrated), when the role of moral factors is demonstrated they often suggest that these can be incorporated into neoclassical analysis by assuming that they are contained in the preferences or affect the "constraints." In effect, such a "concession" is greater than it may at first seem because moral factors are changing. This, in turn, leads one to realize that when economic behavior changes it may be due to changes in preferences, and not merely to those in constraints. For example, there is currently a neotemperance movement in the United States that reduces the "preference" for alcohol. Nor is this the only instance. Without any change in taxes the temperance campaign of Father Matthew around 1850 in Ireland reduced that country's consumption of spirits from twelve million to five million gallons per annum (Hirshleifer, 1980, p. 11), indicative of a major window through which moral explanations may systematically enter the study of economic behavior.

The Irreducibility of Moral Behavior

Not only are there moral acts but their explanation cannot be "reduced" to other explanations because people who seek to live up to their moral commitments exhibit systematically and significantly different behavior from people who act to enhance their pleasures. These qualitative differences were noted by one of the major utilitarian philosophers, John Stuart Mill. He wrote, "certain social utilities . . . are vastly more important and therefore more absolute and imperative than any others are as a class . . ." and these utilities are "guarded by a sentiment not different in degree but in kind" (cited by Nisbett, 1981, p. 42). The essay turns next to spell out the distinctive qualities of behavior significantly affected by moral factors. The characterization is based on both everyday observations and social-science findings.

To the extent individuals act under the influence of moral commitments they are more likely to persevere when circumstances change, as compared to when they calculate costs and benefits. Conversely, the more individuals act in the calculative mode, the more likely they are to modify their behavior as circumstances change. For instance, moral behavior is more tenacious than economic behavior. Translated into economic terms, this suggests that *moral commitments "stretch out" the learning curve and are expected to increase transaction costs* when changes favored by economic rationality are inconsistent with moral conduct.

The learning curve reflects the time lapse and costs involved in improving performance. It demonstrates that people provided with information do not absorb it and act on it instantaneously, as was assumed by earlier—and even some present-day—economists. How long it takes and how many resources are required to achieve full absorption are also reflected. The more sharply it slopes, the lower the learning costs; the more stretched out, the higher. The shape of the curve is affected by nonmoral factors (for example, the complexity of the information to be absorbed). Assuming all these other factors are equal, learning is slower and more costly the higher the moral objections to what is being taught.

The concept of "transaction costs" has been introduced by economists to help explain "stickiness"—the observation that people will not modify their behavior even when such modifications are advantageous if the costs involved exceed the expected gain. Moral commitments are among the factors that affect the level of transaction costs. For instance, the stronger the moral commitment, the higher the return needed before the individuals involved will violate their implicit contracts in the face of changed economic circumstances that favor such a violation, and they will absorb more of an economic loss in order to live up to their obligation. For example, it is considered "improper" for professors to accept an offer in May from a competing university to start teaching in September in the same academic year (because it makes it difficult to replace such faculty so late in the year). The norm is said to be stronger in some universities (Ivy League?) than in others (Red Brick?). Hence, in May, it would take a larger salary differential to move a professor from the first kind of university than from the second. In short, moral behavior is "stickier" than amoral behavior.

Intrapsychic conflict between the pleasure and moral valuation of an item, whether the specific psychic mechanism that is activated is guilt, denial, or some other, *results in intrapsychic stress,* which in turn exacts costs that are not typical information or transaction costs: *they diminish the capacity of the actor.* A large body of research shows that under stress, people's decision making becomes less rational—if by acting rationally one means using available information, drawing proper conclusions, and so on. (For a masterful review of the findings, see Janis and Mann, 1977.) A major source of stress is "selling out" virtues one believes in, "prostituting" one's self.

"Dirty" Preferences and Encumbered Trades

Due to moral factors choices do not reflect simple, one-dimensional, preferences but are *multifaceted.* Economists tend to assume that all units of a specific item (at any one point in time) have one price; all offers and bids are made simultaneously, all bargains are struck, prices are set, and the market clears in a flash for the whole process to start over again ("comparative statics"). However, everyday observations and experiments show that many purchases are accompanied or followed by feelings of guilt, shame, regrets, and other such feelings that, we shall see, are not merely ephemeral states of mind but have significant behavioral consequences. That is, preferences and behavior are often ambivalent, *and* moral factors which conflict with urges or drives or quests for pleasure are a major source of the ambivalence.

A simple example illustrates the point. It involves dieting, the activity in worship of the body on which millions of members of industrialized societies, especially those better off, focus their moral-like efforts: They feel guilty when they indulge (i.e., experience pleasure) and virtuous when they abstain (pain). One may observe a person who usually does not have desserts order them on three occasions in a row (say, during a holiday season) and then skip lunch on a fourth. An economist may suggest that the price of desserts first fell, and subsequently their cost sky-rocketed (assuming no change in income and other prices). It seems more explanatory to realize the connection between the events, the accumulation of, at first not visible, guilt being worked off (and "revealed in behavior" on the fourth occasion). It also will be more predictive. Guilt is, of course, not the only "accompanying" feeling of choice that has subsequent observable effects. The example is given but to highlight that a one-dimensional ranking overlooks much of what there is in a choice, including the role of moral factors that may not be revealed in every single choice, if viewed as unidimensional and complete unto itself.

Evidence of the existence of ambivalence, whether its source is moral conflict with pleasure or competing pleasures or otherwise, poses a difficulty for neoclassical economics. It is supposed to arise, in the "standard" model, only when consumers are indifferent among combinations of commodities. A lead article in an issue of the *American Economic Review,* the official scholarly publication of the American Economic Association, is dedicated to the puzzle of people whose behavior is said to reflect at one and the same time *two incompatible preferences* (Schelling, 1984). For instance, a man, who goes to a cocktail party, tells the host that when he gets drunk, the host should refuse his request for his car keys. What is the guest's preference? To drive drunk—then why ask to be refused the keys? Not to drive drunk—then why ask for the keys? Many more examples are given and considerable deliberation has been devoted to the dilemma. It exists, of course, only because the theory assumes that people will have one clear preference, reflecting one utility.

Because moral and pleasure "preferences" are qualitatively different, items or means of satisfying them cannot be simply "traded off" or substituted for one another, the way various consumer goods can be, which is an essential assumption for the basic concept of the market. If my marginal utility tells me to buy more oranges and fewer apples, there is no aftertaste (or residue) of guilt, shame, or sense of betrayal. But *when people choose to violate their moral precepts to enhance their pleasures, such post-hoc feelings are expected to accompany their actions* and these feelings in turn *have behavioral consequences.* As Hirschman puts it, in situations where individuals act in line with their preferences but in violation of their "meta preferences," often their moral values, the result is "regret and guilt over having preferred it" (1984, p. 13).

In experiments, people who were induced to tell a lie were twice as likely to volunteer to carry out a chore than those who did not lie. Fifty-five percent of shoppers who believed they broke a camera in a shop offered to help another shopper in a staged incident versus fifteen percent of a control group. (These and other studies are reviewed by Rushton, 1980, pp. 43–44.) The relationship is often more complex: a single transgression may lead to some guilt but only the cumulative effect of several will lead to one act of remorse. If an economic analogue can be given to such behavior it would be akin to charging consumers, retroactively but irregularly, for a random subset of past purchases, an additional mark up on items they already consumed, or charging them "extra" in the said manner, more for an item *other* than the one they bought. Guilt about one act spills over and attaches itself to other, seemingly unrelated, items.

The behavioral consequences are expected to include behavior sequences or cycles in which one or more acts are followed by bouts of morally approved behavior, and/or *an*

*increased search for or commitment to offsetting (or "compensatory"),
morally approved behavior;* for example, contributing to charity.
Several experiments have shown positive correlations between
responding to requests for help and *prior* "transgressions,"
correlations interpreted as the result of "guilt arousal"
(Carlsmith and Gross, 1969, pp. 232–39; Sadalla and Wallace,
1966, pp. 187–94).

Conflicts between economic motives and moral beliefs,
like other situations described by psychologists as governed
by *dissonance*,[2] are expected to lead to inaction (one is caught
between conflicting forces) and to *denial* (one acts one way
but pretends, or firmly believes, that one acts differently). A
simple example of the effects of dissonance is found in
changed attitudes toward debt.

The success of credit cards and bank-check credit is at-
tributable to the fact that they allow people to be in debt
without having to deal with the dissonance between their feeling "debt is wrong" and their desire to use credit (Maital,
1982, pp. 142–43). People do not perceive these as loans or
debt. (On effects of dissonance in the purchase of stocks, see
Klausner, 1984, pp. 71–75.)

The discussion so far suggests that moral commitments
cannot be exchanged for pleasurable acts without inner and
behavioral consequences. It should be noted that many psychologists, from Sigmund Freud to Herbert Marcuse, have argued that the reverse also holds true: Basic urges or pleasures
cannot be sublimated into socially approved behavior with full
success, without residue. This, of course, lends further support to the thesis that the two concepts refer to behaviors that
are substantively different, and are not reducible.

The inner structure of many moral decisions is systematically different from that of typical economic decisions. Unlike many economic decisions, *many moral decisions are difficult to reverse (i.e., are asymmetrical), are very "lumpy" (or highly
discontinuous), and reveal a high "notch effect" (a fear of passing a
threshold that makes behavior sticky before passage but reluctance
much diminished or lost once passage is completed).* Take, for example, the decisions concerning premarital sex many women

used to face. There were basically three morally recognized positions: virginity, being sexually active, and being promiscuous. Each contained a very large range of behavior considered of the same basic merit; i.e., the decision was very lumpy. Also, once a woman "lost her virtue," or was known to be promiscuous, she found it almost impossible to reverse her moral status. Moreover, acts that had great value before passing the threshold (an incident of intercourse), have a much lower significance, lower value, once the transgression has occurred. That is, there is no standardization of the item at issue.

The same basic observations can be made about joining welfare. Before one joins, a welfare dollar may be worth only 80 cents, but once one joins, and one is stigmatized, the very next dollar will be worth the full (or nearly) 100 cents. And, even if one gets off welfare and no longer receives stigmatized income, the stigma is likely to linger. Taking out the first loan, for people who feel being in debt is a moral evil, is different from extending it or taking out a second one. (Denial here takes the form similar to that of using credit cards, which people do not consider in the same way [Maital, 1982, pp. 143ff.].) Selling one's home, especially if it is the first move, moving to a different city, especially if it is the first relocation, and first voluntary change of job may all reveal such a structure due to moral (and emotional) factors, all in sharp contrast to what economic transactions are assumed to be.

Conclusion

This essay presents conceptual reasons and empirical indications for advancing a multiple-utility conception for the study of economic behavior, one that recognizes at least two sources of value: pleasure and morality. Attempts to accommodate moral behavior within the monoutility model strain it. These efforts have pushed economists first to dilute the substance of the concept of utility to the point it ceased to differentiate. The concept of utility came to include both love for self and for others. In the process, Adam Smith's thesis, which assumes economic behavior is based on self-interest, is, in effect, abandoned. Later attempts to view the concept of utility as a completely contentless, formal concept render it a-empirical as all logical and mathematical concepts are, unless related to some other symbol.

The qualities of moral acts have been indicated and the often, but not necessarily, conflicting relationship between morality and pleasure was explicated. Evidence of authentic altruistic behavior has been cited. The role of moral factors in a variety of economic behaviors was indicated. Moral considerations, such as the arousal of guilt, were found to encumber preferences and choices. The level of morality was shown to be inversely related to the level of transaction costs. Limits that moral factors imposed on market relations were also discussed. In short, the distinction between pleasures and morals seems to be not only conceptually sound but also productive in accounting for the factors that drive economic behavior.

Notes

1. A reviewer pointed out here that if one's altruism encompasses one's children, there is still a need for the invisible hand to order the relations among the households. This is quite true. However, to the extent that altruism encompasses those with whom one transacts, it supplements or replaces self-interest as the ordering mechanism. For evidence, see below.
2. On the term, see Festinger, 1957; for an application by economists, see Akerlof and Dickens, 1982.

References

Akerlof, George, and William T. Dickens. 1982. "The Economic Consequences of Cognitive Dissonance." *The American Economic Review* 72:307–19.

Barry, Brian. 1978. *Sociologists, Economists and Democracy.* Chicago: University of Chicago.

Benedict, Ruth. 1934. *Patterns of Culture.* Boston: Houghton Mifflin.

Bentham, Jeremy. 1948. *An Introduction to the Principles of Morals and Legislation.* New York: Hafner.

Boulding, Kenneth E. 1978. *Ecodynamics: A New Theory of Societal Evolution.* Beverly Hills: Sage.

Bowie, Norman E., and Robert L. Simon. 1977. *The Individual and the Political Order.* Englewood Cliffs, NJ: Prentice-Hall.

Buchanan, James M. 1978. "Markets, States, and the Extent of Morals." *American Economic Review* 2:364–68.

Carlsmith, J. M., and A. E. Gross. 1969. "Some Effects of Guilt on Compliance." *Journal of Personality and Social Psychology* 11:232–39.

Cheal, David J. 1984. "Wedding Gifts and the Making of Money." Paper presented at the 79th Annual Meeting of the American Sociological Association, San Antonio, August 27–31.

———.1985. "Moral Economy: Gift Giving in an Urban Society." *Winnipeg Area Study Report no. 5.* (January) Winnipeg: University of Winnipeg.

Childress, James F. 1977. "The Identification of Ethical Principles." *Journal of Religious Ethics* 5:39–68.

Curtin, Richard T., and Thomas S. Neubig. 1979. "Outstanding Debt Among American Households." In *Survey of Consumer Attitudes* (April). Ann Arbor: University of Michigan, pp. 1–2.

Denison, Edward F. 1979. *Accounting for Slower Economic Growth.* Washington, DC: Brookings.

Derlega, Valerian J., and Janusz Grzelak (Eds.). 1982. *Cooperation and Helping Behavior: Theories and Research.* New York: Academic Press.

Douglas, Mary, and Baron Isherwood. 1979. *The World of Goods.* New York: Basic Books.

Dyke, C. 1981. *Philosophy of Economics.* Englewood Cliffs, NJ: Prentice-Hall.

Elster, Jon. 1979. *Ulysses and the Sirens: Studies in Rationality.* New York: Cambridge University Press.

Etzioni, Amitai. 1984. *Capital Corruption.* Orlando, Fla.: Harcourt Brace Jovanovich.

Fellner, C. H., and J. R. Marshall. 1968. "Twelve Kidney Donors." *Journal of the American Medical Association* 206:2703–7.

Festinger, Leon. 1957. *A Theory of Cognitive Dissonance.* Stanford, CA: Stanford University Press.

Fishkin, James S. 1982. *The Limits of Obligation.* New Haven, Conn.: Yale University Press.

Godwin, Kenneth, and Robert Cameron Mitchell. 1982. "Rational Models, Collective Goods and Nonelectoral Political Behavior." *Western Political Journal* 35:161–92.

Goodin, Robert E. 1980. "Making Moral Incentives Pay." *Policy Sciences* 12:131–45.

Harsanyi, John C. 1955. "Cardinal Welfare, Individualistic Ethics, and International Comparisons of Utility." *Journal of Political Economy* 63:309–21.

Heath, Anthony. 1976. *Rational Choice and Social Exchange.* New York: Cambridge University Press.

Hirschman, Albert O. 1977. *The Passions and Interests: Political Arguments for Capitalism Before Its Triumph.* Princeton: Princeton University Press.

———. 1984. "Against Parsimony: Three Easy Ways of Complicating Some Categories of Economic Discourse." *Bulletin: The American Academy of Arts and Sciences* 37(8):11–28.

Hirshleifer, Jack. 1976. *Price Theory and Applications.* Englewood Cliffs, NJ: Prentice-Hall.

———. 1980. *Price Theory and Applications,* 2nd ed. Englewood Cliffs, NJ: Prentice-Hall.

———. 1985. "The Expanding Domain of Economics." *The American Economic Review* 75(6):53–68.

Hornstein, H. A., E. Fisch, and M. Holmes. 1968. "Influence of a Model's Feelings About His Behavior and His Relevance as a Comparison of Other Observers' Helping Behavior." *Journal of Personal and Social Psychology* 10:222–26.

Hornstein, Harvey. 1976. *Cruelty and Kindness.* Englewood Cliffs, NJ: Prentice-Hall.

Hornstein, Harvey A., Hugo N. Masor, and Kenneth Sole. 1971. "Effects of Sentiment and Completion of a Helping Act on Observer Helping: A Case for Socially Mediated Zeigarnik Effects." *Journal of Personality and Social Psychology* 17:107–12.

Janis, Irving, and Leon Mann. 1977. *Decision Making: A Psychological Analysis of Conflict, Choice and Commitment.* New York: Free Press.

Juster, F. T. 1985. *Preferences for Work and Leisure.* Ann Arbor: University of Michigan, Institute for Social Research.

Kagel, John H., H. Rachlin, L. Green, R. Battalio, R. Basmann, and W. R. Klemm. 1975. "Experimental Studies of Consumer Demand Behavior Using Laboratory Animals." *Economic Inquiry* 13 (March):22–38.

Klausner, Michael. 1984. "Sociological Theory and the Behavior of Financial Markets." In Patricia A. Adler and Peter Adler (Eds.), *The Social Dynamics of Financial Markets.* Greenwich, CT: JAI Press.

Kohlberg, Lawrence. 1968. "Moral Development." In David L. Sills (Ed.), *International Encyclopedia of the Social Sciences,* vol. 10, pp. 483–93. New York: Free Press.

Laitner, John P. 1979. "Bequests, Golden-Age Capital Accumulation and Government Debt." *Economics* 46:403–14.

Latane, B., and J. M. Darley. 1970. *The Unresponsive Bystander: Why Doesn't He Help?* New York: Appleton-Century-Crofts.

Lindenberg, Siegwart. 1983. "Utility and Morality." *Kyklos* 36:450–68.

Lipsey, Richard, and Peter Steiner. 1975. *Economics.* New York: Harper Collins.

Little, I. M. D. 1957. *A Critique of Welfare Economics.* Oxford: Clarendon.

Maital, Shlomo. 1982. *Minds, Markets, and Money.* New York: Basic Books.

Margolis, Howard. 1982. *Selfishness, Altruism and Rationality: A Theory of Social Choice.* Cambridge: Cambridge University Press.

Moffit, R. 1983. "An Economic Model of Welfare Stigma." *American Economic Review* 73:1023–35.

Nisbett, Robert A. 1981. "Replies to Steven Kelman." *Regulation.* March/April: 42–43.

Piliavin, I. M., J. Rodin, and J. A. Piliavin. 1969. "Good Samaritanism: An Underground Phenomenon?" *Journal of Personality and Social Psychology* 13:289–99.

Rushton, J. Philippe. 1980. *Altruism, Socialization, and Society.* Englewood Cliffs, NJ: Prentice-Hall.

Sadalla, E., and J. Wallace. 1966. "Behavioral Consequences of Transgression." *Journal of Experimental Research in Personality* 1:187–94.

Samuelson, Paul A. 1980. *Economics.* 11th ed. New York: McGraw-Hill.

Schelling, Thomas. 1984. "Self-Command in Practice, in Policy, and in a Theory of Rational Choice." *American Economic Review* 74(2):1–11.

Schwartz, Shalom H. 1970. "Elicitation of Moral Obligation and Self-Sacrificing Behavior: An Experimental Study of Volunteering to Be a Bone Marrow Donor." *Journal of Personality and Social Psychology* 15(4):283–93.

Scitovsky, Tibor. 1976. *The Joyless Economy.* New York: Oxford University Press.

Sen, Amartya K. 1977. "Rational Fools." *Philosophy and Public Affairs* 6(4):317–44.

Shorrocks, Anthony F. 1979. "On the Structure of Inter-Generational Transfers Between Families." *Economica* 46:415–25.

Simmons, Roberta G., Susan D. Klein, and Robert L. Simmons. 1977. *Gift of Life: The Social and Psychological Impact of Organ Transplantation.* New York: Wiley.

Smith, Adam. 1937 (1776). *Wealth of Nations.* New York: Random House (Modern Library Edition).

Solow, Robert M. 1980. "On Theories of Unemployment." *American Economic Review* 70(1):1–11.

Stigler, George J. 1966. *The Theory of Price.* 3rd ed. New York: Macmillan.

Thaler, Richard, and H. M. Shefrin. 1981. "An Economic Theory of Self-Control." *Journal of Political Economy* 89:392–406.

Thompson, Michael. 1979. *Rubbish Theory: The Creation and Destruction of Value.* New York: Oxford University Press.

Thurow, Lester C. 1983. *Dangerous Currents.* New York: Random House.

Walsh, Vivian Charles. 1970. *Introduction to Contemporary Microeconomics.* New York: McGraw-Hill.

Walzer, Michael. 1983. *Spheres of Justice.* New York: Basic Books.

Wells, A. 1970. *Social Institutions.* London: Heinemann.

The Moral Dimension
in Policy Analysis

A policy analyst suggested that in order to reduce the incidence of skin cancer in the United States, blacks ought to be asked to occupy the seats on the sunny side of sports arenas (blacks are regarded as being biologically less sensitive to the sun's rays). The analyst added that he recognized that such a policy would encounter "some social difficulty in implementation." From a perspective of efficiency (or narrow utilitarianism) alone, it is difficult to fault the suggested policy. It would clearly raise the total well-being of society at a low cost. Some would argue that policies should be designed in such a way as to improve the well-being of some, but only as long as they do not reduce the well-being of any. This is possibly a worthy rule but practically always impossible to follow. Attempts to fault the proposal on grounds of inefficiency (the policy may lead to riots and hence to high costs) fail because the estimated probability of such riots is undetermined or low. Instead, most would reject the policy on the basis of our first reaction, our moral intuition; it *sounds* outrageous. On examination, they (and I) would reject it because it is unfair to ask those who suffered long and still do to take on yet one more burden (a disproportionately small but yet additional amount of skin cancer), especially to do so in order to help a group that has historically been imposing many disadvantages on the targeted minority, the blacks. Many also oppose policies that deliberately impose an illness on a specific group of people, especially one defined by racial criteria. The sug-

Note: This essay, which has not previously been published, grew out of extensive dialogue with Mark Kleiman. I am indebted to Judith Lurie for editorial assistance.

gested policy is therefore judged morally inappropriate even if it is efficient.

Another policy option highlighting the same points is the suggestion to hang each year, at random, one hundred drug dealers in order to reduce the sale of illegal drugs (Kleiman, 1988, pp.14,16). When this policy idea was discussed at a seminar on values and public policy at the John F. Kennedy School of Government, a professor of ethics suggested, to further point out the moral unacceptability of such a proposal, that since drug dealers are hardened souls, they already accept the risk of death as part of their trade—hanging drug *users* would cut even more drug sales and would therefore be more efficient.

Both of these proposals conflict with values that most Americans adhere to, values that suggest that we not hang people because of transactional crimes (as distinct from those that directly and deliberately involve the taking of life). Furthermore, these values reject (as a matter of principle) deliberately meting out harsher punishments to a few chosen at random, than to others who committed the same crime. For the same reason, most Americans oppose shooting *young,* likely recidivistic offenders, which would be much less costly than paying for their jail terms, even though from a narrow efficiency perspective, with jail terms running at $20,000 per year or more per offender, the younger the offender, the higher the saving to result from executions.

These policy proposals are extreme, perverse products of a thinking that extols efficiency and leaves moral judgments to individuals who, it is assumed, express their preferences through the market, an approach that forswears moral consideration. True, most—indeed, practically all—neoclassical economists and other neoclassicists would be quick to reject these policy proposals. Nevertheless, it is not accidental that those few who explore them are neoclassicists; the extolling of efficiency *über alles* points in this direction of narrow utilitarianism and consequentialism.

We strive to significantly correct this way of thinking with a paradigm based on a deontological ethic, one that sees individuals as responding to moral and social values, in *addition* to rational drives toward maximizing utility, and that encompasses moral examination in its framework. A new discipline, socioeconomics, combines analysis of economics and efficiency with factors of social and moral values. By viewing human motivations as *co*determined (by a quest for economy or efficiency and by moral and social factors), socioeconomics seeks to improve the descriptive and normative bases of policy analysis.

We turn below to the many questions that come to mind: Where does one find these moral factors? Why have they been missing from policy analysis? What, more specifically, do they represent? According to *whose* moral values should one evaluate and design policy? Once the applicable moral values are located, how are their conflicting claims to be balanced? How can one reach one policy conclusion when the validity of two criteria—efficiency and morality—are recognized?

Omnipresence of the Moral Dimension

For the policy proposals discussed so far, the relevancy of the moral dimension seems quite evident. When the moral intuition reacts rather strongly, it is not very taxing to explicate, nor is it difficult to provide its basis in careful reasoning and established moral principles. Normally, though, the moral dimension is not as obvious, nor is the moral judgment. Nevertheless, rarely if ever is the moral dimension absent; furthermore, it requires a separate mode of analysis above and beyond evaluation of efficiency. True, some proposals, such as whether we should paint highway dividing lines white or yellow, are highly technical and they seem to lack a moral dimension. These are, however, implementing decisions, not true policy proposals. In effect, we cannot come up with a single genuine policy proposal in which the moral dimension is not present. For instance, as a rule, changes in economic policy affect some groups differently than others, as illustrated by inflation, an often cited example, which hurts pen-

sioners (because of their inflexible incomes) more than workers (whose pay tends to rise with prices). Hence, economists
are regularly making equity decisions that have moral implications: Should we hurt groups x, y, and z to advance groups
a, b, and c? Similarly, many policies affect the environment
(often considered a "public" good): Should we allow it to be
diminished? By how much? How fast? Also related are labor
policies, such as giving employees decision making opportunities, that have the potential to raise human dignity and self-
esteem.

A typical example of the presence of the moral dimension is the policy debate over whether to raise the speed limit
on highways. In part, the question is one of cost-benefit analysis of efficiency. The more time we spend on the road, as a
result of slower driving, the higher the costs of the policy,
because we "waste" people's valuable time and spend more
money in truckers' wages (Kamerud, 1988, pp. 343, 346). In
part, it is a question of moral judgment: Should we deliberately switch from a public policy that saves lives to one that
saves fewer?

Reductionism

Throughout human thought, from the Cynics to Karl Marx
to Gary Becker, attempts have been made to deny the significance or autonomy of the moral dimension. In the neoclassical tradition, there is little or no room left for authentic altruism or other "pure" moral motivations. At every step,
utilitarian thinking imputes some calculating motive and
hence diminishes the moral dimension; every action is depicted as a result of self-interest. An early tale captures the
approach: When Thomas Hobbes was asked why he gave
money to a beggar and whether this was not because of Christian ethics, he responded that he did so "with the sole intent
of relieving his own misery at the sight of the beggar" (Losco,
1986, p. 323).

Neoclassical policy analysts do not normally deny the
presence of the moral dimension, but they often argue that

we need not study moral and social values as a separate category because they are already reflected in preferences, and one need not study what lurks behind these preferences. "In the usual neoclassical formulation, a person is simply a bundle of preferences, and his moral ideals, if they enter the analysis at all, enter simply as some among his preferences— his taste for honesty being on a par with his taste for peanut butter" (McPherson, 1984, p. 243.) Hence, when the utilitarian model heaps all preferences and desires into one pile and attributes them to self-interest, it in effect absorbs the moral dimension and loses it in the shuffle.

Moreover, these attempts to reduce moral motivations to self-interested efficiency drives break down in the face of both much evidence to the contrary (Mansbridge, 1989) and everyday examples. A poignant example: By standard exchange theory, the husband or wife of an ailing Alzheimer's patient has no reason to stay with his or her mate; he or she gets nothing in return. Victims of Alzheimer's (a disease without as much as a dim hope for a cure) slowly lose their memory, first of events and names of simple objects, and finally to the point at which they cannot recognize even those members of their own family who care for them. Eventually, they require constant care and become incontinent and abusive. This means that spouses of these patients labor and nurse with no promise of reciprocal care, with no thanks, or, even worse, with abuse in return. Nevertheless, nearly all husbands and wives of Alzheimer's patients stay with their spouses throughout their illness. Exchange theorists may try to explain this behavior by arguing that they stay rather than endure the neighbors' gossip. Yet weighed against all of the hardships endured in caring for an Alzheimer's patient, this argument seems quite unconvincing. People seem to stay mainly because it is the right thing to do. That is, certain courses of action present themselves to these individuals as morally necessary (Charles Fried, 1964, refers to this in his article "Moral Causation").

Voting behavior serves as further evidence. Neoclassicists argue that normally there is little reason for people to vote because they get nothing in exchange; they cannot reasonably expect that their vote will make a difference. They may vote, therefore, only when the election is close, when they feel that their individual vote will make a difference. There is, however, only weak evidence in support of this correlation between voter turnout and closeness of the election. And, obviously, many millions vote when the elections are not close. The explanatory and predicting factor, on the contrary, turns out to be a moral commitment: People vote because they feel that it is their "civic duty" (Barry, 1978, p. 17).

The Multiple Self

Utilitarian neoclassical psychology, with its view of individuals as orderly and rational bundles of preferences and desires, is similarly reductionistic. These psychologists assume that people are unitary, that they are driven by one overriding preference (usually for "pleasure" or some other monistic "utile"). Deontological psychology, on the other hand, recognizes that, like policy proposals, people also have a moral dimension. It is increasingly realized that humans, unlike animals, are constituted of "multiple selves" (Elster, 1985): Their behavior is controlled by two layers of preferences, one (the metapreference) used to evaluate the other (the regular preference), and when these two come into conflict, a typical struggle ensues. The simple statement "I would *like* to go to a movie but *ought* to visit my friend in the hospital" captures the common tension. Moral values are the most important source of these scrutinizing metapreferences.

While it is possible to systematically study the forces behind the two levels of preferences, the outcome of the struggle rarely lands on one side or the other. Rather, human behavior is frequently conflicting and not consolidated; choices are multifaceted events. If the friend is neglected, guilt nags; if the movie is skipped today, it may appeal more strongly the next time a duty calls.

Typically, the presence of the moral dimension is reflected in terms of "ought" statements and thoughts (although not all "ought" statements are morally based). For example, the statement "I would like to spend more money now (say, on a car) but ought to save so as not to be dependent on the government or my children" reflects the moral dimension's influence. To be accurate and normatively effective, policy analysis ought to encompass this conflict. Policies should be designed to appeal to moral values and evaluated in terms of their moral standing (in addition to the efficiency factors). For example, the government may appeal to the public's obligation to future generations to encourage saving, a policy that generates no immediate pleasure. Relying only on economic factors, such as tax deductions for those who save in IRAs, is both limited in appeal and costly, if a sense of obligation can carry part of the policy load. Since two major kinds of factors affect people, policies should encompass both.

What Belongs in the Moral Dimension?

If a major source of metapreferences is moral, how is one to distinguish between moral and other voices? Despite many hundreds of years of hard labor, philosophers have still not produced a fully satisfactory definition of what is moral. Many, though, agree that statements are to be viewed as moral if they meet the following four criteria: first, people who act on the basis of moral metapreferences sense that they "must" behave in the prescribed way. Their moral acts are experienced as "imperatives," things they must do because they are obligated, duty bound. Most of us are familiar introspectively with this experience, doing something because it is right, as distinguishable from doing it because it is enjoyable.

The notion of an imperative is supported by the observation that people set aside certain realms as commanding a special, compelling status. Durkheim (1947) points to the fact that people treat certain acts as "sacred" (which need not mean religious.) Such sacred moral principles characteristically repudiate the instrumental rationality, which includes cost-benefit analysis; that is, people feel obligated to save a life or donate blood without calculating the potential payoffs (Goodin, 1980.)

The need for additional criteria to characterize moral acts arises out of the fact that there can also be non-moral imperatives; for example, obsessions with an un-requited love or even with an object, such as an illegal drug or the object of a fetish. The addition of second and third criteria helps here to separate moral imperatives from others (Childress, 1977).

Second, individuals who act morally are able to *generalize* their behavior—they are able to justify an act to others and to themselves by pointing to general rules. Statements such as "because I want it" or "I need it badly" do not meet this criterion, because no generalization is entailed in them. "Do unto others as you wish others to do unto you," on the other hand, is a prime example of a generalized rule.

Third, moral preferences must be *symmetrical* in that there must be a willingness to accord other, comparable people, under comparable circumstances, the same standing or right. (Otherwise, the moral dictum is rendered arbitrary. Such an arbitrary rule would state "This rule applies to Jane but not to Jim, although there is no relevant difference between them.") Racist ideologies, although they otherwise have the appearance of moral systems in that they are compelling (to their believers) and possibly generalizable, fail to qualify as moral by this test.

Finally, moral preferences affirm or express a *commitment,* rather than involving the consumption of a good or a service. Therefore, they are intrinsically motivated and not subject to means-end analysis (Dyke, 1981, p.11). (The fact that there are nonmoral acts that are intrinsically motivated does not invalidate this criterion. It only shows that the universe of such acts is larger than that of moral acts, and hence, as was already indicated, that this criterion is necessary but not sufficient in itself.) As to the argument that moral acts themselves are not impulsive acts but reflect deliberations and judgments (especially evident when one must sort out what course to follow when one is subject to conflicting moral claims), these deliberations are not of the same kind as means-end considerations; they require judgments among moral ends.

Whose Morals?

These criteria are useful in excluding some claims on moral appropriateness; for example, authoritarian statements such as "I did it because the president ordered me to" is rejected because it is not symmetrical. Also, those claims derived from some version of humanistic psychology, such as "because it feels right," can properly be excluded because they are not generalizable. This still leaves open the question: Policy alternatives should be evaluated according to whose morals?

Combining the above described criteria with a coherent moral theory discriminates the field of applicable moral judgments one step further. The result, though, depends on which moral theory one embraces. One theory, not widely shared in the contemporary United States, holds that there is an *absolute* set of values (sometimes referred to as "natural") by which we all must abide. Some religious thinkers, for example, may insist that the Ten Commandments are an absolute moral code, applicable to all people in all circumstances. In secular circles, absolute moral codes have been embodied in France's revolutionary Declaration of the Rights of Man and later in the American Declaration of Independence in the belief in the "natural" equality of all men and their consequent rights to freedom, security, and the pursuit of happiness (McDonald, 1984, p. 27). Contemporary libertarians extrapolate individual rights from these fundamental doctrines—basic laws considered valid "natural facts" irrespective of their societal context and despite the fact that they cannot be verified.

Another position, one that takes its lead from empirical data rather than dogmatic reasoning, asserts that there is a *universal* set of values that all people reaffirm. Those include the value of life, health, human dignity, even comfort. Inkeles and Smith (1974), for instance, found that people in very different cultures wanted basically the same things. After an extensive empirical study of the impact of modernity on six Third World countries, they conclude that "These separate cultures may give the individual personalities in each distinctive context, but we believe those cultures do not alter the basic principles which govern the structuring of personality in all men. We believe certain pan-human patterns of response persist in the face of variability in culture content. These transcultural similarities in the psychic properties of individuals provide the basis for a common response to common stimuli" (p. 12). Various attempts have been made to construct lists of these basic human needs. Those traits may include the universal desire for affection (solidarity, love), recognition (self-esteem, approval), context (orientation, meaning), and repeated gratification (the length of time varies, but all people seem to demand rewards for their activities) (Maslow, 1954; Etzioni, 1968, pp. 623–626).

Many hold that values are relative to particular cultures and periods, although they are not without guidance—they can draw on a procedural position. They use the consensus in the community for which the policy is intended as their guide to what is morally appropriate. Accordingly, for most issues, if the legislature has enacted a law—after proper deliberations and a vote—we normally owe it allegiance even if we disagree with its content. The consensus method encompasses not only shared values but also a recognition of the right to differ on certain matters (for example, it leaves room for conscientious objections even when a war is declared legitimate)—even to engage in civil disobedience. Still, on most matters, for most people, at most times, consensus forms the moral standard.

In addition, when the relevant community cannot reach a consensus, policy analysts may turn to moral reasoning to help form a consensus or serve as guidance in its absence. This branch of ethics provides guidance as to how to sort out what is morally appropriate when there are conflicting moral claims. Moral reasoning typically draws on competing ethical theories (act and rule utilitarianism, act and rule deontology, and so on; see Beauchamp, 1982). One may use one or a mix of those competing theories to sort out which position to follow. Granted, this might be difficult to accomplish, because it leaves open to justification the choice of the general moral principle from which the reasoning takes off. The example of the Harvard Business School seminar on truth telling discussed in the first essay in this book illustrates how the ethical theory that one embraces will color one's ethical reasoning and policy conclusions.

A different form of moral reasoning seems more suitable. One can start off with a well-established principle and use it to sort out conflicting claims. Goodin (1989, pp. 574–624) provides an important example. He asks whose rights should prevail, the rights of the smoker or the nonsmoker? The issue is, of course, relevant to the formulation of such policies as prohibition of smoking in public facilities (offices, schools, buses, trains, and planes) as well as public support of antismoking messages (banning ads, stronger surgeon general's warnings). Goodin suggests that the rights of nonsmokers should take precedence; his reasoning takes off from the moral position that one's liberty does not entail a freedom to violate another's. He quotes the popular phrasing "My right to extend my fist ends at your nose." Therefore, since the conduct of the nonsmoker does not violate the rights of the smoker, but that of the smoker does violate the rights of the nonsmoker (the smoke literally enters his or her nose), Goodin concludes that sovereignty should be given to the rights of the nonsmoker.

To the extent that a policy proposal promotes some value already endorsed by the community, its acceptance is "home free." When, however, such a consensus is absent, values cannot simply be inserted into the population in order to gain approval of the policy; the moral principles must come first, followed by policies that build on them. Or the policy analyst may draw on his or her own values and promote a policy based explicitly on his or her opinion, without attempting to legitimize it through consensus. Finally, policies may be presented as a menu of options, each in accord with respective moral standards. For example, to promote public health, a policy analyst may suggest that either the industry should introduce voluntary warning labels about the dangers to fetuses of consuming alcohol or the government should impose such labels.

Moral Appropriateness and Efficiency

The discussion so far has focused on the moral dimension because it is often neglected. However, it is not suggested that it ought to replace considerations of efficiency or that the latter are inappropriate. Rather, the point is that policy analysis ought to encompass both kinds of considerations. Thus, when cost-benefit analysis points to opportunities for significant economies and there are no moral hindrances, this factor surely should guide policy.

Consider as an example the findings on lives saved by expenditures on encouraging citizens to wear seat belts versus lives saved by expenditures on improving drivers' skills. The Public Health Service estimated that its program to encourage seat belt use, which cost $2 million from 1968 to 1972, averted nearly 23,000 deaths over that period, resulting in a "cost per death averted" of $87; in contrast, driver education programs, which ran $750.5 million over the same period, were estimated to have prevented a little over 8,500 deaths, or $88,000 per death averted (Drew, 1967, p.16). As long as we agree that education to voluntarily use seat belts is not morally inferior to other modes of driver education, such a policy is clearly to be preferred.

We argue that analysis ought to proceed on two levels: considerations of costs and benefits or other indications of efficiency and considerations of moral appropriateness. For example, a recent study on the costs of smoking and drinking approached the problem from both perspectives (Manning et. al., 1989). The study found that from a narrow efficiency viewpoint, taxes on cigarettes are high enough because they more than pay for their harms (the external costs to society are 15 cents per pack, but taxes are set at 37 cents per pack) because a pack of cigarettes increases medical costs but reduces life expectancy by 137 minutes, lowering the amount of pension payments collected. However, when the study broadened its purview to encompass moral criteria, it found reasons that might support raising the taxes on cigarettes. One argument is that even if one accepts uncritically that one ought not to interfere in private choices, there is still some room to consider it morally appropriate to act to discourage smoking. The authors point out that the young, when they "choose" to smoke—and become addicted—often are not fully informed about the consequences of their choice; hence, to help them stop smoking is, in effect, to act according to their latent preference (our terminology, not theirs). Second, the fact that many smokers try to quit signals their "true" desire. It would be quite a different matter to, say, impose chastity upon them, since there is little indication that this is what they desire.

There is no reason to argue that it is logically necessary or productive to assume that there are only two main sources of evaluation and no others may be considered. For example, aesthetic satisfaction might be another criterion (something might be efficient, and moral—and ugly). The main question, though, is not whether one can discern a third (or fourth or fifth) utility in addition to efficiency and moral values but whether one can keep the *number small* to avoid overdetermination, to preserve parsimony. And one must ask for the *criteria* for introducing into one's paradigm new utilities versus subsuming an observed motive, drive, or preference in a utility that is already a component of one's paradigm or theory.

In part, the question is pragmatic. Criteria of evaluation are not found in nature or in the brain; they are concepts that we introduce to organize our thinking and the evidence that we generate. The question is hence, in part, a matter of what "works," what is productive. No attempt is made here to formulate a list of evaluative concepts. It is sufficient to establish that a multiple but small number is preferable to a single one and to a larger list. (For additional discussion, see Etzioni, 1988, chaps. 2 and 3.) Here we limit the discussion to two, although the procedure for three or four is not basically different.

The question arises: Once each analysis is completed in its own track, so to speak, how does one proceed? To the extent that a particular policy proposal is both more efficient and more morally appropriate than another (or than an existing policy—for example, it enables people to get off welfare and to gain meaningful and well-paying work without neglecting their children—there is obviously no difficulty. To the extent that a policy is both morally unacceptable and inefficient (compared to some others), again, the choice (assuming all other things being equal) is easy. In cases, however, where the two criteria point in opposite directions and when one is very strong and the other is weak, the stronger will tend to and often ought to carry. For example, few would favor retaining a profit-making corporation to arrange for executions (Donahue, 1989).

In other situations, the moral and efficiency considerations collide head-on. A recent discussion in the *New York Times* (Mydans, 1989, p. A1) of new policies to combat drug abuse provides examples of both kinds. Among the drug enforcement policies considered by some to be relatively less offensive is the suggestion to ban loitering and gathering in a group of two or more in certain areas of Washington, D.C. Among those policies considered by the author of the article to be "more extreme" is the proposal to allow public whippings.

When the two criteria strongly conflict, when what is much more efficient is significantly more morally dubious or what is morally preferable is significantly less efficient than some other policy, a typical result is a deadlock. For example, we do not expect the more extreme antidrug policy to be implemented. Temporary inaction is an intelligent policy conclusion under these circumstances. For example, the U.S. Supreme Court frequently defers hearing cases on issues not deemed ripe for consideration. Congress and other legislators often table issues, bottle them up in committees, go through first and second but not final readings, and so on. True, other purposes are served this way. However, such a stance is clearly neither unusual nor without merit. Policy analysts should recommend it more often. In such cases, the first obligation of the policy analysts is to inform the client and/or community of the conflict and urge a quest for a third option or limited partial resolutions that circumvent the problem. (Before abortion was legalized, it was allowed in certain states for women under unusual stress.) In the meantime, an effort is made to evolve consensus, push for new technological development (for example, the French pill RU 486), change economic conditions, or alter some other major factor that will allow a resolution to the stalemate by enabling a policy option that is efficient and morally appropriate.

Conclusion

In conclusion, I agree with Hirschman (1984): there can be too much parsimony. Policy analysis surely suffers when only criteria of efficiency are introduced and moral considerations are either ignored or lumped together with a myriad of other considerations. Specifically, it is wise to examine each policy from at least two distinct viewpoints: its efficiency and its moral appropriateness. This view draws on the recognition that human nature is best perceived not as a unitary bundle of preferences but as a multiple self, one in which metapreferences vie with preferences over which will control behavior. The most important sources of metapreferences are moral and social values. While these do not always provide an unambiguous guideline, philosophers have developed criteria to distinguish that which is moral from that which is not and have even found ways to deal with conflicting moral claims.

How is one to combine the two (often conflicting) criteria into one policy conclusion? When the two criteria are mutually enforcing (that is, when the action is both moral and efficient or is neither), it is rather easy (although third considerations may intrude); when one provides a strong endorsement and the other a weak hindrance, the conclusion is still relatively evident. In those cases in which the two criteria clash head-on ("deadlock"), a search for third options is called for.

References

Barry, Brian. 1978. *Sociologists, Economists, and Democracy*. Chicago: University of Chicago Press.

Beauchamp, Tom. 1982. *Philosophical Ethics: Introduction to Moral Philosophy*. New York: McGraw-Hill.

Childress, James F. 1977. "The Identification of Ethical Principles." *Journal of Religious Ethics*. Vol. 5, no. 1, pp.39–68.

Donahue, John. 1989. *The Privatization Decision: Public Ends, Private Means*. New York: Basic Books.

Drew, Elizabeth. 1967. "HEW Grapples with PBS." *Public Interest*. No. 8, pp. 9–29.

Durkheim, Emile. 1947. *The Division of Labor in Society*. New York: Free Press.

Dyke, C. 1981. *Philosophy of Economics*. Engelwood Cliffs, NJ: Prentice-Hall.

Elster, Jon. 1985. *The Multiple Self*. Cambridge: Cambridge University Press.

Etzioni, Amitai. 1968. *The Active Society*. New York: Free Press.
———. 1988. *The Moral Dimension: Toward A New Economics*. New York: Free Press.

Fried, Charles. 1964. "Moral Causation." *Harvard Law Review*. Vol. 77, no. 77 (May), pp. 1258–1270.

Goodin, Robert E. 1980. "Making Moral Incentives Pay." *Policy Sciences*. Vol. 12 (August), pp. 131–145.
———. 1989. "The Ethics of Smoking." *Ethics*. Vol. 99 (April), pp. 574–624.

Hirschman, Albert O. 1984. "Against Parsimony: Three Easy Ways of Complicating Some Categories of Economic Discourse." *Bulletin: The American Academy of Arts and Sciences*. Vol. 37, no. 8 (May), pp.11–28.

Inkeles, Alex, and David H. Smith, 1974. *Becoming Modern: Individual Change in Six Developing Countries*. Cambridge: Harvard University Press.

Kamerud, Dana. 1988. "Benefits and Costs of the 55 MPH Speed Limit: New Estimates and Their Implications." *Journal of Policy Analysis and Management*. Vol. 7 (Winter 1988), pp. 341–352.

Kleiman, Mark. 1988. "Dead Wrong." *New Republic*. Sept. 26, pp. 14, 16.

Losco, Joseph. 1986. "Understanding Altruism: A Critique and Proposal for Integrating Various Approaches." *Political Psychology*. Vol. 7, no. 2, pp. 323–348.

Manning, Willard G. et.al. 1989. "The Taxes of Sin: Do Smokers and Drinkers Pay Their Way?" *Journal of the American Medical Association*. Vol. 261, no. 11, pp. 1604–1609.

Mansbridge, Jane. 1989. *Beyond Self-Interest*. Chicago: University of Chicago Press.

Maslow, Abraham H. 1954. *Motivation and Personality*. New York: Harper Collins.

McDonald, Margaret. 1984. "Natural Rights." In Jeremy Waldron (ed.), *Theories of Rights*. New York: Oxford University Press.

McPherson, Michael S. 1984. "On Schelling, Hirschman and Sen: Revising the Conception of the Self." *Partisan Review*. Vol. LI, no. 2, pp. 236–247.

Mydans, Seth. 1989. "Powerful Arms of Drug War Arousing Concern For Rights." *New York Times*, Oct. 16, 1989. pp. A1, B10.

INDEX